Authorized Agents

SUNY series, Native Traces
JACE WEAVER AND SCOTT RICHARD LYONS, EDITORS

Authorized Agents

Publication and Diplomacy in the Era of Indian Removal

FRANK KELDERMAN

Portions of chapter two have appeared in an essay titled "Rock Island Revisited: Black Hawk's Life, Keokuk's Oratory, and the Critique of US Indian Policy," *J19: The Journal of Nineteenth-Century Americanists* 6, no. 1 (Spring 2018): 67–92.

All author royalties on this book will be donated to the American Indian College Fund, a nonprofit organization that supports American Indian students and tribal colleges.

Cover art: detail, "Council of the Sacs and Foxes, at Washington City," by Ferdinand Pettrich. Ink and wash on paper. Ferdinand Pettrich Sketchbook, c. 1842. Edwin E. Ayer Collection, Newberry Library, Chicago.

Published by State University of New York Press, Albany

© 2019 State University of New York

All rights reserved

No part of this book may be used or reproduced in any manner whatsoever without written permission. No part of this book may be stored in a retrieval system or transmitted in any form or by any means including electronic, electrostatic, magnetic tape, mechanical, photocopying, recording, or otherwise without the prior permission in writing of the publisher.

For information, contact State University of New York Press, Albany, NY
www.sunypress.edu

Library of Congress Cataloging-in-Publication Data

Names: Kelderman, Frank, 1984- author.
Title: Authorized agents : publication and diplomacy in the era of Indian
    removal / Frank Kelderman.
Description: Albany : State University of New York Press, [2019] | Series:
    SUNY series, Native traces | Includes bibliographical references and index.
Identifiers: LCCN 2018052660| ISBN 9781438476179 (hard-
    cover) | ISBN 9781438476193 (e-book) |
ISBN 9781438476186 (pbk.).
Subjects: LCSH: Indian Removal, 1813-1903. | Indians of North
    America—United States—Historiography. | Indians of North America—
    Government relations—1789-1869.
Classification: LCC E93 .K245 2019 | DDC 973.04/97009034—dc23 LC
    record available at https://lccn.loc.gov/2018052660

10 9 8 7 6 5 4 3 2 1

For my parents

CONTENTS

List of Illustrations — ix
Acknowledgments — xi

Introduction: Indian Removal and the Projects of Native American Writing — 1

1. "Kindness and Firmness": Negotiating Empire in the Benjamin O'Fallon Delegation — 31

2. "Our Wants and Our Wishes": Frontier Diplomacy and Removal in Sauk Writing and Oratory — 73

3. "The Blessings Which We Are Now Enjoying": Peter Pitchlynn and the Literature of Choctaw Nation-Building — 123

4. Rewriting the Native Diplomat: Community and Authority in Ojibwe Letters — 167

Afterword: The Indians in the Lobby — 213

Notes — 221
Index — 259

ILLUSTRATIONS

Figure 1.1. The House of Representatives, by Samuel F. B. Morse, 1822. 32
Figure 1.2. Portrait of Benjamin O'Fallon, by an unidentified artist, c. 1833. 36
Figure 1.3. *An-Pan-Tan-go or the Big Elk, a Maha Chief*, after Charles Bird King, 1838. 38
Figure 1.4. *Hayne Hudjihini, the Eagle of Delight*, after Charles Bird King, 1838. 49
Figure 1.5. *Petalesharoo, a Pawnee Brave*, after Charles Bird King, 1838. 53
Figure 1.6. Frontispiece of I. G. Hutton, "The Generous Chief," 1823. 54
Figure 1.7. *Shar-I-Tar-Ish, a Pawnee Chief*, after Charles Bird King, 1838. 60
Figure 2.1. *View of the Great Treaty Held at Prarie* [sic] *du Chien, September 1825*, 1835. 74
Figure 2.2. Daguerreotype portrait of Keokuk, by Thomas M. Easterly, 1847. 78
Figure 2.3. Portrait of William Clark, by George Catlin, 1832. 80
Figure 2.4. *The Grand National Caravan Moving East*, by Hassan Straightshanks (David Claypoole Johnston), 1833. 88
Figure 2.5. Portrait of Black Hawk, after Robert Matthew Sully, 1903. 90
Figure 2.6 *Council of the Sacs and Foxes, at Washington City*, by Ferdinand Pettrich, c. 1842. 106
Figure 2.7. *Council of the Sacs and Foxes, at Washington City*, by Ferdinand Pettrich, c. 1842. 106
Figure 2.8. Ioway map of the Mississippi and Missouri River Valley, c. 1837. 108

Figure 2.9.	Portrait of Robert Lucas, by Robert H. Yewell, c. 1858.	116
Figure 3.1.	*P. P. Pitchlynn*, by Charles Fenderich, 1842.	128
Figure 3.2.	Page from the diary of Peter Pitchlynn, 1828.	133
Figure 3.3.	*Tenskwatawa "The Prophet,"* after James Otto Lewis, 1835.	135
Figure 3.4.	Phrenology and physiognomy of Col. P. P. Pitchlynn, 1846.	141
Figure 4.1.	Portrait of Ozhaguscodaywayquay.	172
Figure 4.2.	Portrait of Jane Johnston Schoolcraft.	175
Figure 4.3.	*Shin-gua-ba-wossin*, after James Otto Lewis, 1827.	180
Figure 4.4.	*Shin-ga-ba-w'ossin, Image stone*, after James Otto Lewis, 1838.	180
Figure 4.5.	Portrait of George Copway, from a daguerreotype by McClees & Germon, 1850.	192

ACKNOWLEDGMENTS

Since this book is about the collaborative nature of publication, it is a particular joy to thank everyone who helped me complete this work, in ways that they may not realize but that I will not forget. I am grateful to my colleagues in the English Department at the University of Louisville for helping me see this project to completion. I am particularly grateful to Susan Griffin, Timothy Johnson, Mark Alan Mattes, Susan Ryan, Stephen Schneider, and Joseph Turner for reading parts of this book. Many thanks are due to my department chair, Glynis Ridley, and to Andrew Rabin, Annelise Gray, Sherry McCroskey, and Taleia Willis for their support of my research. I am also grateful to John Gibson of the Commonwealth Center for the Humanities and Society and to Kimberly Kempf-Leonard, dean of the College of Arts & Sciences.

I started this work at the University of Michigan, and I owe a deep debt of gratitude to Julie Ellison, Scott Richard Lyons, Philip Deloria, and Mary Kelley. They are extraordinary mentors who understood this project before I did, and have offered superb guidance to help me see it through. Along the way, I also received much wisdom from James W. Cook, Gregory Dowd, Joseph Gone, Kristin Hass, Tiya Miles, Margaret Noodin, and Michael Witgen. At Michigan, I benefited from workshops with the Native American and Indigenous Studies Interdisciplinary Group and was lucky to have a supportive community in Stefan Aune, Michelle Cassidy, Courtney Cottrell, Joseph Gaudet, Becky Hill, William Hartmann, Sophie Hunt, Emily McGillivray, Steve Pelletier, and Christie Toth.

As a postdoctoral fellow at Oberlin College I received much support from Naomi Campa, Evangeline Heiliger, Shelley Lee, Amy Margaris, Kathryn Miller, Pablo Mitchell, Afia Ofori-Mensa, Gina Pérez, Chie Sakakibara, and Danielle Skeehan. Most of all, I thank Wendy Kozol for invaluable advice and encouragement.

Over the years, many archivists and library staff have aided my research in numerous ways. In particular, I wish to thank Clayton Lewis and Terese Austin at the William L. Clements Library (Ann Arbor), Renee Harvey at the

Helmerich Center for American Research (Tulsa), and Delinda Buie Stephens at the University of Louisville Archives and Special Collections. I would also like to thank archivists and staff members at the Bentley Historical Library (Ann Arbor), the Center for Arkansas History and Culture (Little Rock), the Filson Historical Society (Louisville), the Iowa State Historical Society (Iowa City), the Library and Archives Canada (Ottawa), the Missouri History Museum (St. Louis), the National Archives and Records Administration (College Park, MD), the National Portrait Gallery (Washington DC), the Newberry Library (Chicago), the Oberlin College Library, and the University of Oklahoma's Western History Collections (Norman).

The field of Native American and indigenous studies has been a remarkable and welcoming intellectual community, and I wish to thank Angela Calcaterra, Alicia Cox, René Dietrich, Scott Manning Stevens, Caroline Wigginton, and Kelly Wisecup for meaningful conversations that have helped me develop this project. I have learned much from conversations with fellow panelists and audience members at the American Indian Workshop, the American Studies Association, C19: The Conference of Nineteenth-Century Americanists, the Native American and Indigenous Studies Association, the Native American Literature Symposium, and the Western Literature Association. The Heidelberg Center for American Studies and the D'Arcy McNickle Center for American Indian and Indigenous Studies provided unique opportunities to workshop early versions of this work.

At SUNY Press, I am indebted to Amanda Lanne-Camilli for her faith in this project, and to Jace Weaver and Scott Richard Lyons for giving it a place in the Native Traces series. I am also grateful to the anonymous reviewers for their invaluable comments on the manuscript. Many thanks are due also to Ryan Morris, Anne Valentine, and Daniel Otis for helping me see this book to publication.

In Louisville, I've cherished my writing sessions with Byron Freelon, Cynthia Ganote, Melanie Gast, Mary Greenwood, Katherine Massoth, Andrea Olinger, Anna Browne Ribeiro, and Oliver Rollins. Beyond Louisville, I'm grateful to my family and my friends, especially Liz Harmon, Jenny Kwak, Calvin McMillin, Lisa Jong, Chris Broughton, Alexander Olson, Nicolette Bruner, Lisa and Kirk Maki, Meghan Wind, and Jason Ness. Wish you all lived right around the corner. To Gavin Rienne, the person-without-whom, thank you for your love and support.

INTRODUCTION

Indian Removal and the Projects of Native American Writing

In 1821, several American newspapers published the transcript of a speech by a Pawnee tribal leader who had recently paid a visit to Fort Atkinson, an American army post on the Missouri River. Identified by the scribe as Shun-kah-kihe-gah, the Pawnee leader had sat in council with Benjamin O'Fallon, the American subagent at the Upper Missouri Indian agency at Council Bluffs, in the heart of Indian country. In his speech, he addressed his people's political relations with the United States, reflecting on the first time that the four Pawnee bands had entered into treaty with the Americans, when in 1818 they declared themselves "under the protection of the United States of America, and of no other nation, power or sovereign, whatsoever."[1] Adhering to a convention of diplomacy between Native leaders and American officials, Shun-kah-kihe-gah addressed O'Fallon as "My Father" and recalled a remarkable moment of historical transformation: "We considered [the Pawnees] to be the first nation on the earth; we had always appeared so conspicuous as almost to obscure the other nations around us, but when you came to this land, followed by so many war chiefs and soldiers, whose glistening appeared like a fiery son of heaven, I almost shrunk within myself; I thought I discovered my mistake, and, consulting the safety of my people, I opened my ears to your words, and became an American."[2] The Pawnee leader recalled a moment when the potential of diplomacy with the United States seemed limitless, when the parade of American soldiers promised either imperial domination or protection. Yet he swiftly deflated this narrative by pointing out the limits of American

1

influence in the Pawnee homelands. Although three of the Pawnee bands had allied with the United States, the Skidi band continued to raid American traders in the Upper Missouri Valley, and O'Fallon's failure to punish the culprits caused unrest among the Pawnees: "Since I have been an American," Shun-kah-kihe-gah said, "my influence with my nation weakens, as you hesitate to punish every insult offered your people . . . you, altho' a great chief, have not the control of them."[3] The words of the Pawnee speaker pointed to a disconnect between the rhetoric of American empire and the messier realities it buried. As he recounted the waxing and waning of US influence in the span of just three years, Shun-kah-kihe-gah suggested to O'Fallon that the protection of his American "father" amounted to little on the ground.

The Indian agency at Council Bluffs was not the Pawnee's exclusive audience: his words made their way east from Indian country to readers in American cities, who encountered them in magazines and newspapers such as *Niles' Weekly Register*, the *Washington Gazette*, and the *Richmond Enquirer*. In these publications, the speech was advertised under the succinct heading of "Indian Eloquence," a standard phrase by which editors categorized the oratory of Native leaders. For American readers, the speech promised the distinctive rhetoric of an Indian Other, laden with powerfully vivid metaphors of the body, from open ears and rejoicing hearts to spilt blood and naked bones. Intimating that tribal leaders governed their people "with their tongues" while punishing enemies "with their arms," the Pawnee's rhetoric must have resonated with romantic images of eloquent Indian chiefs and fearless warriors. At places like the Council Bluffs agency, however, such idiomatic language was a regular feature of the interactions between Native leaders and Indian agents, traders, and interpreters. Even as they became part of a bourgeoning American print culture, speeches like Shun-kah-kihe-gah's harkened back to the cross-cultural exchanges that were central to Indian diplomacy. By speaking to government scribes and interpreters, the Pawnee leader brought an indigenous perspective on US-Indian relations into American governmental networks. In doing so, he emphasized that his words represented not just his own views, but the deliberations of his community: "I did not leave my village in the dark but with the knowledge of my people, and after having consulted my chiefs and warriors." And as he explained the failures of the American government in dealing with the Skiri band, he realized that his speech conveyed an uncomfortable reality: "My father, I come to tell you truth, but it will be unpleasant to your ears."[4] Construing his own words as Pawnee communal knowledge, Shun-kah-kihe-gah offered his political allegiance along with a critique of how the Americans were managing their diplomatic affairs.

The circulation of the Pawnee speech reflects the stakes and conditions of early Native American literatures in English, the publication of which was closely connected to the world of Indian diplomacy.[5] Although it has never been central to mainstream narratives of American culture, Indian diplomacy had profoundly shaped North America since the early days of the Atlantic fur trade. As early as the sixteenth century, representatives of indigenous nations engaged in diplomatic exchange with emissaries of European empires. After the American Revolutionary War, Indian nations found themselves engaging in diplomacy with the United States, a nascent empire that was gradually expanding westward. As treaty after treaty reduced the land base of Indian nations, the figure of the Native diplomat became a ubiquitous actor in a continental history of exchange and dispossession. By the nineteenth century, scenes of treaty-making had become a fixture in increasingly romanticized cultural narratives about US-Indian encounters, from popular depictions of William Penn's 1683 treaty with the Lenni Lenape to the "Indian deed" discovered in Nathaniel Hawthorne's *House of the Seven Gables* (1851). The Indian diplomat gradually came to be understood as the quintessential colonial dupe: dignified and noble, but not artful enough to wield the upper hand in negotiations, and ultimately deceived by colonial adversaries. As a variation on the "vanishing Native American," Indian diplomats were worthy of commemoration more than anything, immortalized by artists such as Charles Bird King and James Otto Lewis, whose famous portraits of Native delegates extended a discourse of cross-cultural friendship. Steadily the Indian diplomat became a trope in a nationalist story that popularized a distorted or even sanitized version of the colonial relations between Indian nations and the United States.

The records of Indian diplomacy often echo such tropes of international friendship. When Shun-kah-kihe-gah sat in council with O'Fallon, for instance, the transcription of his speech ended with his statement that "I only aspire to be your friend, and wish to *live* in your *estimation*."[6] Yet this rhetoric of friendship belies a more complex history of diplomatic relations, and early Native American literatures in English reveal a detailed record of indigenous critiques of American institutions that had become central to Indian diplomacy. After 1790, the United States government established what Phillip H. Round calls lasting "institutions of Indian policy" in the War Department, the Office of Indian Trade, and—after 1824—the Office of Indian Affairs. These institutions carried out a broad attempt to "appease" Indian nations in the western territories, carrying out "intense diplomatic efforts" that took place in a "charged atmosphere." By participating in these interactions, American Indian diplomats came to model what Round calls the "emerging indigenous speaking subject in American political discourse."[7] More than simply extending the rhetoric of cross-cultural amity, Native diplomats used writing and oratory to bear witness to the concerns of individual Indian nations and the state of intertribal relations, in ways that affirmed indigenous sovereignty within American institutions of diplomacy. Through the collective efforts of indigenous representatives, Indian diplomacy gave rise to an important tradition of indigenous literature.

Authorized Agents examines how nineteenth-century Native American writing and oratory extended the forms and substance of Indian diplomacy into new publication contexts. In the chapters that follow, I explore the works of American Indian writers and orators from the nineteenth century who insisted on the need for continued diplomatic relationships that were responsive and politically meaningful to Indian nations. As they traversed diplomatic networks, figures such as Sharitarish (Pawnee), Ongpatonga (Omaha), Hardfish (Sauk), and Peter Pitchlynn (Choctaw) worked with interpreters, traders, religious leaders, and delegates from other indigenous nations, and in doing so they secured a political voice within colonial institutions. Through these efforts, they contributed to a substantial yet much-overlooked body of Native American literature in English, the publication of which wavered between textual collaboration and institutional critique.

The literary history of Indian diplomacy adds important inflection to the study of indigenous people's agency in colonial regimes of representation. In nineteenth-century North America, Native people frequently entered the colonial record through translation and collaboration, and often by speaking alongside indigenous and settler participants in formal negotiations. They worked with scribes and interpreters, joined delegations, sat in council with American officials, wrote petitions, gave speeches, and engaged in ceremonial exchanges. Because such diplomatic negotiations typically took place between representatives who spoke different languages, they worked by scripted and ceremonial routines. While many representatives of Indian nations were able to read and write in English, others depended on the work of government interpreters and saw their oratory transcribed by field agents of the Office of Indian Affairs. At the same time, these interactions also extended indigenous protocols and ceremonies: whether held in Washington or in Native villages, Indian diplomacy incorporated oratory, parades, gift giving, tobacco smoking, and the display and exchange of regalia and uniforms. These practices represented a discursive space that was shaped by the possibilities and limitations of the diplomatic encounter. As Richard White shows in his influential history of the Great Lakes region, the frequent misinterpretations that ensued in these settings forged a "middle ground" of interaction, a new cultural plane that emerged from the mutual adaptations and misunderstandings between European and Native protocols and rhetorics.[8]

This is not to say that Indian diplomacy took place on a neutral playing field. Rather than dealing with Indian nations on an equal footing, nineteenth-century US policymakers consistently undermined the domestic and intertribal politics of Indian nations, grouping autonomous bands and tribes together to treat with clearly legible constructs of "nations."[9] In doing so, the United States claimed more extensive diplomatic relations than their negotiations actually established on the ground, to project a further reach of US imperial power. This practice reflects that, as György Ferenc Tóth writes, the category of the *nation* is "not natural but *performed* in cultural representations, government policy, and international diplomacy." Indian diplomacy is thus "the performance of the nation through 'representation'—the standing in of an individual or a team for the interests and positions of a larger 'imagined community,'" which means that the representation of nationhood in scenes of diplomacy depends on a situational performance.[10] While the performance of Indian diplomacy affirmed international political ties between sovereign nations, however, American policymakers translated indigenous sovereignty into a diminished form of sovereignty, meaningful only within the confines of its colonial relation to the United States. Following the War of 1812, moreover, not only did the United States divest from Indian diplomacy more and more, the conduct of diplomacy—especially by organizing delegations to Washington—became an opportunity to intimidate Native leaders with the size of American cities, arsenals, and shipyards, to demonstrate the military strength of the expanding settler nation. With federal Indian policy aimed at the erosion of Indian nations' sovereignty and land base, indigenous diplomats typically worked in a context of limited agency or even coercion.[11]

Authorized Agents examines the works of indigenous writers and orators who pushed back against these asymmetries. One such intervention is the work of the Sauk warrior Black Hawk, who in 1833 narrated his life story for the bestselling autobiography *Life of Ma-ka-tai-me-she-kia-kiak*. The publication of this book depended on the work of a government interpreter at the Rock Island Indian agency, but it also criticizes the interpreter's involvement in the history of Sauk dispossession. Meanwhile, the Sauk tribal leader Keokuk held frequent councils with government officials at Rock Island and St. Louis, which enabled him to establish an important body of oratory in which he outlined the shortcomings of US Indian policy. In the Choctaw Nation, the diplomat Peter Pitchlynn wrote a report on his survey of Choctaw lands in Indian Territory, in which his reflections on intertribal diplomacy became a defense of his people's land claims west of the Mississippi. And in the early 1840s the Ojibwe missionary Peter Jones brought a petition to the British crown that challenged philanthropic discourses of "pity" for

Native subjects, offering a rationale for indigenous education that was sanctioned by local networks of Ojibwe government. Far from dupes who were played upon by colonial administrators, these writers and orators were apt readers of institutional networks and discourses, who contributed to an innovative body of literature about intertribal and colonial relations in North America.

The fact that such literatures of diplomacy were typically edited and published by colonial institutions—including the Indian Office, missionary organizations, and territorial governments—has often left their authors to be misread, discredited, or simply ignored. Yet these writings deserve critical attention because they point us not only to the dialogic and colonial contexts of Native literatures, but also because they are attuned to their intertribal dimensions. Indian diplomacy generated a rich body of indigenous literature that was both tribally specific and inherently international in outlook, resistant to colonialism while also incorporating Euro-American ideologies and writing practices. Although shaped by intercultural protocols, Indian diplomacy nevertheless legitimized the representational work of indigenous diplomats who articulated concrete political goals, even when these cannot be ascribed to a singular, original "author." Recognizing these tensions, this book revisits a body of indigenous literature that might otherwise be dismissed as merely an extension of the bureaucratic discourses of the settler state. Reading the history of Indian diplomacy back into these texts, it traces the fraught collaborations that forged them and the contributions they made to the archive of nineteenth-century indigenous literature.

INDIGENOUS PUBLICATION PROJECTS

In examining the relation between indigenous literatures and diplomacy, this book explores what it meant for Native authors to "publish" in the nineteenth century. Indian diplomacy depended on forms of communication in which indigenous people and settlers alike shaped the forms and substance of meaning making, through oral performance, manuscript writing, and nontextual forms of communication. In this sense, the practice of Indian diplomacy was part of what Matt Cohen and Jeffrey Glover term "colonial mediascapes," the complex interactions of textual and nontextual materials that formed the basis of communication between Native people, settlers, and other newcomers to the Americas.[12] Scholars such as Andrew Newman and Birgit Brander Rasmussen have examined how early Native American literatures hinged on collaborative forms of writing, including wampum belts, treaties, and petitions.[13] Resisting what Craig Womack criticizes as the facile "oppositional thinking" about orality versus literacy, this work points to the ways in which settlers and indigenous people in the Americas participated in multimedia "publication events," Matt Cohen's generative term for performative interactions in which neither Native people nor Europeans fully controlled the "customs and rhetorics" of cross-cultural interaction.[14]

In the nineteenth century, American Indians gradually gained more control over the publication of their own printed works, reflecting the changes in a media landscape that was increasingly shaped by a cross-regional market for print.[15] The emergence of an expansive print culture in the mid-nineteenth century brought Native writings and oratory from councils and delegations into a wider cultural realm: into printed books, magazines, petitions, and newspapers. As Michael Warner argues in *The Letters of the Republic*, the potentially unlimited circulation of printed matter had long modeled the sense of abstraction and disembodiment that is central to what Jürgen Habermas calls the "public sphere," the free, rational-critical discourse through which private individuals come together to critically reflect on state power and to offer a counterweight to it.[16] American Indian writers, too, mobilized the close connection between print and the public sphere. Between 1828 and 1834, the Cherokee writer Elias Boudinot published the newspaper *Cherokee Phoenix* in New Echota, the capital of the Cherokee Nation, raising public awareness about the political question of Cherokee removal and, more generally, the relations between the United States and Indian nations.[17] In 1829, the Pequot author William Apess published his autobiography *A Son of the Forest*, and four years later Black Hawk published his as-told-to autobiography *Life of Ma-ka-tai-me-she-kia-kiak*.[18] In other words, Native authors were quick to respond to innovations in publishing, and the cross-regional reach of print made their publications an important factor in the history of nineteenth-century American letters.

Throughout the nineteenth century, Native authors carried the social and political questions of Indian diplomacy into this expansive print culture, and in doing so they fashioned new kinds of collaborations. After all, historians of print culture have shown that print publication is a relational and situational act. In the words of Elizabeth Maddock Dillon, the publication of a book represents a "series of collective interchanges" that involve "authors, editors, printers, publishers, consumers, booksellers, reviewers, and readers not to mention technologies related to such matters as paper production, printing presses, typefaces, and transportation."[19] But as Eric Cheyfitz reminds us, in the context of American Indian literatures the term "collaboration" often carries a "nuanced range of . . . meanings from cooperation to coercion," and as such the entangled questions of authorship, translation, and sponsorship also represent the power dynamics of indigenous-settler relationships.[20] To recognize these tensions it helps to consider

Arnold Krupat's seminal work on American Indian autobiography, in which he posited a series of analytical questions to examine the collaborative contexts of Native American literature:

> How many workers ... were involved in the production of the final text, and what did each contribute to it? ... Under what auspices was the text produced, and what claims were made for it? ... Was it paid for by the government or by a private individual? Was it sponsored historically or legally, in relation to a particular event or a particular claim? ... What were the apparent intentions of the producers and what benefits did they derive from their collaborative project?[21]

Krupat's questions are an early call for what we could name a book-historical perspective in indigenous literary studies, linking questions of book production and dissemination to the relational or institutional contexts of early Native print publication. If print publication is the product of networks of people and technologies, the collaborative dimensions of publishing are more than merely background or "context," pointing us instead to the ways Native authors traversed these networks in order to raise public notice.

Even in the nineteenth century, however, the printed book remained but one of many avenues of publication. Despite an expanding, cross-regional market for printed books, this technology of publication stood alongside manuscript writing, oratory, and performance—modes of cultural production that were "composed of events bound in time and framed in space."[22] For Native writers, too, manuscript writing and oral performance remained equally important forms of publication, as is reflected in the career of William Apess, one of the most widely studied Native writers of the nineteenth century. After he became a Methodist minister in 1829, Apess promptly finished an autobiography titled *A Son of the Forest*, published the same year, in which he recounted his conversion and offered a rebuke of Euro-American colonialism and racial prejudice. Traveling around New England to preach to ethnically mixed congregations, he became involved in the political situation of the Mashpee Wampanoag of Cape Cod, who had been placed under supervision by white overseers while white settlers encroached on their lands. The Mashpee protested their conditions during what has come to be known as the "Mashpee Revolt" (1833–1834), and Apess supported their cause by speaking out publicly on their behalf in local meetings, petitioning the Massachusetts State government, and writing letters to Harvard College to contest the appointment of the minister who served the Mashpee community.[23] As he secured favorable coverage in the *Boston Advocate*, the affair consolidated his reputation as a writer, orator, and preacher. In short, his career as an author did not depend on his print autobiography alone but also on how he navigated networks within the Methodist church, colonial and indigenous governments, educational institutions, and the lecture circuit. It is through these different forms of publication (encompassing manuscript writing, oratory, and print) that Apess contributed to the public discourse on Indian affairs in Massachusetts—a debate that was rooted both in colonial institutions and in Mashpee community contexts.

The career of Apess reminds us that the writing and publishing of literature is a networked affair. In *Indigenous Intellectuals*, Kiara M. Vigil argues that in the realm of writing and cultural production, a network can be understood as a "structure, with individual centers of gravity," in which "ideas flow through both interpersonal and mediated communications."[24] Much of what we now call early American literature extended interpersonal networks within institutions and associations, including reform societies, conversational clubs, evangelical groups, academies, and seminaries.[25] Accordingly, studies by Susan Scott Parrish, Sean Harvey, and Kelly Wisecup have emphasized how indigenous people had long been creators of knowledge within the networks of learned societies, religious organizations, and governments.[26] As Richard Brodhead argues in *Cultures of Letters*, "writing is always an acculturated activity" and it is therefore important not to delimit the networks from which acts of writing emerge as merely a matter of "context." Rather, the act of writing

> always takes place within some completely concrete cultural situation, a situation that surrounds it with some particular landscape of institutional structures, affiliates it with some particular group from among the array of contemporary groupings, and installs it [in] some group-based world of understandings, practices, and values. But this setting provides writing with more than a backdrop. A work of writing comes to its particular form of existence in interaction with the network of relations that surrounds it: in any actual instance, writing orients itself in or against some understanding of what writing is, does, and is good for that is culturally composed and derived.[27]

Indian diplomacy represented a crucial network of relations through which Native writers and orators extended the communication networks of indigenous nations. In *Ethnology and Empire*, Robert Lawrence Gunn examines nineteenth-century literatures of US-Indian interaction from the American borderlands, showing how the institutional networks of the US state fostered "interanimating networks of peoples, spaces, and communication practices" that carried Native people's words and ideas "across western borderlands regions and metropolitan centers of knowledge production and power."[28] As "vehicles of power [and] instruments of conquest," Gunn explains, these networks produced writings that originated in "unstable, shifting borderlands" but were filtered through the "seemingly dry imperial matters of bureaucracy, law, and policy." In this respect, Gunn argues, they reflected colonial relations that were simultaneously "local and national, individual and systemic, [and] firmly terrestrial yet deeply vested in the cultural imaginary of nineteenth-century US imperialism."[29] For Native writers and orators, then, "publication" did not necessarily mean engaging a national mass market for print, but depended largely on networks of Indian diplomacy and colonial bureaucracies, as well as closely related spheres outside of government.

Besides Gunn, several scholars of early Native American literature have remarked on the links between indigenous publication and the workings of Indian diplomacy. In *The Common Pot*, Lisa Brooks argues that American Indians in the Northeast used petitions, political writings, and oratory to regain land rights and to assert anticolonial mappings of Native space. In particular, Brooks draws attention to a genre of Native writing that can be understood as "treaty literature," consisting of "oratory protocol guided by mnemonic wampum belts and birchbark scrolls that contained the records of international exchange."[30] Even though it was inherently transnational in outlook, treaty literature also registers political projects that were deeply shaped by the lives of local indigenous communities. The conduct of Indian diplomacy was therefore a powerfully motivating context for indigenous speech acts. Phillip H. Round's *Removable Type* traces how "diplomatic publics" emerged from new connections between tribal leaders and diplomats (from different Indian nations), agents of settler governments (at the federal, state, and territorial levels), and representatives of religious organizations. While not synonymous with indigenous publics, diplomatic publics were an important factor in the efforts "to formulate a nascent set of American Indian 'publics,'" as Indian nations found ways to "negotiate with each other, argue with colonial adversaries, and preserve for posterity their motives and deliberations during diplomatic struggles."[31] Sometimes these diplomatic publics represent what Nancy Fraser calls "strong publics," having a direct influence on political decision-making, while at other times they constituted "weak publics," playing only advisory or even tokenistic roles in diplomatic settings.[32] In either case, the writing and oratory that emerged from these settings became meaningful in and *because of* the diplomatic situation. But if Native authors channeled the discourses of colonial networks, they also modified them according to culturally specific political objectives. As James H. Cox argues in *The Red Land to the South*, diplomacy ultimately "has an end game." It operates by cautious interaction and "patient, tactful advocacy," but it is also an overtly political form of cultural mediation: diplomats cannot afford to "alienate" their audience, but at the same time they need to "advocate for a specific position."[33] In sum, Indian diplomacy worked by moments of exchange that were situational and inscribed by colonial relations, but it also organized indigenous publics that were politically motivating, since it was an increasingly rare discursive space for public debate on the present and future of indigenous communities.

The publication of indigenous writing and oratory was thus organized within institutional landscapes, and indigenous diplomats and tribal leaders created texts that showcased an astute awareness of the administrative functions and malfunctions within colonial bureaucracies. Through collaborative acts of publication, they carried out projects to pursue meaningful change in diplomatic institutions, thereby intervening in the relations between Indian nations and the settler state. To capture these situational and goal-oriented logics of Indian diplomacy, I use the term "projects" to describe acts of publication that were institutionally embedded but also forward-looking and oriented toward future change. But what does it mean to think about writing and publication as a "project"? In a study of technological and scientific projects in eighteenth-century Britain, the literary scholar David Alff argues that to carry out a project requires "a thinking through of possibility" to make one's "proposed endeavor seem plausible in the context of the future." A project, Alff suggests, depends on individuals weaving together "strategies of rhetorical persuasion, publication, and embodied action," in an effort to apply "their faculties of imagination to achieve finite goals."[34] This goal-oriented nature is also central to other definitions of projects, which typically indicate a relationship between imaginative acts and their impact in the social world. In *Phenomenology of the Social World* (1932), the Austrian philosopher Alfred Schütz defines a project as the "phantasying" of social action that precedes a person's agency, an imagining of the impact that one's action will make in the social world. Schütz argues that social action depends on the ability to theorize for oneself a "project" that can be visualized as a completed, fully realized act, and is thus motivated by how individuals imagine their actions will effect meaningful change.[35] In this respect, there is an inherently social component to the notion of a project. In her work on South American youth movements, for instance, the cultural sociologist Ann Mische draws on Schütz's work to theorize projects as imagined possibilities that motivate collective social action, what she calls an "imaginary horizon of multiple plans and possibilities."[36]

But if there is a social component to the idea of a project, there is an institutional one as well.[37] In organization theory, the concept of a project concerns the making and remaking of organizational structures. The organization theorists J. Rodney Turner and Ralf Müller define projects as "temporary organizations" that depend on the workings of existing organizations but also modify them. In their definition, projects are collaborative and short-term endeavors that often operate under a sense of urgency, and that tap into the resources of existing organizations to "deliver beneficial objectives of change."[38] This usage helps to understand projects as goal-oriented and often collaborative endeavors that are shaped by the institutional networks of Indian diplomacy, even as they work toward discursive and political change within them.

Drawing on these different usages, I argue that nineteenth-century Native American writers and orators generated what I term *indigenous publication projects*: mediated forms of indigenous representation that are produced with non-Native collaborators, which take place in institutional and diplomatic networks but also intervene in them. They are *indigenous* not because they authentically give voice to the ideas of indigenous actors, but because these mediated forms of publication nevertheless construct indigenous counter-discourses within colonial scenes of interaction. And they are forms of *publication* not because they necessarily hail a potentially unlimited audience, but because they organize politically meaningful publics within existing communication networks. Finally, I define them as *projects* because they are collaborative forms of textual production, directed at some measure of institutional change. Indigenous publication projects organize various forms of writing and speaking in the context of diplomatic interaction, but if they are shaped by institutional structures and discourses, they also inflect them. In the nineteenth century, Native authors circulated their critiques by working closely (sometimes problematically so) with collaborators such as Indian agents, administrators, and missionaries, who often imposed their ideas and political goals onto these attempts to gain public notice. Even as their projects were sponsored by American policymakers, however, they were important interventions in existing institutions, constituting crucial attempts to claim a place for Indian nations in North America. By considering Native American publication as a *project*, then, I emphasize the political and intellectual goals of indigenous writers and speakers while being realistic about the process and conditions of their path to publication. To approach such acts of writing and speaking as indigenous publication projects emphasizes the strategic agency of Native authors who navigated diplomatic publics within government and civil society—communication circuits that included coauthors, amanuenses, translators, printers, and participants in treaty councils. These networks provided the discursive means by which their texts were disseminated within a range of (intimate) networks, but they were also inflected by the efforts of Native writers who pushed back against their very structures.

In the era of Indian removal, indigenous publication projects negotiated different visions for the political and economic organization of tribal nations. These projects extended but also modified the long history of indigenous writing in North America, which since the first days of colonial encounter had been shaped by the practice of treaty-making and the confines of colonial law. In an important survey of American Indian literatures, Eric Cheyfitz suggests that the form and content of US-Indian treaties reflect deeply rooted colonial conditions, revealing how "Indian communities are subject to, even as they resist, cultural, social, economic, and political translation."[39] And since treaties became central to the official status of Indian nations under American law, federal Indian law itself can be seen as an early form of "collaborative American literature."[40] In the nineteenth century, Native writers proved themselves deeply aware of the political implications of how Indian nations were constructed in American law. As Maureen Konkle has shown in *Writing Indian Nations*, Native American intellectuals engaged with the history of treaty-making to affirm the existence of tribal nations as modern nations living in historical time, holding undiminished claims to political sovereignty.[41] Writers from Elias Boudinot to George Copway recognized that treaties represented a central site of contestation over the meaning of Indian nationhood in relation to American empire. In this respect, such projects extended a distinctive tradition of Native American literature that engaged the history of US-Indian treaties and thereby asserted the political sovereignty of Indian nations.

Yet if US-Indian treaties and federal Indian law had a profound shaping influence on indigenous literatures, they were not the only diplomatic contexts that Native writers and speakers engaged. Indeed, Cheyfitz reminds us that American legal institutions were by no means the only state apparatus that affected Native people's lives profoundly, and indeed the White House and the United States Congress had a more immediate impact on the conduct of Indian policy and diplomacy.[42] Since Indian diplomacy was a situational affair, taking place in different locations in and beyond Indian country, indigenous publication projects emerged from a wide range of diplomatic settings: intertribal councils, the offices of Indian agents, delegations to Washington, speeches in the US Congress, collaborations with state governments, and meetings with the leaders of religious organizations. It was in these multivalent sites of diplomacy that Native writers and orators intervened in the institutions of the early American republic. The writings that came out of these settings were not defined by a US-Indian dyad but were profoundly shaped by negotiations within and among Indian nations. Through these diplomatic networks, Native representatives generated an important tradition of indigenous writing that was both tribally specific and intertribal, chronicling the failures of American policy and diplomacy while articulating new possibilities for Indian nations in a colonial situation.

INDIAN REMOVAL, SETTLER COLONIALISM, AND INDIGENOUS SOVEREIGNTY

That Native writers and orators were shrewdly aware of institutional structures and rhetorics was an important recourse for Indian nations, in a colonial culture that sought to extinguish indigenous people's social and physical place. A good case in point are the removal-era writings of the Cherokee elder Nancy Ward (Nanye'hi, c. 1738–1822), who contributed to a longstanding tradition of political petitioning in the Cherokee Nation. In June 1818, Ward called a meeting of thirteen women to discuss the Cherokees' shrinking land base and the possibility of their removal to the trans-Mississippi West. For years, the Cherokees had faced pressure and intimidation from American settlers and speculators, and treaty commissioners now urged them to abandon their homes in Georgia to remove to Indian country. The women drafted a petition to the Cherokee National Council, urging it to take a firm stance against the prospect of removal: "We have heard with painful feelings that the bounds of the lands we now possess are to be drawn into very narrow limits. The land was given to us by the Great Spirit above as our common right, to raise our children upon, & to make support for our rising generations. We therefore humbly petition our beloved children, the head men & warriors, to hold out to the last in support of our common rights, as the Cherokee nation have been the first settlers of this land; we therefore claim the right of the soil."[43] Ward was a logical choice to present the petition to the council, having played a long-standing role as a diplomat. Having once fought in battle, she was allowed to speak in council on national affairs, and she had made speeches to American treaty commissioners going back to the years of the American Revolutionary War.[44] Faced with an increasingly urgent debate over removal, Ward used her status as a diplomat to mediate between the Cherokee women and the National Council and, ultimately, to intervene in the workings US-Cherokee diplomacy.

Still, there was another strand to the Cherokee women's argument as well. While they protested the sale of Cherokee lands, their petition also testified to the influence of Euro-American narratives of "civilization" as a rhetorical defense against indigenous displacement: "Our Father the President advised us to become farmers, to manufacture our own clothes, & to have our children instructed. To this advice we have attended in every thing as far as we were able. Now the thought of us being compelled to remove [to] the other side of the Mississippi is dreadful to us, because it appears that we shall be brought to a savage state again, for we have ... become too much enlightened to throw aside the privileges of a civilized life."[45] In rejecting the prospect of removal, they embraced the rhetoric of civilization as promoted by "Our Father the President," arguing that the Cherokee's accomplishments in arts, science, and agriculture brought their nation "enlightenment" and in fact reinforced their claims to their lands. Recognizing that the concept of "civilization" was an important argument in asserting national sovereignty, the Cherokee women marshaled their pride in these agricultural and educational accomplishments to speak out against removal.

The Cherokee petition underscores that Indian removal was both an immediate political crisis and a wider ideological debate over indigenous sovereignty and "civilization." The Cherokee removal treaty, signed at New Echota 1835, and the subsequent Trail of Tears (1838) loom large in American Indian history, as do the presidency of Andrew Jackson and his signing of the Indian Removal Act in 1830. Yet these were by no means isolated events in the history of removal, nor was this a crisis that affected the Cherokee exclusively. Indeed, the timeline and geography of removal extend far beyond the 1830s and the Cherokee Trail of Tears. Indian removal involved the long-standing displacement of Indian nations by making treaties that extinguished indigenous land title, and as legal historian Stuart Banner notes, this practice had predated Andrew Jackson's presidency by some 200 years.[46] In the early 1800s, however, removal became a more standardized policy for the American government than it had been before. In 1804, following the Louisiana Purchase a year earlier, the United States Congress authorized the American president to negotiate with Indian nations for the exchange of their lands, a resolution that was renewed in 1817. This meant that if Anglo-Americans had previously used money and goods to expropriate lands from Indian nations, "now they would be purchasing it with other lands," as Banner puts it.[47] In essence, removal policy meant that the United States made treaties with sovereign Indian nations, forcing them to abandon their lands in the East in exchange for lands west of the Mississippi. The exploratory expeditions of Lewis and Clark (1804–1806) and Stephen Harriman Long (1817–1823) provided the knowledge needed to work out the logics of relocating Indian nations, as well as the boundary line that would separate American society from Indian country.[48]

In the two decades following the Louisiana Purchase, the US government effected removal on a regional rather than cross-continental scale, pushing for relatively smaller land cessions and relocations on a more local level. After the War of 1812, Secretary of War John C. Calhoun first pursued plans for large-scale removals and in 1824 President Monroe proposed to Congress the idea of a territory west of the Mississippi that could offer a potentially permanent home for eastern Indian nations. After Andrew Jackson assumed the presidency in 1829, the American government pursued the relocation of all eastern nations on a grand scale. In 1830, following a fierce debate in Congress, Jackson signed into law the Indian Removal Act, which reasserted the president's power to directly negotiate removal treaties with Indian nations and appropriated $500,000 to fund removals.⁴⁹ In his State of the Union address that year, Jackson considered the government's policy "not only liberal but generous," arguing that it "kindly offers [the American Indian] a new home, and proposes to pay the whole expense of his removal and settlement."⁵⁰ American policymakers assumed Native people's moral inferiority and thereby their incapacity to determine their own futures, which allowed them to pitch removal as a humanitarian project. They promoted removal as part of the country's paternalistic duty toward Native people, arguing that it would offer them a chance to "catch up" with civilization in the West before they were overrun or corrupted by white settlers in the East.

On one level, then, Indian removal was a time-tested practice that consolidated policies, racial ideologies, and imperial narratives around the goal of extinguishing Native land title. But Indian removal also refers to a more specific period—roughly between the War of 1812 and the American Civil War—when the forced relocation of Indian nations became a defining policy goal for the United States government in its dealings with indigenous people. During Andrew Jackson's presidency (1829–1837), removal became a more prominent political debate in the United States, and the Indian Removal Act of 1830 made removal the go-to policy for handling what came to be known as "the Indian problem." In 1834 the Indian Trade and Intercourse Act established the lands west of the Mississippi as "Indian country" (often used interchangeably with the term "Indian Territory") and designated the trans-Mississippi region as a zone for removed indigenous nations. However, in his historical study of Indian country, William E. Unrau notes that already by the end of the 1830s, the "weak administration" of Indian affairs and the "chronic violations of the new Indian code" meant that even those lands that had been designated for removed tribes were taken, once again, by white settlers. The US government frequently reduced the size of reservations, which soon led to the "blatantly illegal white penetration" of the eastern parts of Indian Territory.⁵¹ As historian Christina Snyder observes, removal should therefore not be seen as "a single act of Congress" or the "lone experience" of the Cherokee Nation, but as "a thousand betrayals, a series of dispossessions, an ethnic cleansing designed to radically restructure North America."⁵² The policy of Indian removal echoed narratives of American empire that increasingly depended on ideas of white supremacy. According to Snyder, Andrew Jackson's presidency marked a key moment when the racist ideologies of his constituency combined with new concepts from scientific racism, crystallizing a "new brand of racism that would empower a core republic of whites." Indian removal logically became a key principle for "a continental empire where people of color could be marginalized as perpetual subjects or, worse, chattel."⁵³

The debate over removal cast sharp divisions not only in Indian nations but also among white policymakers and religious reformists. Historian John P. Bowes notes that the politically controversial case of the Cherokee Nation profoundly influenced the wider public debate over removal, which was shaped by the Cherokees' "language of resistance" as much as the rhetoric of those who promoted removal.[54] As Bowes argues, the dominant rhetoric about removal was shaped by four different if overlapping discourses: the Cherokee constitution's assertion of sovereignty, the American government's policy deliberations, wider debates around removal in the public sphere (which was dominated by white missionaries), and a body of "legal ideologies and judicial rulings."[55] Yet the polarizing responses to removal policy did not reflect fixed lines of ethnicity or tribal affiliation. Many prominent missionaries vehemently opposed removal in word and deed, such as Jeremiah Evarts of the American Board of Commissioners of Foreign Missions, who worked in the Cherokee Nation during the 1820s and widely publicized his arguments against removal.[56] Other religious leaders, such as the Baptist minister Isaac McCoy, promoted removal to Native leaders and worked with territorial and federal agents to negotiate removal treaties.[57] Similar divisions existed within Indian nations. While many tribal leaders and intellectuals opposed removal, others found reasons to sign off on it, and if many of them moved to Indian Territory with their people, others stayed behind and became citizens under American law.

The ideology and practice of removal thus depended on local and regional dynamics, and on the often limited and contextual powers of white Indian agents and administrators.[58] To understand the relation between Native writing and diplomacy therefore requires an effort to recuperate the iterative and uneven histories of Indian removal and those who negotiated it. For the Southern nations that became known as the "Five Civilized Tribes"—the Cherokee, Choctaw, Chickasaw, Creek, and Seminole—removal represented an immediate political crisis when state legislatures threatened to impose their laws over Indian nations. In May 1830, Choctaw representatives signed the Treaty of Dancing Rabbit Creek, which ushered in the first large-scale removal to Indian Territory since the Removal Act of 1830. Perhaps most famously, a Cherokee faction signed the Treaty of New Echota in 1835, which led to their removal three years later. An estimated 4,000 Cherokee people died on their march to Indian Territory, known today as the "Trail of Tears." The removal of the Southern nations in the 1830s, however, is part of a longer and more regionally varied history of removal. In areas that were less densely populated with white settlers, such as Michigan Territory, removal followed a different timeline and geography. Members of the Ottawa, Potawatomi,

Shawnee, Sauk, and Meskwaki nations signed removal treaties relatively early—in the 1830s and 1840s—and were relocated to Indian Territory. Yet many of the Ojibwe tribes in the Great Lakes region fended off removal as late as the 1850s and relocated to smaller tracts of land nearer to their original homelands.

Despite such local and regional differences, the policy and practice of Indian removal was a central factor in the history of settler colonialism in the nineteenth century. Briefly put, settler colonialism is a form of colonialism in which the structuring imperative is not the domination of native labor (as is the case in extraction-based colonialism), but rather the extinguishing of an indigenous presence.[59] In an influential formulation, Patrick Wolfe defines settler colonialism as "an inclusive, land-centred project that coordinates a comprehensive range of agencies, from the metropolitan centre to the frontier encampment, with a view to eliminating Indigenous societies."[60] This logic of elimination, Wolfe argues, has manifested historically in a range of tactics to erode indigenous peoples' sovereignty and land title, including treaty-making, military violence, assimilationist policies, and boarding-school education. In other words, settler colonialism does not indicate a historical "event"—not an "invasion," "encounter," or "period"—but a continuous relationship of indigenous nations to colonial rule, one that may have changed over time but remains a structuring relation as long as there exists a settler demand for indigenous lands. In North America, settler colonialism has followed the pattern of what Carole Pateman calls the "tempered logic of the settler contract," as distinguished from the "strict" logic. Under the strict logic, settlers do not recognize the sovereignty and land title of indigenous nations but render their lands "vacant," thereby relinquishing the need to make treaties with them. The United States, however, upheld the "tempered logic" of settler colonialism in which agents of the settler state made treaties with sovereign indigenous nations that were part and parcel of how their land title was extinguished.[61] Under the tempered logic of settler colonialism, the government *did* recognize indigenous sovereignty and the imposition of a settler state operated *through* US-Indian negotiations.

Pateman's analysis points to the vexed status of indigenous sovereignty in North America. Native studies scholar Amanda J. Cobb argues that in critical discourse, the term "sovereignty" is often used "in the same manner as terms like 'freedom' and 'liberty'—passionately evoked but rarely accorded precise definition or practical meaning."[62] In a settler-colonial context, indigenous sovereignty is an elusive category because it generally refers to two closely related concepts. First, it names Native people's self-determination, their right and ability to determine their own political, social, and cultural affairs; second, it names a more circumscribed legal status of Indian nations as sovereign entities *within* the United States. These settler-colonial logics were reinforced in US law with Chief Justice John Marshall's ruling in *Fletcher v. Peck* (1810), which decided that indigenous land title was temporary, subject to being extinguished by the United States government, even if it did not specify any process by which that could occur. More famously, in the early 1830s, three of Marshall's Supreme Court rulings on Indian sovereignty—the "Marshall trilogy"—codified the status of indigenous nations as "domestic dependent nations" within the United States.[63] Scholars have long grappled with this status of Indian nations as "domestic dependent nations" vis-à-vis the American government. The anthropologist Audra Simpson explains indigenous sovereignty in terms of a "nested sovereignty," a political status that is paradoxically "within and apart from settler governance."[64] And the political theorist Kevin Bruyneel has argued that after the United States stopped making Indian treaties in 1871, Indian nations' appeal to US-based rights, and at the same time their resistance to colonialism, created a "third space of sovereignty" that codified Indian nations as both external and internal to US rule.[65]

This paradox of indigenous sovereignty shaped the workings of Indian diplomacy in the nineteenth century. On the one hand, by making treaties Indian nations reaffirmed their inherent sovereign status as nations external to the United States. On the other hand, the American government recognized indigenous sovereignty only within the context of the colonial relationship between Native people and the United States: for instance, it did not recognize Indian nations as sovereign powers that could engage in formal diplomatic relations with other foreign powers. This also meant that Indian nations were directly affected by American policies, acts of Congress, and legal rulings at the federal level—and often in drastic ways. In Native American studies, therefore, the vexed status of indigenous sovereignty has become a central paradigm for examining indigenous literary and intellectual productions, as evidenced in influential frameworks such as Robert Warrior's "intellectual sovereignty" and Scott Richard Lyons's "rhetorical sovereignty."[66] This scholarly recentering of sovereignty has spurred a proliferation of critical heuristics evoking the concept of sovereignty to emphasize the issue of self-determination in Native cultural productions, including "visual sovereignty," "temporal sovereignty," "sonic sovereignty," and "data sovereignty."[67] This work has opened up new and productive avenues to explore Native American writings as not beholden to narrowly defined notions of indigenous "culture" or tribal traditions, but to the political life of sovereign nations that have always known social and linguistic diversity, different religious traditions, historical change, and transnational relations.

Yet the emphasis on sovereignty as a critical heuristic has also tended to make this concept legible in mostly a metaphorical sense, evoking Indian self-determination without engaging the matter of tribal governments or their political representation vis-à-vis the United States. By focusing on questions of diplomacy I mean to center a more strictly political notion of indigenous sovereignty in the study of nineteenth-century Native writing. Because Indian diplomacy negotiated conflicting indigenous and settler claims to land, it exposes the discursive spaces where Native speakers critiqued US-settler colonialism and represented indigenous sovereignty within colonial institutions. If American ideologies regarded Indian nations' land title as temporary and prone to be superseded by the settler state, Native writers and orators entered an ideological debate in which they consistently challenged the colonial assumptions that buttressed Indian policy.[68] These debates took place in a wide array of institutional settings, well beyond the United States Supreme Court. Congress, the White House, treaty councils, and Indian agencies were among the scenes of Indian diplomacy that directly influenced US-Indian relations, even more so in the era of Indian removal. The Office of Indian Affairs also played a central role in the life of Indian nations after its founding in 1824.[69] Its first director, Thomas McKenney, saw in removal a fundamentally humanitarian policy, calling it "one of the kindest that has ever been perfected," because it would "perpetuate the Aboriginal race, elevate it to its proper dignity, and impart it to a perpetuity of happiness."[70] By the time Andrew Jackson's administration ousted him from office in 1830, McKenney had already promoted removal by championing the Removal Act and by personally negotiating removal treaties with various nations.[71]

Such diplomatic interactions often happened far away from the Indian Office in Washington, typically taking place in councils in or near Native communities, or at the offices of Indian agents or superintendents of Indian affairs. For Native authors, then, to critique Indian policy meant navigating a range of institutions that were loosely structured and often poorly connected. When it was established in 1824, the Office of Indian Affairs was quite literally an office: the director, his two clerks, and his office managers shared only one room in the War Department building in Washington. By the 1850s it fared not much better, with its staff sharing "seven shabby offices."[72] Until its bureaucratization after the Civil War, the Indian Office represented a loose network of US officials, traders, field agents, and members of religious organizations, who conducted policy through oral conversations, letters, and councils with Native leaders. Indian policy relied on the local diplomacy of its employees—field agents, traders, translators, and regional superintendents—and because Indian agents were political appointees, these networks were continually being made and remade. This does not mean that removal happened in the *absence* of federal power. In his history of the nineteenth-century administration of Indian affairs, Stephen J. Rockwell argues that the Indian Office relied on a "culture of discretionary authority and localized decision making."[73] In this regard, the policy of removal operated through the general logics by which the United States managed Indian affairs, which was "fragmented and filtered through a diverse set of political, economic, and regional interests."[74]

The open-ended government structure of the Indian Office calls attention to the porous line between what Antonio Gramsci famously termed "political" and "civil" society.[75] Whereas the former typically includes state apparatuses such as the military, the legal system, and the government bureaucracy, the latter includes "voluntary" or at least "non-coercive" affiliations, including schools, religious organizations, and reform organizations.[76] Although the category of "civil society" is often considered autonomous from the state or even a potential correction to it, William Novak argues that in the nineteenth-century United States it was not a self-organized sphere that existed autonomously from federal policy. While often imagined as a sphere of "freedom, community, democracy, and dissent," American civil society depended on legal frameworks and fiscal policies that actively enabled the creation of associations and organizations in civil society.[77] In terms of its Indian policy, too, the American government encouraged an active role for groups within civil society, relying on the participation of missionary organizations and other religious and reformist groups to execute its Indian policy. For instance, the government's "civilization policy" hinged on enlisting missionary societies to carry out its social policy for Indian nations, especially in the realm of education. In 1819 a congressional act established the Civilization Fund, providing $10,000 annually to support the establishment and support of schools in Indian country, mostly manual labor schools. These funds complemented treaty-stipulated appropriations for Native American education and encouraged missionary organizations to provide teachers for day schools, academies, and seminaries in Indian country.[78] Thus the federal government effectively outsourced the implementation of its "civilization policy" to reform-minded groups in civil society, which worked according to religious principles to effect change in Indian country, acting as mediators between indigenous governments and the United States bureaucracy.

The involvement of nongovernmental entities in Indian affairs also extended to capitalist enterprise. Going back to the seventeenth century, European and American trading companies secured the participation of Native people in the transatlantic fur trade, while white traders often married into indigenous families and even gained roles in tribal leadership. Much like the women they married, traders became important intercultural brokers and consolidated diplomatic ties between Indian nations and settler governments.[79] Traders also often worked as Indian agents and government translators, which means that the local administration of Indian affairs came to lean heavily on the capitalist enterprise of trading companies such as the Chouteau Company and the American Fur Company.

These companies, in turn, encouraged the exploration and settlement of Indian country and forged expedient connections between land speculators, civil chiefs, colonial administrators, and military leaders.[80] By the time the fur trade collapsed in the 1820s, many Indian nations had become indebted to trading companies, and American administrators made this fact an important policy tool, since these debts put Indian nations in a weaker bargaining position when negotiating about land cessions. Regardless, the role of trading companies was not typically seen as a policy tool but as a matter of free association. If "association" typically denotes "cooperative communities based on religious or socialist principles," by the 1830s it came to include capitalist enterprise, bringing about what historian Michael Denning calls a problematic conflation between "intellectual and moral associations" and "manufacturing and trading companies," a slippage that allowed trading companies to occupy a position as "one of many civil associations, whose free activity [was] necessary to the preservation of equality and freedom."[81] In short, the capitalist enterprise of fur trade companies, and their influence on the government's administration of Indian affairs, was easily defended as being a sphere of free democracy rather than a machination of federal Indian policy.

Given the decentralized nature of Indian policy, Native diplomats and tribal leaders did not deal with a clearly defined "settler state," but with a number of dispersed and problematically connected agencies, from tribal councils and US government agencies to religious organizations and trading houses. They found themselves forced to protest removal through face-to-face and written negotiations with a bewildering range of individuals and groups, not only governmental figures such as the commissioner of Indian Affairs but also field agents, translators, territorial governors, traders, citizen groups, missionaries, and other religious groups within American civil society. These divergent arenas of policy came together in scenes of Indian diplomacy, where Native representatives engaged in a Gramscian war of position, a struggle not directed at a monolithic state to be seized and overthrown, but at what cultural theorist Stuart Hall calls "a complex *formation* in modern societies"; Native intellectuals and political leaders found themselves in "an arena of different social contestations" where they had to adopt "a number of different strategies and struggles."[82] In this light, the publication projects of Native writers and orators were not simply records of a "clash" between indigenous and settler values or perspectives, nor did they focus on removal as an isolated political issue. Instead, they reflected what Frederick Hoxie suggests was a "a series of confrontations" that involved "a complex array of collaborators, mediators and deal-makers operating on all sides of the confrontation."[83] Calling attention to these diplomatic struggles will help to uncover the shape-shifting projects and publics of Native writing in the nineteenth century.

AUTHORSHIP AND AUTHORITY IN REMOVAL-ERA NATIVE WRITING

If the literatures of Indian diplomacy worked through intricate institutional networks and collaborations, how did Native writers and orators interpret their own acts of publication in these colonial contexts? When the Ojibwe missionary George Copway published his autobiography in 1847, he included in his book a telling critique on the politics of representation as he experienced them. Copway's life and career gave ample opportunity to reflect on these. Born in Rice Lake, Ontario, Copway had converted to Methodism in 1830, and after his education began to work as a missionary, predominantly in Ojibwe and Dakota communities in the Midwest. He gained fame as a public speaker on reform, temperance, and Native American history, and his rising celebrity resulted in the publication of his *The Life, History, and Travels of Kah-Ge-Ga-Gah-Bowh* in New York in 1847. By the time his book came out, however, Copway had fallen from grace as a missionary. In the Ojibwe communities of Saugeen and Rice Lake he was charged with mismanaging tribal funds and embezzlement in his capacity of overseer of a manual labor school and as council clerk. When Ojibwe leaders reported him to the Indian Department, Copway spent several weeks in a Toronto prison and was ousted as a member of the Canada Conference of Methodist Missionaries.[84] With his reputation in question, Copway's autobiography was an opportunity to defend his character.

But Copway also rebutted accusations of a different kind, challenging critics who argued that Copway had misrepresented himself as a "chief" of the Ojibwe in order to insert himself into Ojibwe politics—an accusation made most prominently by the Methodist publication *The Christian Guardian*.[85] To defend his actions, Copway reprinted a letter from the Ojibwe leader Joseph Sawyer stating his initial appointment as overseer of the manual labor school, for the "benefit and instruction of those, who have been so kind as to insinuate, or assert, that I was not an *authorized agent* to forward the interests of my poor people."[86] Copway emphasized the important role he played in national affairs and claimed a newfound intellectual independence from the Canada Conference of Methodist Missionaries. He suggested that it was not up to the missionary organization to determine who could speak for the Ojibwe: "Those who have been the loudest and most active in this slander, have done the least, in rendering the Indians any essential service. Let them go on, with their gossippings, [*sic*] while I go on my way rejoicing in doing all I can for my poor people, independently of the Canada Conference. Neither have I any disposition to court the favor of this Conference. Indeed, my heart has often sickened at the divisions and subdivisions of the Canada Methodists."[87] In effect, Copway argued that the Canada Conference was not essential to the cause of meaningful Indian reform, while his own career as a writer and speaker rendered "essential service" to his people. Rejecting established Methodist networks, Copway suggested an alternative path to carrying out his role as a public intellectual, independently from the approval the Canada Conference.

For Copway, to be an "authorized agent" meant taking on a representational role in a racialized regime in which Native people were expected to carry some measure of "authorization" from indigenous communities and/or colonial institutions. Like Copway, Native writers and speakers were expected to explain their own ability to speak publicly about Indian affairs (and about their own nations in particular), and they did so in various ways: by testifying to their own education and institutional knowledge, by emphasizing their role within councils, or by performing what American interlocutors would see as a culturally legible notion of the "Indian chief." In short, in a culture in which Native intellectuals and writers were read as representatives of Indian nations, they engaged the expectations and stereotypes of white publics in order to represent what Phillip H. Round calls a "public, political Indianness."[88] However artificial this may have been, such outside "authorization" mattered materially for the purpose of being taken seriously as an intellectual and political authority, rather than as merely an example of the eloquent yet tragically vanishing Native American. Copway recognized the workings of a colonial culture in which Native writers and speakers were asked to speak to the links between authority, authenticity, and textual representation.

Copway's defense of himself as an "authorized agent" raises the question of how Native writers and speakers claimed political relevance as historical actors and textual producers. As social historian William H. Sewell explains, "to be an agent means to be capable of exerting some degree of control over the social relations in which one is enmeshed, which in turn implies the ability to transform those social relations to some degree." It is in relation to larger social structures that agency becomes analytically meaningful. In Sewell's words, "agents are empowered to act with and against others by structures: they have knowledge of the schemas that inform social life and have access to some measure of human and nonhuman resources."[89] In this sense, agency "arises from the actor's knowledge of schemas" and thus the ability to apply these to "new contexts." Agency, then, should not be seen as simply an abstract human capacity for action but as a negotiation between the structural and the situational, through the ability to wield "control of resources" and to "reinterpret or mobilize" them.[90] However, the ability to engage and transform existing structures was not seen as a capacity of Native people in a colonial culture that denied them a role as meaningful historical actors. As Beth H. Piatote writes, the term *agency* "will never function as a neutral term for

Indians" since nineteenth-century federal Indian law hinged on Native people's "legal wardship" and a governmental system that "assigned Indian agency to Indian Agents."⁹¹ The concept of Native agency is inflected by "the ghosts of Indian Agents," government workers whose role in managing Indian nations predated the American state and separated Native people from the very concept of agency in an institutional sense:

> The notion of an Agent as part of a "civilizing" mission and a government representative among the Indians was established in American law in 1793, with the second Trade and Intercourse Act.... In 1831 the US Supreme Court ruling *Cherokee Nation v. Georgia* produced the legal structure of Indian wardship that legitimated the unequal distribution of agency, and as the reservation system expanded through the mid-nineteenth century, so did the power of Agents over Indians. As symbol and structure of this shift, the physical space of the reservation was organized around its central seat of power, the Agency, a building that dispensed Indian Agents but denied Indian agency.⁹²

By presenting himself as "an authorized agent," then, Copway refused a logic in which Native agency was beholden to representatives of the settler state. As an author and public speaker, he insisted on new ways for Native people to carry out the diplomatic relationship—for the Indian speaker to remain an "agent" in representing his or her nation.

This is not to suggest that the discourses of Native writers and speakers only mattered in moments when they *resisted* colonial logics. In a reflection on the writing of histories of slavery, Walter Johnson challenges the interpretive mode of "redress," in which the scholar recognizes the subaltern's stolen agency and tries to return that agency "to its rightful owners."⁹³ This mode of redress risks generalizing "historically and culturally situated acts of resistance" into manifestations of agency as an "abstract human capacity." Johnson argues that this not only obscures how historical actors theorized their own actions in sophisticated ways, but also the "practical process" by which those actions produced new ways of conceptualizing oppression and resistance.⁹⁴ While histories of slavery and indigenous dispossession are not the same, I mean to suggest that Native responses to settler expansion, too, do not represent an abstract form of resistance that we can now reclaim as a fundamental dimension of human agency. Moreover, a too narrowly defined notion of agency-as-resistance risks filtering out the important institutional navigations of Native authors past and present. To echo Maureen Konkle's argument in *Writing Indian Nations*, analyzing the literatures of Indian diplomacy will require us to surrender an interpretive framework in which Native authors signify tragic figures caught between two worlds and fighting against the onset of modernity—an image that has long obscured the political and intellectual questions Native authors raised.[95]

The literatures of Indian diplomacy offer alternative representations of Native agency, re-inscribing the figure of the indigenous diplomat as an agentic subject whose words carried political weight in concrete institutional situations. And no matter how artificial their status as "official" delegates was, these literatures constructed Indian diplomats as the *authors* of texts that were collaboratively produced or sponsored by existing organizations. Indeed, even when they were transcribed or translated by non-Native collaborators, these publication projects established indigenous speakers as the originators of discourse, whose political voice could be constructed as a tribal-national one. To be an "authorized agent," in other words, meant gaining an "author function" that legitimized collaborative texts as the products of indigenous speakers. On the one hand, this dynamic was a function of a government system in which the political representation of Native people depended on the authorizing techniques of the settler state. On the other hand, it denied the logic by which only Indian agents—then a strictly non-Native occupation—had agency in scenes of diplomatic negotiation.

What cuts across the following chapters is the question of *how* these authorized agents—diplomats, writers, intellectuals, and tribal leaders—asserted a public, political voice within diplomatic interactions. One aspect of this question is how they addressed the expectations that befell them as they mediated between Native and non-Native interlocutors. Were they the "real" authors of texts that were produced collaboratively? Were they able to speak for—to *represent*—their people, or American Indians generally? Or, for that matter, could they represent other religious, political, or cultural groups they belonged to? This matter of authorization is closely related to the question of whether Native people could be taken seriously both as *authors* and as representatives of their nations, in a culture where Euro-American ideas about indigenous people shaped the commentary on US-Indian affairs. For instance, when in the 1840s the Choctaw educator and diplomat Peter Pitchlynn visited Washington on diplomatic business, his self-performance cut two ways. He insisted on his own status as a property-owning gentleman who had received formal education, but also presented himself as an embodiment of Choctaw political authority by making affective appeals on behalf of "his nation." His political authority depended on his status as a male, propertied, and educated figure, but Pitchlynn also needed to reconcile this with his ability to be seen as culturally "Choctaw."

That some writers and speakers emerged as "authorized agents" and others did not reflects distinctions of power and privilege based in gender, class, and education. Although Nancy Ward reminds us that Native women were not excluded wholesale from public life because of their gender, the authors in the chapters ahead were predominantly men from privileged family backgrounds, sometimes Christians, and often the recipients of formal education. In other words, family, class, gender, religion, and education were all factors that shaped opportunities for publication. Despite the prominent role that women played as diplomats and intercultural brokers, in formal nation-to-nation diplomacy this role was more exclusively the domain of men.[96] To be sure, several women orators and writers took part in these publication projects, including Hayne Hudjihini (Otoe), Ozhaguscodaywayquay, and Jane Johnston Schoolcraft (Ojibwe). More typically, however, these sites of Indian diplomacy were sites of masculinity, depending on Euro-American codes of homosocial interaction and gendered tropes of friendship and fraternity. Beyond the masculinist dimensions of these publication projects, they were exclusive along other axes as well. They did not necessarily reflect community-based ethics of democratic deliberation or indigenous protocols of decision-making, and sometimes—as I show in chapter 2—they played into the settler government's preference for tribal representatives who would help to streamline US-Indian political relations.

From this perspective, to focus on Indian diplomacy as a framework for Native publication imposes certain limitations. That diplomatic interactions depended on tribal leaders and elite men means that it is difficult to write its history "from the ground up," so to speak. And since the question of who was appointed to conduct US-Indian diplomacy depended on codes of class, gender, and political prominence, there was no one-on-one relationship between Native delegates and the communities they represented, especially in Indian nations that were highly stratified economically. Furthermore, Indian diplomacy worked by a logic in which American government officials had to *recognize* these diplomats as representatives of their nations. As such, Native diplomats were not able to work outside of the bind of what indigenous studies scholar Glen Coulthard calls "the colonial politics of recognition," the problem that in a settler-colonial regime, the legal and political status of Indian sovereignty is acknowledged and codified by the settler state.[97] I mention these as genuine caveats to the analyses that follow. At the same time, the work of Indian diplomacy should not be dismissed too quickly as an inauthentic representation of indigenous sovereignty, or as Indian nations' capitulation to the politics of recognition. Copway's rejoinder to the *Missionary Register* reminds us that it is not up to us as present-day commentators to decide who was authorized to speak for Indian nations. Instead, we should take seriously the attempts of Native writers and diplomats to be *heard* within scenes of US-Indian diplomacy, on their own terms and in recognition of their limitations.

There was much at stake in those efforts. Throughout the nineteenth-century Indian nations were deprived not only of vast amounts of land and opportunities, but also of their negotiating power in relation to the United States. As the United States built a continental empire on cotton and tobacco (and thereby on the labor of enslaved African Americans), their economic relations with Native people who worked in the fur trade became marginal to American economic and political concerns. Moreover, after the War of 1812 it became harder if not impossible for Indian nations to organize large-scale alliances with other indigenous people or European powers, meaning that the military power of Indian nations decreased as that of the United States gradually increased. The subsequent centrality of removal policy in the early nineteenth century signals the US government's increasingly unilateral approach to "the Indian question." In turn, Native diplomats and tribal leaders saw themselves faced with the need to insist on the importance of ongoing diplomatic relationships, to be recognized not as subjects of an American empire but as citizens of sovereign Indian nations.

Returning to the question of Indian diplomacy will therefore extend critical conversations in Native American and indigenous studies about the relationships between agency, sovereignty, and literary representation. How did writers and orators from different tribal nations extend diplomatic interactions through different forms of publishing? Chapter 1 follows the participants in an 1821 delegation to Washington, who hailed from five indigenous nations in the Missouri River Valley. The orators Sharitarish (Chaui Pawnee) and Ongpatonga (Omaha) shared knowledge about the limits of Indian diplomacy in the Upper Missouri Valley and pushed back against ideas of "civilization" that undergirded ideologies of settler expansion. In doing so they exposed the tensions between, on the one hand, the projections of American empire in governmental circles, and on the other hand, the realities of indigenous hegemony in the Missouri River Valley. Chapter 2 traces how different Sauk writers and orators negotiated the ramifications of settler encroachment and removal in the 1830s and 1840s. The tribal leaders Black Hawk, Keokuk, and Hardfish pursued different paths to protesting US militarism and white encroachment onto their lands. Performing sustained critiques of how the Indian Office operated, they created knowledge about the Sauk Nation's economic dependency that resulted from removal and American trading practices. In doing so their publication projects articulated conflicting ideas about the "frontier": whereas American policymakers and treaties understood the frontier as a zone of potential violence and conflict that had to be pacified, Keokuk understood the frontier as a region where different spheres of economic activity (agriculture, trade, hunting, and trapping) could co-exist if managed right.

In other Indian nations, the question of removal refracted wider debates over the development of tribal-national education and institution-building. Chapter 3 examines how the Choctaw diplomat and educator Peter Pitchlynn articulated an innovative strand of Choctaw nationalism. From 1825 to 1855—before and after removal from Mississippi to Indian Territory—Pitchlynn mediated between the Choctaw General Council and the Indian Office, missionary groups, and educational establishments. Championing tribal schools and academies, he developed a notion of Choctaw nationalism that was rooted in an ideology of exceptionalism vis-à-vis other Indian nations. His pragmatic and even imperialist articulation of Choctaw nationalism privileged landowning elites in the nation, but simultaneously worked as a framework for investing in education as a public good. Finally, in chapter 4 I argue that the representation of Native leaders and councils in Ojibwe literature, from 1827 to 1860, became a means to assert indigenous sovereignty within transnational cultures of diplomacy and philanthropy. Ojibwe writers and orators including Ozhaguscodaywayquay, Jane Johnston Schoolcraft, Peter Jones, and George Copway articulated ideas of Ojibwe community that stretched across the border between the United States and Upper Canada, and that lent an Ojibwe nationalist dimension to projects of reform and education. Their literary representation of tribal leadership elaborated a politicized notion of Ojibwe nationhood within the networks of reform organizations that considered indigenous nations either as romantic, organic communities or as objects of pity.

Despite the differences between them, authors such as Sharitarish, Peter Pitchlynn, and George Copway all knowingly addressed the assumptions of contemporary interlocutors who imagined American Indians to be a savage or vanishing race. And both Keokuk and Peter Jones used their institutional knowledge of the Indian Office and missionary organizations to expose their colonial assumptions and injustices. Since settler expansion and removal profoundly shaped debates on nationalism, reform, education, and empire, their publication projects were less centrally focused on matters such as indigenous religious traditions, languages, or cultural practices. To the contrary, many of them promoted Christianity and American-style education and invested in reciprocal relationships with American Indian agents and white missionaries. Does this mean that these authors were "accommodationists," going along with the pressures and policy proposals of white settlers and governmental figures? Were they "collaborators" in a negative sense, gaining personally from working alongside the enemy? Or were they "assimilated" subjects, unmoored from their tribal background and indoctrinated into the tenets of white society? The chapters that follow will complicate these questions, but my aim is not to restore the reputations of these historical figures by locating in their projects a "pure" politics of resistance, or authentic expressions of indigenous cultures. Instead, their publication projects are about "culture" in a broader sense: they make sense of what people think, do, and cause, from ecological and social changes to economic policies and militarized violence. How Native American orators and writers reflected on these things was closely bound up with their attempt to intervene in existing organizational structures. *Authorized Agents* therefore considers the work of Native writers and orators who asserted themselves in diplomatic networks and tried, against great odds, to claim control over the representation of Indian nations in a colonial situation.

These publication projects do not dramatize a collision of cultures but represent slow-moving negotiations in public discourse about US-Indian relations. They contribute to a larger body of Native literature that critiqued the workings of American empire, and they are recuperable when we do not demand from them paradigmatic notions of indigenous resistance. The spectacle of the eloquent chief who cursed the white man in the wake of his own defeat is a colonial simulation that tells us little about the rhetorical strategies that indigenous writers and orators employed. After all, nineteenth-century Indian nations were always complex and highly diverse—multilingual, multiethnic, and multireligious—and existed in a world of transnational exchange and historical transformation. The more their publications challenge our expectations about the histories and futures of Indian nations, the more they tell us about the projects of Native American literature.

CHAPTER 1

"Kindness and Firmness"

Negotiating Empire in the Benjamin O'Fallon Delegation

In a painting titled *The House of Representatives*, the American artist and inventor Samuel F. B. Morse captured a brief but telling moment in the history of US-Indian diplomacy. Years before his invention of the telegraph, Morse had a career as a painter of portraits and historical scenes, and in 1822 he completed his rendering of the chamber of the United States House of Representatives. In much detail, it depicts the House members gathered for an evening session, although their debate has not started yet: the representatives are scattered around the chamber while a custodian is lighting the oil lamps on the chandelier. Yet a closer look at two other figures reveals a more telling moment. On the left side of the canvas, the figure reading from a sheet of paper represents the artist's father, Jedidiah Morse, a geographer and minister who had recently presented Congress with a report on the state of Indian nations in the United States. On the opposite side, by the balustrade next to the farthest-right column, Morse included the warrior Petalesharo of the Skidi Pawnee, his features modeled after a state portrait made by Charles Bird King.[1] Petalesharo had recently visited Washington as part of a delegation of tribal leaders from the Upper Missouri Valley, and by the time Samuel Morse completed his painting, the portrait of Petalesharo had already captured the popular imagination of urban Americans. By including both his father and Petalesharo, Morse captured a certain tension. While Jedidiah Morse is poised to present his authoritative study on Indian country, Petalesharo looks on silently from behind the balustrade. Here at the seat of the United States government, one has a say in Indian policy at the seat of US empire, while the other makes only a brief cameo appearance.

This tension reveals much about the conditions under which Petalesharo and his fellow delegates entered into diplomatic relations with the United States, and into American print culture. Morse's *House of Representatives* alludes to a delegation that was one of the most widely reported events of US-Indian diplomacy in the early nineteenth century. The delegation lasted from October 1821 to February 1822 and was sponsored by the US Department of War, which regulated Indian affairs at the federal level. The delegation was overseen by Benjamin O'Fallon, the subagent at the Upper Missouri Indian agency at Council Bluffs, near present-day Omaha, Nebraska. O'Fallon brought to Washington nine leaders and warriors from three divisions of the Pawnee Nation: the Chaui (often referred to as the "Grand Pawnee"), the Kítkehahki (or "Republican Pawnee"), and the Skidi (Ckírihki Kuuruúriki, or "Pawnee Loups"). Besides the Pawnee delegates, there were also eight representatives from neighboring nations: the Kanza, Otoe, Missouria, and Omaha nations. In Washington and New York, the delegates took part in a number of public and semipublic events, including meetings with policymakers and missionaries and a New Year's reception at the White House. In early February, they sat in council with

FIGURE 1.1   Samuel F. B. Morse, *The House of Representatives*. Oil on canvas, 1822, probably reworked in 1823. Corcoran Collection. Courtesy National Gallery of Art, Washington.

President James Monroe and re-enacted the council five days later in front of a large crowd outside the White House. Before they left Washington in late February 1822, the delegates sat for the artist Charles Bird King to have their portraits painted, which became part of the War Department's "Indian gallery" of portraits of Native diplomats. Although archival records of the delegation are scarce, the diplomatic undertaking generated widespread notice through newspapers, magazine poems, songs, portraits, and government reports. By the time the decade drew to a close, Petalesharo had become the face of the delegation, and King's iconic depiction of the young Native warrior captured the popular imagination and became a symbol for the relationship of Native people to American empire.[2] In a wider sphere of visual and print representations, Petalesharo's celebrity came to overshadow the political oratory of the delegates and evoked instead a sympathetic image of the Indian warrior, promoting an optimistic narrative of American expansion in the trans-Mississippi West.

But what was the meaning of the O'Fallon delegation for the Upper Missouri tribal leaders who took part in it? Although Indian diplomacy was usually conducted in or near Indian nations, by the early 1820s delegations of indigenous leaders to Washington had become a fixture in American culture. In the words of historian C. Joseph Genetin-Pilawa, they were frequent enough to be an almost daily presence in the city, even if the public discourse about them made Native delegates into "curiosities to be beheld by an urbane and sophisticated audience."[3] American commentators interpreted Indian delegations as a "first encounter" between savagery and civilization, refracting American ideas of race, gender, and empire. Yet these stereotypical representations hid a "more complex and more interesting history of Native people engaging with non-Native society in Washington City," Genetin-Pilawa suggests.[4] Delegations to Washington held "critical meaning for Native people" and they refuted the easy narrative of a meeting between two different "worlds" that contemporary commentators projected onto them.[5] The O'Fallon delegation, too, is a reminder that the colonial records of Indian diplomacy register more than simply US projections: the transcripts of the proceedings in Washington are ripe with colonial over-writing but they also present a counterdiscourse of indigenous critiques of US Indian policy and the ideologies that undergirded it. If the delegation was a policy tool for asserting American empire, it also produced an archive of indigenous oratory about the realities of diplomatic relations in the Upper Missouri Valley.

For studies of early Native writing in English, the O'Fallon delegation reflects how diplomatic routines produced a body of writing and oratory that wavers between US imperial projections and articulations of indigenous sovereignty. This chapter explores how the O'Fallon delegation reconciled these diverging projects, as it staged a fraught relationship between the diplomatic and institutional significance of indigenous speech acts and their symbolic meaning in a colonial culture. Arriving in Washington at a moment when federal Indian policy was undergoing crucial change, the delegates were introduced to the policy tenets of the "civilizing mission," by which the American government sought influence over Indian nations in the West through peace treaties, Christianization, and education. Given the actual hegemony of Indian nations in the Upper Missouri Valley, however, the delegates inflected these interactions by insisting on forms of Indian diplomacy that were more responsive to local contexts. Against ideologies that assumed indigenous vulnerability, delegates such as Sharitarish (Chaui Pawnee) and Ongpatonga (Omaha) tested the limits of a new Indian policy that was based in the discourse of education and reform. In this respect, if the O'Fallon delegation extended the bureaucratic discourses of the Indian Office, these performative interactions also relayed indigenous critiques of them, revealing the problematic interplay between federal Indian policy and the situational logics of Indian diplomacy in the West. Beyond the romanticizing gaze of American commentators and spectators, the delegates brought critical local knowledge into scenes of US-Indian interaction, demonstrating the need for diplomacy that recognized Indian nations' real historical situations. Interrupting the proposals of the Indian Office at a liminal moment of American empire, the delegation brought the dialogues of Indian diplomacy into a wider sphere of readers and writers in the early US republic.

FAMILY NETWORKS AND DIPLOMATIC PUBLICS: ORGANIZING THE O'FALLON DELEGATION

The delegation arrived in Washington on November 30, 1821, but its story begins in the Upper Missouri Valley, where the Indian agent Benjamin O'Fallon (1793–1842) oversaw the trade and diplomatic relations between the United States and Indian nations in the region. Appointed by Secretary of War John Calhoun in 1818, his role was to support the Americans' "important military movements ... on the Missouri," which would be "greatly facilitated or impeded by the friendliness or hostilities of the Indians." In his letter of appointment, Calhoun recommended that O'Fallon adopt a "combination of kindness and firmness," arguing that Native leaders would "not be disposed to hostilities" unless they were provoked by "illicit traders."[6] O'Fallon's work as Indian agent was in line with a wider US Indian policy in the trans-Mississippi West. The War Department had authorized Stephen Harriman Long's exploratory expedition into the region in 1817 and established Fort Atkinson at Council Bluffs on the Missouri River in 1819. Meanwhile, the governor of Missouri Territory, William Clark, worked with the fur trader Pierre Chouteau to negotiate a slew of peace treaties with Indian nations in the Upper Missouri Valley, including the Pawnee, Otoe, Missouri, Kanza, and Omaha.[7] In the written treaties, the undersigning chiefs and warriors declared themselves to be "under the protection of the United States of America, and of no other nation, power or sovereign, whatsoever."[8] On paper, the identical language of the different treaties suggested a uniform American policy toward Indian nations, demanding the safe passage of American traders and allegiance to the United States. Four years after the conclusion of the War of 1812, these treaties projected a sole imperial power in the region. As presidential friendship medals "flooded the frontier," the routines of Indian diplomacy became a cornerstone of the effort to "gain the loyalty of the Indians of the Great Lakes region and on the Upper Mississippi and Missouri."[9]

However, the political situation in the Upper Missouri River Valley was more volatile than these peace treaties suggested, and to maintain peaceful relations depended on continuous diplomatic labor on the ground. Historian Anne F. Hyde has shown that although negotiating treaties with Native leaders was important to ensure the well-being of American traders' own families and businesses, it did not necessarily secure the safe passage of other Americans, let alone affirm a US imperial presence in the region.[10] At Council Bluffs, too, Indian diplomacy was a decentered affair, shaped to only a small degree by federal policy from Washington. Whatever imperial inroads the United States government imagined, Americans still found themselves in a region where Indian nations, and the complex intertribal relations between them, dictated the conditions of interaction. The Pawnees alone, for instance, consisted of four divisions. The "South Bands"—the Chaui, the Kítkahahki, and the Pitahawirata—generally lived in villages along the Republican and Platte Rivers, west of the Missouri in present-day Nebraska. Members of the Skidi Federation, the fourth division, lived to the north and spoke a distinct dialect of the Pawnee language. To the east of the Pawnee villages was the territory of the Omahas, Otoes, Kanzas, and Missourias. Navigating this complex intertribal space was a challenge if only because of its linguistic diversity: while the eastern nations spoke Siouan languages, the Pawnees spoke a Caddoan language.

To navigate this complex social world, Indian agents like O'Fallon depended on extensive networks of families and trading companies to gain a foothold in Indian diplomacy in the West. Born in Kentucky, O'Fallon was the nephew of William Clark, who became his legal guardian when O'Fallon was in his teens. After his diplomacy with Indian Nations during the Lewis and Clark expedition (1804–06), Clark was a central figure in the government's dealings with Indian nations west of the Mississippi, first as governor of Missouri Territory (1813–1820) and after 1822 as superintendent of Indian Affairs in St. Louis. O'Fallon entered

FIGURE 1.2 Portrait of Benjamin O'Fallon, by unidentified artist. Oil on canvas, c. 1833. National Portrait Gallery, Smithsonian Institution. Partial gift of Edward Gesuele Peterson and Nancy Gesuele Peterson.

the family business of Indian trade and diplomacy, trading with Sioux nations on the St. Peters River, running a mill establishment, and serving as Indian agent at Prairie du Chien, in present-day Wisconsin. His brother, John O'Fallon, was an army sutler in the Council Bluffs region and one of the American signatories on the treaties that Clark and Chouteau negotiated with the Pawnees in 1818. This diplomatic work depended on ongoing efforts to seek influence with prominent families in Indian nations, as O'Fallon recognized when he organized the 1821 delegation. From the Chaui Pawnee, he invited Sharitarish the Younger, the son of a principal chief also named Sharitarish and the brother of Tarecawawaho. Another delegate was the Omaha tribal leader known as Big Elk, identified in the colonial records as Ongpatonga (1770–1846 or 1853). A member of a prominent Omaha family and an ally of the Americans during the War of 1812, Ongpatonga had been a frequent partner in diplomacy. Moreover, according to some sources, his daughter Mitain had a child and a long-standing relationship with Manuel Lisa, an American fur trader in St. Louis, while his other daughter, Meumbane, married the fur trader Lucien Fontenelle, who later operated a trading post near the Upper Missouri Agency.[11] Since both Lisa and Fontenelle were involved with the Missouri Fur Company in St. Louis, they were partners in business with Pierre Chouteau and William Clark, who were among the company agents in St. Louis. Such intimate relationships between fur traders and indigenous women were recognized in legal documents and forged "important connections for their husbands and were accorded a great deal of respect in the fur-trading world."[12]

By cultivating such relationships, US administrators of Indian affairs hoped that indigenous leaders might consent to buy into the benefits of American trade relations, particularly valuable trade items such as guns and gunpowder. At the federal level, too, the administration of Indian Affairs depended on connections that were forged locally between American traders and tribal governments. In 1795 Congress had established the "factory system" as the bedrock of Indian affairs: a network of trading houses through which the government provided Indian nations with a range of goods in exchange for furs—the kind of "soft power" that US hegemony depended on.[13] By the 1820s, however, this system was in decline. The US Congress had never seen the factory system as a great priority, and with the decline of the fur trade and the Panic of 1819, it decreased funding to support the system, which led to its abandonment in 1822. This left Secretary of War John Calhoun continuously scrambling for funding for Indian affairs from Congress, and it left Indian agents such as O'Fallon in a precarious position as they struggled to make treaty-stipulated payments to Native nations.[14] To make matters worse, by the late 1810s, the illegal encroachment of traders into the territories of Indian nations had put diplomatic relations on edge. Although in the

FIGURE 1.3
An-Pan-Tan-go or the
Big Elk, a Maha Chief,
after Charles Bird King.
Lithograph by Lehman
& Duval, after Charles
Bird King. In Thomas L.
McKenney, *History of the
Indian Tribes of North
America, with Biographical Sketches and Anecdotes
of the Principal Chiefs*,
vol. 1 (Philadelphia,
1838). Archives and Special Collections, University of Louisville.

wake of the War of 1812 Secretary of War John Calhoun had established a series of military outposts on the Missouri and Mississippi Rivers, the Panic of 1819 had halted his fortification scheme, meaning that O'Fallon's agency at Council Bluffs remained the only military outpost west of the Missouri, exposed in a region of "some fourteen tribes, including the militant Blackfeet, Sioux, Assiniboin, and Pawnee."[15] The lack of an American military presence in the area "emboldened" the Indian nations in the region, who were "alert to what they considered American failures" and ready to capitalize on moments when "American force or resolution weakened."[16] O'Fallon thus understood that any influence on Indian nations in the West depended on ongoing diplomatic processes, rooted in the networks of families and trading houses, and he had learned the limitations of American empire in the Upper Missouri Valley, where treaty councils with native leaders effected only situational agreements rather than long-term political alliances.

O'Fallon's 1821 delegation to Washington thus came at a time when his agency was clinging to existing diplomatic relationships in an effort to retain a foothold in the trans-Mississippi West. A delegation of tribal leaders to Washington was a relatively cost-effective way to display American hegemony to Native leaders from a region where such hegemony was tenuous at best. Already in 1819 O'Fallon had made a request to Secretary of War John Calhoun to visit Washington with fifteen chiefs from what he deemed to be the more belligerent nations in the Upper Missouri Valley.[17] His plans were accelerated a few months later following the deadly attack by a party of Skidi Pawnee warriors on nine fur traders near the Arkansas River. Calhoun wrote that the perpetrators ought to "feel the displeasure of the Government," but he also recognized Americans' precarious position in the Council Bluffs area and considered it unwise to respond to the attack with actual military force.[18] Promising to raise the issue of the "imperfect provisions" for Indian Affairs in Congress, Calhoun approved O'Fallon's plan to bring the Upper Missouri leaders to Washington, affirming once again that "by a proper combination of kindness and firmness the conduct of the Indians towards our citizens may be much improved."[19]

The delegation to Washington brought the situational logics of Indian diplomacy at Council Bluffs into a setting where the government could project a semblance of American empire. The makeup of the intertribal delegation reflected the complex geography of the Upper Missouri region, and although their names were translated and transcribed by American government agents, a number of the Native delegates entered the historical record. Although official records of the delegation are scarce and unreliable, some of its participants can tentatively be identified. With nine delegates, the Pawnee bands were most strongly represented: the Chaui were led by Sharitarish, along with Peskelechaco of the Kítkehahki and Petalesharo of the Skidi Federation.[20] The delegation also included representatives from the Omaha, Kanza, Missouria, and Otoe nations—all nearby nations that O'Fallon hoped would remain on friendly terms with the Pawnee and the United States. The principal chief Ongpatonga led the Omaha delegation; Monchousia represented the Kanza Nation; and Choncape and Shaumonekusse represented the Otoe Nation, along with the latter's wife, Hayne Hudjihini. O'Fallon and the delegates were furthermore accompanied by James Graves, an African American hired cook, and Louis T. Honoré, the interpreter and secretary to William Clark.[21] The fact that the Pawnee bands were overrepresented in the delegation—bringing nine of the seventeen delegates—underscores their geopolitical importance in the region: their villages along the Platte and Loup Rivers were consistently occupied and flourishing, they were estimated to number more than 10,000 people in the early decades of the nineteenth century, and they had become infamous for sending out war parties to raid horses, including from the powerful Comanche to the south.[22]

John Calhoun's approach of "kindness and firmness" thus points to a central ambivalence of US empire in the early decades of the nineteenth century. The O'Fallon delegation allowed the American government to portray a notion of empire in the region and, more practically, to show off its military power by taking the delegates to the shipyards and military arsenals on the East Coast. But the policy goal in the Missouri River Valley was not white settlement, but rather the safe passage of American traders in an area that was by and large indigenous space. The timing of the delegation was opportune: after the collapse in 1821 of the Spanish empire, the Mexican government opened up trade with New Mexico, and Americans were hoping for safe passage on the new commercial corridor known as the Santa Fe Trail, which led through western Comanchería and several nations to the north, including the Pawnees.[23] As such, when the delegation went on its way to Washington in October 1821, newspapers on the East Coast reprinted a letter from the Upper Missouri Agency expressing the hope that the delegation would silence "all the disquiet, as well as the frequent petty warfare ... among the remote Indians" and would open up "a road to the richest fur region in the world."[24] While the American government did not seek to impose direct colonial rule in the Upper Missouri region, the treaties and diplomatic relations it forged there aimed to make the region part of the United States's sphere of influence, even if not directly "domestic" to the United States. Although Washington policymakers envisioned a strong American influence through trade, diplomacy, and the threat of military force, from the vantage point of the Indian agent at Council Bluffs any such influence was limited and temporary, and depended on repeated diplomatic interactions with Native leaders. If the O'Fallon delegation meant to project a notion of US empire onto the Upper Missouri River Valley, it also registered the aspirational nature of that very goal.

COUNCIL BLUFFS IN WASHINGTON: WESTERN DIPLOMACY AND THE "CIVILIZING MISSION"

When O'Fallon brought the Upper Missouri delegates to Washington in the late fall of 1821, the ensuing interactions staged an encounter between the situational logics of Indian diplomacy in the West and the policy proposals of federal policymakers in the US capital. Most important, the delegates were introduced to Thomas McKenney (1785–1859), a key figure in US Indian policy whose office was the "de facto center of Indian Affairs."[25] A Quaker from Maryland, McKenney played a central role in the American government's formulation of a coherent policy for Indian affairs, first as supervisor of the War Department's factory system beginning in 1806, and as Superintendent of Indian Trade after 1816. In this capacity, McKenney had codified more regular procedures to ensure that Indian agents carried out a consistent policy in a branch of government that was dependent on officials who were political appointees.[26] When the factory system collapsed after the Panic of 1819, McKenney redirected US Indian policy toward an active promotion of the "civilization program" that was aimed at agricultural education and the Christianization of Native people. The program hinged on outsourcing much of the management of Indian affairs to organizations in civil society, particularly missionary groups. Promoting a joint effort between government and religious organizations, McKenney's efforts reflected a wider pattern by which, in Susan M. Ryan's words, the "rhetoric of benevolence penetrated political and bureaucratic circles."[27] The civilization program was made policy when Congress passed the "Act Making Provisions for the Civilization of the Indian Tribes Adjoining the Frontier Settlements" in 1819. As historian William E. Unrau writes, the act provided appropriations to fund the work of "so-called benevolent white societies" that would "educate the Indians and rescue them from their moral depravity and instruct them in the techniques of white agriculture and land speculation."[28]

Embracing the potential for religious organizations to play a part in Indian affairs, McKenney saw agricultural education as the cornerstone of a policy of religious and economic reform in Indian country. To this effect, he organized a meeting in New York between the delegates and the Reverend Philip Milledoler of the United Foreign Missionary Society (UFMS), which was among the first Protestant missionary organizations to play an active role in the new federal program.[29] The UFMS had begun to experiment with missionary education in western nations in 1821, when they established the Harmony Mission school at the Fort Osage trading post in present-day Missouri. Although not very successful, the Harmony school received wide coverage in national newspapers and helped missionary societies like the UFMS make the case "that they could do a better job of 'civilizing' the Indians than either the government or private enterprise had done so far."[30] McKenney and Milledoler had discussed plans for another mission school for American Indians in the West, and they set up a meeting in New York on December 15, to gauge the delegates' ideas about a school near the Upper Missouri Agency.[31] With eleven other UFMS board managers, Milledoler met with the delegates at their lodging, the City Hotel in New York. They also brought O'Fallon letters of introduction for two missionaries, Jonathan Lesslie and Salmon Giddings, who were appointed to "visit the tribes to which these chiefs and warriors belong" and would hopefully "lead eventually to the introduction of Civilization and Christianity" in their nations.[32]

To sell the delegates on this educational scheme, McKenney took them on an inspection of the Lancaster School in Georgetown, a public school that had opened in 1811.[33] The school was named after the British educator Joseph Lancaster, who pioneered a system for mass public education based on discipline, efficiency, and rote memorization.[34] Although this system left little opportunity for independent thinking, with students moving "in regimental order" and being "rarely allowed to move or speak out of turn," Lancaster schools could also be "run cheaply, expanded indefinitely, and operated as models of efficiency."[35] Given their expansive ambitions for Indian education, missionary organizations were interested in their potential for efficient and easily replicable forms of instruction. When the Upper Missouri delegates visited the Georgetown school, McKenney explained its importance "for their children, and of instruction in the arts and habits of civilized life."[36] McKenney made an impassioned plea to the delegates on behalf of agriculture and education, offering nothing less than a continental narrative of Indian reform:

> Where the great cities now stand, the Red Skins once had their wigwams. All was woods—there were deer and beavers, and bears and wolves. But now they are all gone.... Your country has much game in it now, but a good many moons hence the game will be gone.... You will be gone too.... It is time to begin to show your children how to do when the game is gone. You must teach them to make corn, and to raise animals like the White Skins, and to build houses.... How can your children have all these things if the White Skins do not teach them?[37]

With the image of a wigwam replaced by a wooden house, McKenney mobilized familiar ideas of the nomadic savage and Indian country as an uncultivated "wilderness." Yet this rather stereotypical metonymy also recognized the rhetorical conventions of fur trade interactions, in which metaphor was an important device for cross-cultural dialogue.[38] Moreover, McKenney addressed a problem that was quite real for Indian nations in the West, who were facing the depletion of game populations in their hunting territories due to an increased trade in skins. McKenney's argument was that, ultimately, the core of this problem was the state of Native people's education—they had been "cheated by the White Skins. If you had been taught, you could not be cheated."[39] According to McKenney's logic, it was only because Native people had not received formal education that they were taken advantage of.

The UFMS published the delegates' response to these plans in their house publication, the *American Missionary Register*, positioning them as both participants and foils in a dialogue about indigenous futures in the Missouri River Valley. A "Grand Pawnee" delegate—possibly Sharitarish, the leader of the Chaui delegation—was the first to speak after McKenney. The speeches were translated either by Louis T. Honoré or O'Fallon's interpreter John Dougherty. In either case, since the delegates represented two different language groups, the interpreters probably had to translate all the speeches twice, thus making these performative interactions slow and deliberate work.[40] As recorded in the *Register*, the Chaui delegate affirmed his understanding of McKenney's words as they were translated to him:

My Brother, I have heard your words. I am glad I have heard.... It appears you want to take pity on us. The Great Spirit permitted you to make that talk.... I will not forget your words. They are in my heart. I will hold them there.... When I get home I will tell what you say, to my friends and relations. I will talk to them.... I am glad to hear what you promise. If it can be done, I wish my children to learn to write and read like your children.... When I get home and tell my people all this, their hearts will be glad, and they will want to learn.⁴¹

This bodily metonymy suggests that the Chaui Pawnee delegate internalized McKenney's arguments and aptly picked up on the commissioner's rhetoric of "pity," a sense of moral and religious obligation that expressed a paternalistic attitude toward Native people. Although the delegate stated that he would first have to "get home and tell my people all this," he nevertheless communicated an understanding of McKenney's project and perhaps an openness to it.

Yet the leader of the Kanzas was more skeptical of the educational experiment. Probably referring to the delegate known as Monchousia or White Plume, the *Register* published a short speech in which a Kanza speaker doubted the Americans' willingness or ability to follow through on Indian education. Even if the direct material benefits of agricultural education appealed to him, he considered the words of McKenney as primarily "good talk":

Everything you have said, I have heard with pleasure. I am glad. This is good talk, but I want to see done what you promise. I fear. You say we must learn to plough and do like the white skins. I fear you will not learn us. All you have said I have got in my heart. I would be glad if all can be done you talk about. I hold it as if it was shut up in my hands I will not let it go.... I would be glad if all could be done you talk about. We want cattle. I am afraid you will not give us cattle. If you do, we will thank you.⁴²

Such responses expressed both an interest in the civilization project and a failure of these interactions to fully endorse it. Similarly, one of the Otoe delegates resisted the idea that the delegation in Washington was an effective tool for gaining tribal leaders' consent. "I am glad I ever heard your words—it is good," the delegate noted, but he added, "I am no chief: my brothers are chiefs. What I have heard I will take to them. I have heard your talk, and will take it home.... You say our children will be learned to write. I cannot speak of that. My brothers will hear what I have heard, and they will act."⁴³

Of course, the acts of translation and editing on display here reflect that the publication of Native oratory during this period was often a function of diplomatic and missionary networks. Prone to editorial intervention and mistranslation, these speeches were part of the promotional mission of the *American Missionary Register*, and the description of McKenney's words as "good talk" would certainly have met with approval from the UFMS board. Meanwhile, the use of choppy sentences, errors ("our children will be learned to write"), and reverse translations (referring to the White House as a "wigwam") rendered the delegates as untutored, and thus in need of missionary education in the first place. In this written record of diplomatic exchange, however, these interactions also laid bare the fault lines between US policy proposals and the workings of diplomacy in Indian country. By explaining that "my brothers are chiefs," the Otoe speaker reminded McKenney not only of the difference in rank between warriors and chiefs, but of the fact that in his nation, political decision-making was rooted in family networks. The Omaha delegate—possibly Ongpatonga—similarly pushed back against the meaning of his participation in the delegation, in which he was presumed to represent the Omaha nation. "I have very little knowledge," he was recorded as saying. "I am glad at what I have heard—but I am a little afraid.... I am not alone. There is a heap of young men in my village. I am afraid to promise, lest my young men would not comply."[44] Ongpatonga explained that his own position as tribal leader depended on the counsel of young warriors, who typically had a say in diplomatic and military matters. To underscore this point, he reverted to the type of metonymy that was a fixture in fur trade interactions, stating "you see I am big body. You think I am great man. But I am not a great man." The Omaha delegate pushed back against the idea that these missionaries were sitting down with the "heads" of their nations. If the political purchase of the O'Fallon delegation was rooted in the image of nation-to-nation dialogue and agreement, Ongpatonga exposed how this diplomatic strategy hinged on a form of misrepresentation.

The notion that the O'Fallon delegation represented the political leadership of these nations was thus something of a fiction: in the Upper Missouri region, decision-making lay with councils of multiple chiefs and warriors and was rooted in the life of families and clans. Policymakers in Washington were unlikely to have a firm grasp of such internal politics. Yet by sitting in council with a select number of delegates they could project a notion of American influence in the West, by casting these different leaders as heads of their *nations* who showed allegiance to the United States. The delegates' pushback against this idea came to the fore also when they met with the board of the United Foreign Missionary Society in New York on December 15, 1821. As reported in the *Religious Intelligencer*, the meeting began with the board secretary touting their recent efforts at the Fort Osage mission school and outlining their plans to bring two missionaries to Council Bluffs next summer. The Kanza delegate Monchousia—identified in the transcript as "White Plume"—responded to the secretary's speech, professing an openness to these plans but also arguing that any decision-making about them ought to take place in Indian country:

> "*Brothers*—We are Chiefs and Warriors of different tribes. I will speak for the whole.... We have long since been told, that the red men would one day live like white men, and have houses and food like them.... These things are long coming to pass. I wish it was so. I am now growing old, and have not seen it.... We like your Talk. We must consult our Chiefs and Brothers at home. We cannot now act for them. We will tell them your Talk, and send you word."[45]

Reminding the UFMS board of the importance of each nation's democratic consent through tribal councils, the delegates challenged the relevance of the delegation as a representation of US-Indian diplomacy. By asserting the importance of community-based deliberation, they articulated the idea that indigenous sovereignty in the Upper Missouri region was not an abstract notion, but a fundamental principle of diplomatic conduct.

Again, such critiques did not resist diplomatic relationships wholesale. To the contrary, if the speeches intervened in the policies of McKenney and the UFMS, they also spoke in favor of the role of Benjamin O'Fallon, their agent at Council Bluffs. In conversation with McKenney in Washington, a Kítkahahki Pawnee delegate stressed the material benefits of US influence as well as his trust in O'Fallon's work:

> I am a poor man. There is my father (pointing to Major O'Fallon) who knows me. I follow up behind. He is in light, I am in darkness. That is the reason I am poor. But I am with my father, and I don't fear any thing.... Long time I did not know what blanket was—no knife—no handkerchief. I had on me hard Buffaloe [*sic*] skin. I want you, my father and brother, to be quick and decide on what to do. I want to clothe better—I like your clothes.[46]

The metonymy of "light and darkness" would have aligned well with the missionaries' ideas about Christian conversion as a form of salvation, or even tropes of the "naked savage." But this passage speaks to something other than an assent to civilization policy. The Pawnee's statement that O'Fallon "knows me" was not mere deference or even submission to the Indian agent: he reminded McKenney of the diplomatic channels that were already in place in the Upper Missouri Valley, affirming that the Pawnees considered their ongoing relationships with their agent as beneficial. Ongpatonga likewise pointed to Major O'Fallon to insist on the agent's importance: "There is my father, (pointing to Major O'Fallon, the agent) what he tells me I will do."⁴⁷ For the delegates, the problem with the civilizing mission was not necessarily that it would bring about cultural conversion or the historical change that Thomas McKenney outlined. More likely, the federal government's turn to a standardized policy could potentially sidestep the authority of agents like O'Fallon, who may have been emissaries of US influence but who also had an ear to the ground regarding the needs of Indian nations, and who recognized their sovereignty and diplomatic protocols.

What the UFMS eagerly promoted as an endorsement of the civilizing scheme, then, also captured the failure of federal policy rhetoric to implement meaningful changes on the ground. McKenney and the UFMS sought to construct the delegation as a decision-making body that could consent to the civilization policy as they explained it to them. Yet the records of these interactions register a fear that the policy tool of the "civilizing mission" would bypass established avenues of decision-making at home—both in national councils and in scenes of diplomacy at the Upper Missouri Agency. The delegates' interactions in Washington thereby brought to light the ambivalent workings of American influence through diplomacy. For O'Fallon and the delegates, the visit to Washington was an opportunity to inflect ongoing practices of diplomatic exchange in the Missouri Valley in ways that spoke to the social and political situation in Indian nations there. McKenney, however, was testing the waters for a federal policy hinged on Christianization and agricultural education. Responding to this recent policy in the management of Indian affairs, the delegates highlighted a key problem with this model: it jeopardized the ability of Indian nations to represent their own situations and political projects in existing networks of Indian diplomacy. These transcripts, of course, do not represent the authentic "voices" of indigenous orators and we should not assign any authorship to these texts unproblematically. Still, the publication of these speeches captures the political tensions that surfaced in this diplomatic situation, as the O'Fallon delegation brought the dialogic nature of these performative interactions into print. Through established conventions and rhetorics of Indian diplomacy, the Upper Missouri delegates brought indigenous forms of decision-making to bear on the formulation of Indian policy in Washington.

STAGING THE INDIAN BODY

The meetings with Thomas McKenney and the UFMS were only one aspect of the O'Fallon delegation, and its representation in American print culture took place in other publications besides the journals of missionary societies. Throughout their stay on the East Coast, the delegates participated in the social gatherings of prominent Washingtonians. Between December 1821 and the end of February the next year, the delegates performed an intertribal dance on the White House lawn, attended social gatherings, and were at the center of ceremonies—including oratory, dances, and gift-giving—that were a corollary to their meetings with American officials. These performances were disseminated through letters and newspapers, which explained the tenets of the "civilizing mission" to wider reading publics. Staging a dialectic about the delegates' character, newspaper commentators asked what role Native people played in a colonial narrative of replacement, and there was no fixed answer to such a question. As Philip J. Deloria argues in *Playing Indian*, American ideas about the Indian "Other" were never assembled merely along the positive or negative axis of the "savage" or "noble savage," but also along different axes of interiority versus exteriority and of similarity and dissimilarity.[48] The coverage of the delegation in American print culture was not simply a celebration of conquest but negotiated more ambivalent feelings about US-Indian relations. If it resonated with a narrative of the eventual displacement of an uncivilized racial Other, it also activated "humanitarian" ideas about the moral compatibility between settler society and indigenous people who displayed civilization's virtues.

Reports of the events surrounding the delegation were initially published in the *Daily National Intelligencer* and the *Georgetown Metropolitan*, and widely reprinted in a range of newspapers such as the *American Mercury* (Hartford, Connecticut), the *Independent Statesman* (Portland, Maine), and the *Republican Gazette* (Fredericktown, Maryland).[49] Newspaper commentators described the public events using familiar tropes, linking the physical description of the delegates to a commentary on the character of the *Indian*. One commentator remarked that the delegates were "of large stature" and "very muscular," but also had "fine open countenances, with the real noble Roman nose, dignified in their manners, and peaceful and quiet in their habits."[50] The *Washington Gazette* enthused that the delegates "possess the true aboriginal cast of feature; and many, though in the rough mould of nature, have a commanding yet an expressive countenance."[51] Newspapers presented the delegation as an original "first encounter" between US civil society and the "spectacle" of indigeneity. They asked whether the delegates' conversation and self-presentation conformed to the codes of politeness of upper-class Washingtonians. Responding to the already widespread stereotype of the "drunken Indian," the British writer William Faux commented that there was "no instance of drunkenness" among them and praised the delegates' easy wit.[52] He recalled how the Otoe delegate Shaumonekusse and his wife Hayne Hudjihini had "taken tea with and frequently visited us. She was a very good natured, mild woman, and he shewed [sic] great readiness in acquiring our language, being inquisitive, retaining anything that he was once informed."[53]

In these newspaper commentaries, the O'Fallon delegation became a vehicle for ideas that Americans held about their own society's relation to Indian nations. Shari M. Huhndorf argues in *Going Native* that the figure of the *Indian* had long represented "civilized society's inferior 'other' " in American culture, but this image was also one that Euro-Americans turned to in order to "define themselves and their nation."[54] In American newspapers, the O'Fallon delegation generated meditations on the norms of American civil society, in which the delegates became tropes in a dialectic on American civilization and indigenous displacement. The *National Intelligencer* wrote that their council with Monroe was worth noting since it represented a society superseded by American expansion: "With some vices, and much grossness, they possess many fine traits of character; and we never can forget that they were the native lords of that soil which they are gradually yielding to their invaders."[55] Ultimately, it was "impossible to see these people, and believe, as I do, that they are destined, in no very long lapse of time, to disappear from the face of the earth, without feeling for them great interest."[56] The *Intelligencer*'s commentary inflected the delegation with an ambivalent attitude regarding American Indians: although it suggested that they will inevitably "disappear," it also considered Native people as the "lords" of their country and Americans as its "invaders." Such commentaries thus concreted not only an image of the *Indian*, but also of the urbane reader/spectator who reflected on US-Indian relations with "great interest" and a measure of regret.

Furthermore, the *National Intelligencer*'s emphasis on visual confirmation is an example of how commentators interpreted the bodily rhetoric of the delegates—their gestures, clothing, and physiognomy—to support conjectures on their potential for successful education and civilization, or else their imminent disappearance. As Karen Halttunen explains, in the course of the nineteenth century the United States became a more mobile and regionally dispersed society, and as interactions with strangers became a more prominent feature of everyday life, judging another person's character depended increasingly on immediate visual perception.[57] In the context of cross-cultural interactions, this logic entered a racialized regime in which the nonwhite body was read to determine whether they could validate white audiences' ideas about the potential for civilization of the racialized Other.[58] In this visual sphere, people of color were seen as staging a bodily performance that could prove the correctness of white Americans' ideas about nonwhite populations, and the Upper Missouri delegates became an opportunity for a visual confirmation of Native people's propensity for "civilization." Indeed, the bodies of the Native leaders took center stage in the commentary on the delegation, and much of it centered on their regalia. When the delegates sat in council with President Monroe in early February 1822, the *Intelligencer* described in detail Sharitarish's headdress of turkey feathers, as well as an "elderly chief of the Missouri tribe" who wore a headdress made of "a profusion of horse hair, stained, of a bright scarlet, and surmounted ... with two polished taper *horns*, as long as those of an ox."[59] When the delegates were prompted to put on American army uniforms, the *Intelligencer* described how they appeared "in complete American costumes" except for their hair and face paint.[60] The Otoe delegate Hayne Hudjihini, the wife of the tribal leader Shaumonekusse, generated particular notice. Describing her as "dressed in scarlet pantaloons, and wrapped in a green cambric cloak, without any ornament on her long black hair," the *Intelligencer* reported that she asked President Monroe "to be dressed as a white woman if her great Father would give her a new dress." For the newspaper commentator, this plea was "as natural as her blushes and smiles" and proved that "the love of finery is not created by civilization; it merely becomes more chaste and discriminating."[61] Hayne Hudjihini's participation underscored the gendered dimensions of the delegation as a performance of masculinity: where the male delegates' dress mattered as an iteration of diplomatic

FIGURE 1.4
Hayne Hudjihini, the Eagle of Delight, after Charles Bird King. Lithograph by I. T. Bowen. In Thomas L. McKenney, *History of the Indian Tribes of North America, with Biographical Sketches and Anecdotes of the Principal Chiefs*, vol. 1 (Philadelphia, 1838). Archives and Special Collections, University of Louisville.

ceremony, Hayne Hudjihini's request to be included in this exchange was read as a superficial interest in "finery."

This scrutiny of the delegates' bodies and clothes allowed readers to project their own ideas about race and gender onto scenes of Indian diplomacy. On February 9, 1822, the delegates performed a public dance on the White House lawn, which was preceded by a "mock" council in which the delegates and the presidential party rehearsed the council they had held days earlier. Continuing for three hours, it was the most public of all the events, a display of Indian diplomacy as popular entertainment. These staged spectacles illustrate how American city-dwellers forged ideas about national identity through spectatorship, parades, and public performances: in the nineteenth-century republic, ethnically and regionally diverse Americans elaborated their version of American nationalism through celebrations, parades, oratory, and other public social events, constituting what David Waldstreicher has called a "national popular political culture."[62] Urban Americans' ideas about social relations depended, as Susan G. Davis writes, on their participation in "collective gatherings" such as public readings and speeches, festivals, mass meetings, and parades.[63] As an opportunity to reflect on the relations between American and indigenous people, the intertribal dance became an event confronting Washingtonians with a spectacle of savagery. The *Providence American* described the dance as "a rude kind of leaping, governed, in some measure, by the sullen sound of a sort of drum. They uttered shocking yells, and writhed and twisted their bodies in frightful contortions. They were painted in a savage style, and presented a truly ferocious aspect. The scene excited interest from its novelty, and as an exhibition of man in a purely savage state."[64] This equivocal language ("a rude *kind of* leaping"; "in some measure"; "a *sort of* drum") captures the transgressive nature of the visual spectacle: as the dance defied representation by conventional means, the commentary could only approximate an accurate description. Overall, however, the dance suggested to the commentator the "untamed fierceness of sinful passions, and the ferocious character of savage character, unhumanized by any arts or maxims of civilized society."[65]

For other commentators, the intertribal dance allowed for a wider reflection on cross-cultural relations in American cities. One "whimsical account" in the newspapers read the performance on the White House lawn as a scene of racial mixing. In front of a "promiscuous mass" of "white, black, red, yellow and half breed" spectators, the dance revealed white women's desires for the naked Indian body: "Figure to yourself five or six great strapping fellows all beautifully bedusted with party colored paint, & bunches of feathers sticking *a posterioribus*, resembling a nicked peacock, and then you have a tolerable idea of their appearance. Our ladies gazed very intently and sighed as they reflected they might look in vain for as much bone, sinew, muscle in their more civilized but less athletic husbands. Oh, thought I, what a charm there must be in a red skin."[66] In spite of their "more civilized" appearance, the bodies of their white husbands could not match the more desirable and virile bodies of the "nicked" delegates. But when one dancer struck the ground, "several ladies shrunk back at this sight, some behind the windows, others behind their husbands, exclaiming; Oh shocking! Oh the infidelity of these vile squaws."[67] The author acknowledged the women's right to "peep at any natural curiosity," but, echoing Shakespeare's *Macbeth*, also cast the dance as a demonic spectacle: "I cannot bear the idea that the Metropolitan ladies 'Should preserve (only) the natural ruby of their cheeks / 'When they look on sights, that would appal [sic] the devil.' "[68] As a scene of sexual tension and racial mixing, the dance tested boundaries between propriety and indecency, and the *Providence American* wrote that although "no person of liberal and philosophical curiosity would willingly have missed seeing" the spectacle, "no one who viewed it ... would choose to witness again." It described the delegates' mock council on the White House lawn according to similarly ambivalent tropes, noting that "the gestures of the Indian speakers were violent, but energetic, and frequently graceful; affording a striking specimen of native oratory."[69] The delegates' bodies thus stood in for a set of contradictions, with the *Intelligencer* reporting that a Chaui delegate's gestures were simultaneously "violent and excessive" and "never ungraceful, and always appropriate."[70] The use of contradictory adjectives to describe their bodily rhetoric—simultaneously "violent" and "graceful"—expressed the tension of the scene, which resonated with tropes of savagery while also being poetically pleasing.

By projecting such contradictions onto the delegates, newspaper commentators made their bodies diffuse the ideological tensions around representations of *Indianness*. As Robert Lawrence Gunn argues in *Ethnology and Empire*, nineteenth-century commentaries on such indigenous "semiotics of embodiment" dovetailed with a racial politics rooted in Enlightenment-era discourses of "primitivism," in which "differences of human endowment" were measured on a "developmental" scale and were assumed to be conditioned by differences of "environment."[71] So if the dance was described as a spectacle of savagery, a warlike display of an irredeemable Otherness, the delegation as a whole could be interpreted as a display of primitivism that was still redeemable by the civilizing mission. In other words, the Upper Missouri leaders came to represent tropes in debates about the character of Native Americans as well as white Americans' own norms of race and gender. Were Native people capable of civilization, or irredeemably savage? And were their moral sentiments compatible with those of American civil society? In prompting these questions, the delegation invited reflection on Native people's propensity for civilization even as it held up a mirror for white Americans to reflect on their own capacity for cross-cultural identification.

"HER RELIEF AND RESCUE": PETALESHARO AND THE PERFORMANCE OF FRIENDSHIP

In the course of the delegation to Washington, American ideas about *Indianness* particularly came to bear on the representation of the Skidi Pawnee warrior Petalesharo, who became the delegation's most celebrated participant and the focus of an ideological debate on the place of Native people in an American empire. Although the historical record is scant, several accounts suggest that the person referred to as "Petalesharo" was born in 1795 or 1797 in a village on the Loup River, near present-day Fullerton, Nebraska. He was the son of the Skidi leader identified in many historical sources as Lachelesharo, and he first made his name during a confrontation with a Chaui chief, when he helped his father Lachelesharo negotiate an agreement between the Chaui and Skidi bands.[72] The historical records are spotty and sometimes contradictory, and Petalesharo (often translated as "Man Chief") was only one of several names by which he was known.[73] Regardless, the Skidi Pawnee's story went practically viral in the 1820s and 1830s and Charles Bird King's portrait of Petalesharo became a prototype for the figure of the youthful, fearsome, yet friendly Native hero, and it introduced a striking image of the feather headdress as a signifier of *Indianness*. King's portrait was adapted for the frontispiece of Jedidiah Morse's *Report to the Secretary of War* (1822), Isaac Garner Hutton's song "The Generous Chief" (1825), Samuel Gardner Drake's *Biography and History of the Indians of North America* (1833), and McKenney's own *History of the Indian Tribes of North America* (1837). Across these different adaptations, his facial features regularly changed, but they consistently displayed his headdress and the friendship medal on his chest, marking on the one hand Petalesharo's image as a remote and romantic warrior-figure, and on the other hand his proximity to American society through diplomatic relations.

By the time he arrived in Washington, Petalesharo was already familiar to readers on the East Coast, because newspapers had reported the sensational story of how, in 1817, he interrupted the Skidi Pawnee's Morning Star ceremony to save a captive Comanche girl from ritual sacrifice. Widely disseminated, the account of Petalesharo's rescue played into American readers' interest in traditional ceremonies as a subject of ethnological interest and moral commentary. Held on several occasions throughout the 1810s, the Morning Star ceremony was a ritual of the Skidi Pawnees that took place over several days during the winter. Through the ritual sacrifice of a young woman, it paid tribute to the union of the Morning Star (Upirikutsu) and Evening Star (Cupirittaka), who had given birth to the Girl Child, the first human.[74] The ceremony restored "the balance of contentious but complementary male and female powers that had first brought human life to the world," and on another level reflected the role of the Pawnee tribes in an economy of captivity and exchange that stretched from the Southwest Borderlands to the Great Lakes.[75] As both captors and as captives, the Pawnee were part of a multiregional network of human exchanges that recognized sacred, familial, military, and market-driven motives for the forcible capture of men, women, and children.[76] According to historian James F. Brooks, the Morning Star ceremony offered "intertwined displays of violence, honor, and gender" that expressed the Pawnee cosmology and the geographically expansive social mixing that occurred through violent encounters.[77] The narrative of Petalesharo was first recorded by Captain John Bell, a member of an 1819 expedition to the Rocky Mountains, and his account eventually received widespread coverage in newspapers in Washington, Virginia, Massachusetts, Rhode Island, New Hampshire, Connecticut, New Jersey, Vermont, New York, Maryland, Maine, Georgia, and Pennsylvania.[78] The most widely reprinted account of the story, from Jedidiah Morse's *Report to the Secretary*

FIGURE 1.5
Petalesharoo, a Pawnee Brave, after Charles Bird King. Lithograph by Lehman & Duval. In Thomas L. McKenney, *History of the Indian Tribes of North America, with Biographical Sketches and Anecdotes of the Principal Chiefs*, vol. I (Philadelphia, 1838). Archives and Special Collections, University of Louisville.

FIGURE 1.6 Frontispiece of I. G. Hutton, "The Generous Chief: Written and Adapted to the Music of Lochinvar" (Washington City, 1823). Lithograph by Henry Stone. William L. Clements Library, University of Michigan. The music of this song was that of "Young Lochinvar" by the British composer Joseph Mazzingghi, which in turn was based on Sir Walter Scott's *Marmion: A Tale of Flodden Field* (1808), a historical romance in verse form. In this light, Isaac Garner Hutton's adapting this song suggests that Petalesharo's story offered a uniquely American variation on the genre of the historical romance. The portrait on the title page, by the Washington lithographer Henry Stone, is based on Charles Bird King's portrait of Petalesharo; the background scene depicts the Skidi Pawnee sacrifice he famously halted.

of War (1822), described Petalesharo as twenty-one years old and of "fine size, figure, and countenance," and stressed that his intervention was the act of one person against a Pawnee mob:

> Just when the funeral pile was to be kindled, and the whole multitude of spectators were on the tip toe of expectation, this young warrior ... rushed through the crowd, liberated the victim, seized her in his arms, placed her on one of the horses, mounted the other himself, and made the utmost speed towards the nations and friends of the captive. The multitude, dumb and nerveless with amazement at the daring deed, made no effort to rescue their victim from her deliverer. They viewed it as the immediate act of the Great Spirit, submitted to it without a murmur, and quietly retired to their village.[79]

Morse suggested that the Morning Star ceremony had been abandoned ever since Petalesharo's intervention: "Of what influence is one bold act in a good cause!"

Given Petalesharo's dramatic interruption of the ceremony, Morse ascribed to Petalesharo a singular and heroic role for setting in motion cultural changes among the Pawnees. However, he did not account for the fact that the Morning Star was already a controversial practice among the Pawnees. The ceremony took place only on rare occasions, and it was only practiced by the Skidi Pawnees and had been abandoned by the other Pawnee bands.[80] The explorer Edwin James reported that Petalesharo's father Lachelesharo "had long regarded this sacrifice as an unnecessary and cruel exhibition of power," which suggests that even among the Skidi it was already a politically contentious issue.[81] Nor was Petalesharo's intervention unique: when a captive Mexican boy was set to be sacrificed to the Morning Star in 1818, this event, too, was aborted after a council was convened to debate the issue.[82] In this light, Petalesharo's intervention was probably sanctioned by factions that opposed the ceremony to begin with, and Richard White suggests that warriors such as Petalesharo—often called "braves" by Americans—were members of the village *nahikut*: soldiers who were authorized by chiefs to employ the *raripakusus* (the village police) to "take decisive action even when opposition existed within the tribe."[83] In this respect, the opposition to the Morning Star sacrifice was not, as the anthropologist Melburn Thurman puts it, "a vague 'humanitarianism'" but the result of negotiations between Native leaders, American traders, and Indian agents.[84] Rather than one individual halting an uncontested tradition, the Morning Star episode refracted a wider political debate over the meaning of traditional customs in light of historical change and new alliances.

Yet as American coverage of the episode pitched him as the unique, singular hero who had halted a "savage" practice, Petalesharo became a figurehead for the "civilizing mission" as a shared undertaking of government and civil society.

The gendered dimensions of the account—in which a male Native hero saved a young woman of another tribe—further amplified the story's implications about the moral sentiments of indigenous people, and Petalesharo was invited to a makeshift diplomatic ceremony hosted by a seminary for young women in Washington, identified in newspapers as "Miss White's female seminary." The meeting took place at the house of Daniel Rapine, the former mayor of the city, and although little is known about the participants, it appears that Petalesharo was accompanied by Thomas McKenney.[85] The ceremony tapped into the formal registers of Indian diplomacy: the mayor's daughter, Mary Rapine, gave a speech and presented Petalesharo with a variation on the customary peace medal—a staple of Indian diplomacy—in honor of his rescuing the Comanche girl. The medal was engraved with illustrations of the Morning Star ceremony story: one side depicted Petalesharo leading the Comanche girl away to safety on one side, with the inscription "to the bravest of the braves," and the other side portrayed an empty scaffold with five Pawnee figures looking on.[86] Offering the friendship medal, Mary Rapine urged Petalesharo to "accept this token of our esteem—always wear it for our sakes, and when again you have the power to save a poor woman from death and torture—think of this and us, and fly to her relief and rescue."[87] In her speech, she expressed a colonial narrative in which the male Native hero's protection of a woman signaled his people's potential for civilization and moral sentiment:

> Brother, we have heard of your humanity in rescuing a young squaw of the Paduca nation from a cruel death and still more cruel torture, and leading her back to her home and tribe. It was the influence of the Great Spirit operating on your heart, and may it always so operate. Your white brethren admire and honor such virtue, and will always esteem their red Brethren in proportion as they display this generosity and heroism. You see we are all young, but we love and admire benevolence and courage, whatever the color of the skin that covers them.[88]

Rapine's speech evoked a shared commitment to "benevolence" that coded white men and women as sympathetic to Native nations, and Petalesharo as the friend of women. She proclaimed that "the report of this good action has filled us with esteem for you and your nation. Wherever you go, the white man and white woman will be your friends; because you have been a friend to one in distress and danger; and because they love and respect those who do good to each other."[89] Rapine's speech recalls the gendered tropes that, as Gayatri Chakravorty Spivak has famously argued, often function as a defense of colonialism: the savior narrative of "white men saving brown women from brown men."[90] As a variation on this trope, the speech reads Petalesharo's story as one in which the indigenous actor extends the colonizer's savior role by rescuing Native women from other Native men.

This performance of diplomatic exchange thus reflects how policymakers such as McKenney envisioned a role for associations in civil society in the work of the civilization program—including associations in which educated white women took an active part. In a speech that was presumably transcribed by an interpreter, Petalesharo responded to Rapine's words in a way that affirmed her message and suggested that these interactions in Washington society confirmed the true meaning of his actions. Addressing the participants as "brothers and sisters," he explained that the friendship medal gave him "more ease than I ever had, and I will listen more than I ever did to white men."[91] Furthermore, he suggested that he would have been "ignorant" of his good deed without the medal: "I am glad that my brothers and sisters have heard of the good act that I have done. My brothers and sisters think that I did it in ignorance, but I now know what I have done. I did it in ignorance and did not know that I did good; but by giving me this medal I know it."[92] As hinted at in the record of his speech, his heroic act displayed an innate potential for moral behavior that was left unexamined by Petalesharo himself, and it was up to white civil society to explain its underlying morals by rewarding him. The ceremony thereby enacted a paternalistic ideology in which Native people were deemed capable of proper moral sentiments, as long as American civil society could show them their potential for redemption.

As American commentators dug for messages of friendship and pacification in Petalesharo's narrative, this ideological work resonated with a vision of US-Indian relations that federal policymakers promoted. The representation of Petalesharo expressed the tenets of the civilizing mission that President Monroe, Thomas McKenney, and the UFMS all subscribed to, and by presenting an optimistic narrative about the position of indigenous people in an American empire, it ironed out the political tensions at the heart of the delegation. Shari M. Huhndorf has argued that in the nineteenth century, "images of Native peoples, though never monolithic, grew increasingly ambivalent," and the story of Petalesharo resolved ideological anxieties about race, gender, and empire that the delegation presented to American readers and spectators.[93] Were they part of the narrative of "civilization" as actors who actively shared in this project, or as foils to be conquered? Would Indian country become part of the United States or would it always lie beyond its boundaries? American commentaries on the delegates mobilized tropes of race and gender to assess whether the delegates were similar to Americans and whether they understood the virtues of "civilization." This ideological game was at once the work of groups in American civil society who gazed at the physical spectacle of the Indian delegation, and of missionaries and policymakers who articulated a new approach to Indian policy. Petalesharo was not given much to say during the delegation, but his very presence generated the narratives of American empire that were promoted in Washington.

"WE ARE NOT STARVING YET": ORATORY, FUTURITY, AND REFUSAL

Amid these narratives and mistranslations, the political agency that the delegates wielded in Washington was tenuous indeed. Given the mediation that met the Upper Missouri delegates, the oratory that came out of the delegation depended on an opaque publication process, making it difficult to determine how exactly the delegates assessed the policies they were introduced to in Washington. Still, the literary record that the O'Fallon delegation left behind reminds us of the strong link between Indian diplomacy and the representation of indigenous nations in American literature. Indeed, one of the most famous speeches by a nineteenth-century Native orator—one often reprinted in anthologies of American and Native American literature—came out of the delegates' council with President Monroe on February 5, 1822. The council took place in the Red Room of the White House and, according to one report, was witnessed by the Supreme Court justices. President Monroe opened the council with brief remarks alluding to a visit the delegates had made to the military arsenals and shipyards. After this, several of the Upper Missouri delegates gave speeches in which they were encouraged by Benjamin O'Fallon to "speak with the same freedom that they would use in their own village."[94] The proceedings ended with an exchange of gifts, a staple of diplomatic interactions between indigenous leaders and American officials. Several days after the council, the speeches by the delegates were published in the *Daily National Intelligencer* and reprinted widely on the East Coast.

This publication process depended on the editorializing of American commentators, and in a culture where Indian delegations offered a visual spectacles more than anything, the oratory of the Upper Missouri leaders became detached from the political content of diplomatic interaction. Of the council with President Monroe, for instance, one newspaper commentator regretted that "I had not thought of taking notes, or even of impressing on my mind what was said by each. As it is, I can only recal [sic] some of their most striking remarks, without always remembering by which speaker they were made."[95] Were others listening in the same way? Were the delegates' speeches just another opportunity to admire the eloquent Native body? After all, American newspapers published these speeches under the rubric of "Indian Eloquence," emphasizing the curiosity of Indian oratory more than the political question it addressed.[96] This practice of testifying to native eloquence was a commonplace in early national magazines and newspapers, where Native speeches were printed under such rubrics as "Indian Eloquence," "Fine Specimen of Indian Eloquence," or "Interesting Specimen of Indian Eloquence." As historian Steven Conn argues in *History's Shadow*, "even the most avid admirers of Indian eloquence rarely translated their admiration into a sense of social or political equality." Instead, they paid "homage to eloquent Indians" while articulating a narrative of American progress that was "dependent on Indian decline."[97] Collecting Native oratory allowed white readers' to assuage a sense of guilt about Indian "vanishing" and to record the peculiarities of Native eloquence, a decidedly antiquarian project.[98]

These ambivalent ideas about the relation between Native people and American society mirrored the status of Indian nations in the US legal system, which in the early nineteenth century was in an ongoing process of definition. Between 1801 and 1835, the Supreme Court under John Marshall made several key rulings that came to define and limit the sovereignty of Indian nations in North America. The most widely known of these are Marshall's trilogy of court cases pertaining to the Cherokee Nation—*Johnson v. M'Intosh* (1821), *Cherokee Nation v. Georgia* (1831), and *Worcester v. Georgia* (1833)—which defined Indian nations as "domestic dependent nations" in the United States. The legal relationship between Indian nations and the United States was less rigidly defined at the time of the O'Fallon delegation, but Marshall's opinion in *Fletcher v. Peck* (1810) was an early ruling that codified Indian nations' land title in American law. In *Fletcher*, the future president John Quincy Adams argued that Native people's right to their lands was merely a "right of occupancy ... for the purpose of hunting" and was "not like our tenures." Adams reasoned that Native people had "no idea of a title to the soil itself. It is overrun by them, rather than inhabited. It is not a true and legal possession. ... It is a right not to be transferred but extinguished."[99] Adams believed that American Indians did not practice agriculture and that, therefore, their right to their territories could be superseded by the American state, which would make "proper" use of their land. John Marshall's ruling followed Adams's logic by setting the legal precedent that "the nature of the Indian title" was to be "respected by all courts until it be legitimately extinguished."[100] The ruling in *Fletcher v. Peck* thus considered Indian nations as having only a temporary claim to their own lands—one that institutions of American government could extinguish based on premises that were not at all defined. As Eric Cheyfitz writes, these Supreme Court rulings acted as a "rubber stamp" for the efforts of the US Congress and other branches of government to craft an Indian policy that coded Indian nations as inherently vulnerable.[101] In American law and government, Indian nations' legal presence came to signify what Jodi Byrd calls the "transit of empire," a paradigmatic yet always fleeting presence, bound to be superseded by the ascendency of American empire.[102]

When the *Daily National Intelligencer* published the speeches from the council with Monroe, this too was an opportunity to "preserve" Native oratory at the unique moment of its delivery. "Considering the race to be thus transient," the commentator wrote, "I have often wished that more pains were bestowed, and by more competent persons, in recording what is most remarkable and peculiar among them, now that those peculiarities are fresh and unchanged by their connection with us."[103] The delegation offered the opportunity to observe and commemorate a transient race, as the delegates possessed "many fine traits of character" and were "the native lords of that soil which they are gradually yielding to their invaders."[104] Yet the published speeches from the O'Fallon delegation—particularly those of the Chaui Pawnee and the Omaha delegates—interrupted such ideas about Native vanishing, as they insisted on the dominance of indigenous nations in the Upper Missouri Valley and the ongoing need for Indian diplomacy.

FIGURE 1.7
Shar-I-Tar-Ish, a Pawnee Chief, after Charles Bird King. Lithograph by I. T. Bowen, after Charles Bird King. In Thomas L. McKenney, *History of the Indian Tribes of North America, with Biographical Sketches and Anecdotes of the Principal Chiefs*, vol. II (Philadelphia, 1838). Archives and Special Collections, University of Louisville.

According to contemporary accounts of the delegation, a "Pawnee chief" was the first to respond to Monroe. Evoking the intentions of the Great Spirit in creating Native/white difference, the speech suggests a rhetoric of separatism that resists American influence:

> The Great Spirit made us all—he made my skin red, and yours white; he placed us on this earth, and intended that we should live differently from each other. He made the whites to cultivate the earth, and feed on domestic animals, but he made us, red skins, to rove through the woods and plains, to feed on wild animals and to dress with their skins. He also intended that we should go to war to take scalps—steal horses from and triumph over our enemies—cultivate peace at home, and promote the happiness of each other.[105]

On one level, the Pawnee speech was a call for maintaining a traditional economy based in seasonal hunting, trade, horse raids, and the tenets of warrior culture.

But who was the delegate making this call? Contemporary accounts attributed the speech to a "Pawnee Chief," but ever since W. C. Vanderwerth included it in a 1971 anthology of Native American oratory, it has often been referred to as the speech of Petalesharo. This attribution was repeated by—among others—the editors of the *Norton Anthology of American Literature*, which indeed notes that "we do not know whether 'Petalesharo's speech' was in fact delivered by him or by an unnamed 'Pawnee chief.' "[106] As other scholars have argued, however, a more likely source was the delegate referred to in the record as the Chaui Pawnee delegate Sharitarish.[107] Although there are few reliable biographical facts about the life of Sharitarish, it seems that he was the son of a Chaui tribal leader of the same name. When his brother Tarecawawaho refused to come to Washington, Sharitarish was promoted to the role of head delegate of the Pawnee, which is probably why he was the first to speak after President Monroe.[108] In that case, the speech was probably interpreted either by William Clark's assistant Louis T. Honoré or perhaps O'Fallon's interpreter John Dougherty.[109] So was Sharitarish the speaker of the Pawnee speech? Historian David Bernstein suggests that some of the incongruities in its references to Pawnee economic life make it possible that the speech was not actually performed by a delegate during the delegation at all.[110] In either case, the lack of clarity about the speech's origins—both in the 1822 newspapers and in subsequent critical commentary—reminds us that misunderstandings and mistranslations were a central feature of diplomatic exchange and its representation in American letters.

My attribution of the speech to "Sharitarish," then, is closer to what Michel Foucault calls an "author function," an organizing term by which discourse is organized, even if it does not name an authentic speaking subject.[111] Nevertheless, it is important not to write off the transcripts as merely white ventriloquism of Native speech, even if the mechanisms behind the speech's publication remain opaque. For one, the American commissioners and translators attributed to this "Pawnee chief" a role as an authorized agent—an indigenous representative whose words were read as expressions of indigenous perspectives within scenes of diplomacy. Moreover, the *Daily National Intelligencer* noted that the speeches were translated sentence by sentence into English and then into the various languages spoken by the delegates, which suggests that there was sufficient time for the interpreters and scribes to record the delegates' words with an eye for detail.[112] Finally, for at least two of the people present—Secretary of War John Calhoun and Indian agent Benjamin O'Fallon—there would have been much at stake in getting accurate translations of the delegates' speeches. Both of them knew the limitations of federal Indian policy in the Upper Missouri Valley, as they faced widespread distrust of American officials because of hunters and squatters trespassing in Indian country. Since O'Fallon's agency at Council Bluffs was vulnerable in a region of some fourteen Indian nations with varying degrees of allegiance to the United States, maintaining positive diplomatic relations demanded careful attention to the wishes and critiques of Native leaders.

What, then, may the speech of Sharitarish or the "Pawnee Chief" tell us about the role of indigenous oratory within these diplomatic networks? In the first place, it made a case for established channels of diplomacy to safeguard Indian nations' political position. As in the speeches to the UFMS board, the Pawnee speaker affirmed his trust in the Indian agent Benjamin O'Fallon, arguing that it was important that the Indian department keep him stationed where he was. Insisting on O'Fallon's good intentions, Sharitarish thought it crucial to maintain close relations with his agency: "My Father has a piece on which he lives," he stated, "and we wish him to enjoy it—we have enough without it—but we wish him to live near us to give us good counsel—to keep our ears and eyes open that we may continue to pursue the right road."[113] It would be easy to read such praise for O'Fallon's "good counsel" as the delegate bowing to US imperial aspirations, or perhaps even the Indian Office's self-congratulation. However, this confidence in the agent more likely signaled a desire to keep control over the process of Indian diplomacy: to retain local and mutually responsive relations between Native leaders and American officials in the Missouri River Valley. Sending missionaries to Indian country looked a lot like an unnecessary entangling of diplomatic relations, and Sharitarish reminded Monroe that "you have already sent us a father; it is enough, he knows us, and we know him."[114] The only Indian agent he desired was the one his people already had long-standing ties with, who understood the complex routines of Indian diplomacy and made it possible for them to maintain control over these interactions.

The Pawnee speech therefore did not simply reject US Indian policy, but affirmed that diplomacy was only meaningful if conducted with American agents who had deep knowledge of the political and historical situations in Indian country. Upper Missouri leaders were deeply knowledgeable about the displacement of Eastern Woodlands Indian populations, the increasing presence of white Americans in the region, and changes in the bison population—and the Pawnee speaker outlined the effects of these ecological and social changes in the region. His speech recognized the ripple effects of American trade on Pawnee subsistence:

> There was a time when we did not know the whites—our wants were then fewer than they are now. They were always within our control—we had then seen nothing which we could not get. But since our intercourse with the *whites* (who have caused such a destruction of our game), our situation is changed. We could lie down to sleep and we awoke [and] we would find the buffalo feeding around our camp—but now we are killing them for their skins, and feeding the wolves with their flesh to make our children cry over their bones.[115]

Sharitarish pointed out that the increasing trade in hides had brought about new customs of hunting for bison: not for sustenance, but to sell the skins and leave the rest of the carcasses behind. The social ramification of these changed practices was that hunting expeditions now had to travel farther and farther from their villages during the summers and winters to find bison, which posed a challenge for social cohesion in the Pawnee villages.[116] Sharitarish therefore emphasized the value of local environmental knowledge, sketching a changed use of natural resources, new forms of subsistence, new ways of dealing with wants and plenitude, and a changed relation to the market. In doing so he explained the alienating effects of a transition to new forms of social and economic organization, which was not directly imposed by American policy but nevertheless the result of American expansion and increased trade in Pawnee country. As ethnohistorian Loretta Fowler notes, since the 1790s, the Upper Missouri nations had witnessed the ripple effects of American westward expansion: Delaware and Shawnee people had moved into the territory of the Osages, who, in turn, were moving westward. Moreover, smallpox had decimated the Skidi village in 1801 and raids by the Teton Sioux increasingly rattled life in the Pawnee villages in the subsequent decades.[117] Bearing the brunt of these disruptions and population movements, the Pawnees became increasingly receptive to American influence.

But what did it mean for Sharitarish to argue that "our wants were then fewer than they are now"? The rhetoric of "wants" would probably have resonated with American policymakers' ideas about Native vulnerability, and the need for agriculture and education to "salvage" Indian nations. Such an interpretation is common in a settler colonial situation, in which, as Lorenzo Veracini argues, the central imperative is the replacement of indigenous societies and Native people are thus "routinely perceived and represented" according to "a paradigm of fragility."[118] At this moment of American expansion, the rhetoric of civilization and the legal doctrine of the right of occupancy coded Indian nations as having only a precarious presence in their homelands, unless they were aided by white Christians to claim a more permanent place. As historian Richard White puts it, Americans "assumed the Pawnees starved and suffered . . . because they had always starved and suffered"—that this simply revealed the "exigencies of the Indian economy."[119] Following this logic, only a radical reconfiguration of indigenous modes of subsistence would ameliorate their condition. Yet the Pawnee speaker shifted the contours of the debate, seeing scarcity and suffering not as reflective of a "primitive" condition, but as the result of white encroachment in Indian country. His statement that the Pawnees' wants had increased worked alongside his more militant statement that "we have everything we want. We have plenty of land, *if you will keep your people off of it.*"[120] Here the delegate walked a fine line, enumerating how American expansion led to ecological change and occasional scarcity, yet without playing into the notion that those problems demonstrated an inherent vulnerability of Native societies and, therefore, the need for the civilizing mission.

The speech of Sharitarish, then, did not necessarily resist US influence, but it challenged the tropes of indigenous vanishing that shaped American approaches to diplomacy. Sharitarish told his audience that "[i]t is too soon, my Great Father, to send those good men among us—we are not starving yet. We wish you to permit us to enjoy the chase until the game of our country is exhausted—until the wild animals become extinct. Let us exhaust our present resources before you make us toil and interrupt our happiness—let me continue to live as I have done."[121] Here the speech seems to encode an assumption about the eventual decline of resources, and the expectation that starvation, suffering, and, ultimately, agricultural education would be imminent. "We are not starving yet": the speech of the Pawnee speaker suggested an inevitable narrative of declension. But what would that assumption have been based on? Richard White has argued that it was not until much later, in the mid-nineteenth century, that crop failures or unsuccessful hunts became an immediate threat to the Pawnee way of life. In a mixed economy of horticulture and hunting, there was security against starvation unless ecological chaos affected both horticulture and hunting simultaneously.[122] Historian David

Bernstein notes that because of the crises that the Pawnees faced in the second half of the nineteenth century—which was marked by "massive dispossession, population decline, and cultural devastation"—it is "tempting" to read the speech "as part of a Pawnee strategy of geopolitical resistance to U.S. expansion" or as an "example of the Pawnees' stoicism in the face of massive population and land loss."[123] Yet the Pawnees "neither feared American encroachment nor wanted to bar them from their country," and since the bison population in Pawnee country "may have actually increased during the 1820s," the speech's argument about ecological and economic decline may in fact have been hypothetical.[124] Perhaps, then, the assertion that "we are not starving yet" mainly echoed the assumptions about Native vulnerability and disappearance on the part of American missionaries and policymakers.

This means that the speech attributed to Sharitarish should not be taken literally as an expression of the Pawnees' historical situation. Indeed, its remarks about starvation probably harkened back to the rhetorical conventions of fur traders, in which the word *starve* had a continuum of meanings that did not always denote the immediate threat of physical harm. The ethnohistorian Mary Black-Rogers has delineated the ways in which fur traders used the verb *to starve* for different rhetorical purposes. It could have a literal meaning, entailing "messages about lack of adequate food," or a technical meaning, relaying information about the business of the fur trade in regard to scarcity of food. But there was also a manipulative usage of the verb *to starve*, a metaphorical employment of the literal or technical usage as part of "certain ritual routines."[125] The translators of the speech may have been familiar with interactions in which professing vulnerability was part of a shared idiom for negotiating reciprocal relationships, rather than an expression of a state of imminent want or vulnerability. After all, Richard White notes that the Pawnees numbered well over 10,000 people, and their village sites on the Platte and Loup Rivers were consistently occupied for a remarkably long period.[126] Moreover, the crop failures and famines the Pawnees suffered later in the mid-nineteenth century resulted from "historical conditions that verged on chaos" rather than "any inherent shortcomings of the Indian economy that forced them to rely on whites as soon as white aid became available"[127] So as the Pawnee speaker negotiated between a critique of the ramifications of Americans expansion on the one hand and the risk of validating ideologies of Native vulnerability on the other, his rhetoric of Native "wants" modified a diplomatic debate about ecological changes and scarcity.

By embracing a notion of historical contingency, the "Speech of the Pawnee" challenged American historical narratives that saw Native people as unwitting victims of modernity and the civilizing mission as an inevitable remedy. Reiterating his call for an uninterrupted way of life, the Pawnee speaker pleaded with his American interlocutors to "let us exhaust our present resources before you make us toil and interrupt our happiness. Let me continue to live as I have done."[128] On one level, this rhetoric suggests a lack of concern for the problem of depleted resources, which American policymakers might have read as evidence of an inherent incapability on the part of indigenous leaders to manage lands and resources. Yet it also qualified this narrative of continuity by anticipating the likelihood of historical change. The speaker argued that "after I have passed to the Good or Evil Spirit from off the wilderness of my present life, the subsistence of my children may become so precarious as to need and embrace the assistance of those good people."[129] Whether this was a literal usage or a figurative usage referring to tribal members as "children," Sharitarish insisted both on indigenous autonomy—to make use of their available resources and live an uninterrupted life—while recognizing the possibility that the precepts of the "civilizing mission" *could* become desirable if their mode of subsistence were to change. Either way, by insisting on the contingency of such a situation, Sharitarish suggested that any embrace of US policy tools would have to be based in indigenous understandings of historical and environmental changes, and locally responsive forms of Indian diplomacy.

That American administrators did not necessarily take this view is apparent from the commentary of Jedidiah Morse, a Congregationalist minister who included the delegates' speeches in his *Report to the Secretary of War of the United States, on Indian Affairs* (1822). Appointed by Secretary of War John Calhoun in 1819, Morse was asked to report on the present condition of Indian nations from New York to the Mississippi River, and he laid out a set of recommendations for the federal government's civilization policy.[130] He included the speeches not as serious engagements with the government's policy proposals, but as foils for a policy that already carried institutional support. For Morse, the speeches were evidence of Native people's resistance to education, which he held to be "natural in their state of ignorance of the value and necessity of the blessings offered them." Making an impassioned argument for Native education, Morse suggested that the Pawnee speeches were evidence that the tribe' resistance posed "no serious obstacle to a prudent commencement of an Education Establishment among them, under the protection of the Government."[131] Morse supposed that Native people's "ignorance" of the value of education actually made a good case to support his policy proposals: their refusal of the rhetoric of civilization demonstrated the very need for Indian education.

Morse's editorializing notwithstanding, the delegates' speeches offered more than simply a response to the civilization program, being rooted in the situational diplomacy of the trans-Mississippi West. While Jedidiah Morse filed away its rejection of the civilizing mission as "ignorance," Sharitarish insisted on ongoing diplomatic relations between the Pawnee and the United States. During the council, these relations were reaffirmed with an exchange of gifts, in which the delegates offered robes and necklaces made from bear claws, among other valuable objects. In his speech, Sharitarish asserted a measure of control over the meaning of this exchange: "The robes, leggins, mockasins, bears-claws [sic], &c, are of little value to you," he explained, "but we wish you to have them deposited and preserved in some conspicuous part of your lodge, so that when we are gone and the sod turned over our bones, if our children should visit this place, as we do now, they may see and recognize with pleasure the deposites [sic] of their fathers, and reflect on the times that are past."[132] With the phrase "as we do now," he emphasized that later generations of Pawnee delegates would come to Washington in the same way he himself did, as political representatives of their people. And the gifts he left behind were not to be preserved as tokens for Americans to mourn over: they established political ties and were a visible link to the Pawnees' future as ongoing political actors. As such, the Pawnee speech offered an alternative to what Johannes Fabian's terms the denial of Native people's "coevalness," or the impulse to assign them either to the past or to an eternal present.[133] It challenged American ideas about indigenous disappearance by articulating a notion of Pawnee futurity that developed in historical time, and that centered on the Pawnees' response to changing historical circumstances.

A different speech attributed to an "O'maha chief" echoed the perspective of the Pawnee speaker, outlining a social and economic situation that belied the rhetoric of indigenous vulnerability. As with the speech of Sharitarish, its authorship is not certain, but the fact that Ongpatonga was the leading Omaha delegate—and a well-known orator—makes it possible that the speech originated with him. Like the speech of Sharitarish, the Omaha speaker argued that there was no need to change his people's mode of subsistence: "I believe that when the Great Spirit placed us upon this earth he consulted our happiness. We love our country—we love our customs and habits. I wish that you would permit us to enjoy them as long as I live."[134] Arguing that the Great Spirit supported their use and occupation of their homelands, he communicated an ideological conviction that countered American ideas about indigenous land claims being tenuous and temporary. He also made clear, however, that historical conditions were prone to change, and while he refuted the idea of immediate "civilization" at the hands of missionaries, matters of historical contingency could make missionary education more appealing in the future. "When we become hungry, naked, when the game of our country becomes exhausted, and misery encompasses our families, then, and not till then, do I want those good people among us. Then they may lend us a helping hand—*then* show us the wealth of the earth—the advantages and sustenance to be derived from its culture."[135] The speaker outlined these historical changes to consider the Omahas' understanding of their past, present, and future: the Omaha were not a people who were "stuck" in time, forever resistant to the onset of modernity and hence doomed to either "assimilate" or to fade away before the tide of "civilization." Instead, he argued that the Omaha lived in historical time, recognizing that historical changes might persuade them to adopt the principles of agricultural education, or other projects of reform.

These historical contingencies were a reminder of the intertribal geography in the Upper Missouri Valley, where social and political life depended on the long-standing interactions between multiple indigenous nations and trading empires. And understanding historical change in the Missouri Valley had little to do with American narratives of progress and civilization. In a passage of his speech that Jedidiah Morse, tellingly, did not include in his *Report to the Secretary of War*, Ongpatonga drew attention to the military and geopolitical ramifications of white expansion in the Upper Missouri Valley, emphasizing the deteriorating Omaha-Sioux relations as an important concern that Indian policy had failed to address. "I am fond of peace, my Great Father," the Omaha delegate offered, "but the Sioux have disturbed my repose. They have struck upon me and killed two of my brothers, and since more of my bravest warriors, whose deaths are still unrevenged. . . . I am forced to war, my Great Father, and I am in hopes you will assist me; I am in hopes that you will give some arms to my Father to place in the hands of my braves to enable them to defend their wives and children."[136] The Upper Missouri nations were deeply affected by the intertribal conflicts that were the ripple effects of Indian removal and American expansion in the East. According to the Omaha delegate, Monroe's imperial projections mattered less in a social world that was increasingly marked by the westward expansion of the Sioux. In making this argument he displayed little sympathy to the position of the Sioux, who themselves were facing pressures from American expansion, from the relocation of eastern nations, and from Indian nations that allied with the United States against them.[137] Still, the Omaha speaker made the important argument that effective diplomacy could only take place if one understood the ripple effects of American expansion on intertribal relations and conflicts.

The speeches that came out of the O'Fallon delegation thus insisted on the importance of the local and situational forms of diplomacy that were a mainstay of political life in the Upper Missouri Valley. And they argued that such diplomacy ultimately benefited the Americans as well—the Omaha speaker called on his audience to look at his own hands as evidence of the Omaha's peaceful intentions: "Look at me, look at me, my father, my hands are unstained with your blood—my people have never struck them. It is not the case with other red skins. Mine is the only nation that has spared the long knives."[138] If the speech was indeed delivered by Ongpatonga, this may have referred to his alliance with the Americans during the War of 1812, but in either case, his claim that his people had spared the Americans (the "long knives") was a reminder of Omaha hegemony and American vulnerability. Moreover, as he represented the political power dynamics in the Upper Missouri Valley, Ongpatonga downplayed the importance of councils held in Washington, stressing that even though he was the main Omaha delegate, he could only represent his nation to a limited extent: "I am chief, but not the only one in my nation; there are other chiefs who raise their crests by my side."[139] To establish friendship with one delegate in Washington did not automatically entail peace with the entire nation: the city of Washington, far away from their villages and the Upper Missouri Agency, was not the center for US-Omaha diplomacy but rather the periphery.

Notwithstanding the questions surrounding their publication, the speeches published during the O'Fallon delegation elaborated a critical conversation on the tensions between the rhetoric of US Indian policy and the situational knowledge and interests of Native leaders. It would be easy to overstate the direct influence of delegates such as Sharitarish and Ongpatonga on Indian policy, but although missionaries of the UFMS went to the Upper Missouri in 1823 with plans to set up schools in the region, these plans failed to materialize. So in spite of its shift toward "civilization" policy, in the short run the Indian Office did not manage to effectively promote a regionally comprehensive, standardized program for Indian reform in the West. If the O'Fallon delegation was a decentered, collaborative project for generating public notice, we may see that it represented more than simply a "staged" form of Indian diplomacy or a trope in the narrative of American empire. Whereas Jedidiah Morse's *Report to the Secretary of War* filed away their speeches as a demonstration of "ignorance," the delegates found an opportunity to circulate knowledge about intertribal affairs, historical changes in the Missouri Valley, and the importance of Indian diplomacy in the trans-Mississippi West.

In addition, the delegates introduced a notion of Native futurity that was imagined in historical terms—neither a naive idea about a stable continuation of present conditions, nor an anticipation of Native vanishing. If Sharitarish and Ongpatonga were the authors of these speeches, they did not merely dismiss the idea of missionaries and agricultural education, but held the door open to future negotiations about them, as might be dictated by historical and environmental changes. They acknowledged the possibility that Indian nations could adopt agricultural education and other aspects of civilization policy, albeit on their own terms and at their own time. In doing so they articulated an alternative to the American assumption that Indian nations would historically be superseded by American empire, an ideology that rendered Native people historically vulnerable and politically subordinate. Looking beyond a narrative in which historical change was a pretext for indigenous disappearance, the oratory from the O'Fallon delegation refused the civilizing scheme to the extent that it presumed Native people did not have any agency in debating it as a policy proposal. By resisting the idea that "civilization" was something that Americans introduced at a time of their choosing, they projected a future for Indian diplomacy in which Indian nations would continue to be taken seriously as partners in exchange and as historical agents.

"A REMOTE AND SAVAGE HERO"

The translations and mistranslations at the center of the O'Fallon delegation reflect how Indian diplomacy negotiated the fraught interactions between representatives of a fledgling American empire and those of sovereign Indian nations from regions outside of direct US influence. In Washington, the delegation elaborated an optimistic narrative about the spreading outward of a continental empire of civilization, even if attitudes toward the place of Native people in that empire were highly ambivalent. Although the US government standardized its Indian policy during the Monroe era, its ideological and political hold on Indian nations in the West was nebulous. In this respect, the delegation to the US capital was more than merely a display of American hegemony but also affirmed the importance of lasting and locally responsive forms of Indian diplomacy. The oratory of Sharitarish and Ongpatonga expressed only an ambivalent commitment to the newly emerging tenets of federal Indian policy. In doing so, they presented a counternarrative of the history and future of indigenous people in the trans-Mississippi West, interrupting the assumptions that undergirded American policy proposals. They looked beyond colonial logics that saw Washington as the center for US-Indian dialogue and the Missouri Valley as the periphery. Against ideas about indigenous vulnerability and Native disappearance, they articulated a future in which Native people continued to be dealt with as political actors on an equal plane.

After the delegation, Benjamin O'Fallon remained at Council Bluffs for several years until 1826, when he resigned from public office and returned to St. Louis. Ongpatonga remained tribal leader of the Omaha until his death in 1846. Sharitarish died not long after coming home from the delegation to Washington and was succeeded by his younger brother. But it was Petalesharo whose celebrity lingered on in the course of 1820s. Years after the O'Fallon delegation, writers and artists frequently revisited his story to articulate ideas about American nationalism and empire. In 1825, Petalesharo's Morning Star narrative was revisited in "The Generous Chief," a song written to honor the Revolutionary War hero Marquis de Lafayette, who conducted a celebratory grand tour of American cities in 1824 and 1825. The lyrics were written by the Washington bookseller Isaac Garner Hutton, who turned Petalesharo's story into a narrative of Indian pacification in the West. The song ends with the "Generous Chief" returning the captive maiden to her home village after saving her from ritual sacrifice. When he brings her home, he offers her people a peace pipe, made by a white man, and speaks the following words:

"Take this pipe (it was made by the white man of peace)
To thy people now so scattered. Let war ever cease
"Full soon shall we prove that the Sachem spoke lies
Mississippi no longer the white man defies."[140]

Carrying the pipe and speaking words of peace, Petalesharo is imagined as the embodiment of a commitment to peaceful relations, both on the part of American settlers and Indian nations in the West.

By the end of the 1820s, then, Petalesharo had come to stand in for American ideas about the place of Indian nations in North America, literally and figuratively. The American novelist James Fenimore Cooper modeled his Pawnee hero Hard-Heart from *The Prairie* (1827) on Petalesharo, whom he had met in 1821 in the dining hall of the City Hotel in New York.[141] Cooper later reflected in *Notions of the Americans* (1828) on the "reputation of this remote and savage hero," which had "spread beyond the narrow limits of his own country."[142] Even if the author considered him a "savage," Petalesharo displayed a physical and moral superiority among a "humbled and degraded" race, and was a reminder that it was possible to find "specimens of loftiness of spirit, of noble bearing and of savage heroism."[143] Petalesharo exemplified that Indian nations west of the Mississippi displayed the "finer traits of savage life," whereas eastern nations had fallen victim to "the abuses of civilization without ever attaining to any of its moral elevation."[144] But there was also a narrative of empire at play in Cooper's reflection: he suggested that the only way to keep in check the "constant diminution in the numbers of the Indians" was to remove Indian nations west of the Mississippi. There they could establish a territorial government and live with little interference or corruption from whites.

As an emblem of Indianness, Petalesharo supported the newly prevalent idea that only the westward migration of Indian nations would allow them to "catch up" to civilization on their own time, away from the influence of white society. Cooper saw this "humanitarian" project of removal as an antiquarian one as well, writing that "if the plan can be effected, a race about whom there is so much that is poetic and fine in recollection will be preserved."[145] The commentary on Petalesharo thereby accomplished what the collaborative publication project of the O'Fallon delegation had not, reinforcing ideologies of Native vulnerability and promoting the need for the civilizing mission. The cult of Petalesharo articulated what had been an underlying response to the public events of the O'Fallon delegation, validating the idea that American Indians were poetically pleasing but politically inconvenient. The image of the Pawnee warrior—brave and fearsome, yet friendly and morally upright—was an opportunity for Americans to project ideological narratives that were politically more expedient. Constructing an image of western tribes as less "degraded" than those in the East, the image of Petalesharo allowed Americans to rationalize the removal of the eastern tribes to the unorganized territories west of the Mississippi.

But if American commentators and policymakers came to interpret the O'Fallon delegation through such colonial projections, the delegation itself was more akin to the scene Samuel Morse painted in *The House of Representatives*: a liminal moment before the action, a moment of ambivalence that defied a clear narrative of empire. The short time that these delegates and policymakers overlapped in Washington reflects the temporality of the delegation as a *project*, a collaborative effort that was limited in duration but that nevertheless inflected ongoing diplomatic relationships. For the delegates, American hegemony was not a foregone conclusion, and their performances failed to bolster the idea of Indian nations as vulnerable and imminently vanishing. Capturing these shifting colonial dynamics, the O'Fallon delegation reproduced the ambiguous space between indigenous sovereignty and American empire.

CHAPTER 2

"Our Wants and Our Wishes"

Frontier Diplomacy and Removal in Sauk Writing and Oratory

In June 1825, the Indian agent Henry Rowe Schoolcraft observed the proceedings at a historic treaty council at Prairie du Chien, near the confluence of the Mississippi and Wisconsin rivers. Although the council at Fort Armstrong brought together more than a thousand people from a host of nations—the Sioux, Menominee, Ioway, Ho-Chunk, Ojibwe, Ottawa, and Potawatomi—Schoolcraft was singularly taken by the Sauk civil chief Keokuk. With some lyricism, he recalled how the tribal leader "stood as a prince, majestic and frowning," representing the "wild, native pride of man, in the savage state." But it was the delivery of his oratory that impressed Schoolcraft most: Keokuk "stood with his war lance, high crest of feathers, and daring eye, like another Coriolanus, and when he spoke in council, and at the same time shook his lance at his enemies, the Sioux, it was evident that he wanted but an opportunity to make their blood flow like water."[1] Schoolcraft's commentary is a reminder of American writers' fondness for the spectacle of indigenous oratory, but it also tells us that Keokuk was in his element at councils such as this. Through his oratory, he came to hold a prominent position in the networks of the Indian Office and built a long career as tribal leader and diplomat. Keokuk's participation in the Prairie du Chien councils reflects that Indian diplomacy depended on seasoned indigenous diplomats who, over the course of long careers, became adept at navigating diplomatic networks. Over the course of the removal era, Keokuk's position became both a source of power and a point of contention for the Sauk and Meskwaki people.

FIGURE 2.1 *View of the Great Treaty Held at Prarie* [sic] *du Chien, September 1825*, after James Otto Lewis. Lithograph by Lehman and Duval, 1835. Rare Book and Special Collections Division, Library of Congress. The full title states that "upwards of 5000 Indian Warriors of the Chippeways, Sioux, Sacs & Foxes, Winnebagoes, Pottowattomies, Menomonies, Ioways, & Ottawas tribes were present," with "Gov. Lewis Cass of Michigan and Wm. Clark of Missouri Commissioners on the part of the United States." James Otto Lewis included this work in *The Aboriginal Portfolio: A Collection of Portraits of the Most Celebrated Chiefs of the North American Indians* (Philadelphia, 1835).

As the first in a series of intertribal councils at the same location, the 1825 council at Prairie du Chien suggests that although delegations to Washington were a fixture in US-Indian relations, the routines of Indian diplomacy more typically took place in Indian country. The Prairie du Chien councils were also an important factor in the diplomatic literature of the Sauk and Meskwaki Nations—also commonly known as the Sac and Fox Nations—and the history of their removal from Illinois to Iowa Territory in the 1830s, and to Indian Territory in 1842.[2] At the center of this history is Keokuk, whose role as civil chief and diplomat was cemented in the period following the War of 1812. During a time when white settlement in Illinois posed an immediate threat to their sovereignty and livelihood, Keokuk's negotiations with American administrators were the fulcrum of Sauk and Meskwaki representation to the US government. Over the course of almost two decades, from 1825 to 1842, Keokuk's oratory within the Indian Office bureaucracy recorded the imperial aspirations of the United States in the Old Northwest, as well as a sustained critique of Indian policy. His role was not uncontested, however. Running counter to Keokuk's diplomatic projects, the Sauk leaders Black Hawk (Ma-ka-tai-me-she-kia-kiak) and Hardfish (Wishecomaque) challenged Keokuk's influence on the conduct of US-Sauk diplomacy. Through petitions, letters, speeches, and autobiography they rallied public opinion to counteract Keokuk's influence, offering alternate paths for contesting the logics of US Indian policy and its designs for Sauk and Meskwaki removal. Produced in the offices of Indian agents and at intertribal councils, these diplomatic writings were intimately shaped by the logics of the treaty system and the history of Sauk and Meskwaki dispossession.

Their efforts took place in the wake of the violence of the Black Hawk War (1832), a brutal American campaign against the Sauk and Meskwaki people that had cost the lives of hundreds of American Indian men, women, and children, and that accelerated Indian removal in the Midwest. The most famous Sauk text from this period is the as-told-to autobiography of Black Hawk, titled *Life of Ma-ka-ta-me-she-kia-kiak* (1833), which he produced in collaboration with the editor John Barton Patterson and the interpreter Antoine LeClaire. In this bestselling account of the war of 1832, Black Hawk shared his perspective on the causes of the war and offered a powerful critique of the treaty system in the process. That Black Hawk's *Life* successfully shaped the written history of the war is evident from the fact that there is something of a straight line from Black Hawk's suspicions of Keokuk to the analysis of later historians and critics. As Mark Rifkin argues, the book's criticism of Keokuk's "smooth tongue" cemented his reputation as an "extension of the bureaucratic discourse" that imposed US territorial mappings onto Indian country.[3] In the words of Thomas Burnell Colbert, Black Hawk has consequently been remembered as "a noble Native American leader trying to save his culture," while Keokuk has been dismissed as "a self-seeking sycophant to whites, especially the government of the United States."[4] From this vantage point, Keokuk's communications within American bureaucratic networks were a handmaiden to the project of settler colonialism, betraying an assumed cultural and political unity among the Sauk people.

Instead of sorting out whether Keokuk deserved this verdict, this chapter seeks to expand the literary archive of Sauk removal by examining Black Hawk's *Life* alongside the writings and oratory of Keokuk and Hardfish and their textual collaborators. The comparison of their respective publications offers a new perspective on the question of indigenous agency and representation as it played out in the history of removal. Given the prominence of Black Hawk's *Life* in literary history, studies of Native American literature have depicted the history of Sauk removal as being more or less synonymous with the Black Hawk War of 1832. But if Black Hawk's memoirs are only one instance in a series of collaborative publication projects—including councils, speeches, and petitions—the colonial records of the Indian Office reveal a more substantial body of Sauk writing that critically engaged with the long history of Sauk-Meskwaki removal and the advent of a settler colonial regime in the Midwest. The writings of Black Hawk, Keokuk, and Hardfish cataloged the various ways the US treaty system imposed new tribal borders, reconfigured the economic place of Indian nations, spurred new intertribal and internal conflicts, and exacerbated existing ones. And even as they offered powerful critiques of the failings of Indian policy, they called for renewed diplomatic relations, insisted on an Indian policy that was responsive to Sauk and Meskwaki lifeways, and proposed economic policies that might consolidate their social and political place in a region that was being opened up to white settlement. Despite their diverging political projects, Keokuk, Black Hawk, and Hardfish all complicated American officials' understanding of the western "frontier" as a place where different stages of civilization clashed. Against this notion, they articulated alternative visions of their future place in North America, and carried on critical conversations about borders, economic organization, and the need for indigenous voices in diplomatic networks. In tracing these fraught negotiations, this chapter locates the places and publics of Sauk writing in the era of removal.

WILLIAM CLARK AND KEOKUK, COAUTHORS

If we can consider the transcription of Native oratory as a form of literature in English, the civil chief Keokuk (c. 1780–1847) may be the most prolific Sauk author during the era of removal. The record of his oratory—delivered at treaty sites and in diplomatic councils—is a substantial part of the archives of the Indian Office's diplomacy with the Sauk and Meskwaki people. According to historian Thomas Burnell Colbert, Keokuk was born in 1780 or 1781 in the village of Saukenuk, near the confluence of the Mississippi and Rock Rivers; while his father's identity is unknown, his mother was "of mixed Sauk and French ancestry."[5] Having distinguished himself in battle—especially in conflicts with the Eastern Dakota—Keokuk's status as a warrior led him to take on an important diplomatic role. Colbert notes that as a young man he became the "guest-keeper" at the village of Saukenuk, in which capacity he hosted official visitors, which made his lodge "the center of social activity" and allowed him to "hone his diplomatic skills."[6] During the War of 1812, Keokuk initially urged his people to remain neutral, but when in 1813 the Sauk were planning to abandon Saukenuk due to a recent American attack nearby, he urged the council to stand firm and defend the village. Although the attack did not materialize, Keokuk's oratory so impressed the tribal council that he gained the title of war chief. This new status led him to become the official diplomat of the tribe to the United States, beginning with a peace delegation to St. Louis in 1816.[7] After that Keokuk engaged in frequent councils with the Indian agent Thomas Forsyth and Superintendent of Indian Affairs William Clark, and in 1824 he took part in a delegation of Sauk and Meskwaki leaders to Washington.[8]

By that time, however, there was already ample reason for the Sauk and Meskwaki people to regard US-Indian diplomacy with suspicion. Decades earlier, in 1804, a delegation led by the Sauk leader Quàshquàme had come to St. Louis, ostensibly for the release of a Sauk person who was a murder suspect. Unprepared for the negotiations about land cessions, the delegation ended up signing a treaty that ceded to the United States the majority of Sauk and Meskwaki lands in present-day Illinois, Missouri, and Wisconsin.[9] The treaty was not immediately enforced, but in 1816, with the steady influx of white settlers into the region, American treaty commissioners persuaded several Sauk and Meskwaki leaders to reaffirm the treaty, and Keokuk and Black Hawk were among the signatories. Keokuk urged the majority of the Sauk and Meskwaki to remove to the Iowa River, since their homelands around Rock Island were overrun with white settlers. But Black Hawk held that the treaty had been wrongly explained to him and persuaded his followers not to give up the village of Saukenuk but to resist American expansion in the Rock River region. The resulting conflict led to the events now known as the Black Hawk War, in which a volunteer army of American settlers committed a brutal massacre to suppress the return of Black Hawk and his followers to the Rock Island region. Following Black Hawk's defeat, the Sauk and Meskwaki people suffered a series of removals: in 1832 they were first forced to relocate to their lands on the Iowa River and they removed further west to the Des Moines River four years later. Finally, in 1842, Keokuk and a council of Sauk and Meskwaki chiefs signed a removal treaty that ushered in their relocation to Indian Territory, in present-day Kansas.[10]

Keokuk's prominent role in these treaties closely ties his historical legacy to the project of US settlement in the Mississippi Valley, and his long career as a diplomat involved many fraught diplomatic interactions in which American officials pressured Sauk and Meskwaki leaders to cede lands to the United States. Keokuk's influence as civil chief and diplomat was especially pronounced in four intertribal treaty councils held at Prairie du Chien between 1825 and 1830. The councils at Prairie du Chien were a response to the fact that the intertribal geography of Indian country was constantly changing, due to white settlement, territorial wars, intertribal conflicts, and the continual redrawing of Indian nations' borders. The goals of these councils were daunting: they were meant to establish new borders and neutral hunting grounds between different tribes and to bring "an end to any ongoing or future warfare between Native peoples in the northwest interior."[11] In

FIGURE 2.2 Daguerreotype portrait of Keokuk, by Thomas M. Easterly. Daguerreotype, 1847. Thomas Easterly Daguerreotype Collection, Missouri Historical Society, St. Louis. This portrait of the Sauk civil chief Keokuk is the most widely reprinted work by the American daguerreotypist Thomas Martin Easterly (1809–1882). Made in 1847, it depicts Keokuk late in life, a year before he passed away on the Sauk and Meskwaki reservation in Kansas. The daguerreotype was taken in Easterly's studio in St. Louis, where he had established a temporary gallery and studio space that year. Keokuk was joined on his trip to the city by Appanoose and several other Sauk and Meskwaki leaders. As Dolores Ann Kilgo notes, the combination of Easterly's expertise as a daguerreotypist and his subject matter made his Native American portraits a major attraction during the artist's time in St. Louis. See Dolores Ann Kilgo, *Likeness and Landscape: Thomas M. Easterly and the Art of the Daguerreotype* (St. Louis: Missouri History Museum, 1994), 15.

particular, for the Sauk delegates the aim was for the Sioux to agree to "a series of intertribal boundaries suggested by Keokuk."[12] Conflicts between the Sauk and the Sioux had intensified as white settlement reshaped the borders of Indian nations in the western territories and the neutral hunting grounds between them. For Native people in the region, this meant that diplomacy with other Indian nations and the United States became an all too regular feature of political life.

Keokuk's work as a diplomat reflected the compromised role Native leaders played in the networks of the Indian Office, as his visits to Washington and his conversations with US administrators left him with a pessimistic view of staving off settler expansion. Well informed about Indian removal in the East, he knew about the growing population and military strength of the United States and became "more fully convinced that the only prudent political position was for his people to ally with the Americans."[13] One of Keokuk's most important informants and interlocutors was William Clark, the superintendent of Indian Affairs in St. Louis, whom he frequently visited throughout the 1820s and 1830s. In his capacity as superintendent, Clark was a key agent in reshaping Native North America on both sides of the Mississippi. He controlled Indian agents—such as Benjamin O'Fallon, Thomas Forsyth, Lawrence Taliaferro, and Pierre Menard—and his office issued licenses and passports, provided payments for injuries and injustices, arrested and punished lawbreakers, surveyed boundaries, distributed annuities, and conducted treaty councils.[14] As Jay Buckley observes, Clark's position was such that many American Indian leaders deemed treaties invalid unless they were conducted with him personally, and over the course of his tenure as superintendent he presided over the removal of some 80,000 American Indians from the East to the trans-Mississippi West.[15]

In his interactions with William Clark, Keokuk constantly tried to gain control over the conduct of Indian diplomacy, in an attempt to accomplish his diplomatic goals without ceding too much of his own authority. For instance, at the 1829 treaty council at Prairie du Chien, Keokuk asked Clark to organize a delegation of Sauk and Meskwaki leaders to Washington, to speak directly with the president, the newly inaugurated Andrew Jackson. Although the Indian Office received a list of chiefs to take part—including Keokuk and the Meskwaki leader Wapello—by March of the next year the secretary of war had failed to authorize the delegation. In council with William Clark in the St. Louis office in March of 1830, Keokuk reiterated his request: "We asked at the Treaty of Prairie du Chien last summer to be permitted to go to Washington City. We repeated this request to our Agent, and to you yourself last fall. We have it much at heart, & cannot get it out of our mind."[16] When Clark asked him about the specific purpose of the delegation, however, Keokuk refused to explain it to him; although he hinted at conflicts with the Sioux over their tribal borders, he explained that "when we return to our Village, a council will be held by [the Sauk and Meskwaki] Tribes, we will then be united & agree upon our plan and the object of our visit will be made known."[17] By withholding his precise reasons for requesting the delegation, Keokuk prevented Clark from being the only deciding voice in authorizing the delegation, instead allowing the Sauk and Meskwaki chiefs to formulate the precise goals collectively in council. Yet although Clark told Keokuk he would "send on your talk to your Great Father & recommend that you be permitted to go see him," the delegation did not materialize and, as Thomas Burnell Colbert writes, "a disgruntled Keokuk returned to Iowa."[18]

These interactions between Clark and Keokuk attest to the intricate power dynamics of the diplomatic situation at the St. Louis superintendency. Keokuk's silence placed Clark in a position where he was forced to adopt the Sauk political perspective and enumerate the problems of settler encroachment in Sauk country. "I know all that you people want," Clark declared, and he proceeded to list many of the pressures and problems that Keokuk frequently addressed in the decade

FIGURE 2.3 Portrait of William Clark, by George Catlin. Oil on canvas, 1832. National Portrait Gallery, Smithsonian Institution. Made by an artist who specialized in portraits of American Indians, George Catlin's (1796–1872) portrait of William Clark (1770–1838) pictures him in his role as superintendent of Indian Affairs in St. Louis, where his office was a major hub for Indian diplomacy, as well as an important base for Catlin during his travels in Indian country during the 1830s. The rolled-out manuscript on the table is the text of the 1830 Prairie du Chien treaty, and the bound volume on the floor, leaning against the globe, reads "Indian Treaties."

to come: the better management of borders between Indian nations; financial compensation for the lands they had lost; a halt to the liquor trade; to be recognized and respected as a sovereign nation; more transparency and accountability with regard to treaties; and to reduce the nation's debts. Having enumerated all of these things, Clark asked Keokuk, "Have I not guessed pretty nearly your wants?" Keokuk answered affirmatively, saying that Clark had "described exactly our wants & our wishes."[19] This collaborative speech act affirmed that Keokuk's political goals were legible to Clark, even when the Sauk leader refused to tell him. If Clark implied that the management of Indian affairs was in capable hands with him, he also made Keokuk's "wants" and "wishes" legible in a bureaucratic context that was deeply shaped by American policy goals. First, the tribal debts Clark alluded to had been incurred over decades, during which trading houses extended credit to Indian nations for goods and provisions they needed for their seasonal hunting expeditions. But ever since Thomas Jefferson's presidency, the American government had encouraged the massive accruement of tribal debts, using these as powerful tools of leverage during negotiations about land cessions. Second, Clark also made Keokuk the official representative of both the Sauk and Meskwaki people, to treat with them as a singular political unit and thereby streamline these diplomatic relationships. In this respect, by approving of Clark's list of his people's "wants" and "wishes," Keokuk endorsed a controversial diplomatic role that ignored the political autonomy of the Meskwaki people and facilitated the policy goals of the Indian Office.

The interactions between Clark and Keokuk connected indigenous governance and US administrative networks, but they took place on an interpersonal plane that was neither private nor public. For instance, in the March 1830 council with Keokuk in St. Louis, the superintendent professed himself to be a "friend," offering his "personal" advice to Keokuk to persuade him to authorize more cessions of Sauk lands to the United States: "As we are now in private council, I will give you my opinion (my private opinion, & that from the Govt) of what you should do. You should offer to sell to the Government a piece of your land on the Mississippi for the purpose of enlarging your annuities, to enable you to pay your debts, & to assist you in farming.... These are my private opinions, as your friend, not being authorized thereto by the Government. You should sell lands enough to get a sufficient annuity."[20] Although Clark described the conversation as a "private" council, in this moment terms such as "public" and "private" do not adequately explain these interactions. That Clark's advice simultaneously expressed "my private opinion, & that from the Govt," implies that these personal conversations *were* public discourse, even as they sidelined Sauk and Meskwaki publics by speaking to Keokuk "in private."

Clark's diplomacy at the St. Louis office reflects that in the early nineteenth century, the Office of Indian Affairs was a loose network of American and Native participants in councils and treaties, and as Stephen Rockwell writes, its operators were typically "more innovative, more independent, and more autonomous" than in later times, wielding a bureaucratic autonomy in which interpersonal communication was still central to exerting political influence.[21] In this instance, Clark tried to make this fact work to his advantage, pressuring Keokuk in this "private" setting to make further land cessions.

The record of their interactions suggests, however, that Keokuk was acutely aware of these dynamics and worked to resist them. Three months later, Keokuk held a council at Clark's office in St. Louis that upended their interactions by turning the superintendency into the site of an "ad hoc" Sauk-Meskwaki public sphere. The occasion for this council was the murder of Peahmuska, a Meskwaki chief who had been one of the signers of the 1829 treaty of Prairie du Chien. An Indian agent stationed at the Sioux agency had invited Peahmuska to come to Fort Crawford on official business, but he was killed by a party of a Sioux warriors on the way there. When Keokuk met with Clark to address the affair, he brought 200 Sauk and Meskwaki people into Clark's office in St. Louis, effectively staging a public performance of indigenous sovereignty.[22] Keokuk, who often made similarly dramatic entrances during intertribal councils, turned Clark's office and the grounds surrounding it into a public spectacle—a reminder of Sauk and Meskwaki hegemony in their region.[23] If Clark had tried to make his earlier meeting in March a "private" council, away from the scrutiny of Keokuk's people, this time around Keokuk staged their interaction in a public arena, challenging the use and purpose of Indian diplomacy if it failed to secure the "protection" that the Americans promised in their treaties. Before an audience of Sauk and Meskwaki spectators, Keokuk voiced his refusal to attend the next treaty council at Prairie du Chien, which was scheduled for July 1830. "My Father," he asked, "How is it possible for our people to go to P. du Chien? When [Peahmuska] went to Washington the President gave him a Flag, a medal & some other things; when he was going to P. du Chien he took these things with him to show who & what he was, but he was fallen upon by murderers, and his flag, Your Flag, the Flag of the United States was trod under foot & then burned."[24] Keokuk questioned the meaning of these diplomatic symbols in light of the Americans' failure to uphold the promises they made: Peahmuska's American flag, trampled and burned, revealed the Indian Office's inability to provide the protection that had been negotiated at Prairie du Chien. Although Clark urged Keokuk to attend the upcoming council, Keokuk stated his refusal to participate: "My Father: We have never before refused you anything, you have always said true (ever had your own way) but now we cannot go.... I am firm and immovable in my determination not to go to Prairie du Chien."[25]

Keokuk's oratory, then, was a form of institutional intervention, making use of the routines of Indian diplomacy in St. Louis while also questioning their efficacy. Keokuk challenged the legitimacy and practical use of treaty councils if the diplomatic relations they established had little meaning on the ground. "My Father," he spoke, "I now tell you from the bottom of my heart that I cannot go to Prairie du Chien & hope I will say true, and have my way in my turn, for once. I am done."[26] His decided tone registered a moment when the conversational back-and-forth of his councils with Clark made way for an uncompromising statement of an absolute position. Noting that "we have our homes, & can do business very well there," Keokuk sought to change the conditions of interaction with the United States, suggesting that the upcoming council be held in Sauk political space, on their own terms.[27] His critique forced Clark to acknowledge the failings of the US administration of Indian affairs, and Clark acknowledged that Peahmuska was killed "at an unfortunate time for his people, & by bad management they were deceived ... by the ignorance of a man who had no authority to do as he had done."[28] Clark's use of the passive voice muddled agency and accountability, but Clark nevertheless acknowledged that the death of Peahmuska was the result of the "bad management" of Indian affairs.[29] Implicating his office's failure to manage the volatile political situation in the region, Clark explained that the subagent at Prairie du Chien displayed an "ignorance of Indian affairs," and that he would "recall him from among you—alltho' [sic] I had nothing to do in his appointment. He never shall again be the cause of injury to you."[30] In front of a large audience of Sauk and Meskwaki warriors, the council at St. Louis became a showcase for the Indian Office's failures as well as Keokuk's influential role in pointing out these failures.

Through these performative interactions Keokuk addressed the Indian Office's management and mismanagement of the new intertribal borders in the region, which were brought on by American expansion as well as the geopolitical power of the Sioux. Keokuk's diplomacy aimed to gain control over the communications in these bureaucratic networks, to insist on American officials' accountability for the actions of their agents, and to be responsive to the Sauk and Meskwaki's political concerns. The result of this work was a mixed bag. On the one hand, Keokuk secured from Clark a payment of $1,000 in trade goods to "cover the dead": as compensation for the loss of Peahmuska and to prevent young warriors from seeking retaliation. On the other hand, Keokuk did cave and attended the council at Prairie du Chien the next month, where Clark had told him he would "hear the words of the President." Although a new intertribal peace was negotiated there, it reduced the Sauk and Meskwaki's land base even further, to provide for a neutral zone between the Eastern Dakota and the Sauk and Meskwaki people.[31]

Keokuk's negotiations with Clark did not escape the colonial logics of the treaty system, but he found new ways to mediate among the Sauk and Meskwaki chiefs, the council grounds at Prairie du Chien, and Clark's office in St. Louis. His publication projects were attempts to bring the negotiations with the superintendent into a mixed indigenous-settler public sphere, in which his oratory carried tribal authorization and resisted being co-opted by the agenda of the settler state. Yet his political voice also depended on recognition from William Clark, and as such these diplomatic interactions reflect that, as Eric Cheyfitz notes, the word "collaboration" activates a range of meanings from cooperation to coercion.[32] The fact that Keokuk and William Clark were practically coauthors of these texts means that they were not just "intercultural" texts that registered a convergence of Sauk and American cultural traditions. Rather, they were *diplomatic* forms of writing—the result of interactions that were ceremonial and staged, and that offered self-consciously politicized representations of national interests that were necessarily reductive. Such were the conditions of publication for tribal leaders like Keokuk, who in raising public awareness about US-Indian relations relied on the networks of the settler state. Yet if these interactions ultimately reaffirmed the decision-making power of William Clark, they also revealed the strategies of his coauthor Keokuk, whose role as an authorized agent of the Sauk and Meskwaki Nations, I will argue, gradually became an index of dissent among his own people.

BLACK HAWK'S AUDIENCES AND THE IMAGE OF THE FRONTIER

If Keokuk's diplomatic efforts sought to preserve close relations with US government officials, the Sauk warrior Black Hawk (1767–1838) challenged his influence by resisting settler encroachment in a more direct way. A veteran of the War of 1812, Black Hawk was not a hereditary chief but had gained much status as a warrior in raiding parties and intertribal conflicts. During the War of 1812, Black Hawk and his followers had sided with the British against the Americans and their allies, and commanded the Native American forces, which consisted of some 200 Sauk warriors and members of the Kickapoo, Potawatomi, Ho-Chunk, and Ottawa nations. Because of his role as commander in the War of 1812, American administrators came to refer to Black Hawk and his followers as the "British Band." In the decades after the war, which ended in 1815, white settlers advanced rapidly into the Sauk and Meskwaki homelands, and Illinois achieved statehood in 1818. By 1830, some Sauk and Meskwaki people held out on the western edge of Illinois, but they faced intense pressure to relocate altogether across the Mississippi, into what the Americans called "unorganized territory"; it became Wisconsin Territory and Iowa Territory later in the decade. While Keokuk urged the Sauk and Meskwaki people to resign themselves to the Treaty of 1804 and leave the village of Saukenuk on the Rock River, Black Hawk defied the treaty and urged his followers to do the same. Between 1830 and 1832, he led his followers back east across the Mississippi to Saukenuk after their seasonal hunts, even though by 1830 the village was surrounded by white settlers, who tried to keep out its original inhabitants by burning their crops and destroying their settlements.

The expulsion of the Sauk and Meskwaki people from Illinois reflects a larger pattern in which settlers viewed Native people as "outsiders" in their own territories, effectively turning their homelands into a "frontier." Believing that the return of Black Hawk and his followers to Saukenuk would usher in immediate conflict, Illinois citizens on the Rock River wrote a petition to Governor John Reynolds asking for "protection against the Sac and Fox tribe of Indians, who have again taken our possession of our lands near the mouth of Rock River and its vicinity." The settlers wrote that they had been "burning our fences, destroying our crops of wheat," and "threaten[ing] our lives if we attempt to plant corn." According to the petition, Black Hawk and his followers were "determined to exterminate us, provided we don't leave the country."[33] By 1832, the United States was prepared for such conflict, and Edmund P. Gaines, the commander of the western territorial army, had mobilized troops in an attempt to intimidate Black Hawk and his followers. In April 1832, Black Hawk led approximately 500 warriors and 600 civilians—mostly Sauk, Meskwaki, and Kickapoo—across the Mississippi, back to Saukenuk. American officials assumed their intentions were hostile and they mobilized an army of settler volunteers against them. In St. Louis, William Clark showed no tolerance for Black Hawk's band and defended what he called a "war of extermination" against the warrior and his followers: he suggested that "the peace and quiet of the frontier, the lives and safety of its inhabitants *demand* it."[34] Although Keokuk's influence kept the majority of his people outside of the conflict, the American response to Black Hawk's defense of Saukenuk ushered in the deadliest conflict between Americans and Native Americans since the Creek Wars of 1813 and 1814. The fighting began when settler volunteers attacked a party of Native people on May 14, 1832. Under the command of General Henry Atkinson, the Americans defeated Black Hawk and his followers in August 1832, during the Battle of Bad Axe. More a massacre than a battle, settler volunteers shot dozens of Native men, women, and children as they were trying to cross back over across the Mississippi to the west. Although estimates vary, it is believed that the Sauk and their allies suffered 450 to 600 casualties, against 77 losses on the American side.[35]

The American victory forced the Sauk and Meskwaki chiefs to sign a new treaty in the fall of 1832. The treaty stipulated a surrender of all Sauk lands east of the Mississippi, including the principal village of Saukenuk, with only a 400 square-mile tract of land on both sides of the Iowa River to be kept as a reservation. The remaining Sauk lands east of the Mississippi were opened for white settlement beginning in June 1833.[36] Moreover, the treaty proclaimed "peace and friendship" with the Sauk and Meskwaki people, but with the noted exception of "the hostages before mentioned," meaning Black Hawk and several other leaders of his "British band" whom the Americans had taken captive.[37] This wedge between Black Hawk's band and the rest of the nations is a critical move in the treaty's narrative of pacification, allowing the United States to proclaim ongoing friendship while asserting that it had "subdued the said hostile band" and secured "the future safety and tranquility of the invaded frontier."[38] The 1832 treaty thus interpreted the war as a symptom of Indian lawlessness that had threatened an "invaded frontier" that was imagined as being part of US territorial space. Reading Black Hawk as a "lawless and desperate" leader who was now "conquered and subdued," it carried out a narrative of conflict and pacification that ultimately served to legitimate the land cessions in the eyes of the American government.

In the aftermath of the 1832 war, Black Hawk became part of the US government's attempt to use the spectacle of Indian diplomacy to promote an image of the pacified frontier. After the war, Black Hawk was taken to the city of Washington along with four other leaders of his band: his eldest son Nasheaskuk, the Sauk-Winnebago Wabokieshiek and his son Pamaho, and the Sauk principal chief Neapope.[39] The War Department held them in Fort Monroe in Virginia for five weeks, after which they took them on a widely publicized tour of Eastern cities. As J. Gerald Kennedy writes, the captivity tour had three important goals: to "humiliate the Indians," to "convince them of the uselessness of warring with a far more numerous and powerful people," and to demonstrate "President Jackson's control over his Indian policy."[40] Like Petalesharo a decade earlier, Black Hawk became something of a celebrity, through public spectacles in eastern cities and portraits made by artists, including Charles Bird King and Robert Sully. Newspaper articles generated a flurry of publicity about his captivity tour, with one newspaper editor even coining the phrase "Blackhawkiana" to describe the coverage. And like Petalesharo a decade earlier, Black Hawk came to represent the figure of the defeated Native warrior in this enactment of American empire, in which the bodies of the captive leader signified either a pacified frontier or the mistreatment of Native people at the hands of the United States. Indeed, the mock diplomacy of the captivity tour made Black Hawk a familiar trope in a vehement debate about western expansion and Indian dispossession. When Andrew Jackson signed the Indian Removal Act into law in 1830, he advanced a policy agenda to actively pursue removal, while the American victory in the Black Hawk War vindicated his aggressive pursuit of US expansion. That Jackson's policies toward Indian nations were politically controversial, however, is apparent from a political cartoon published not long after the end of the war, in which Black Hawk figures prominently. Under the pseudonym "Hassan Straightshanks," the cartoonist David Johnston published a cartoon satirizing President Andrew Jackson's administration and the program of westward expansion he vigorously championed. Titled "The Grand National Caravan Moving East," it depicts a crowd watching a parade led by Jackson and Vice President Martin Van Buren. Black Hawk and his party are carried off in a cart with iron bars, while Black Hawk exclaims "Home Sweet Home" and a banner ironically proclaims the "Rights of Man."[41] Through such depictions, Black Hawk became a current symbol for American Indians who were on the receiving end of Jackson's Indian policy at a pivotal moment in US territorial expansion.

The coverage of Black Hawk's tour in US newspapers resolved ideological tensions about the recent war and Americans' relation to Native people in the western territories. Some commentators understood the end of the war as a moment of Indian pacification on the frontier. *Niles' Register* reported how Black Hawk met Andrew Jackson in Washington, where the president explained they would be confined "until it was ascertained that the stipulations of the treaty had been complied with by their people, and all the bad feeling which had led to the bloody scenes on the frontiers banished."[42] Other newspaper accounts stressed a newfound potential for peaceful relations. The *New York Evening Post* reported that Black Hawk "addressed the people assembled" and wished them "the greatest prosperity." He assured them of "a kind remembrance of their friendship, and, when restored to his tribe, of a more amicable disposition towards their white Brethren."[43] The report of a meeting between the Sauk captives and several Seneca leaders similarly reinforced the War Department's narrative of pacification: Black Hawk proclaimed that he had seen "how great a people the whites are. They are very rich and very strong—it is a folly for us to fight with them." He advised his people "to be quiet and live like good men," and affirmed his intention to "walk the straight path for the future, and to content ourselves with what we have, and with cultivating our lands."[44] This narrative of pacification, however, emerged alongside those that projected Euro-American ideas of savagery onto Black Hawk's party, such as a *New York Evening Post* article arguing that Black Hawk had "no

FIGURE 2.4 *The Grand National Caravan Moving East*, by Hassan Straightshanks (David Claypoole Johnston). Print; lithograph on wove paper, 1833. Prints and Photographs Division, Library of Congress, Washington DC. This illustration by the American cartoonist David Claypoole Johnston seems to comment on three interrelated phenomena: the public spectacle of Black Hawk's "captivity tour" in eastern cities, the blind pursuit of American expansion and Indian removal under president Andrew Jackson, and the centrality of parades and pageants in American democratic culture. Passing in front of a crowd of spectators, Jackson leads the parade with Vice President Martin Van Buren seated behind him on the same horse, while a devil playing a fiddle follows them on a second horse. Finally, two horses pull a wagon that carries a cage with six American Indian figures inside it, ostensibly depicting Black Hawk and his party, one of whom utters the phrase "Home sweet home." The context of the Black Hawk War is further alluded to by the fiddling devil, who comments, "When wild wars deadly blast was blown." Meanwhile, several other elements ironically undercut this scene of captivity and conquest, including a banner reading "Rights of Man," a liberty cap (which was a symbol of manumission), and a drunken man lying prostrate in the street exclaiming "[h]ail! Columbia, happy land."

other aim or object than the gratification of blind revenge, in the slaughter of women and children."⁴⁵

Whereas American commentators took Keokuk seriously as a diplomat and orator, the coverage of the captivity tour did the opposite for Black Hawk. Whether they considered him pacified or still a "savage," the writers of "Blackhawkiana" boosted the warrior's celebrity but rendered him irrelevant as a political figure. A brief note in the *Washington Globe* imagined Black Hawk speaking out publicly on the controversy over the US National Bank, the rechartering of which was famously vetoed by Andrew Jackson. But it ridiculed the notion that Black Hawk could have an informed opinion about this political controversy: "It is understood that the celebrated BLACK HAWK has declared himself decidedly in favor of re-chartering the United States Bank. The Hawk and his party visited the Bank on Thursday, inspected the books, expressed through his interpreter his satisfaction of its conduct, and retired amid the crowd of boys and negroes about 2 o'clock. The stock will look up to-morrow in Wall-street."⁴⁶ Another piece of "Blackhawkiana" ridiculed the group of captives through tropes of laziness and drunkenness. One writer recounted an attempt to have "a religious conversation with the sons of the forest," writing that Nasheaskuk "had just thrown himself on a sofa . . . saying, 'I lazee—I lazee,'—covered his head with a blanket, and fell asleep."⁴⁷ If the representation of the captives wavered between tropes of American Indians as fierce savages and as degraded drunkards, in either case they were figures to be discredited.

As a public figure, then, Black Hawk was denied the status that Keokuk enjoyed: that of an authorized agent seen as capable of representing the Sauk nation within diplomatic networks. On his return from the East Coast, however, Black Hawk claimed an alternative path to such public authority, narrating the story of his life and career to a translator and a clerk at the Rock Island Indian agency. His memoirs were published in book form as *Life of Ma-ka-tai-me-she-kia-kiak, or Black Hawk* in 1833, and as the preface by the editor John B. Patterson explains, the book was intended to correct Black Hawk's image as "lawless" and a "desperate leader": "Several accounts of the late war having been published, in which he thinks justice is not done to himself or his nation, [Black Hawk] determined to make known to the world, the injuries his people have received from the whites—the causes which brought on the war on the part of his nation, and a general history of it throughout the campaign. In his opinion, this is the only method now left him, to rescue his little band . . . from the effects of the statements that have already gone forth."⁴⁸ If the book was indeed an attempt to restore Black Hawk's image as a political figure, it may have been quite successful. After it was published in Cincinnati in 1833, the *Life* was reprinted many times, becoming an enduring bestseller. It is no surprise that American reading audiences were so captivated by Black Hawk's narrative at this crucial moment of American western expansion: Gordon M. Sayre has amply demonstrated the popularity of literary writings about indigenous leaders who resisted empire, a genre that the *Life* certainly fits within.[49] Its success further inspired other publications about the Black Hawk War, including the historian Benjamin Drake's *Life and Adventures of Black Hawk* (1838) and Elbert Herring Smith's narrative poem *Ma-ka-tai-me-she-kia-kiak* (1848).[50]

The publication of Black Hawk's *Life* extended the workings of US-Indian diplomacy at the Rock Island Indian agency. A prefatory note to the book states that Black Hawk narrated it at the agency to a "US Interpreter for the Sacs and Foxes," meaning that, as Timothy Sweet puts it, its immediate audience was not an abstract reading public but "the United States government as represented in the person of the interpreter LeClaire and the physical space of the Rock Island Agency."[51] Importantly, the physical space of Rock Island reflected several overlapping spheres of Indian diplomacy: it housed the Indian agency, the military

FIGURE 2.5
Portrait of Black Hawk, after Robert Matthew Sully. Photogravure by G. Barrie and Sons. 1903. Author's collection. This portrait of Black Hawk was one of several portraits of American Indian figures by the artist Robert Matthew Sully (1803–1855). According to Patrick J. Jung, the portrait was made in 1833 when several artists visited Black Hawk's party while they were detained at Fort Monroe in Virginia. Patrick J. Jung, *The Black Hawk War of 1832* (Norman: University of Oklahoma Press, 2008), 193.

post Fort Armstrong, and the trading house of George Davenport. The roles of these different agencies were firmly intertwined, and it is important to note that Antoine LeClaire—a protégé of William Clark—worked for both Davenport the trader and the Indian Office.[52] Black Hawk's editor John Barton Patterson, meanwhile, had moved to Rock Island only recently, in 1832, but when he began the publication of Black Hawk's *Life* he was also working as a clerk in Davenport's trading house.[53] In this respect, the fact that Black Hawk narrated his memoirs to LeClaire and Patterson meant that he was engaging two agents of the Indian Office and the trading companies that worked closely alongside it. Black Hawk's memoirs therefore represent a departure from other "as-told-to narratives," a thriving genre of books that detailed the interesting life stories of (often) nonwhite subjects and thereby catered to a voyeuristic interest in the tales of misfortune of a cultural Other.[54] Rather, Black Hawk was publishing his own political memoirs through the institutional networks of Indian diplomacy, not as a mere informant but as what William Boelhower calls "a rhetor self-consciously speaking in public."[55]

The collaboration with Patterson and LeClaire at Rock Island allowed Black Hawk to occupy a position similar to Keokuk's: to be taken seriously as a political figure within these administrative networks and to represent Sauk collectivity in a public performance of diplomacy. In a further parallel to Keokuk's role, the *Life* expresses an institutional critique of these very networks, implicating the Indian agent, trader, and interpreter in the mismanagement of Indian affairs. Recalling how white settlers destroyed the Sauk women's cornfields in 1830, Black Hawk represents this moment as a turning point in the history of the war, the moment when a military standoff between Black Hawk's band and American settlers began to seem inevitable. Yet he emphasizes that in spite of his own efforts to engage in diplomacy, the agent, interpreter, and trader offered him only one option: "I visited Rock Island. The agent again ordered me to quit my village. He said, that if we did not, troops would be sent to drive us off. . . . The *interpreter* joined him, and gave me so many good reasons, that I almost wished I had not undertaken the difficult task that I had pledged myself to my brave band to perform. In this mood, I called upon the *trader*, who is fond of talking, and had long been my friend, but now amongst those advising me to give up my village."[56] As the literary scholar Neil Schmitz observes, in this passage the trader, agent, and interpreter are "spoken of almost as a single identity, because what they say to the Sauks is always the same."[57] Schmitz points out that even the replacement of the Indian agent does not change this discourse. In 1830 the Indian agent Thomas Forsyth was dismissed from his office after criticizing William Clark, and was replaced by the much younger Felix St. Vrain, yet Black Hawk remarks that "the young man who took the place of our agent, told the same old story over, about removing us."[58] He recounts how Davenport asked him twice whether "some terms could not be made ... for us to remove to the west side of the Mississippi," after which he gave in and "agreed, that I could honorably give up."[59] Meanwhile, Black Hawk writes, William Clark in St. Louis "would give us *nothing!*—and said if we did not remove immediately, we should be *drove off!*" In rendering the words of these administrators, Black Hawk suggests that the conflict was exacerbated by the impossibility of dialogue within the structures of the Indian Office, and by making this critique he turns his account of the war's origins into a diagnosis of institutional failures. Black Hawk's *Life* thereby criticizes a bureaucratic discourse of removal different from the policy rhetoric that promoted removal as a "humanitarian" project of civilization and Indian reform. Rather, the book critiques the rhetoric of a bureaucracy that sees the Sauk lands as already ceded and holds no room for negotiation—a government apparatus in which there is no more space for diplomacy.

So if Black Hawk sees white settlers' encroachment onto Sauk lands as the main offense, another is the refusal of American officials to recognize his openness to diplomatic options, and to take him seriously as a political representative of the Sauk people. His description of a council with the American general Edmund Gaines is a key moment in this critical account. When the Sauk leaders Wapello and Keokuk convene with Gaines at Rock Island, Black Hawk and his band are summoned to come to the council grounds, where the general urges them to remove peacefully "from the lands you have long since ceded to the United States," to "leave the country you are occupying" in order to prevent military conflict. In the exchange that follows, Black Hawk responds by insisting on the political autonomy of his own band of followers, one that is not recognized by Gaines: "I replied: 'That we had never sold our country. *We* never received any annuities from our American Father! And *we* are determined to hold on to our village!' The war chief [Gaines], apparently angry, rose and said:—'Who is *Black Hawk?* Who is *Black Hawk?* I responded: 'I am a *Sac! my forefather was a Sac! and all the nations call me a SAC!*"[60] As Mark Rifkin notes, in this pivotal moment Black Hawk turns Gaines's pronoun "you" into a more specific "we" referring specifically to Black Hawk's followers, who never assented to the sale of Sauk lands. His words thereby signal a political notion of a Sauk authority that is based not in the diplomatic channels sanctioned by the US government but in "traditional Sauk notions of identity and territoriality."[61] The passage registers Black Hawk's performance of what Arnold Krupat calls a "synecdochic" mode of self-identification, in which the speaker's identity is important foremost as a representation of a larger collectivity.[62] Yet his riposte is more than a statement of a collective identity, as it criticizes the communication channels within the networks of Indian diplomacy.

By citing Gaines's repetition of the question "Who is *Black Hawk*?" he emphasizes the general's lack of knowledge of the complicated questions about political representation within US-Sauk interactions. Having just made his way down the Rock River to attend the council at Rock Island, Gaines quickly dismisses the political relevance of Black Hawk, since he is not recognized by American officials as civil chief. In response, Black Hawk hints at the failure of this diplomatic network to recognize the important political faction that he represents, pointing out an institutional failure to pay attention to conflicts and issues of leadership within the Sauk and Meskwaki tribes.

In his account of these interactions, Black Hawk exposes the limits of US-Indian diplomacy in Sauk country, which Americans began to see as the western "frontier." He sees Indian removal not only as a policy that was formulated by politicians and religious reformers on the East Coast, but as a historical injustice that transpired because of administrators in the field, who blindly reaffirmed policy decisions without taking seriously the indigenous leaders who protested them. If this is a critique of US officials, Black Hawk also implicates Keokuk, whom he sees as an extension of US bureaucratic networks: "All the whites with whom I was acquainted, and had been on terms of intimacy, advised me contrary to my wishes, that I began to doubt whether I had a *friend* among them. Ke-o-kuck, who has a smooth tongue, and is a great speaker, was busy in persuading my band that I was wrong—and thereby making many of them dissatisfied with me."[63] As several scholars have pointed out, Black Hawk's description of Keokuk's "smooth tongue" echoes his earlier reflection on white Americans, when he notes "how smooth must be the language of the whites, when they can make right look like wrong, and wrong like right."[64] Recognizing in both Keokuk and the Americans an ability to manipulate language and unduly influence tribal members, Black Hawk criticizes Keokuk's acquiescence to abandoning the village of Saukenuk. "We were a divided people," Black Hawk writes, "forming two parties, Ke-o-kuck being at the head of one, willing to barter our rights merely for the good opinion of the whites; and cowardly enough to desert our village to them. I was at the head of the other party, and was determined to hold on to my village, although I had been *ordered* to leave it."[65] Timothy Sweet observes that Black Hawk's refusal to leave and his "centeredness within the traditional tribal worldview" is in stark contrast to the actions of Keokuk, a "nonwarrior who repeatedly violates Sauk traditions," and whose negotiations with American officials advance the extinguishing of Sauk land title.[66]

Black Hawk's *Life*, then, offers a critique of diplomatic conduct that is rooted in colonial hierarchies. Mark Rifkin argues that his challenge to Keokuk's leadership is a critique of the "logic of the treaty-system" and he articulates "an alternative, decentralized vision of Sauk politics" by challenging his adversary's singular position as the leading diplomat.[67] This is not to say, however, that his memoirs disregard Indian diplomacy altogether, or consider armed resistance as a more expedient path. In a key passage, Black Hawk narrates the moment when he begins to see military action as a necessary alternative to US-Sauk diplomacy, when the Sauk principal chief Neapope tells him that the Winnebago "Prophet" Wabokieshiek has guaranteed that Potawotami and British fighters will come to their aid. At this moment, Keokuk tries to convince him that he has "been imposed upon by *liars*, and had much better remain where I was and keep quiet." When he realizes Black Hawk's resolve, he requests Clark to authorize a delegation to Washington, to have their "difficulties settled amicably."[68] However, they hear "nothing favorable from the great chief at St. Louis" and Black Hawk keeps his warriors mobilized as he believes that Keokuk's "peacable disposition" has been "the cause of our having been driven from our village."[69] But even as the narrative here builds to a moment when Black Hawk gravitates to armed resistance, he does not dismiss the work of Keokuk in exploring diplomatic avenues. "Every overture had been made by Ke-o-kuck to prevent difficulty," he recalls, "and I anxiously hoped that something would be done for my people, that it might be avoided."[70] Indicating a more systemic problem, Black Hawk writes that "there was bad management somewhere, or the difficulty that has taken place would have been avoided."[71] With this emphasis on "bad management," the *Life* echoes a phrase that was also used by William Clark in council with Keokuk, which suggests how the rhetoric of both men was shaped by acts of translation in the Indian Office. While this bureaucratic phrase obscures individual accountability, it points to a wider mismanagement of information within the Office of Indian Affairs as a cause of the conflict, implicating a fundamental inefficiency in the communication circuits of traders, Indian agents, government officials, and Native representatives. Black Hawk resists not diplomacy, but inefficient diplomacy; not the management of Indian affairs by the American government, but their "bad management" of Indian affairs.

With his *Life of Ma-ka-tai-me-she-kia-kiak*, Black Hawk brought into American print culture a critical representation of Indian diplomacy in the West. By lambasting the imbrication of Indian agents, traders, and interpreters, Black Hawk challenged the conduct of diplomacy as well as the very networks that the publication of his own book depended on. Through this collaborative publication project, he challenged the narrative of "frontier violence" that was established by the petition of white settlers in Illinois, the Treaty of 1832, and the newspaper accounts of his captivity tour in the East. That Black Hawk published his story through the agency of Patterson and LeClaire should not prompt us to regard his memoirs simply as an act of colonial imposition or mistranslation. Indeed, the fact that LeClaire and Patterson were both agents of the settler state was the very point of telling them his story, and to publish his narrative in these fraught circumstances was better than to be reduced to a newspaper cartoon.

Due in part to the powerful narrative in Black Hawk's *Life*, the history of Sauk removal has long been associated with what historian Alvin M. Josephy once termed "the rivalry of Black Hawk and Keokuk."[72] If we consider their respective publications as forms of institutional critique, however—as projects of intervening in diplomatic routines—the easy binary of the "peacable" Keokuk and the "warlike" Black Hawk begins to break down. By writing his life story, Black Hawk located the origins of the 1832 war in institutions of Indian diplomacy that refused to own up to the fraudulence of the 1804 treaty and that failed to take seriously the decentralized forms of decision-making in Indian country. Like Keokuk's oratory, Black Hawk's publication project was aimed not at an abstract audience of American readers, but at the networks of Indian diplomacy at the Rock Island agency, to condemn the ways in which it extended a system that had eroded the Sauk and Meskwaki's place in western Illinois. And like Keokuk, Black Hawk recognized the need to assert and reassert diplomatic relations, to ensure a more accurate representation of Sauk collectivity in the political spaces where this mattered. Seeking out the few routes to publication that were available to him, Black Hawk offered a corrective account of the frontier violence against Native people and the institutional failures that brought it on.

KEEPING RECORDS: POWER AND PLACE IN THE ORATORY OF KEOKUK

After the 1832 treaty and the publication of the *Life*, Black Hawk's role in Sauk political life came to an end, save for a purely ceremonial role during an 1837 delegation to Washington. Even as Black Hawk exited the public eye, however, the Sauk and Meskwaki people's struggle for their lands and their existence continued, through diplomatic engagements in which Keokuk continued to play a significant role. Throughout the 1830s, Keokuk was faced with the dramatic reduction of Sauk and Meskwaki lands per the Treaty of 1832, with his people confined to a small reserve on the Iowa River, in a region that was rapidly flooding with white settlers and that became organized as Wisconsin Territory in 1836 and as Iowa Territory in 1838. The historian William T. Hagan once described this period—from the Black Hawk War to the Sauk and Meskwaki's removal to Indian Territory in 1845—as the "Iowa interlude," suggesting that it was merely a transitional period between two more significant historical moments.[73] But this decade was an important liminal moment, holding new opportunities for the Sauk and Meskwaki people to claim a permanent place in their homelands, a project that depended deeply on the work of Indian diplomacy. This was a period when the US government carried out a profound remapping of the region around the Mississippi, Iowa, and Des Moines Rivers: white settlers expanded westward into indigenous territories while intertribal conflicts prompted efforts to redraw the boundaries and neutral grounds between them. During this period, Keokuk's oratory in councils and delegations negotiated between the need to address US colonialism in a constantly changing intertribal geography. His speeches and councils in the records of the Indian Office, then, also document the intertribal dimensions of Indian diplomacy, reflecting that, as Arnold Krupat reminds us, Native literatures "have always-already been implicitly transnational."[74] Aimed at power struggles on different fronts, Keokuk's oratory registers the drastic effects of settler colonialism in Indian country—the dispossession of indigenous lands in tandem with the assertion of US bureaucratic control—and how this dovetailed with the border conflicts between different Indian nations and the problematic remapping of indigenous space through US-Indian diplomacy. As Keokuk made these issues central to US-Sauk diplomacy, his oratory represents a persistent effort to intervene in the networks of the Indian Office, to gain communicative control over its problematic management of Indian affairs.

But what did "influence" and "control" mean for tribal leaders in a colonial network of administrators? How did power work in these settings, and to what extent did Keokuk wield it? As Kate Flint argues, a profound upheaval for American Indians in the nineteenth century was their new role as "subjects, rather than agents, in the formations and development of a huge nation-state and their subjection to externally imposed bureaucracy."[75] In a region that was being transformed from indigenous space into American territory, leaders like Keokuk worked within the confines of an administrative system that secured Indian "pacification" through various means—including financial policy and military violence—and thus thrived on relationships of power that were fundamentally unequal. Yet this does not mean that they were unilateral. Historian Gregory Dowd explains that North American indigenous understandings of power typically emphasized its interactional and relational character. "Power lay at the center of all concerns," Dowd writes, and "most fundamentally, power meant the ability of an individual to influence other people and other beings. Power meant successful interactions."[76] This conception of power may be similar to Michael Witgen's explanation of *manidoo*, the Anishinaabeg concept of power that names "the ability to make things work in the world in a way that an ordinary human being was not capable of doing on his or her own."[77] Importantly, human beings could also "possess manidoo in the sense that they controlled access to a source of this extraordinary power," which was an important factor in how indigenous people regarded emissaries of European empires—from traders and governors to kings and presidents. As Witgen explains, "whether manidoo rested in a material object or in providing or denying access to things that helped human beings to survive, it represented a power of control exercised over the world at large."[78] This is not to suggest that Keokuk was locked into a cultural framework that shaped his decision-making, but to recognize that within these diplomatic interactions, Keokuk probably recognized many gradations of power between wielding it as a sovereign or else "accommodating" existing centers of power.

Negotiating with colonial administrators was an effort to achieve "successful interactions" by tapping into existing sources of power in Indian Office networks. For Keokuk, the work of the interpreter Antoine LeClaire was one such source of power. The French-Potawatomi interpreter was a critical part of Keokuk's navigation of Indian Office networks, and in 1834 Keokuk objected to a proposed reduction of LeClaire's pay by an act of Congress. As transcribed by the Indian agent Joseph Street and the trader George Davenport, Keokuk pushed back against these organizational changes in the Indian Office, which had been imposed from above without input from tribal leaders:

> This Man is our Interpreter we have long used him, he speaks our language well, and when we want to speak to our Father we know he will get all say correctly, and that that what is said to us will be truly repeated. We have great confidence in him for he never deceived us. He now tells us you have reduced his pay so much that he will not be able to Interpret for what you offer him any longer. You and Gov. Clark tell us it is all the Great Council of the White People at Washington have advised the President to give & he has told you to give one interpreter no more. We are very sorry for this. For we can have no other Interpreter but this man.[79]

Keokuk urged Congress to place the public good of his people above their financial considerations, explaining that he had "no confidence that our talk, and yours, would be truly understood . . . if this man is not by to talk between us. We hope our Great Father will consider this and the danger there will be and not deprive my Nation of their interpreter to save a little money."[80] Only with adequate financial resources might the Sauk and Meskwaki begin to cope with the economic and social pressures they were facing: as they had "sold most of our country to the President, our land is small, the game is getting very scarce and it takes all our money to support us. . . . If we also have to pay our interpreter we must take it from our money and our wants and sufferings will be greater."[81] There is certainly a hint of nepotism in this collaborative text, given the fact that Keokuk, Street, and Davenport all depended on LeClaire's translation work in their business and public affairs. But in a geography that was rapidly and dramatically transforming, the continuity that LeClaire represented was an important source of power for Keokuk in negotiating the Sauk and Meskwaki's place in the Iowa River region.

These negotiations concerned the historical legacy of the intertribal councils at Prairie du Chien between 1825 and 1830, and the reduction of the neutral hunting grounds between the Sauk and Meskwaki people to the east and the Sioux (the Eastern Dakota) to the west. Given the long-standing conflicts between the two, it became increasingly dangerous for Sauk and Meskwaki hunters to go on their seasonal hunts, which were a cornerstone of their economy. As a result, young Sauk and Meskwaki warriors often advocated warfare against the Sioux to regain their position in the region. In this light, Keokuk found himself caught between the pressure from his warriors to enter battle with the Sioux and the directives from William Clark and the Indian Office to preserve peace at all costs. In December 1832, several months after the end of the Black Hawk War, Keokuk addressed this position in a letter to William Clark, sent from the upper rapids of the Des Moines River. Translated by Francois Labusier and Edward Brishnelle, it explained that the Sioux had "advanced within our boundaries ... which have been agreed upon by all the parties of the Prairies du Chien Treaty." He added that the Sioux had not "deigned to give us the smallest signs or tokens of peaceful intentions," and the Sauk had "kept ourselves in great distrust of them, and have even withdrawn ourselves from our own hunting grounds in order to avoid all difficulties with them."[82] Keokuk urged Clark to take "such measures as will oblige the Sioux to keep within their own limits, for without this, it is impossible for a peace to last."[83] Appealing to a sense of national honor, he argued that it was "too humiliating for the Sac Nation to allow the country to be taken possession of without attempting to defend it. Father! We must defend our homes, or die."[84] From Keokuk's vantage point, American expansion had caused not only the direct loss of Sauk and Meskwaki lands to white settlers, but also a decrease in neutral hunting grounds between them and other Indian nations.

Over the course of the 1830s, Keokuk repeatedly addressed the conflicts with the Sioux but did not see his complaints addressed by Clark or the Indian Office. For Keokuk, the problem of Sioux encroachment was an effect of different Indian agents working at cross-purposes, and thus part of a structural failure on the part of the US government to manage Indian affairs:

> Our Great Father the President had us all gather together at Prairie-du-Chien three different times to talk to us—and every time I expressed my wish that the Commissioners sent by the President could make known to the Sioux's that they were not to come on our land ... last fall when Genl

Scott made a treaty with us I requested him to tell the Sioux's to keep off our land—last spring I came to see Genl Clark and repeated the same words to him—and came here and repeated the same words to you.[85]

This institutional mismanagement affected the Sauk and Meskwaki's ability to successfully hunt during the winters, which posed a direct threat to their livelihood. Keokuk explained that this situation was no longer tenable: "These people," he argued, "have injured us much by intruding on our lands, attacking our people, and destroying our game. We have not but little land—not more than sufficient for ourselves. On this land we wish to hunt in peace; but are determined to hunt there at all events. And as I do not wish to be misunderstood, or to deceive you, I now state, that if we find the Sioux on our lands, we will kill them."[86] Clark advised Keokuk not to attack under any circumstance, explaining that he was "aware of the efforts which he and other Chiefs had used already to preserve peace" and gave them "full credit for their efforts & urged him still to persevere in the same course." He noted that "the Sioux might be ignorant of the Sac boundary line, but that this line would be soon run & marked."[87] Investing in the clarity of a marked boundary line, Clark professed his faith in his administration's work to demarcate the ever-changing boundaries of Indian country.

Besides the threat of Sauk-Dakota war, Keokuk was also faced with white Americans who were again encroaching onto Sauk lands. White settlement in Illinois proved to be incessant, and in January 1834 Keokuk and three other tribal leaders—Pashepaho, Wahcamme, and Peat-Tshe-Noi—collaborated on a letter to William Clark to protest the presence of white hunters in Sauk country. Translated by Francois Labussier, it addressed the lack of an institutional response to the problem of white encroachments onto Sauk lands: "We have recourse to this paper to inform You that here is some white people hunting on our land since last fall and their intention is to remain all this winter and the next spring. We have informed our father the Agent of our Tribes of it. But we received no satisfactory answer. We have recourse to you. We know father your exertion to do justice to the Indians and we appeal to your Benevolence to remedy our right that is violated by the White peoples."[88] Although he was critical of white encroachment, however, Keokuk saw the continuous threat of all-out warfare with the Sioux as a more immediate issue. By the summer of 1834 Keokuk saw himself again forced to return to the matter, noting that "we are almost tired of keeping peace. I stay in my lodge for several days at a time thinking how I shall keep my young men out of difficulty with the Sioux's and let them hunt on our land ... we can't keep peace any longer with the Sioux's—and we hope that the President will release us from the treaty [of Prairie du Chien] and let the Sioux's and our nation settle our difficulties in our own way—as we used to do."[89] In council with General Henry Atkinson, the military commander at Jefferson Barracks near St. Louis, Keokuk was joined by the Meskwaki leaders Wakashawske, Poweshiek, and Wopeshiak. In what was the longest speech of the day, Keokuk implicated the Sioux agent in the deterioration of Sauk-Sioux relations. Explaining that the Sauk agent and trader had gone "the straight road," he believed the conflicts "must be the fault of the Sioux Agent and trader who advise the Sioux to go on the Sac land and hunt... the Sioux Agent and Trader tell the Sioux's to go anywhere they can find game."[90] Caught "between the American hammer and the Sioux anvil," as historian Thomas Burnell Colbert put it, Keokuk highlighted the failure of the treaty councils at Prairie du Chien to prevent the deteriorating border conflicts between Indian nations.[91]

Keokuk's repeated criticism of the US government established a physical record of the shortcomings of the Indian Office's management of intertribal affairs, diagnosing a failure to take responsibility for the military and political problems caused by the Americans' remapping of Indian country. In pursuit of this project, Keokuk showed no apparent distrust of the translated, written word. To the contrary, his speeches considered written documents as holding the potential for accountability, and Keokuk continually insisted on a written record of oral interactions and responses in writing. Recognizing that the Sauk Nation had moved into a new situation where the written word was increasingly central to diplomacy, he insisted that his words be written down on paper and sent to the American president. For instance, in a council at Jefferson Barracks in 1834, Keokuk affirmed his confidence that his words would "go straight" to the authority of President Andrew Jackson and Secretary of War Lewis Cass, appealing to a higher authority to manage the conflicts with the Sioux. "I hope what I have said, and what I am going to say will go straight," he stated. "As soon as this talk reaches the President & Secretary of War I hope they will consider it."[92] Imagining that the written records of his oratory would reach Washington, Keokuk believed in their capacity to be passed on in a reliable, standardized way. Similarly, he stated that when he and the accompanying Meskwaki delegates shook hands with US officials, "in shaking hands with you we shake hands with the Great Father the President. What we say to you now we wish you to put down on paper, so that the president may know what we have said to you."[93] Earlier that year, when Keokuk dictated a letter to Clark to protest the presence of white hunters on Sauk lands, he urged Clark to send back "an answer of the content of the said information if you saw it" and even specified which postmaster to send his letter to.[94]

For Keokuk, control over such communication routes was a key condition of successful diplomacy. Because written documents were a public, material record of the Indian Office's failures to effect policy, only the complementary use of oratory and writing could make councils politically relevant. Keokuk thus embraced the convergence of various communication strategies—oratory, translation, letter writing, and the postal service—as technologies that might prevent the inauspicious manipulation of spoken language, and which would help him establish a record of the governmental failures to respond to the problems of settler encroachment. In St. Louis in the summer of 1837, for instance, Keokuk complained that the United States Congress and President Jackson had made a large number of amendments to the language concerning payments in a treaty made the year before. "We are now told that the Great council of the White people & the President have altered the Treaty we made with Governor Dodge," Keokuk explained. "We never authorized any person to alter it, and we still hope the council of the white people will let our Treaty remain as it was made by us and Governor Dodge."[95] The alteration was a betrayal of the very thing these councils were supposed to enact, and Keokuk reminded the Indian Office that "when you make treaties, you put them on paper and the paper cannot lie."[96]

The problem was not, then, that the Sauk and Meskwaki leaders did not understand written documents of treaty councils, or that diplomats like Keokuk were ultimately "dupes" of the treaty system and the American government. They *did* understand these documents, and Keokuk, for one, saw their existence in written form as one of their more appealing aspects, since this made it possible to establish a permanent record. Indeed, he regarded written papers as material objects that affirmed the meaning of oral councils, and as such they had a function similar to that of ceremonial objects such as peace pipes and wampum belts.[97] As he saw it, however, the fundamental problem with Indian diplomacy was that this material record did not seem to matter much to American officials at the end of the day. Still, his negotiation of power within the Indian Office was an important attempt to stay plugged in—to ensure his people's continued representation within its networks. Knowing the institutional discourses of the Indian Office gave him a measure of institutional leverage, and Keokuk transcended the limits of the figure of the Indian diplomat as colonial dupe, asserting control over his own representation within the bureaucracy of the Indian Office. Keokuk's demands and strategies mattered materially as he established a lasting record of its institutional failures—a project that complements the bound and printed pages of Black Hawk's *Life*.

NATIONS, BORDERS, AND THE RECONFIGURING OF NATIVE SPACE

Notwithstanding Keokuk's efforts to modify the workings of the Indian Office, it would be wrong to claim his agency as an autonomous form of resistance against American political interests. The diplomatic work of tribal leaders like Keokuk was bound by a settler colonial project in which US government officials continually pressured them into selling lands. Faced with tribal debts and his people's weakened military position vis-à-vis the United States, Keokuk signed off on significant land cessions on numerous occasions. In 1834 he consented to the sale of their reservation on the Iowa River, reflecting the vulnerable social position of the Sauk and Meskwaki Nations in a region being drastically reconfigured by American expansion. At that point, Keokuk sat in council with Indian agent Joseph Street at Rock Island, arguing that "when we made a Treaty & sold our country on the West border of the Mississippi we reserved a piece of land on the Ioway River where are our villages and corn fields—we did so because it is a fine country and good to live in & raise our corn & we did not wish to remove." However, the reserve was "small and surrounded by that we sold, and great numbers of white persons are settling around and near our villages," while the influx of settlers around the reserve meant that "trouble about whisky... is commencing and might end in mischief."[98] Given these problems, Keokuk stated in no uncertain terms that he assented to the sale of the Iowa River reserve, and to remove to the Sauk and Meskwaki villages on the Des Moines River. His vision was that this location might allow them to maintain a workable distance between their nation and the white settlements, to "prevent white men from intermeddling."[99]

Keokuk's emphasis on the problems that arose from white settlement outlined an alternative understanding of what Americans called the "frontier," as he noticed a clash between two social-economic systems in Iowa. In his essay "The Significance of the Frontier in American History" (1893), the historian Frederick Jackson Turner famously interpreted the white settlement of the American West as an evolution of democratic society spreading westward through various stages. Turner read the continuous crises that Native people were faced with in the nineteenth century through the lens of conjectural history, tracing a teleological narrative on a macrohistorical scale. In doing so, he charted the evolution of economic systems from the stage of the "Indian and the hunter," to the "pastoral stage" of ranch life, that of "exploitation of the soil... in sparsely settled farming communities," the "intensive culture of the denser farm settlement," and, finally, to the stage of "manufacturing organization with city and factory system."[100] In Turner's model, the "frontier" was what he called "the outer edge of the wave—the meeting point between savagery and civilization."[101] In *Nature's Metropolis*, however, historian William Cronon reconsiders this framework to argue that what Turner interpreted as the teleology of American nation-building can be better understood as the contiguity of different zones of economic activity.[102] What to Turner were "stages" in the progress of civilization, Cronon argues, were in fact coexisting and interrelated spheres of economic and social organization—different spheres of economic life that were defined not by stages of historical progress but by such matters as the availability of open lands and the proximity of different industries and infrastructures. From this vantage point, the Iowa "frontier" in the 1830s was not the setting of a historical drama in which American "civilization" replaced the obsolete era of the "Indian and the hunter." Rather, the Sauk and Meskwaki people were dealing with the daunting challenge of reconciling two different forms of economic organization in the same region: an indigenous economy centered on the seasonal round and a settler economy centered on intensive agriculture.

For Keokuk, the upshot of his diplomatic efforts was to find a way to reconcile these different economic systems in a region that was drastically changing. His role as a diplomat thereby points to a central tension within the literatures of Sauk diplomacy: namely, that the diplomatic effort to negotiate a new physical place for tribal nations was usually tethered to massive lands sales that tribal leaders like Keokuk authorized. In 1836, the Sauk and Meskwaki chiefs sat in council with Colonel Henry Dodge, the governor of Wisconsin Territory, which now encompassed the Sauk reserves. Dodge attempted to "persuade the Indians to cede their entire claim to Iowa," but ultimately only secured the purchase of Keokuk's reserve "at bargain rates."[103] Keokuk articulated the difficulty—if not impossibility—of conveying the value of land in monetary terms, stating "we do not know the value of land, and we are unable to put any price upon it." He noted that "a large country on both sides of the Mississippi has been sold by the Sac & Fox Nation, but we have never been asked to put a price on the land before; and we cannot put a price on this piece." Keokuk added that if his people had been able to "enjoy it free from any interruption from white men," the lands would have been "of great value to us," but since they were "surrounded by white men," the reservation was "of little value to our Nation."[104] He thereby suggested a tension between two different types of value: first, the ability to use and "enjoy" the land without interruption from white settlers, and second, the ability to "put any price" on the lands.[105] Promoting the idea that the tribes should consolidate at the Des Moines River, he argued that the lands on the Iowa River had been rendered valueless in the former sense, but might still have a value to his people in the latter.

Keokuk's diplomatic interactions were about claiming a place for the Sauk and Meskwaki people even if the goal was not to remain fixed to one area in particular: at least for Keokuk, more important was the ability to continue the seasonal round and to keep their distance from white settlements. In 1837 he agreed to sell the remainder of the Sauk reservation on the Iowa River, arguing that "if we can get rid of our lands on the reserve the Indians must all come back to the Desmoines and all will be well."[106] Keokuk's suggestion that he wanted to "get rid of" the reservation stands out as an odd phrase, conveying an eagerness to sign away lands that had been rendered valueless. To "get rid" of these lands was different from selling them: rather than signing away ownership of something that has inherent value, "to get rid of" the lands suggested disposing of something that was had no inherent value and had become cumbersome to hold on to. This did not mean that Keokuk simply calculated the value of the Iowa reserve in monetary terms. Rather, the proximity to white settlers diminished the value of the land as a source of livelihood for his community, because it hindered his people from sustaining an existing mode of life. "Our land is getting very small and white men are crowding close upon us," he explained. "Game is getting scarce and our money is not sufficient to support us. When we sell the reserve we hope our Gr. Father will remember all the land he had got from us on both sides of the Mississippi, and give us a liberal price for this place. Then we shall have more to live on, and not roam so far [for] hunting."[107] Keokuk saw the lands he agreed to sell as already being devalued by the encroachment of white settlers, which made it impossible for them to continue a way of life that depended on seasonal patterns of agriculture and hunting.

The incessant demand of settlers for agricultural lands had created a playing field where Native leaders were forced to make deals in light of profound regional changes. White settlement was transforming an area that had long harbored a diverse indigenous economy into a primarily agricultural region with Indian reservations inside it. The Sauk and Meskwaki chiefs hoped that their people could live as they had before: to rely on the seasonal hunt, to live in their villages outside of the hunting seasons, and whenever necessary, to visit their traders, blacksmiths, and Indian agent for trade and diplomacy. Such an economy depended on the seasonal abandonment of their villages, and this was not a secure prospect in a white-dominated region. A main objective for Keokuk was therefore to maintain a physical distance from white settlement while having their trading houses, blacksmith shops, and Indian agent nearby. "We cannot come so far through the white settlement to get our work at the shops, & to see our Agent," Keokuk explained in 1834. "We hope the president will have our shops removed, give us permission to have one Trader a good home amongst us when he can have a Farm and live as he desires, and that he will give us an Agent near to us."[108] To continue a traditional economy in a settler colonial context, in short, involved minute negotiations about land, to make sure that the towns of the Confederated Tribes remained far away from white settlements but relatively close to blacksmiths and traders, who provided essential provisions for their hunting expeditions. To have the shops and the Indian agency located near the Sauk towns on the Des Moines River would help secure access to goods and information without requiring travel through white-dominated areas. Caught in a contestation over land in a rapidly transforming region, Keokuk was engaged in his own struggle to reshape the physical space of Indian country, articulating a vision of what a mixed Native and white economy on the Iowa River might look like. This vision depended on a distance from white settlers, positive trade relationships, and an Indian diplomacy that was responsive to the social and political needs of Indian nations.

Such a vision also depended on negotiations between different Indian nations, and in 1837 Keokuk took part in a large delegation of midwestern tribes to Washington. At the behest of the Commissioner of Indian Affairs, Carey Allen Harris, a delegation of Sauk, Meskwaki, Sioux, and Ioway leaders came to the capital, in a diplomatic effort that had the twin goals of brokering a new peace between the Eastern Dakota and the Sauk and Meskwaki Nations, and—for the United States—of expropriating more Indian lands. Keokuk led the Sauk and Meskwaki delegation and was joined by his former adversary Black Hawk, who was again presented to audiences in American cities and sat for another portrait by Charles Bird King.[109] The official business of the delegation failed to secure a meaningful peace with the Sioux Confederation, and for Keokuk's delegation the most consequential outcome was an additional cession of more than a million acres of land, to the west of those ceded after the Black Hawk War.[110] During the treaty negotiations, Keokuk explicitly resisted the "civilization" program that the United States promoted. While the Sauk and Meskwaki delegates agreed to funds being allocated toward mills, blacksmiths, and agricultural tools, they rejected any funds to be used for missionary education and other programs aimed at cultural change.[111] This rejection of the civilization program spoke to Keokuk's attachment to a form of social and economic organization in which agriculture was not the center but existed in combination with the seasonal round and US-Indian trade.

The negotiations in Washington in 1837 did not take place in a vacuum of US-Sauk relations, however, and in a region that was home to many different Indian nations, the land cessions that Keokuk authorized per treaty brought on new contestations with other tribes. While the American government began to see the region as the Iowa "frontier" and as US territory, the question remained regarding which tribal nations they would recognize as having an original claim to these lands, and therefore the ability to enter into treaty with the United States. The Ioway delegates argued that the Sauk and Meskwaki people did not have the original claim to the reservation on the Iowa River that they sold to the United States. At that point, the Ioway had been removed from a wider region in present-day Iowa to the area surrounding the Great Nemaha Agency,

FIGURES 2.6 & 2.7 *Council of the Sacs and Foxes, at Washington City*, by Ferdinand Pettrich. Ink and wash on paper. Ferdinand Pettrich Sketchbook, c. 1842. Edwin E. Ayer Collection, Newberry Library, Chicago. These two figures comprise a depiction of the treaty negotiations held in Washington in October 1837. It is one of thirty-five drawings of American Indian leaders and delegates from the sketchbook of the German sculptor Ferdinand Pettrich (1798–1872), and appears to be a study for a plaster frieze that ultimately ended up in the collections of the Vatican. According to the annotations, the figure of the delegate extending his arm is Keokuk; the figure standing next to him is the interpreter. The right half of Pettrich's sketch depicts the American treaty commissioners, with Secretary of State John Forsyth smoking the peace pipe and Secretary of War Joel Poinsett holding the quill.

near Fort Leavenworth in Kansas. The Sauk and Meskwakis' expansion into the Mississippi Valley, they argued, meant that they occupied lands that had historically belonged to the Ioway, who therefore deserved monetary compensation for the lands that were sold to the United States. To underscore their argument, the Ioway leader Na'hjeNing'e ("No Heart of Fear," 1797–1862) presented a map depicting the Ioway's historical occupation of villages in the Mississippi and Missouri Valleys. Drawn in ink, the map was made by an unknown draughtsman, but probably with the aid of an Indian agent.[112] The map depicted the Mississippi River and the Missouri River branching off near St Louis. To the east side of the Mississippi, it depicted, among others, the Illinois River, Rock River, and Wisconsin River, with the Des Moines, Iowa, and Cedar Rivers in the middle of the map, and the Platte River on the west side. On this landscape of rivers and lakes, the mapmakers overlaid the Ioway's historical village sites and migration routes, visualizing a history of Ioway presence and movement. They used empty circles to depict lakes, dotted circles to represent populated villages at different moments in their history, and dotted lines to show their historical migration routes. Because their map depicted the region between the Mississippi and Missouri in most detail, the Ioway delegates emphasized the period from about 1780 to 1824, when the Ioway claimed a prominent hold in the region around the Des Moines and Iowa Rivers.

At the 1837 council in Washington, then, the Ioway delegates presented the Sauk and Meskwaki homelands as a site of territorial contestation, challenging the tribes' claim to the region as well as the logics by which the United States validated those claims. The map took seriously the mobility of Ioway life as a basis for their land claims, displaying rivers and migration routes that marked an alternative to US territorial mappings of Indian country. It thereby disrupted the cartographic logic of US empire, which, as Adam Jortner writes, privileges notions of "the empty continent" or displays American state and territorial borders in order to render the US empire as "a settled state of affairs."[113] Of course, the Ioway map did not offer a radically alternative depiction of the region or an authentically indigenous or Ioway perspective: its visual representation of the Mississippi Valley was very much shaped by the diplomatic situation. As Mary Kathryn Whelan argues, although the map drew on a "centuries-old tradition" of Native American "spoken maps"—orally constructed texts that blended "natural and cultural information"—it was also "a contemporary product, generated as a rhetorical tool to help persuade US government officials during treaty talks." The delegates blended traditional methods with "elements familiar to them from western maps of the time," turning to technologies of writing that they imagined "would be compelling to their EuroAmerican

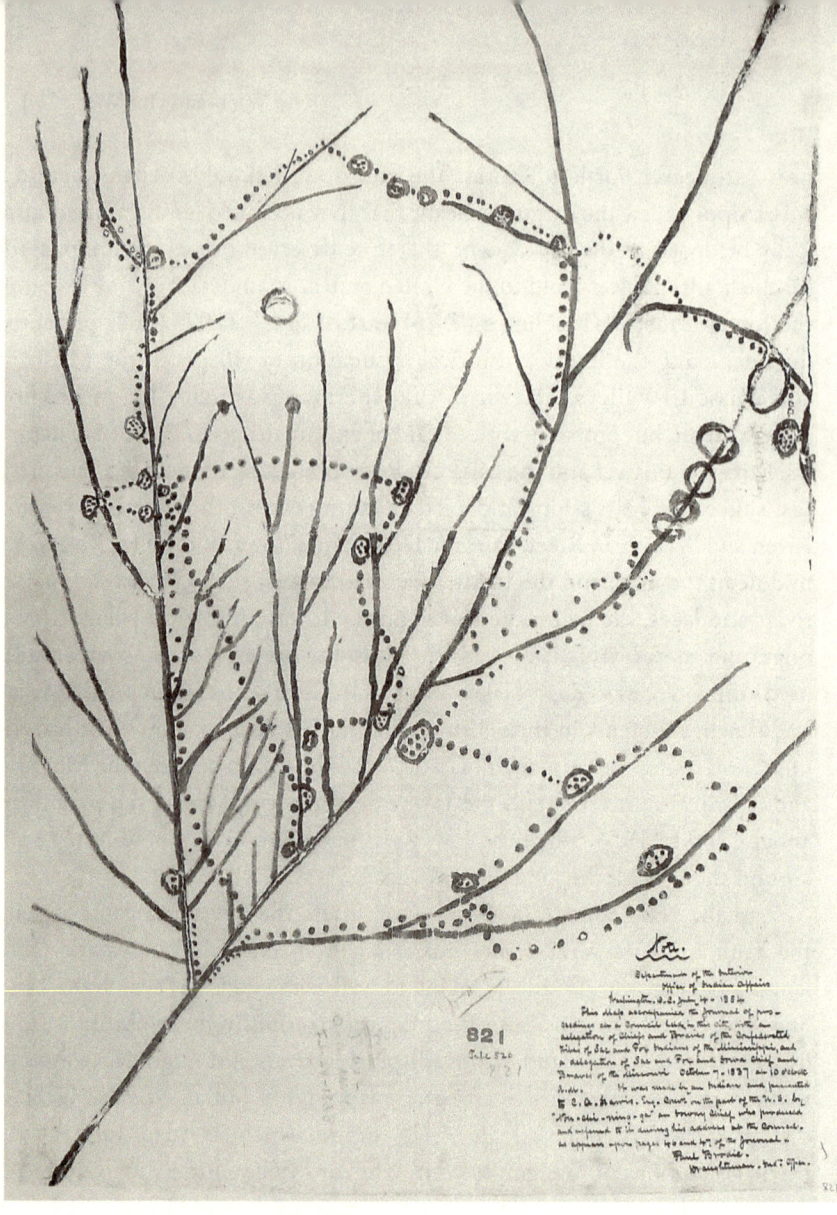

FIGURE 2.8 Ioway map of the Mississippi and Missouri River Valley, c. 1837. Record Group 75, Map 821. National Archives and Records Administration, Cartographic and Architectural Branch, College Park, MD. The annotations on the map—written by a Bureau of Indian Affairs official in 1884—are as follows: "This map accompanied the Journal of proceedings at a Council held in this city with a delegation of Chiefs and Braves of the Confederated Tribes of the Sac and Fox Indians of the Mississippi, and a delegation of Sac and Fox and Ioway Chiefs and Braves of the Missouri October 7, 1837 at 10 o'clock A.M. It was made by an Indian and presented to C. A. Harris, Esq. comr. On the part of the U.S. by 'Non-chi-ning-ga' an Ioway Chief who produced and referred to it during his address at the Council, as appears on pages 46 and 47 of the journal." Although it is by no means certain that Na'hjeNing'e created the map, it is worth noting that the Bureau of Indian Affairs insisted on his authorship at this time.

audience."[114] After all, for the Ioway delegates there was a concrete end game in showing their map of the Mississippi: to decenter the territorial claims of the Sauk and Meskwaki delegates and Keokuk in particular.

Despite the map's rhetorical power, however, it was Keokuk who ultimately proved more persuasive to American commissioners in this landscape of diplomatic relations. He defended his people's claims to their lands in present-day Iowa by arguing that they had been won by right of conquest: when Secretary of War Joel Poinsett confronted him with the claims of the Ioway, Keokuk argued that "it is true we have fought with the Iowas and taken a part of their land. If they want it back again, let them come and try to take it again." As historian Greg Olson writes, "Keokuk admitted that the land had once indeed belonged to the Ioway, but argued that the Sac and Fox owned it because they had forced the Ioway out. 'We have always pushed them before us,' Keokuk proudly stated. 'That is the reason they have marked so many villages on their map.'"[115] Keokuk, in other words, probably assessed the rhetorical purpose of Na'hjeNing'e's map accurately, recognizing that its layering of geographical and historical details was an effective means of persuasion. Still, the fact that the American government sided with Keokuk despite this historical document speaks volumes about his influence in Indian Office networks, and indicates that it was more important for the US government to placate the Sauk and Meskwaki leaders. From the Ioway perspective, Olson notes, "the treaty negotiations in Washington had become a diplomatic debacle," and the Ioway delegation angrily left Washington before the negotiations were even concluded.[116]

Despite this victory, Keokuk's influence did not resist the process by which the Indian Office used the treaty system to extinguish indigenous land title: his diplomatic success in the 1837 delegation was little more than a rubber stamp for land cessions he had already negotiated. And his continued diplomatic work kept in place structures within the Indian Office that had solidified the colonial administration's hold on Indian country, through treaties and land cessions, and—during the Black Hawk War—with military force. For Keokuk, however, retaining control over the relations between indigenous nations and the Indian Office depended on a measure of institutional continuity. He navigated these diplomatic avenues in an attempt to maintain a traditional economy based in the seasonal round, trade, and redistribution—a social system that was closely embedded in Sauk cultural and political life, however difficult it proved to maintain. Keokuk's oratory thereby presents something of a problem for literary and historical scholarship: the notion that agency also comes in the form of an effort to keep things going as they are. This might make Keokuk a problematic figure for us as twenty-first-century readers, since he did not exhibit the type of Native agency that we may be most eager to see. As Walter Johnson has argued, historical interpretation tends to favor the types of agency that are clearly recognizable as forms of "resistance" to systems of oppression or existing institutions.[117] With the benefit of historical hindsight, it is easy to see the process of settler colonialism as a completed fact, and Keokuk's agency as a key factor in the historical events of indigenous dispossession. And given Keokuk's commitment to established routines of diplomacy, it is easy to read his rhetoric as that of the "anti–Black Hawk"—the accommodationist who sold out to the settler state and white traders.

Anyone looking to find in Keokuk someone who collaborated with the United States will certainly find it, yet we should also take seriously the possibility that his diplomatic work was not merely a cynical deal with the settler state. Keokuk's diplomatic strategies tried to make the colonial legacies of the treaty system work for an indigenous project to secure a permanent presence in what was now Wisconsin Territory, a region that was transforming into an area of white settlement and agriculture. Keokuk's oratory reflects the double bind of Native leaders who worked through colonial administrative networks, in which their protests against settler encroachment played into the hand of the Indian Office, which enlisted the agency of tribal leaders in an effort to expropriate indigenous lands. But at least in part, Keokuk's diplomatic efforts sought to continue an existing mode of social and economic organization that was rooted in the traditions of Sauk life. No matter how compromised they were, his textual collaborations asserted a Sauk political voice within the networks of the colonial government—one that was limited and controversial, but also a necessity to secure continued diplomatic representation at a moment of profound dispossession and displacement.

"INDIAN DEPREDATIONS" AND THE RACIAL IMAGINARY OF THE FRONTIER

Besides the colonial and intertribal dimensions of Indian diplomacy, the literary record of the Sauk and Meskwaki Nations testifies to debates and schism within the tribes that shaped the publication projects of indigenous writers and orators. If *Life of Ma-ka-tai-me-she-kia-kiak* had expounded the political disagreements between Black Hawk and Keokuk, by the second half of the 1830s, the tribal leader Hardfish, a follower of Black Hawk, stepped up to publicly challenge Keokuk's policies and his role as the leading Sauk-Meskwaki chief. Particularly around the issue of how treaty-stipulated annuities were distributed by the tribal leadership, Hardfish managed to rally a large contingent of his people against Keokuk and the other civil chiefs. In a wider sphere of US-Indian interactions, however, American

"Our Wants and Our Wishes" | 111

administrators eagerly interpreted such political disagreements as signs of an inherent lack of governance or even lawlessness in tribal nations. In the remainder of this chapter, I explore how Hardfish spearheaded a series of publication projects that sought an alternative path to Sauk and Meskwaki nation-building, and in the process challenged the economic policies that Keokuk championed. In doing so, Hardfish forged new collaborations between tribal publics, American citizen groups, and the territorial government of Iowa, even if his efforts were undermined by a racial imaginary that decoded such internal political disagreements as a threat to the Iowa "frontier."

The crux of the disagreement between Keokuk and Hardfish centered on the use of the annuities that were stipulated in US-Indian treaties. When the Sauk chiefs signed the Treaty of Washington in 1837, this intensified an intratribal controversy about how annuities should be distributed to the Sauk and Meskwaki people. The treaty stipulated that $100,000 would be paid toward the tribes' national debts; $67,000 toward mills and farming assistance; and $10,000 toward annuities.[118] Prior to 1834, there had not been a fixed policy: some annuities were paid in money, some in goods; some were made to the chiefs, and others to the heads of individual families. In 1834 Congress investigated a new organization of Indian policy regarding annuity payments and recommended that they be made to the chiefs. However, the resulting laws still allowed for the possibility of individual payments, since payments could be made in any manner specified by the principal chiefs.[119] These policy changes led to a conflict between Sauk and Meskwaki leaders about whether treaty-stipulated annuity payments should be paid to the principal chiefs or to the heads of individual families. In September of 1840 tensions flared up when Keokuk advised Joshua Pilcher—William Clark's successor as superintendent of Indian Affairs at St. Louis—to remove the annuity moneys from Sauk and Meskwaki country until the disagreements were settled. By 1840 this controversy not only caused "bitter confrontations within the tribal councils" but "disrupted the federal administrative apparatus in Iowa."[120]

At its core, the annuity controversy was a debate among Sauk and Meskwaki tribal leaders and citizens about how to politically and economically organize the tribes in the face of settler expansion and removal. Keokuk argued that the annuities would be a resource for the nation as a whole if they were kept as a collective fund. During an 1833 council with William Clark at St. Louis, where he was joined by all the principal chiefs and some ninety warriors, Keokuk had argued in favor of the existing system, which sanctioned payments to the chiefs. He asked, "When anything happens between us & the whites or between us & other Indians, to whom do you apply? When difficulties are to be settled, treaties to be held, or any business of consequence to be transacted, you apply to the Chiefs.... The annuities should be paid in the old way—all concerned will be benefitted by it."[121] In particular, the tribal funds would be a resource for preventing further conflicts with other Indian nations. Keokuk explained that "in case of the deaths of a brave, or any other national occurrence, the Chiefs can buy the necessary articles to bury him. It is also the only means which the Chiefs have of turning back a war party of young men—by paying them."[122] Centralized control of the annuities, Keokuk argued, would allow the chiefs to pay off warriors who might otherwise be persuaded to go on the warpath as part of the traditional practice of "covering the dead": when a warrior was killed or lives were lost in battle, it was customary to organize a war party to capture or kill people from the tribe responsible. He also understood that successes in battle often led to an increase in rank, which meant that there was often a social incentive for young warriors to take part in such raids. Keokuk frequently regretted his own inability to control "young men" who were eager to make their mark; given the volatile conflicts caused by the remapping of the region, this situation was a major threat to peace. In addition, the payments to the chiefs would benefit those who were socially vulnerable and help to curb the consumption of alcohol. At a council at the Rock Island agency in the summer of 1833, Keokuk suggested that "there is but a small portion of these annuities coming to each of us, and this mode of distributing it individual would ruin my people: as there are many among them who would take their money and buy Whiskey, instead of such articles of necessity, as they would otherwise receive."[123] Instead, Keokuk argued, tribal control over the annuities would offer a social safety net: in case a "poor family are suffering for Provisions or clothing, the Chief then has to buy and give to them. Old men who cannot hunt, old women who cannot work, or find support have to be fed & clothed by the heads of the nations, and if the Chiefs have no more means to afford the required relief, than others, the helpless and miserable must suffer."[124] For Keokuk, then, this model of control over the annuities would continue the traditional system in which civil chiefs redistributed goods to their people, a system that was central to the social and political life of the tribe, even as it also consolidated power in the hands of the chiefs.

Keokuk's position on the matter led to substantial resistance, and in 1834 the Meskwaki chief Appanoose spoke out against his leadership by dictating a letter to the United States president. Appanoose held that ever since the treaty of 1832, the Meskwaki chiefs no longer received a proportionate amount of the annuities, claiming also not to have been informed that the annuities had been distributed at St. Louis. Furthermore, he argued that Keokuk himself "received all the Annuities, and paid it ... for debts contracted previously, by themselves, with the American Fur Company." He challenged Keokuk's appointment as the government liaison for both the Sauk and Meskwaki, which he argued eroded the latter nation's autonomy. Much like Black Hawk in *Life of Ma-ka-tai-me-she-kia-kiak*, Appanoose sketched Keokuk as a figure who fomented dissension and acted in his own interests, while being kept in power by the settler government: "Ke-o-kuck (acting as principal chief of the Sac Tribe, having been made such by commissioners appointed by our Great Father to treat with our people in the Summer of 1832, and without being a descendant of any of our former chiefs, or in any manner connected to them, and contrary to the customs and laws of or Nation throughout all time)— has been using all his influence to reduce my Band and create dissatisfaction among my people."[125] In this transcription, the long parenthetical aside captures a telling dynamic between Appanoose as speaker and the scribe in the Indian Office. On the one hand, by placing much of the critique of Keokuk between parentheses, it subordinates this information to the main thrust of the argument, which is that Keokuk had used his influence to erode Meskwaki autonomy. On the other hand, the length of this parenthetical aside makes this list of grievances highly visible in the record. Moreover, the argument that Keokuk was "acting as principal chief of the Sac Tribe, having been made such by commissioners" clearly registered the critique that his validity as civil chief was in question. If the Indian Office had singled out Keokuk as the authorized agent to his people, it also recorded the beliefs of other chiefs that he was an untrustworthy interloper who failed to act in the interest of his people.

Perhaps the most vocal critic of Keokuk was the Sauk leader Hardfish (Wishecomaque), who carried on a political campaign against Keokuk into the 1840s. Hardfish was a member of the Sturgeon clan, which had traditionally supplied the Sauk civil chiefs, and in fact his father had been civil chief before Keokuk. As a former follower of Black Hawk, he challenged Keokuk's leadership position when in an 1836 council several Sauk and Meskwaki leaders approved Hardfish's appointment as principal chief in Keokuk's place.[126] When the Indian agent Joseph Street annulled this decision, Hardfish and his followers subsequently defied the chiefs and the Indian Office in another way. For one, the Treaty of 1832 stipulated that those who had been part of Black Hawk's "British Band" had to live in one of the established towns: Keokuk's Town, Appanoose's Town, or Wapello's Town. But Hardfish and his followers openly defied this stipulation and established Hardfish's Town in 1840, on the east shore of the Des Moines river, north of the existing villages.[127] In doing so, Hardfish effectively channeled the public opposition to Keokuk and the Indian Office into an alternative form of social and political organization.

Countering Keokuk, Hardfish rallied public opinion against the centralized disbursement of the tribal annuities. Already in 1835 he had presented a memorial to the United States Congress urging the annuities to be paid to individuals rather than the chiefs. Under "the existing regulations respecting the payment of our annuities," Hardfish argued, "we have *again* been deprived of our just rights as members of the Sac and Fox nation."[128] By 1838, what had previously been Wisconsin Territory became part of the newly formed Iowa Territory, and in February 1840 Hardfish published a "Notice to the Public" that appeared in the *Iowa Territorial Gazette*. In it, fifty "chiefs and representatives" of the Sauk and Meskwaki signed a statement speaking out against Keokuk's authority. Transcribed by an American army interpreter, the memorial argued that Keokuk was not "authorized" to represent them politically, nor to pay national debts out of the tribes' annuities: "The Chiefs and Representatives of the Sauk and Fox tribes of Indians, caution the public from trusting Keokuk, as he never was authorized by our nation, so to do since we have begun to sell our country to government, or to contract any debts in the name of our nation, though for years we have suffered with patience his encroachments on our rights, we have kept silent in seeing him acknowledge great sums of money as our national debts due to his friends among the white people."[129] Declaring himself to also be "under great obligations to our friends, among the whites," Hardfish explained to newspaper readers in Iowa Territory that Keokuk used tribal funds to make payments to the American Fur Company and the Chouteau Company, for his own gain and comfort. Hardfish urges Iowans to understand that no more debts contracted by any of the principal chiefs were allowed to be paid from tribal moneys.[130] Through this collaborative publication project, Hardfish extended the intratribal debate about the tribes' economic policy to a wider audience of Iowa settlers.

Since Keokuk had American administrators on his side throughout his career, Hardfish recognized the need for a collaborator who would represent an authoritative voice in the settler government. He turned to Robert Lucas, the governor of Iowa Territory, who in this capacity had jurisdiction over Indian affairs in the region surrounding the Sauk and Meskwaki reserves.[131] His "Notice to the Public" already mentioned that the signers had "an interview with a great wise man the Governor of Iowa, to which we tender our thanks" and two months later, in April 1840, Hardfish and his allies petitioned Lucas to speak publicly on their behalf. The petition pleaded that "all our hope is in you, because since we have had recours to the office of the Government of the United State none of them have shewed us so much compassion for the fate of our Tribes." Suggesting that the federal networks of the Indian Office had not given Hardfish and his allies a fair chance in the annuity debates, they wrote, "If it is not in your Power To make it a Law to pay our Annuities Individualy, we hope that [you] will use your Influence in our behalf."¹³² Keokuk, however, engaged Hardfish on his own terms and sent a petition to President Martin Van Buren with the signatures of more than 500 Sauk and Meskwaki people. The petition acknowledged the controversy as a "difference of opinion of a small portion of our nation" and explained their intention to "respectfully ask our Great Father, to have them ... paid as heretofore to our Chiefs."¹³³

These appeals to Lucas and Van Buren were part of a long history of Native American petitions, which, as Lisa Brooks writes, can be considered "a genre unto themselves."¹³⁴ Petitions allowed Native communities to wield writing as an instrument to appeal to a "political body that has power in relation to themselves," by calling on a "historical relationship of alliance" and "their ally's power to transform" their political situation.¹³⁵ Keokuk's petition followed what was a typical format for Native petitions: first, the "prayer" or "declaration of principle" and second, a "signatory list comprising the written names of those who support the prayer"—in this case the x-marks of more than 500 Sauk and Meskwaki "chiefs, warriors [and] hunters."¹³⁶ As Daniel Carpenter explains, such petitions were documents of recruitment, not only soliciting the support of political leaders but mobilizing citizens politically. Keokuk's petition to Van Buren was a tool to "identify sympathetic citizens and recruit them," and it effectively created a new public of Sauk and Meskwakis who rallied around Keokuk and allied chiefs.¹³⁷ Governor Lucas proved a potent ally for Hardfish, however, as he argued that Keokuk had produced fraudulent signatures, suggesting that there were more x-marks on the petition than he would have been able to garner.¹³⁸ In an effort to delegitimize Keokuk, Lucas accused him of betraying the democratic process of such petitions and sent his own to President Van Buren in support of individual payments, affixing three pages of signatures from white settler "friends" in Iowa.¹³⁹ Lucas's support for Hardfish appeared to be partly successful: according to historian Michael Green, by 1840 "the Governor, the legislature, various citizens' groups, and an important Sac and Fox faction were firmly on record as opposing the prevailing payment system."¹⁴⁰

Eventually the debate ended with a compromise. In 1840 the annuities were paid to the chiefs; in 1841 half of them were paid to the chiefs and half to the heads of families; and in 1842 all of the payments were made to individual families.¹⁴¹ But Lucas's critique of Keokuk carried well beyond the contours of the annuity debate: just as Black Hawk had come to represent the specter of frontier violence, for the Iowa governor Keokuk came to stand for an idea of the corrupt Indian chief who was beholden only to American traders and who let his own people slip into dissipation. In 1840, Lucas presented a report to the War

FIGURE 2.9 Portrait of Robert Lucas, by Robert H. Yewell. Oil on canvas, c. 1858. State Historical Society of Iowa, Iowa City. Robert Lucas (1781–1853) was the first governor of Iowa Territory from 1838 to 1841, after he had been speaker of the Ohio State Senate and then governor of Ohio. George H. Yewell's portrait appears to have been made posthumously in 1858, after a daguerreotype portrait of Lucas. See "Portrait of Governor Lucas," in *Fifth Biennial Report of the Board of Curators of the State Historical Society to the Governor and General Assembly of the State of Iowa* (Des Moines, 1866), 6.

Department on Indian affairs in Iowa Territory—based on government papers, correspondences, and personal conversations—that sketched the annuity debate as a symptom of wider discord and social anomie in the Confederated Tribes. Lucas lambasted the trading houses as a "malign influence that controls the actions of two of the principal chiefs, viz. Keokuck and Appenoose," and argued that this was the cause of "the excitement that has . . . existed among the Indians with regard to the payment of their annuities."[142] He argued that Keokuk funneled annuity moneys to the American Fur Company, suggesting that the traders had co-opted Keokuk's efforts to pay off their tribal debts.[143] Lucas believed that the tribes had long been "under the control of the American Fur Company," their present conditions being "a living commentary upon the paternal policy of that company," which had "for many years controlled this tribe without a rival."[144] In this respect, Keokuk came to be seen as a symbol of a more general problem—the Sauk and Meskwaki's dependency on the trading houses.

Lucas's narrative of dependency, in which Keokuk was a central actor, sketched a pessimistic view of the tribes' social and political situation. "The rapid decrease in the number of this tribe presents a gloomy picture," he wrote. "In

1837 they are reported at 6,400 ... they are now by actual enumeration in 1840 found to number 2,999. The mind is naturally led to inquire, Why this rapid decrease? They formed a gallant band of hunters a few years since, and brought into market upwards of $50,000 worth of peltries annually.... Their annuity at this time amounts to $47,000, and still they are a miserable people."[145] Of course, a logical answer to Lucas's question might have been that the Sauk and Meskwaki were living in a postwar society faced with a dramatic loss of lands and with tribal debts, intertribal conflicts, and the economic uncertainties that came from the influx of white settlers. Yet Lucas placed the origins of the Sauk and Meskwaki's poor economic circumstances not with settler expansion—or, for that matter, with the treaty system and the mismanagement of Indian affairs—but with the tribal leadership's "opposition to the introduction of schools and missionaries among them."[146] Lucas offered the War Department a narrative of declension, suggesting that the Sauk and Meskwaki's current mode of subsistence, and their dependence on annuities, would offer no reprieve, and that their opposition to education made their national prospects bleak indeed.

To make this argument, Lucas pointed to the social geography of the Sauk and Meskwaki Nations to suggest an alternative way forward, holding up Hardfish's Town as a model of successful social organization. He explained that he had visited the new town on the Des Moines River where Hardfish and his faction had established themselves. Lucas stressed the town's prosperous outlook, naming Hardfish's Town "the neatest looking village I have seen in the Indian country."[147] To Lucas, the town represented what the Sauk and Meskwaki people should aspire to: he held it up as the "residence of a set of seceders from the confederated tribes, the remnants of the war party who were endeavoring to establish themselves in violation of the treaty of 1832." However, rather than the rough settlement of a band of squatters, Lucas found it to be "the most thriving and populous village in the nation and inhabited by the most sober and orderly Indians, many of whom declare that they came there to get away from the scenes of dissipation that were constantly carried on at the lower towns."[148] Hardfish's Town even represented a modernizing impulse, as Lucas argued that the townspeople desired to establish schools:

> I made some inquiries relative to the establishment of schools among them. They observed that it would be a good thing, and some of them expressed a desire to have their children taught. I requested them to think on the subject, and told them that if after mature consideration they should think it advisable to have a school established among them that we would endeavor to send some good man to live with them who would not want their money or their land, but whose whole object would be to do them good, and to instruct their children.[149]

The governor saw in the town an indigenous variation on narratives of regeneration through mobility. By escaping the vices of the larger community and established structures of power, the Hardfish faction had blossomed and proven to be amenable to "civilization" in a remote, unauthorized settlement.

For Governor Lucas, this regeneration of Sauk life was predicated on the town's movement away from the corrupting influence of Keokuk and the American Fur Company, and from the tribes' treaty agreements with the federal government. Although Lucas did not actually visit the towns of Keokuk, Appanoose, and Wapello, he nevertheless echoed reports that these established towns offered only scenes of dissipation. "A gentleman who resides in the vicinity," Lucas explained, "informed me that during the summer there appeared to be an almost constant scene of dissipation and revelry, that whiskey by the barrel had been landed on the bank of the river at Keokuck's town, and that from the noise of the confusion kept up at the towns he supposed that upwards of fifty barrels must have been used by them the [sic] season."[150] Lucas argued that the proximity of the established towns to the American Fur Company's trading house caused the Sauk Nation's economic condition, because they were influenced by traders and fell victim to their steady supply of alcohol. Lucas concluded that "the benevolent designs of government toward the Indians" would be useless "until the power and influence of the traders were counteracted"; until that time the established Sauk towns were destined to remain merely the puppets of the American Fur Company.[151] Like Appanoose and Hardfish, Governor Lucas criticized the chief's being beholden to the corrupting influence of the trading houses of the American Fur Company.

It is important to note that Lucas's report recognized many of the same problems that Keokuk also addressed in his oratory: economic hardship, tribal debts, and the influx of hard liquors into Indian nations. For Keokuk, however, the trading houses represented an important measure of constancy in an ever-changing bureaucracy. After all, representatives of the Indian Office came and went: William Clark died in 1837, the Indian agent Thomas Forsyth was forced to resign in 1829, his replacement Felix St. Vrain was killed during the Black Hawk War, and his successor Joseph Street resided in St. Louis the greater part of the year until he, too, died in 1840. Meanwhile, the Sauk and Meskwaki towns were located in a region that became part of newly defined US jurisdictions. It transformed from unorganized territory to Wisconsin Territory in 1836, and to Iowa Territory in 1838, changing the regional administration of Indian Affairs each time. Amid these changes, the trading houses offered relatively constant access to information, goods, and credit. Keokuk was perhaps naively dependent on them—all the more so since American expansion thrived on the promulgation of tribal debts—but to maintain positive relations with traders was simply a necessity for Sauk and Meskwaki survival. Removed from their homelands and experiencing rapid economic and social change, they materially depended on American traders for a variety of goods to sustain a traditional economy based in the seasonal round. The decline of the bison and game population had made the winters less lucrative than in the past, while the westward expansion of white Americans had cut into the neutral hunting grounds between the Sauk and the Sioux, leaving smaller areas to hunt without great risk of conflict.[152] The trading houses were a problematic yet crucial link in this economy, extending credit for the necessary supplies to keep their traditional economic organization alive into the end of the decade.[153]

As compromised as Keokuk's vision was, his close relations to the American Fur Company and the Chouteau Company were a means to claim an economic role for the Sauk and Meskwaki people in Iowa Territory. Lucas, however, argued that the only way forward was what he euphemistically called "emigration." He believed that removal offered the only viable chance of any Sauk and Meskwaki future: "The Sac and Fox Indians, from once being warlike and a terror to their enemies, are fast progressing towards extermination ... nothing but emigration from their present residence can wrest them from the avaricious control of the traders, and the blighting effects of intemperance, which combined are fast hastening to the lowest degree of degradation. I am under the impression that the ensuing year would be peculiarly favourable for treating with them for a cession of their whole country and their removal south of Missouri."[154] In short, the governor's report took seriously the possibility of Sauk and Meskwaki regeneration, but only if it happened somewhere else. The potential that Hardfish's Town had exhibited was already superseded by the promise of a settler state that demanded a complete extinguishing of Native land title in Iowa. Having entered the intratribal debate about the annuity payments, Lucas came to advocate removal to Indian Territory and the wholesale cession of their remaining lands. That Lucas and Iowan settlers publicly supported Hardfish in the annuity controversy should therefore be met with some suspicion. As Michael D. Green explains, they imagined that individual payments would prevent disgruntled Sauk and Meskwaki from coming into white settlements to seek compensation for missed annuities. Settlers in Iowa were thus "concerned largely with justice for themselves. If the annuities were distributed directly, they argued, the Indians would not commit depredations 'to supply themselves with the necessaries.'"[155] Years after the end of the Black Hawk War, Governor Lucas's outline of his Indian policy again evoked the safety and tranquility of the frontier.

Lucas thereby shifted the contours of the annuity debate away from the economic and political organization of the Sauk and Meskwaki Nations, to the peace and safety of the Iowa "frontier." On November 3, 1840, shortly after submitting his report to the War Department, Robert Lucas gave a speech to the legislative assembly of Iowa Territory in which he pitched the annuity crisis as a sign of potential Native hostility. In his address he expressed "little doubt" that the annuities would be "distributed among the different bands justly" and go toward "the liquidation of their just debts." Yet even though the Sauk and Meskwaki were no longer "warlike and a terror to their enemies," he still suggested that any delay in the annuity payments would spur Native violence on white settlers, arguing that the matter now threatened the safety of the "frontier." If the payments were delayed any longer, he argued, "the excitement produced by its postponement will burst beyond the bounds of restraint and thereby endanger the peace of our frontier."[156] In other words, in his speech to the legislative assembly Lucas presumed that the controversy might degenerate into violent conflict and argued that Iowans should be ready to "meet every possible contingency that might endanger the peace of our frontier." The possibility of "Indian depredations" conveniently offered justification to request a territorial army of settler volunteers. Lucas argued for "the expediency of authorizing by law, the organization of a number of mounted volunteer riflemen ... and to provide for calling them into service in case of Indian depredations or threatened invasion."[157] Moreover, he noted that this effort to defend the Iowa frontier from "Indian depredations" would be aided by the War Department's plans for a "depot of public arms and munitions of war" at Rock Island, to help the "citizens of the Territory" defend against "Indian hostilities."[158]

Lucas's rhetoric suggests that the Black Hawk War had become a historical turning point in the history of American settler expansion, as the governor's call to defend the Iowa frontier echoed widespread fears of Native-settler conflict. By soliciting Lucas's help, Hardfish had successfully called on an important figure who could sway public opinion and policy, yet the governor co-opted the annuity debate to pursue his own designs. Perhaps this collaboration can be understood as a publication project gone awry: as he outlined his Indian policy for Iowa Territory, Lucas betrayed Hardfish twice over—first to the federal government, and to the territorial government ten days later. And although the annuity controversy ended in a compromise after eight years of divisions, Lucas ultimately saw this public debate as evidence of Native American lawlessness. For American policymakers, the existence of intratribal factionalism alone was enough to raise the specter of violence and "depredations" on settler communities in Iowa, posing a direct threat to a fledgling settler society. Co-opting Hardfish's efforts to generate public notice about the annuity issue, Lucas saw the political debates about Keokuk and his policies as a confirmation of the idea that Indian nations were an outside threat to the tranquility of the frontier.

BAD CHIEFS

Although Hardfish disrupted the routines of Indian Affairs in Iowa for several years, his alliance with Governor Lucas ultimately served a settler agenda that did not imagine a Sauk-Meskwaki future in Iowa Territory. But as divisive as the annuity controversy had been, in 1841 the Hardfish and Keokuk factions united in the face of the immediate threat of removal. At the annuity payments that year, American commissioners pushed for the Sauk and Meskwaki people to remove to present-day Minnesota. In protest against the commissioners and the removal scheme, Hardfish came to support Keokuk's role as spokesperson for the two nations to the American government, and removal to the north was put off.[159] This provided to be only temporary, however. The tribes did not manage to achieve financial solvency and the debts they incurred to traders started to exceed their annuity payments by 1842. To make matters worse, their hunting expeditions had been unsuccessful, they had lost many horses during the harsh winters, and white squatters had begun to burn their mills.[160] In the face of these compounding crises, the chiefs signed a removal treaty in 1842 that forced them to give up their remaining lands in Iowa Territory and to remove to a tract on the Missouri River, in present-day Kansas, by 1845.[161]

The history of Sauk and Meskwaki removal reflects that the US government's pursuit of territorial expansion was shaped by regional contexts, intertribal relations, and intratribal schisms. Concomitantly, the literatures of Sauk and Meskwaki diplomacy of the 1830s register more than a colonial conflict along a settler-indigenous binary. The publication projects of Keokuk, Black Hawk, and Hardfish were fraught collaborations that mediated between, on the one hand, different individuals and factions within their nations, and on the other hand, publics that were comprised of federal administrators, traders, citizen groups, territorial governments, and diplomats from other Indian nations. Given the decentered nature of Indian diplomacy, tribal leaders who tried to mitigate the effects of US expansion had to wage a campaign of influence in a situation that was marked by poorly connected agencies, miscommunications, and a continually changing geopolitical landscape—not to mention the willful disregard of Native people's collective and individual livelihood.

Keokuk's skill in navigating these complex networks prompted critics such as Black Hawk and Hardfish to regard him as a convenient handmaiden to white interests in the western territories. But perhaps in hindsight he may be viewed as a figure who tried, against great odds, to assert control over the impossible project of fashioning a coherent political and economic plan, to claim a permanent place for the Sauk and Meskwaki people in their homelands. None of this is to suggest, of course, that Keokuk got it "right." After all, he assented to the treaties that signed away many tracts of lands in Iowa, and in the annuity debate he took a side that kept monetary control over the annuities away from individual families. Yet it is important to take Keokuk's oratory seriously, for despite the circumscribed way he entered public discourse, he left a written record that shows that the history of Sauk and Meskwaki dispossession extended well beyond the events of the Black Hawk War. This record complicates the settler narrative of a frontier "clash" between American and Native society, in which the Sauk and Meskwaki people were coded as outsiders in their own homelands. In Philip J. Deloria's words, American ideas about the frontier typically represent US-Indian conflict "as if the United States had been defending its own territory all the time."[162] Such settler colonial narratives thrive on a notion of the frontier as the historical supersession of indigenous societies by the settler state, and they thrive on facile images of "good chiefs" and "bad chiefs" who alternately encoded "pacified" Indian nations or an imminent threat to the peace of the frontier.

Today, Black Hawk's *Life of Ma-ka-tai-me-she-kia-kiak* remains the most famous account of the 1832 war, but we may also recognize it as only one of many Sauk texts that interrogated the legacies of Indian removal. Seen together, the literatures of Sauk diplomacy point to a history of removal that cannot be reduced to a singular moment or treaty, since it took the shape of an endless set of pressures—social, economic, and military—that white settlement brought to Indian nations. Astutely aware of these pressures, Keokuk, Black Hawk, and Hardfish all offered alternatives to the colonial narrative that legitimated indigenous displacement to American settlers and administrators. Against the notion that Indian nations did not have a future in the Midwest, they claimed a place by pushing for indigenous land rights, tribal control over economic policy, and American accountability to treaties. In the process, they established an important written record of anticolonial critique that reminds us that even after the violence of the Black Hawk War, removal was not an inevitable outcome. They seized moments of diplomatic exchange as opportunities for critique and collaboration, and insisted on indigenous futures in a landscape that had been dramatically reshaped by white settlement and colonial violence. In a sustained effort to make the routines of Indian diplomacy accountable to Native people's lives, they carried out critical projects to claim a future for Indian nations in North America.

CHAPTER 3

"The Blessings Which We Are Now Enjoying"
Peter Pitchlynn and the Literature of Choctaw Nation-Building

Arguably the most widely read account of Choctaw removal is that of Alexis de Tocqueville in his classic work of political theory, *Democracy in America* (1835). Traveling in the United States in 1831, the French aristocrat and philosopher witnessed a party of Choctaws crossing the Mississippi in the "depths of winter," carrying along "the wounded, the sick, newborn babies, and old men on the verge of death." A year after the passing of the Indian Removal Act, Tocqueville wryly reflected that Native dispossession was now accomplished in a "regular and, as it were, quite legal manner."[1] His account vividly describes a scene of both desperation and resignation: "Not a sob or complaint could be heard from this assembled crowd; they stood silent. Their afflictions were of long standing and they considered them beyond remedy. Already the Indians had all embarked upon the boat which was to carry them; their dogs still remained upon the bank. When these animals finally saw that they were being left behind forever, they raised all together a terrible howl and plunged into the icy Mississippi waters to swim after their masters."[2] Describing in detail the panic of the dogs, Tocqueville powerfully contrasts this with the Choctaws' silence and resignation in the face of losing their homelands in Mississippi, and their relocation to Indian Territory. By the stroke of a pen, Tocqueville suggests, the Choctaws were forced to accept a future that seemed as inevitable as it was tragic.

Although the case of the Choctaw Nation was the first cross-continental removal of one of the large southeastern nations, it never led to the same vehement national debate that Cherokee removal inspired in American politics and society. Still, Tocqueville's emphasis on the supposed resignation of the removal party disregards the long controversy that the removal crisis brought on in the Choctaw Nation. While Tocqueville's observations have become a standard account of removal, scholars have often overlooked Choctaw writers who engaged with this history directly. This chapter therefore centers on the writings of Peter Pitchlynn (1806–1881), a Choctaw diplomat and educator whose writings and speeches were bound up with the history of Choctaw removal. In the course of four decades, Pitchlynn alternately negotiated removal, protested it, interpreted it historically, and contested its legacies at the seat of the United States government. These roles were part of a longer career as a diplomat that registers the innovations and disruptions of Choctaw life in the removal era. In the 1820s he had been secretary of the meetings in which the General Council established the Choctaw constitution, and in the 1830s and 1840s he conducted diplomacy with other Indian nations and the United States. In the subsequent decade, he renegotiated a treaty to receive a settlement for the lands that many Choctaws had been defrauded of in the aftermath of removal, before ultimately becoming the principal chief of the Choctaw Nation from 1864 to 1866.

Peter Pitchlynn's state papers document a close link between removal-era Choctaw writings and the conduct of Indian diplomacy. Yet although his state papers are some of the most important pieces of Choctaw literature from the nineteenth century, studies of Native American literature have mostly examined Pitchlynn only through his representation in Charles Dickens's *American Notes* (1842). Two of Pitchlynn's manuscript poems are included in Robert Dale Parker's 2011 anthology of early Native American poetry, but most of his writings and speeches are absent from studies of nineteenth-century literature.[4] The lack of engagement with his work may not be entirely surprising. For one thing, Pitchlynn never published his writings in book form, and many of his speeches and petitions were collaborative efforts. Moreover, he is a problematic figure, to say the least: a wealthy slave-owner, Pitchlynn championed his own financial interests as eagerly as those of his nation, and embraced Jackson-era ideologies of race and power in pursuit of his political goals. On a rhetorical level, his writings often express opportunistic strategies that played into existing social hierarchies within Choctaw Nation. More than anything, Peter Pitchlynn's written work reflects that projects of Indian nation-building were often tethered to the interests and political power of educated, propertied men who claimed political prominence.

Starting from this premise, this chapter traces the diplomatic career of a controversial figure who was alternately described by his contemporaries as a "stately and complete ... gentleman of nature's making" and a "man who disregards all rules which bind honorable men together."[5] It would be easy to dismiss Pitchlynn as simply an assimilationist voice in nineteenth-century Native American writing. Yet his writings also represent important perspectives on the interrelation between Indian diplomacy and Choctaw nation-building, as Pitchlynn critiqued the colonial practice of treaty-making and championed tribal control over educational projects. In this respect, the works of Peter Pitchlynn represent a marked contrast to the writing and oratory of Keokuk. The Sauk leader's diplomacy represented an effort to maintain existing structures of power and communication within bureaucratic networks, and insisted on established ideas about the relation between tribal authority and community life. By contrast, Peter Pitchlynn—not unlike authors such as Elias Boudinot (Cherokee) and George Copway (Ojibwe)—insisted on the ongoing educational, governmental, and economic reorganization of the Choctaw Nation, a project of modernization that was modeled after the example of US institutions. Pitchlynn's writings offer important insights into the fault lines of this ideological project, which undergirded new articulations of Indian nationalism during the era of removal. In his political writings, Pitchlynn negotiated between, on the one hand, the pressures of removal and US colonialism, and, on the other hand, the need to build and rebuild Choctaw institutions after removal. By promoting national education, he set up an innovative system of schools in the postremoval Choctaw Nation in Indian Territory, and through diplomacy with the American government he promoted efforts of economic and educational reform. His writings thereby represent a sustained effort to make the colonial legacy of dispossession through treaty-making into a material framework for indigenous nation-building.

In the context of studies of nineteenth-century Native American literature, the writings of Peter Pitchlynn present us with a crucial question: how do we make sense of Pitchlynn's brand of nationalism, which did not articulate cultural resistance or validate Choctaw traditions and ancestry? In studies of American Indian writing, literary nationalism typically names a critical optic that examines the rootedness of texts in tribally specific notions of culture and peoplehood. It has been closely associated with what scholar Craig Womack calls "Native American literary separatism," anticolonial writing traditions that draw on cultural repertoires specific to Indian nations and are distinct from non-Native forms and literary canons.[6] Considered from such a cultural-nationalist framework, however, Pitchlynn's work may easily escape attention, since he rarely valorized Choctaw traditions, and he held a Eurocentric view of what his people should aspire to. Pitchlynn located the idea of Choctaw nationalism not in tribal traditions but in the promotion of modern institutions, and he considered Euro-American ideas about law, property, race, and civilization as the frameworks for new forms of political organization and education. In the course of his career as a diplomat, however, these ideas also undergirded his critique of US-Indian treaty-making and the land theft that followed in the wake of the Treaty of Dancing Rabbit Creek. As a result, Pitchlynn's fraught publication projects show us how the legacies of treaty-making and American racial ideologies became important factors for elite, landowning Choctaws who articulated new ideas about social belonging and tribal organization. These tensions, I argue, are a defining aspect of the work of a controversial Choctaw nationalist who envisioned new paths of indigenous nation-building after the dramatic upheavals of removal.

IMAGINING CHOCTAW NATION IN INDIAN TERRITORY

Peter Pitchlynn's career as a writer and diplomat took shape during a period when Choctaw political power moved away from the hereditary chiefs to a younger generation of elite, educated, and often mixed-race men. In the context of this shift, Peter Pitchlynn, whose Choctaw name was Hatchootucknee ("The Snapping Turtle"), gained prominence in Choctaw political life during the 1820s. He was born in 1806 in the Choctaw community of Hush-ook-wa, in the northeast of present-day Mississippi. His father was the Scottish trader John Pitchlynn while his mother, Sophia Folsom, was the daughter of a white man and a Choctaw woman. Pitchlynn belonged to a wealthy family that owned sixty enslaved African Americans in 1831, making them the largest slaveholding family in the Choctaw Nation.[7] The Pitchlynns held a prominent status due to John Pitchlynn's role as a trader and their relation to Mushulatubbee, the *miko* (district chief) of the Northeastern District. In 1824 Peter married Rhoda Folsom, the sister of the Choctaw leader David Folsom of the Northeastern District, and the same year he was elected to lead the Lighthorse, a tribal police force. In this capacity, he successfully combated the liquor trade and gained the title of "colonel" that he used throughout his life.

Pitchlynn's family background tells a more general story about the relation between race, class, and political power in the Choctaw Nation. Since the late 1700s, elite landowning families had often encouraged women to marry white traders or colonial officials, to forge new diplomatic and trade relations and thus to secure access to new avenues of power.[8] In the course of the early nineteenth century, the increased social stratification along class and racial lines led to what historian James Taylor Carson calls the political tensions between "primordialists" and "cosmopolitans." For the "primordialists," Choctaw cultural and political life centered on the autonomy of the three separate districts: Okla Falaya, Okla Tannap, and Okla Hannali. Although in the past the chiefs of these districts had frequently come together in council, their laws were rooted in the social life of families and clans. The primordialists held that governance should be based in existing models of traditional Choctaw political organization, such as the redistribution of goods by the district chiefs. The "cosmopolitans," however, held that a lack of political unification hindered the nation's political effectiveness when dealing with the rapid expansion of white settlement in Mississippi. They promoted aspects of Euro-American ideas and institutions that would contribute to a centralized form of governance, especially laws codified in writing and a unified political system that would give the Choctaw Nation more legibility as a modern nation in the eyes of the United States government.[9]

This debate over Choctaw modernization was the occasion for Peter Pitchlynn's first public writings, when in 1826—at the age of twenty—he served as secretary to the meetings of the Choctaw General Council. Between August 1826 and August 1828, the Council came together on three different occasions to lay the groundwork for what became the first set of written laws applying to all three districts. The aim was to unify the nation politically by codifying laws regarding criminal punishment, marriage practices, and property ownership, which also included laws related to the ownership and punishment of enslaved African Americans. As Christina Snyder writes, during these council meetings, Pitchlynn played a role similar to that of James Madison during the US constitutional convention, as he "took notes of the proceedings, wrote and edited various drafts, and produced a final copy of the constitution." Pitchlynn was a "logical choice" for this position, since he was "among the most literary Choctaws, had effectively enforced the temperance laws as a Lighthorse captain, and came from a prominent family."[10] Pitchlynn's record of the meetings—which missionaries referred to as the Choctaws' first "constitution"—expressed an emergent form of Choctaw nationalism that was centered on written laws and property ownership.[11] In his transcripts of the meetings, Pitchlynn used the language of value and efficiency to underscore the importance of the project: "What value can we provide for our Nation? This shall be our concern ... that those of us here continue not to be of one mind, and we are ineffective. It is necessary for us to finally conclude that we are certainly not effective at the things we are doing. If we continue to work and to finalize this legislation it shall be worth the time and effort for our nation."[12] If this national reorganization involved emulating American laws and political institutions, Pitchlynn's record of the meetings also stressed the ancestral

FIGURE 3.1
P. P. Pitchlynn, Speaker of the National Council of the Choctaw nation and Choctaw Delegate to the Government of the United States, by Charles Fenderich. Hand-colored lithograph on paper, 1842. National Portrait Gallery, Smithsonian Institution. In 1842 the United States Congress commissioned this portrait of Peter Pitchlynn, during one of his diplomatic trips to Washington. The German-American artist Charles Fenderich (1805–1887) portrayed him in a double-breasted suit, with his hair combed back and a fashionable patterned scarf tied in a loose bow across his chest. The caption identifies him as "speaker of the National Council of the Choctaw Nation" and "Choctaw delegate to the Government of the United States." While the portrait paints him in the role of intercultural broker, his public persona is straightforwardly "Choctaw." At the same time, the portrait is remarkably similar to those Fenderich made of many members of the US Congress, suggesting Pitchlynn's established place in scenes of American government. The portrait may be considered in stark contrast to George Catlin's famous portrait of the Assiniboine delegate Wi-jun-jon in Washington (1832), in which the subject's donning of Euro-American fashion suggests a narrative of effeminacy or assimilation. Fenderich's portrait of Pitchlynn may be uniquely successful among nineteenth-century portraits of Native American leaders, since it resists representing Pitchlynn along such axes of authenticity or assimilation.

precedent for these innovations, noting that "each district has always possessed laws. In the past, our forefathers always had laws for all concerns."[13] Being scribe of the General Council meetings, Pitchlynn had close insight into efforts of nation-building through the codification of new laws and institutions of government.

Pitchlynn benefited materially from the political innovations of the 1820s, which also ushered in an elaborate system of education. Elite Choctaw families saw Western forms of education as "new sources of power and influence" and as a possible solution to the increasing pressure on Choctaw lands from a growing population of white settlers in Mississippi.[14] Two treaties with the United States, made in 1820 and 1825, secured educational funds that were used for a range of different day schools and boarding schools. As historian Clara Sue Kidwell demonstrates in her study of missionary education in the Choctaw Nation, the chiefs of the different districts—including "primordialist" leaders such as Puckshanubee, Mushulatubbee, and Pushmataha—actively promoted mission schools as instruments of nation-building, and by 1830 there were eleven schools in the Choctaw Nation, twenty-nine teachers, and 260 enrolled students. In addition, 250 adults had been taught to read their native language.[15] Yet these educational opportunities also exacerbated social stratification among the Choctaw, since these schools tended to privilege children from rich, landowning families and were more accessible to elite families that did not represent, in Kidwell's words, the "mainstream of Choctaw cultural life."[16] The most significant of these educational projects was Choctaw Academy, an elite school for the advanced education of Choctaw boys. In 1825 the General Council approved its establishment in Scott County, Kentucky, and it was set up according to the Indian Office's regulations for Indian schools.[17] Choctaw Academy was housed on the plantation of the Kentucky senator Richard Mentor Johnson, a well-known commander of the War of 1812. As Christina Snyder explores in her history of the academy, it was managed by Julia Chinn, an enslaved African American woman who was also Johnson's common-law wife.[18] The academy opened its doors in November 1825 with fifty-five students, some of whom were students from other Indian nations or white students from the Blue Springs area.[19]

If Choctaw education was tethered to the diplomatic relationship between the Choctaw Nation and the US government, so was the early career of Peter Pitchlynn. When Pitchlynn enrolled at Choctaw Academy in 1827, it was a springboard for his advanced education and his political career, which depended in part on an education that was sponsored by both the Choctaw General Council and the Indian Office.[20] With the approval of the General Council, Commissioner of Indian Affairs Thomas McKenney paid for his expenses by allocating $500 from the Choctaws' educational funds, most of which went to his clothing and books: a volume on Roman history and a copy of *Paradise Lost*, as well as "books on the Masonic Order, logic, natural philosophy, synonyms, political economy, chemistry, and moral philosophy."[21] Pitchlynn left Choctaw Academy after only three months to enroll briefly at Transylvania University in Lexington, Kentucky, and the University of Nashville, where he attended classes from November 1827 to April 1828.[22] Despite his short stints at these schools, he secured letters of recommendation from Richard Mentor Johnson of Choctaw Academy and Philip Lindsley, the president of the University of Nashville. Johnson, for one, described Pitchlynn—whom he identified as "part Choctaw & part white blood"—as "a gracious man of amiable manners & disposition," endowed with "great & good qualities; industrious & resolute, & more devoted to study than is usual." He had no doubt that Pitchlynn would "pursue his studies with ardor & zeal what will do honor & credit to any student."[23]

Pitchlynn's studies and his work for the General Council set him up to become a key player in the history of Choctaw removal. In 1828 he took part in a diplomatic expedition to survey the Choctaw Nation's lands in Indian Territory, to determine whether Indian removal would be a workable prospect. With the treaties of Doak's Stand (1820) and Washington City (1825), the Choctaw district chiefs had negotiated cessions of lands in Mississippi in exchange for large tracts in the West: the treaties ceded to them approximately one-third of Indian Territory, the southeastern part in present-day Oklahoma. The Choctaw title to these lands put the American government in a position to promote removal to Indian Territory as a future possibility, and in 1827 Thomas McKenney visited Choctaw Nation to negotiate the terms of a removal treaty. Although the district chiefs were not willing to sign one, they agreed to an expedition to Indian Territory west of the Mississippi River, to survey the lands they had gained through treaty and to weigh their options.[24] The General Council appointed Pitchlynn as the leader of the Choctaw delegation, and in November 1828, he set out to explore the Choctaw lands west of the Mississippi.

Like other diplomatic initiatives, the expedition to Indian Territory was sponsored by the United States government, but it reserved an active role for organizations in civil society as well as indigenous leaders. The expedition numbered forty-two people in total. The American army captain George H. Kennerly was in command of the expedition, which also included the topographer Lt. Washington Hood, his assistant John Bell, the physician George P. Todson, and an interpreter to translate from the Osage and Kanza languages. The Choctaw delegation was composed of six delegates—two from each district—and was accompanied by the Indian agent David W. Haley. Twelve Chickasaw delegates were also part of the delegation, along with their Indian agent and their interpreter, and three Creek delegates, who brought along several hired men. The delegates also brought along several enslaved African Americans, and Pitchlynn was accompanied by a personal servant he referred to as "Black Peter."[25] The expedition was overseen by the Baptist missionary Isaac McCoy, an influential figure in the Indian reform movement and a promoter of removal policy. McCoy had long been a Baptist minister in Indian country, and his efforts in promoting removal helped him to get appointed in 1830 as a government surveyor under Andrew Jackson. McCoy was pessimistic about the prospect of meaningful reform as long as Indian nations remained where they were, and he saw removal as the only way to prevent their economic and social degradation, due to the corrupting influence of whites. He had lobbied the Secretary of War and the Baptist Board of Missions since 1824 to promote the view that Indian reform depended on "the concentration of all the tribes in some suitable portion of country, under such guardianship of our Government as shall be found conducive to their permanent improvement; together with the guaranty . . . of said country to them and to their posterity for ever."[26] As Pitchlynn recorded in his diary, McCoy championed the idea of a permanent home for all American Indians where they could gradually adapt to "civilization" while escaping the corrupting influences of whites, as long as the western lands could be permanently guaranteed to Indian nations.

For Pitchlynn, an immediate goal of the expedition was to write a report for the General Council about the lands and people in the West, so the council could decide whether the region was sufficiently rich in resources to make removal a workable prospect. During his travels, from the fall of 1828 to the winter of 1829, he kept a diary in which he recounted his observations and his diplomatic meetings with tribal leaders in the West and with American officials. In his diary Pitchlynn accurately described McCoy's aim as being "to concentrate all the Indian nations within the limits of the U States over on the Western side of the Mississippi," even if he also felt that the Baptist missionary was "upon examination rather superficial in his opinion of things."[27] Pitchlynn found himself at odds with McCoy's official report to Secretary of War Peter B. Porter, which stated that the western lands were of sufficient quality to justify the prospect of Choctaw removal. To be sure, McCoy had some misgivings: the region lacked timber, and he argued that the lands of the Indian nations already in Indian Territory were too large, which he thought would delay their pursuit of agricultural projects. On the whole, however, McCoy reported that the western lands were "adequate to the purposes of a permanent and comfortable house for the Indians," concluding that "whatever may be the obstacles which at present oppose," they could be "located there without recourse to any measure not in accordance with the most rigid principles of justice and humanity."[28] By contrast, Pitchlynn's report had only few positive things to say about the lands and people in Indian Territory, and the expedition returned home even before they had surveyed the bulk of the lands ceded to them. Of particular concern to Pitchlynn was the region's sparse population of deer, a staple of the Choctaw economy, and the lack of cane, which was used to weave baskets and make other equipment.[29] He described the lands he saw with phrases like "principally prairie," "middlin good," "moderately rich," and "generally of the inferior kind." At best, he reported a central ambivalence about the western lands, and, as Christina Snyder notes, on the whole he "could not imagine living in Indian Territory."[30] If Isaac McCoy's report to the secretary of war had been mostly positive, Pitchlynn's appraisal of the territory to the Choctaw Council challenged the recommendations of the Baptist missionary.

As a document of Choctaw diplomacy, however, Pitchlynn's diary appraised not only the potential of the western lands but also the indigenous population that was already there. In considering removal to Indian Territory, one concern was how they could lay a legitimate claim to lands that other indigenous people already lived on. To this effect, the US government also organized the expedition with an eye on conducting diplomatic meetings, which would help promote Indian Territory as a friendly place to the Choctaw, Chickasaw, and Creek delegates. After they met with Superintendent of Indian Affairs William Clark in St. Louis in mid-October, the expedition stayed several days in the new villages of the Shawnees, whom the US government had recently forced to remove to the western border of the state of Missouri, near present-day Kansas City. In his diary, Pitchlynn recounted his meeting with two Shawnee chiefs—William Perry and Peter Cornstalk—and the religious leader Tenskwatawa, the famous "Shawnee Prophet." The Shawnees were newcomers to the region, having settled in their villages only recently, in the spring of 1828, and Pitchlynn recorded a speech by William Perry that professed friendship between the United States and the Shawnees. Pitchlynn summarized that Perry "was glad, he said, that we did not pass his nation as strangers" and "spoke some time of the former interviews they had with our forefathers, and that it seemed the Great Father had ordered it so that we should meet again and take each other by the hand."[31] Perry recalled the War of 1812, when the Shawnee prophet Tenskwatawa's religious visions had spurred his brother Tecumseh's pan-Indian alliance with the British, which stretched from the Old Northwest to the Southern nations, including the Cherokee. The Choctaw chiefs, however, had rejected Tecumseh and Tenskwatawa's alliance. Now, eighteen years after Tecumseh's defeat, Perry "presented to each of the delegations white beads and tobacco as a renewer of our old friendship."[32]

Pitchlynn's report of the meeting with Tenskwatawa reaffirmed the image of the Shawnees as a population that had submitted to the hegemony of American

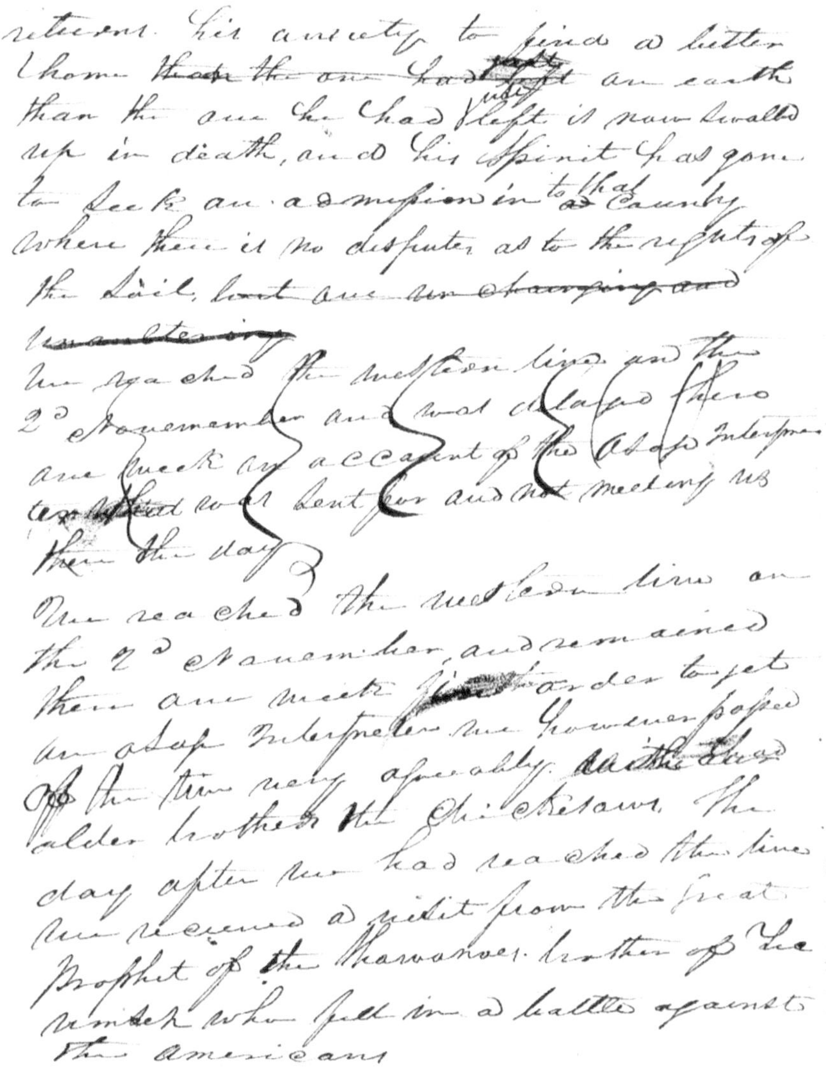

FIGURE 3.2 Page from the diary of Peter Pitchlynn. 1828. Peter Pitchlynn Collection, Box 5, Folder 65, Western History Collections, University of Oklahoma Libraries, Norman, Oklahoma.

rule. After Tenskwatawa had been exiled to Canada after the War of 1812, Michigan's territorial governor Lewis Cass persuaded him to return to the United States in 1824, to lead the remaining Shawnee in Ohio to their reservation west of the Mississippi River. In other words, Cass, one of the architects of federal Indian removal policy, had successfully enlisted the Shawnee prophet to promote the removal scheme to his own people.[33] Having just arrived in their new settlements, Tenskwatawa proclaimed to Pitchlynn a vision of peace between the Shawnees and the United States. As Pitchlynn reported,

> He said that they knew not anything, even that which was good for them. He then spoke of the great wisdom of the President of the United States. He said that he knew what was for their good. Knowing these things to be true, he said that he had given up his own opinion on things respecting the interest of his nation and that he looked to the Great Father, the President, to advise in every thing, and that he obeyed him in all things like an obedient child, and recommended that we should do the same.[34]

Pitchlynn took Tenskwatawa's words as a sign of Shawnee obedience to their Indian agent, William Clark, and the president in Washington. His speech affirmed what the Indian Office would have gladly seen: a pacified nation that adhered to their boundaries and took up an agricultural life. Pitchlynn therefore concluded that the Shawnees would be sure to take up agriculture soon. Although he deemed the Shawnees' new country "by far inferior" to the Choctaw lands in Mississippi, he noticed the advances the Shawnees had made and concluded that "they will in a few years, I think be all tillers of the soil.... Their manners and customs are pretty much as those of the Choctaws with but a few exceptions ... the Shawanoes had located themselves in Towns and had built for themselves nice and comfortable houses of hewed logs and [had] them placed in regular order."[35] By staging these diplomatic interactions, the organizers of the expedition managed to present a positive view of the conditions of a tribe that had faced removal earlier.

Through such efforts, the expedition drew on the customs of Indian diplomacy to render the western lands more "internal" to the Choctaw Nation. What was particularly problematic for the Choctaws was the fact that the treaties of 1820 and 1825 had ceded to them large tracts of land that had previously belonged to the Osages, with whom they had long-standing conflicts over boundaries and hunting rights. Pitchlynn recounted a meeting he held on November 20 and 21 with the Osage leader Belle Oiseau in White Hair's village, an Osage town near the Neosho River. Pitchlynn delivered a speech in which he recognized that "our nations have been at times in enmity with each other, and like men and warriors made the ground red with each other's blood whenever they saw each other."[36] Pitchlynn emphasized that the Choctaw "are thought to be the largest nation of

"The Blessings Which We Are Now Enjoying" | 135

FIGURE 3.3
Tenskwatawa 'The Prophet,' after James Otto Lewis. Hand-colored lithograph on paper, by J. Baricou, 1835. National Portrait Gallery, Smithsonian Institution.

red people in the United States and they, like other red men, love war," but he also told Belle Oiseau that "we have been told by our Great Father, the President, to be at peace with all nations, and teach our young men how to work, and advise them to pursue the ways of the white man."[37] To affirm that the Choctaws had indeed held close talks with the US government, Pitchlynn told them about their meeting with William Clark in St. Louis the previous month, calling him the "great friend of the red man." Mobilizing the rhetorical conventions of Indian diplomacy—to raise the specter of war combined with statements of friendship—Pitchlynn pledged that his people had "laid by everything like war, and wish to be at peace with all nations, and particularly the nations of red people."[38]

Beyond such boilerplate professions of intertribal peace, these diplomatic councils were also an opportunity for Pitchlynn to reflect on the habits and living conditions of the people in Indian Territory, to measure how other nations compared to the Choctaws in terms of manners, language, dress, and education. Reporting on his meeting with the Shawnee chiefs, for example, he described William Perry and Peter Cornstalk's dress as "very poor, being a common course grey coat (frock) worn out at the elbows and course about the skirts." By comparison, Pitchlynn was "much pleased" with the Osages, who were "generally tall and [lean] in flesh," and considered the mixed-race Cherokee diplomat Richard Fields "quite entelignt and a young man of steady habits."[39] However, he described a Kanza woman as "rude and wild in her aspect," and he was generally disappointed by the appearance of the Indian nations he encountered west of the Mississippi. In St. Louis the expedition came in contact with a delegation of Sioux leaders who were visiting William Clark's office, whom he described as a "people but little known to the Choctaws." Although they held a gift-giving ceremony to "claim them as their friends and brothers," Pitchlynn described the Sioux as "a poor and miserable race."[40] This ambivalent appraisal of the people he met in Indian Territory articulated a dialectic on "civilization" that became an ideological rationale for the Choctaws' claim to their lands west of the Mississippi River. Pitchlynn's commentary on these tribes implicitly coded his own people as "civilized" by comparison, capitalizing on the fact that Americans had come to regard the Choctaws as one of the "Five Civilized Tribes," alongside the Cherokee, Seminole, Creek, and Chickasaw. As Christina Snyder writes, that Americans afforded them this status was "a distinction that had nothing to do with race," as other Indian nations in the East "used similar rhetoric to distance themselves from Plains peoples and assert that they, like US citizens, lived in 'civilized nations.'"[41] But their adoption of American institutions and traditions—including alphabetic literacy, legal knowledge, political organization, and written constitutions—would render the Choctaws more capable of claiming social ascendancy among other Indian nations in Indian Territory if they chose to remove there. In short, the contrast between the "civilized" Choctaws and the conditions of the western tribes allowed Pitchlynn to imagine his own people as the eventual successors to the soil.

But even if the rhetoric of "civilization" was more about education and Christianity than about racialized notions of human difference, ideas about race did play a part in Pitchlynn's commentary on Native peoples. Pitchlynn extended his criticism to another southeastern nation as he commented on the Creek people, who were part of the same expedition. By the time the expedition arrived near the Verdigris River in November 1828, Creek removal to Indian Territory had already been underway for some time, and Pitchlynn witnessed the arrival of an estimated 230 Creeks "from the old Nation" to the area surrounding Fort Gibson.[42] Pitchlynn visited their camp on two nights while the Creeks celebrated the arrival of their newly removed fellow citizens. Witnessing their dancing, Pitchlynn regretted the interracial dimensions of this celebration, complaining that "half negro and Creek" people joined in the dance together. Pitchlynn commented that "I am extremely sorry for one thing, that is, to find people of my own color (Indians) so full of vice as I have found the Creeks are. There is no distinction between them and the Negros (that is) with themselves. They mingle together in Society upon an equality. There are among them a great many mixed (half negro and Creek).... They were Negro men and Indian women.... The women of the

Creeks are very lude, &c."⁴³ In Pitchlynn's view, the suggestion of interracial association and miscegenation was a marker of "vice," a transgression of naturalized boundaries of race, sexuality, and class. Characterizing the Creek as being of his "own color," he suggested that their disregard for proper boundaries of race and sexuality made them less civilized than the Choctaws. He commented on the festivities at the Creek camp the next day, further testifying to his assumptions about the Creeks' "vice":

> At sun down I got on my horse and rode over to the Creek Village, where they were dancing. I joined with them in 3 reals and then came off. Just upon my arrival there an old woman died in 20 steps of the place where they had made arrangements to have the dance, owing to which the party moved their dance over to another 3 hundred yards off. From this was proved [sic] that these people are so full of vice that they regard not the death of their nearest neighbour. The party consisted of Indians a few white halfbreeds, Negroes &c.⁴⁴

As to his own participation in the dance, Pitchlynn quickly added that he was there for "proper" reasons—namely to "find out things &c. &c"—but whatever his motivations were, his commentary showed him a critical observer of Native people's moral behavior.

If Pitchlynn's report to the General Council did not endorse removal to Indian Territory, it did express a rationale for why his people would have a legitimate claim to their country west of the Mississippi. In his diary, he articulated a Choctaw variation on what Michael Denning calls "settler exceptionalism," an ideology of national uniqueness that originates in the narrative of settlers' encounter with societies that they intend to replace.⁴⁵ Not only did Pitchlynn claim the Choctaws' title to the western lands based on the treaties of 1820 and 1825, their "civilized" position among other nations in Indian Territory was a basis for wielding what Carole Pateman calls the "settler contract," a rationale for extinguishing Native land title that depends on a replacement narrative, in which the settler transforms wild, uncultivated lands into civil society.⁴⁶ In the logic of the settler contract, settlers not only proclaim lands to be "vacant," but also legitimize their claim to land by professing themselves to be "civilized" and therefore capable of establishing institutions of civil society, such as governments, schools, farms, and borders. For Pitchlynn, the recent innovations in Choctaw education and law helped to articulate a sense of Choctaw exceptionalism that solidified their treaty-based claims to Indian Territory. Based in a notion of a national character that was *civilized* compared to other Indian nations, this notion of Choctaw exceptionalism naturalized the Choctaws' claim to a potential future in Indian Territory, regardless of what would be the General Council's decision on removal.

In his report on these diplomatic exchanges, Pitchlynn championed an abiding sense of Choctaw nationhood, defending their political status as a sovereign nation with legitimate claims to their lands in Indian Territory, which had been ceded to them by treaty. But the other side of this argument was that even if his report did not promote removal for practical reasons, it sanctioned an ideological defense of Choctaw removal that was based in Euro-American codes of race and civilization. Intervening in the networks of US-Choctaw diplomacy, Pitchlynn's removal diary and his diplomatic speeches suggested common ground between a Choctaw project of nation-building and American schemes of indigenous dispossession.

THE RACIAL CODES OF POLITICAL REPRESENTATION

Peter Pitchlynn's removal diary reflects that the political issue of Indian removal emerged alongside new discourses of race and empire in the early US republic, which carried over into the literatures of Indian diplomacy. The expedition to Indian Territory coincided with the 1828 US presidential election between incumbent president John Quincy Adams and his Democratic challenger, the populist Andrew Jackson. The inauguration of Jackson the following year had important ramifications for Native people, since he was on record as supporting a more rigorous policy of Indian removal on a larger scale. One of his signature political acts in office was the Indian Removal Act, which passed in Congress after vehement debate. Signed into law by Jackson in 1830, it allowed the federal government to negotiate removal directly with Indian nations. Of course, as Stuart Banner notes, removal had already been an existing practice for about 200 years, but what was new was "the speed of the process" and the increased appropriation of funds for removal that were authorized by Congress, not to mention the wider political debate about removal in public discourse.[47]

For the Choctaws, however, the more immediate crisis was at the level of the state rather than the federal government: in March 1830 the state of Mississippi threatened to extend its jurisdiction over Indian nations within its borders. As Christina Snyder explains in *Great Crossings*, this meant that Choctaw people would become subject to the laws of Mississippi as people of color rather than as citizens of the Choctaw Nation. The difference was immense: in Mississippi and other states, free people of color were barred from voting, holding public office, or testifying in court. In essence, the application of state law over Choctaw lands would "transform Indians from citizens of a sovereign nation into subjects of an increasingly racist empire."[48] In this light, tribal leaders who supported removal generally did so because the extension of state law "would destroy the Choctaw Nation—if not literally, then at least politically."[49] Given this immediate political crisis, tribal leaders ultimately signed a removal treaty at Dancing Rabbit Creek in September 1830, despite widespread resistance to removal among them. In a widely reprinted newspaper address, the Choctaw lawyer George W. Harkins explained that his people had been forced to choose between "two evils": either to give up their ancestral homelands, or to extinguish Choctaw sovereignty by becoming subject to the laws of Mississippi.[50] Harkins believed that his people "rather chose to suffer and be free, than live under the degrading influence of laws, which our voice could not be heard in their formation."[51]

For Peter Pitchlynn, these events ushered in five decades of wrangling with the historical legacy of Choctaw removal. Although it is not certain whether he signed the Treaty of Dancing Rabbit Creek, afterward he led a "nation-wide protest" to nullify the treaty, which was quashed when the Indian agent William Ward called on the Mississippi militia to break it up.[52] Although the rebellion was short-lived, it gained Pitchlynn much popular support among the Choctaw people, who elected him to temporarily serve as chief of the Northeastern district, in order to oversee the process of removal to Indian Territory.[53] In this capacity he witnessed firsthand the traumatic passage to Indian Territory during the first phase of Choctaw removal, which turned disastrous in the winter of 1832 when some 2,500 Choctaws were stranded at an army post on the Arkansas River, exposed to the elements when a long and harsh storm hit them.[54] The situation was exacerbated by poor clothing and provisions, and Pitchlynn wrote to Secretary of War Lewis Cass to demand the necessary goods and support. This succession of events underscores the complex debates that removal generated in Indian country: over the course of only a few years, he had explored the possibility of removal, rejected it, protested it, and, finally, oversaw its actual process.

As a Choctaw leader and diplomat, Pitchlynn thus occupied an ambivalent position as he navigated the overlapping discourses of race, empire, and indigenous sovereignty. But how did he present himself as an authorized agent of the Choctaw people, someone who could speak on behalf of his nation and be taken seriously within institutions of Indian diplomacy? Since Pitchlynn belonged to an elite, mixed-race Choctaw family, it might seem tempting to interpret his diplomatic role as one that reflected the identity of someone who was suspended "between two cultures," a position of liminality between irreconcilable Choctaw and American worlds. But if Pitchlynn articulated any such liminal position, it was more likely to have resulted from how he chose to mobilize ideas of race, nationhood, and civilization in his diplomatic efforts. Throughout his diplomatic career, Pitchlynn fashioned a self-presentation as an indigenous leader who embodied the Choctaws' compatibility with Euro-American ideals of civilization. Reconciling his ideological convictions with political opportunity, Pitchlynn claimed a measure of social prominence by embracing Euro-American notions of race and masculinity.

In the 1840s, for instance, Pitchlynn turned to new scientific discourses to construct this public persona when he solicited a "phreno-physiognomical" report by the physician Gideon Lincecum. A distant cousin of Pitchlynn's father, Lincecum was a former surveyor and a historian of the Choctaw people.[55] In 1846, he examined Pitchlynn using a standardized chart for the "Specific and Proportional Delineation of Personal Traits of Character, as manifested in Physiological Structure," attributed to a Dr. J. L. Berthollet. The use of this standardized chart reflects that physiognomy and phrenology had become popular sciences in the nineteenth century. Phrenology refers to a form of physical examination starting from the idea that the shape of a person's skull provides information about their character and mental faculties; physiognomy is the practice of reading a person's face and body to deduce information about their personal characteristics. Lincecum's report was a full endorsement of Pitchlynn's capabilities. When Gideon Lincecum examined Pitchlynn's cranium, he located a scientific mind: his subject displayed "all the Phrenological organs requisite for studying anatomy, form, size, locality, eventuality, and comparison," as well as a "natural love of Chemistry and Pharmacy, and all studies appertaining to human nature."[56] Lincecum summarized Pitchlynn's facial features, physical attributes, and personal characteristics, and rated them on a numerical scale. He described his features as "round as an egg" but also "symmetrical"—indeed, the symmetry of his person was "exemplary" and "harmonious." Pitchlynn's hair was "thin and fine," his cuticles "soft," and his body "good & strong—able to sustain all that the head demands." On the whole, Lincecum described him as "more attractive than repulsive."[57]

What was the social function of a document such as this? Karen Halttunen has argued that for nineteenth-century Americans, "inner character was believed to be imprinted upon his face and thus visible to anyone who understood the moral language of physiognomy."[58] In societies shaped by differences of race, ethnicity, and class, having a scientifically reasoned summary of one's own physical features allowed for a self-conscious "performance and self-presentation" to control one's own image in the public eye.[59] Phrenology, too, emerged in the 1830s as a scientific discourse that rationalized human difference on anatomical grounds, linking people's emotional and intellectual traits to the size and shape of their cranium. According to Robert Bieder, phrenologists believed that the human brain was "composed of individual faculties that controlled personality, thought, and moral action," and that they could determine the strength of these faculties via

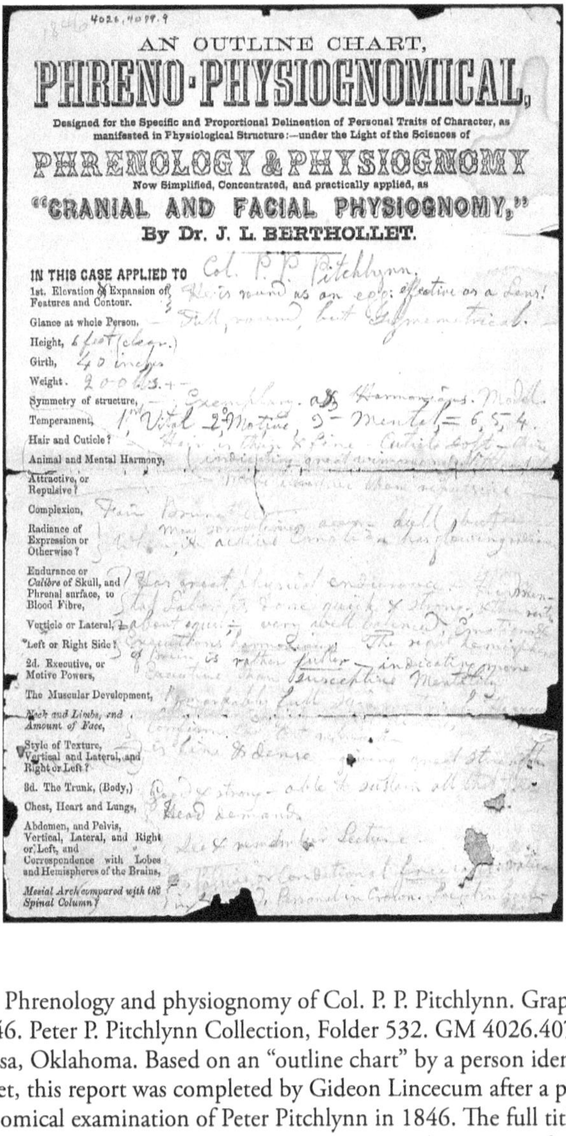

AN OUTLINE CHART,

PHRENO-PHYSIOGNOMICAL,

Designed for the Specific and Proportional Delineation of Personal Traits of Character, as manifested in Physiological Structure:—under the Light of the Sciences of

PHRENOLOGY & PHYSIOGNOMY

Now Simplified, Concentrated, and practically applied, as

"CRANIAL AND FACIAL PHYSIOGNOMY,"

By Dr. J. L. BERTHOLLET.

IN THIS CASE APPLIED TO Col. P. P. Pitchlynn

1st. Elevation & Expansion of Features and Contour.

Glance at whole Person, Full, round, but Symmetrical.

Height, 6 feet (clear.)

Girth, 40 inches

Weight. 200 lbs.+

Symmetry of structure, Exemplary & Harmonious. Model.

Temperament, 1st Vital 2d Motive, 3 Mental = 6, 5, 4.

Hair and Cuticle?

Animal and Mental Harmony,

Attractive, or Repulsive?

Complexion, Fair Brunette

Radiance of Expression or Otherwise?

Endurance or *Calibre* of Skull, and Phrenal surface, to Blood Fibre, Has great physical endurance

Verticle or Lateral,

Left or Right Side?

2d. Executive, or Motive Powers,

The Muscular Development,

Neck and Limbs, and Amount of Face,

Style of Texture, Vertical and Lateral, and Right or Left?

3d. The Trunk, (Body,)

Chest, Heart and Lungs,

Abdomen, and Pelvis, Vertical, Lateral, and Right or Left, and Correspondence with Lobes and Hemispheres of the Brains,

Mesial Arch compared with the Spinal Column?

FIGURE 3.4 Phrenology and physiognomy of Col. P. P. Pitchlynn. Graphite and ink on paper, 1846. Peter P. Pitchlynn Collection, Folder 532. GM 4026.4079. Gilcrease Museum, Tulsa, Oklahoma. Based on an "outline chart" by a person identified as Dr. J. L. Berthollet, this report was completed by Gideon Lincecum after a phrenological and physiognomical examination of Peter Pitchlynn in 1846. The full title of the chart is "An Outline Chart, Phreno-physiognomical, Designed for the Specific and Proportional Delineation of Personal Traits of Character, as manifested in Physiological Structure:—under the Light of the Sciences of Phrenology and Physiognomy Now Simplified, Concentrated, and practically applied, as 'Cranial and Facial Physiognomy.'" The wording of the chart's title reflects the increasing popularization of phrenology and physiognomy as scientific practices. Among the categories that Lincecum completed was "Glance at whole Person" ("Full, round, but symmetrical.") "Symmetry of structure" ("Exemplary & Harmonious. Model."); "Complexion" ("Fair Brunette"); "Radiance of Expression or Otherwise?" ("May sometimes seem dull, but when in active motion has glowing radiance"); and "Endurance or *Calibre* Skull, and Phrenal surface, to Blood Fibre" ("Has great physical endurance").

"protuberances on the skull."[60] Moreover, Britt Rusert argues in *Fugitive Science* that there was a public, performative dimension to phrenological readings: being "popular among both the elite and working classes, phrenological readings of celebrities were widely reported in the press, and readings were often performed in public." Rusert explains that the "dramatic and 'hands-on' element of phrenological examinations—in which a careful exploration of an individual's skull would reveal hidden aspects of their personality and character—made them particularly amenable to stage performances."[61] Although there is no evidence that Pitchlynn's reading was conducted in public, given the performative nature of phrenology and the preservation of Lincecum's report among Pitchlynn's state papers, the document was probably part of his self-presentation as a public figure.

But phrenology had a vexed relationship to American Indian communities, to say the least. Phrenologists believed that each race "manifested its cultural traits through the shape of the cranium" and that "each race possessed a typical, or national, cranium."[62] Most prominently, the ethnologist Samuel G. Morton used Native American skulls to demonstrate his theories about the differences among what he thought were the five races of humankind, which he famously expounded in his *Crania Americana* (1839).[63] Phrenology and physiognomy thus emerged in tandem with the consolidation of scientific racism, a system of knowledge that proposed fundamental biological differences between people of different races, and established a system of classification that consigned American Indians to an inferior status to whites. However, Britt Rusert shows that despite its link to craniology and scientific racism, the practice of phrenology was also adopted by African Americans and Anglo-American women, who attempted to make it a more "radically inclusive and 'democratic' science" and thereby posed a "serious challenge to racial science's attempt to make racial traits fixed and immutable."[64] Likewise, Pitchlynn's phrenology report avoided any hint that his identity meant a status of racial inferiority, as espoused by theories of scientific racism. Lincecum marked Pitchlynn's complexion as "fair brunette" and otherwise did not comment on his mixed-race identity. He also made sure to qualify Pitchlynn's less savory characteristics, neutralizing any interpretation that might activate racialized ideas of "savagery." Writing that Pitchlynn's "spirit of revenge is tremendous," the physician added that it was also "governed by justice." To be sure, Lincecum found him "wanting in that patient plodding application which dwells on one thing, and too apt to fly from subject to subject, jump at one bound from premise to conclusion, find your first thoughts, your best."[65] Similarly, he thought Pitchlynn was too receptive to the praise of others: "Your love of praise is quite large. You get a great deal by the good opinion of others, but not too much by your own good opinion of yourself.... You are proud spirited and high-minded, are not induced to look up to any body, nor down on yourself. Are not conscious of having superiors."[66] Yet Lincecum counterbalanced Pitchlynn's flaws by naming his transparency of character: he was "perfectly candid and outspoken," with not "one shadow of a shade of duplicity in your composition." Indeed, Lincecum concluded that "You possess most excellent motives. No man could mean better than you mean."[67]

Lincecum's report reflected more than Pitchlynn's susceptibility to flattery. The report was a carefully crafted tool that played into the politics of personality and masculinity that had become central to American political life. As Dana Nelson writes in *National Manhood*, in the early American republic, masculinity was the most important pretext for a cross-class, national identification through which white men assumed "the privileges and burdens of national imperatives." In the course of the nineteenth century, an imagined fraternity of white manhood became "carte blanche" for their exclusive claim to civic management.[68] The physician offered a ringing endorsement of Pitchlynn's fortitude, writing in the opening paragraph that he had "one of the very best constitutions in the world." His "most conspicuous feature" was "firmness": Lincecum wrote, "You stand like a rock, in the midst of the ocean, not dashing against the waves, but they are dashing against you, but making no impression. Stability, especially in the cause of right and truth, is . . . your strongest trait."[69] Lincecum's report thus constructed a public persona in which Pitchlynn's performance of masculinity was compatible with racially exclusive codes of civic leadership. Lincecum proclaimed Pitchlynn "capable of going through anything. . . . I am perfectly astonished at your hardihood." This stamina extended also to his love life, with Pitchlynn possessing "the highest order of attachment" to women and being "admirably sexed," "naturally gallant," and a "most devoted lover."[70] With this testament to his physical and mental attributes, Pitchlynn's claim to leadership positions did not rest on a racialized idea of the "Indian chief," but on gendered notions of civic leadership that were typically regarded as the domain of white men.

Through this collaborative text, Pitchlynn and Lincecum remixed codes of race and masculinity that were a prerogative for civic leadership in nineteenth-century America. And if it is unclear whether the report had a readership beyond Pitchlynn himself, it was compatible with a form of self-performance that modified the rigidly defined racial codes of the mid-nineteenth-century United States. In either case, his phrenology report suggests that Pitchlynn's political career was not simply an epiphenomenon of his cultural identity as a mixed-race Choctaw member of the upper class. Like his arguments about intertribal difference, Pitchlynn's embrace of these new sciences reveals how he actively played into racial ideologies to construct a measure of political authority. In doing so, he asserted control over his performance as an "authorized agent" capable of representing Choctaw peoplehood while also carrying authority within institutions of Indian diplomacy. Peter Pitchlynn recognized, then, that the performance of this role depended on the codes of race and gender that determined the political hierarchies of American life.

NATIONALISM AND EDUCATION IN PETER PITCHLYNN'S ORATORY

The most widely read instance of Peter Pitchlynn's self-representation was captured by the famous English novelist Charles Dickens. In the spring of 1842, Peter Pitchlynn was returning home from Washington to the Choctaw Nation and met the British writer on board a steamboat from Cincinnati to Louisville. According to Dickens's reflections in his travelogue *American Notes for General Circulation* (1842), Pitchlynn gave him his business card, and the two men conversed about literature, education, and the history and future of the American Indian. Dickens characterized Pitchlynn as a well-educated gentleman, who had "read many books," and he commented that the poetry of Sir Walter Scott "appeared to have left a strong impression on his mind." He "spoke English perfectly well," the novelist noted, although he had not begun to learn the language "until he was a young man grown." The only thing that Dickens regretted was that he did not see Pitchlynn in "his own attire," dressed as he was in an American suit. Pitchlynn explained that the Choctaws were "losing many things besides their dress" that "would soon be seen upon earth no more," but he assured the author that he "wore it at home" still.[71] From this casual conversation, Dickens constructed a vivid narrative of cultural change, in which Pitchlynn acted as the visible body on which that cultural change was written. Of course, Dickens's account had some important blind spots. It is curious, in fact, that although *American Notes* is essentially a study of American institutions—its system of government, prisons, schools, and hospitals—Dickens did not recognize the important role that Pitchlynn played in promoting institutions of Choctaw education. Indeed, Pitchlynn actively promoted schools as institutions that were embedded in the life of the nation rather than a colonial imposition from outside. In fact, when he met Dickens on the way to Louisville, Pitchlynn was returning home from a diplomatic trip to Washington, during which he had lobbied Congress for more financial control over the education of his people.[72]

Pitchlynn devoted much time to his efforts to rebuild Choctaw institutions in Indian Territory, and in the early 1840s he oversaw some of its most important educational innovations. For him, the cornerstone of a national culture was formal education, which had been a prominent feature of Choctaw life since the first establishment of missionary schools in the late 1810s.[73] In 1842, he dismantled

Choctaw Academy in Kentucky to establish Spencer Academy in their new homelands in the West, which was placed under the direct control of the General Council and became the "training ground for its future leaders."[74] The following year, Pitchlynn wrote an educational act that spearheaded an "elaborate system of schools," consisting of six academies and boarding schools for male and female students.[75] During this period, he gave several speeches on nationalism and education, actively promoting the idea that schools should be seen as institutions embedded in the life of the nation, rather than as a colonial apparatus imposed from outside by US civilization policy. The close connection that Pitchlynn saw between Choctaw nationalism and education was at the center of numerous speeches he made in the early 1840s. In his oratory, he made the tropes of "civilization" and property ownership the hallmarks of new tribal institutions, reclaiming these colonial tropes in his effort to articulate a future path for the Choctaw people.

In promoting the new system of schools, Pitchlynn argued that for education to become a project of indigenous nation-building rather than a colonial imposition, the Choctaws needed concrete control over its execution. Delivering a statement to the General Council in 1841, he spoke in support of administrative independence of their schools as he sought to replace Choctaw Academy in Kentucky with a new academy located within the boundaries of the Choctaw Nation. Pitchlynn argued that "the prosperity and happiness of mankind is ... solely dependent upon schools and literary institutions and that no nation can be prosperous without them."[76] But he also believed that "unless you yourselves establish your schools, appoint your teachers, and jealously watch over them, you may expect nothing from them but what you have experienced heretofore."[77] He held that there were "no public funds belonging to the Choctaws which we should prize more highly than our school funds, and none which we should watch over with greater care and strictness."[78] As Pitchlynn saw it, tribal control over the treaty-stipulated funds for education would wrest Choctaw education away from white American control over their schools; at the time, white American control was typically a prerequisite for using such funds. Instead, he called for Choctaw schools that would be built on "a broad, free and independent foundation," in a school system that would "give the institution all its funds, free and secure from the avarice of speculators, and entirely under the control of your Council and people and never under the influence of white men."[79]

For Pitchlynn these ideas about Choctaw education were closely related to his administrative work in spearheading a new system of schools in place of Choctaw Academy. Although he acknowledged that the academy had been the "most extensive literary institution ... for the benefit of the 'red man,'" Pitchlynn believed that it was not "as successful ... as was anticipated by its projectors."[80]

So when he took on the role of superintendent of Choctaw Academy in the early 1840s, he did so only to disenroll all the Choctaw students, take them back to the Choctaw Nation in Indian Territory, and enroll them in tribally controlled schools. Richard Mentor Johnson, the previous overseer of Choctaw Academy—who had recently served as the US vice president under Van Buren—saw this intervention as destructive. He wrote to the American secretary of war, John Spencer, that Pitchlynn considered himself to have "more power than the Government" and had put "every rule of honor at defiance." If he had praised Pitchlynn fifteen years earlier in his letter of recommendation, Johnson now concluded that he had "never met with a man so base." He asked in vain to keep Choctaw Academy running, believing that Pitchlynn would "stop at nothing to ... lessen the school in value."[81] But not only did John Spencer endorse the new academy in Choctaw Nation, it was even named after him. As one of the six new schools established by Pitchlynn's education act of 1842, Spencer Academy helped to renationalize Choctaw education on an administrative level.

Through these draconian means, Pitchlynn showed a deep commitment to a system of schools, which was part of a larger project of tribal-nation institution building; a strategy for conceiving of Western-style schools as unproblematically *Choctaw*. After all, American commentators still considered Native schools and academies as anomalies, institutions that were somehow at odds with their location in Indian nations. Although there had been mission schools, day schools, boarding schools, and academies in Choctaw Nation for almost three decades, when Spencer Academy opened in 1844 the *Arkansas Intelligencer* insisted on the novelty of seeing "a young savage in the backwoods construing the Commentaries of Caesar!"[82] In an undated address to the Choctaw General Council, Pitchlynn acknowledged that Choctaw education was indeed something "new" and argued that its history was deeply tied to his people's relationship with the United States. "It is only since we have had schools and educated men among us," Pitchlynn argued, "that we have prospered and done well, and it is only by them that we have acquired a name and character abroad and are now placed in advance of all the nations of red people in point of civilization."[83] Conversely, a failure to commit to education would be a relapse to previous conditions: "Take our educated men out of the nation," he warned, "discontinue our schools, and we should soon relapse into the state and condition of our forefathers, and the period would soon arrive when we should be numbered among the Tribes who are no more."[84] The Choctaws had "ascended a hill" where they had an "extensive view ... in the midst of sunshine," with "knowledge growing and spreading rapidly in every portion of our land."[85]

With his appeal for administrative control over Choctaw education, Pitchlynn promoted a pragmatic form of Indian nationalism that centered on present-day material welfare rather than the traditional past. Historian Donna Akers argues that Choctaw education was an attempt at "conversion" of Choctaws into white culture, or a means to achieve cultural assimilation by inculcating Christianity and Euro-American values: "Native people, in order to be 'saved,' had to adopt the culture, values, and language of the dominant white society" even when "missionaries failed miserably in their quest to convert Choctaws into white people."[86] But it is important to note that the expansion of formal education did not in fact achieve the "assimilation" of Choctaws into dominant society, but rather invigorated a new sense of nationalism. Historian Richard White explains that "without the missionaries' intending it or even realizing how it was happening, Christianity became a vehicle for a strain of Choctaw nationalism," and landowning elites promoted mission schools and European-style education as a means to address the economic needs and concerns of the nation.[87] While most of the Choctaw men who promoted education "served their personal interests, protected their wealth, and guaranteed them status and power," White argues that "the nationalism of the mixed-bloods was real nonetheless." The Choctaw nationalists saw traditional practices as halting their prospects for national self-sufficiency, and promoted "thrift and accumulation," "respect for property," and sobriety.[88] For Pitchlynn, then, the project of "civilization" was less about the goal of cultural assimilation and more a means to invest in Choctaw nationalism and futurity.

Yet if Pitchlynn's promotion of education was part of a wider history of Choctaw nation-building, his rhetoric also buried the social and cultural differences that existed in the Nation. In the first place, even though he professed to extend privileges of education to all Choctaws, these privileges did not extend to lower-class Choctaws, or to the more than 100 enslaved people Pitchlynn owned over the course of his lifetime, or, for that matter, to other enslaved African Americans who lived in Choctaw Nation.[89] Moreover, while Pitchlynn insisted on the need for Choctaw schools to be free from white influence, his speeches on nationalism also assumed white superiority and described Choctaw "progress" as an epiphenomenon of European settlement in North America. In 1842, at a temperance celebration in Choctaw Nation, Pitchlynn argued that "if we love our country, we will establish more and better schools in our Nation," but noted that "of all the things which the white man prizes most is their schools and their Bible— it is these that have made them a wise & a great people."[90] Although he refuted the idea that Native people were incapable of economic and political organization, he also considered the initial encounters between Native and non-Native people as a fundamental catalyst of progress. White men had introduced the Choctaws to property and agriculture, he argued, which had set up the framework for Choctaw advancement: "From them they received ... such articles which was to them of no importance, but great for us.... Ever since that day we have gradually been adapting into use the things belonging to the white man and now we want every thing [belonging] to the white man."[91]

Pitchlynn seemed to be aware that others might find this a problematic reading of history and would see such "adaptation" as an outside imposition. "Every good thing we now have is from the white man," he argued, but "still we find among us men who are enemies to improvement. What can they be thinking of?"[92] Yet Pitchlynn saw these historical changes as necessary for adapting to an economic system in which they had previously threatened to slide into economic dependency. His pragmatic nationalism asserted Choctaw autonomy and continuity, but also responded to the profound historical changes of the early nineteenth century. In a speech delivered at a debating society in Eagletown, he embraced a teleological narrative about the progress the Choctaws had made compared to the "former state of the nation"—before the innovations of the early nineteenth century. First, he outlined his vision of the Choctaws' living conditions in the traditional past:

1 [crossed out]
2 they were hunters
3 they did not work
4 they had no property
5 they were ignorant
6 war parties ...

Pitchlynn contrasted these conditions with the accomplishments of the "present time," marked by agriculture, economic development, private property, and education:

7 As a nation we have large farms due us from the government ...
8 we are agriculturist
9 we raise stock and hold property
10 we are daily improving
11 we have mechanics
12 we have educated men among us [93]

Pitchlynn's teleological narrative of "progress" hinged on the personal pronouns "they" and "we," which suggested a discontinuity between Choctaw ancestry and the metonymic "we" of his people as they existed in his own time. In Pitchlynn's view, Choctaw nationalism was inherently linked to the cultural and political changes he saw as underway among his people, and depended on distancing their nation from the way of life of his ancestors, which Pitchlynn believed to be a hindrance to economic development.

By appealing to such dominant ideologies of historical progress, Pitchlynn's disavowal of ancestry represents a form of mimicry, Homi K. Bhabha's term for the ambivalent "play of power" through which colonial subjects access avenues of authority. Catering to the colonizer's desire for "a reformed, recognizable Other," mimicry establishes "a subject of a difference that is almost the same, but not quite."[94] Does this mean, however, that Peter Pitchlynn was a self-hating Choctaw? Had his consciousness been colonized by Western ideas about savagery and civilizations? Historian Donna Akers has suggested that Pitchlynn's work as a diplomat and tribal leader evinces a "syncretic identity," since even though he "continued to assert his identity as 'Choctaw' throughout his life," it was not "that of the traditional people."[95] But Pitchlynn's disavowal of Choctaw ancestry was not simply the rhetoric of a mixed-race leader who felt himself suspended between white and Native culture. To imagine Pitchlynn as wavering between two opposite ends of a cultural spectrum—neither wholly Euro-American nor wholly Choctaw—risks explaining away his rhetoric as merely a "symptom" of his cultural location, rather than taking his writings seriously as public discourse or statements of governmental policy.

Rather, Pitchlynn's speeches on nationalism are part of a wider intellectual tradition in which Native writers problematized the link between present and past generation as *only* a relation of continuity. For instance, in his 1826 "An Indian's Address to the Whites," the Cherokee newspaper editor Elias Boudinot proclaimed the Cherokee Nation's capacity for cultural change in a similar way. Boudinot saw the civilization project as a means to safeguard Cherokee nationhood, and this argument hinged on highlighting the difference between present and past generation of Cherokees. "I am not as my fathers were," Boudinot wrote, since "broader means and nobler influences have fallen upon me. Yet I was not born as thousands are, in a stately dome and amid the congratulations of the great, for on a little hill, in a lonely cabin, overspread by the forest oak I first drew my breath; and in a language unknown to learned and polished nations, I learnt to lisp my fond mother's name."[96] Like Pitchlynn, Boudinot located the Cherokee people's cultural and historical changes in his own person: from first lisping his mother's name to writing his "address," his own education testified to a narrative of change that made him "not as my fathers were." This change, however, was also a catalyst for his patriotic sentiments: "I have had greater advantages than most of my race," Boudinot wrote, "and I now stand before you delegated by my native country to seek her interest, to labour for her respectability, and by my public efforts to assist in raising her to an equal standing with other nations of the earth."[97] Through the metonymy of his own experience, Boudinot tried to disaggregate the idea of Choctaw peoplehood from the need to demonstrate *only* cultural continuity.

In Pitchlynn's speeches, this complex negotiation of national culture manifested as an emphasis on property and technology. If nationalism was a form of relatedness that existed laterally in the present, he urged against romanticizing the Choctaw past without considering the comforts many people enjoyed in the present, as he argued at the temperance celebration in 1842.[98] Again, Pitchlynn concretely outlined the contrasts between the postremoval Choctaw Nation and its ancestral past. Their ancestors, Pitchlynn explained,

> ... had no schools
> No farming utensils, save the most rude kind.
> No horses, no cattle, no hogs, for these came from the white man.
> The only property which they owned was the bow ...
> They had laws, but such as suited only their conditions ... laws regulating ... war parties ...
> We are the descendants of a naked people who knew nothing of the blessings which we are now enjoying.[99]

If Pitchlynn's nationalism was based on an embrace of new knowledge and institutions ("Who would give up his Education for what all our fathers knew? Who is willing to give up our laws for the laws of our fathers?"), it was equally dependent on the availability of goods and technologies, which he saw as a measure of the success or failure of Choctaw civilization. "Who of us is willing [to give] up his plough for the wooden hoe?" he asked. "Who is willing to give up his horse, cattle, and hogs? ... Who is willing to give up his fine clothes and warm blankets now? ... Who is willing to give up the Blacksmith Shops, who is willing to give [up] the spinning wheel?"[100] His preference for present conditions was thus rooted in people's ability to hold property and the availability of goods and animals to own. Suggesting that individual well-being would lead to collective well-being, Pitchlynn translated the discourse of nationalism from one about ancestry and land into one about new institutions, property, and individual welfare.

This argument had implications for his views on the relation between nation and territory as well, since his embrace of all things "new" uncoupled Choctaw nationalism from the idea of an "original" homeland. He argued that although the Choctaw had previously believed there was no other homeland besides "that which we had been driven from," after removal "our country" was in Indian Territory: "It is our home and we love it." If in his 1828 removal diary he had written about Indian Territory with ambivalence at best, now he embraced their lands in Indian

Territory as a new basis for Choctaw identity. "The chief wish of our hearts," he noted, "is to live & remain upon it undisturbed, and rather than be driven from it we would meet any foe that would come to dispossess us from it."[101] In doing so, he even decentered his people's traditional emergence story, which holds that the Choctaws originally emerged from Nanih Waiya, or "Mother Mound," the ancient earthworks in present-day Winston County, Mississippi.[102] Pitchlynn, however, assigned Nanih Waiya to a mythical past that was not necessarily central to Choctaw nationhood: while he acknowledged that some believed that his people "came out of the Earth at Nanih Waiya," he argued that there was no firm "account given us of [the] country from whence we came."[103] Rather than tracing the idea of Choctaw peoplehood directly to cultural traditions, he offered a more complex negotiation of mythology, land, and national origins.

Pitchlynn thus articulated a vision of Indian nationalism that depended on a complex narrative of peoplehood, in which ancestry represented continuity as well as change. As postcolonial theorist Frantz Fanon argues in *The Wretched of the Earth*, the appeal to a "national culture" runs the risk of claiming a cultural essence that has little to do with a colonized people's actual conditions—it may evoke merely a "folklore" in which "an abstract populism is convinced it has uncovered the popular truth."[104] For Pitchlynn, to locate a "popular truth" of nationhood in the past would mean upholding their former living conditions as the "essence" of Choctaw nationhood, which was a problem given the many changes in education, industry, politics, and social life that he had championed. Pitchlynn therefore made the double move of embracing Choctaw ancestry as what Anthony Smith calls the "ethnie," the "preexisting traditions and heritages that have coalesced over the generations," while disavowing the living conditions of these past generations.[105] This double move recalls Homi K. Bhabha's argument that expressions of nationalism do not simply identify a body politic defined by national boundaries, but activate more "complex strategies of cultural identification and discursive address that function in the name of ... 'the nation.'"[106] Suspended between past and present, Pitchlynn's idea of Choctaw peoplehood problematized any facile connection between the *nation* and a cultural essence.

This does not mean that Pitchlynn castigated traditional customs wholesale. In 1843, he publicly decried that Choctaw Academy had exacerbated a loss of culture and language among its students, and that the school's pan-Indian student body had led them to forget "all their customs, their language, their relatives, their national attachments."[107] Overall, however, Pitchlynn's pragmatic nationalism saw traditional knowledge as something that was rather separate from the economic and educational development he promoted. Pitchlynn's embrace of new goods and institutions—and his call not to romanticize the past—expressed a particularly nineteenth-century form of nationalism that evoked what Benedict Anderson terms an "imagined community" rooted in a shared feeling of simultaneity with others, rather than tracing a cultural continuity with the ancestral past.[108] Pitchlynn made it clear that if the historical and mythological origins of the Choctaws offered a measure of cultural cohesion as a nation-people, they were also something to move away from, noting that "nothing will cause us greater sorrow than to see them ignorant and miserable," as he believed their forefathers had been.[109] Rather than an adherence to any soil or cultural essence, nationalism meant an investment in Choctaw institutions, and to love one's country meant to "promote the happiness of our people" by investing in education, labor, and agriculture:

> We will be proud of every child that can read his books.
> We will be proud of our schools, [because] they are lights to a nation
> We will be proud of our churches—
> Mills . . . blacksmith shops, salt works—
> We will love to look upon the good farms in our country,
> And every kind of living stock we see grazing upon our prairies.
> For all is ours—it belongs to our country and helps to give it a good name.[110]

For Pitchlynn, this "we" was the essence Choctaw nationhood—a sense of patriotism through which people were connected to institutions, and that traded on a wider ethics of community responsibility and care.

Pitchlynn's promotion of cultural change, then, was a more complex negotiation than merely a narrative of "assimilation." His speech constructed the project of "civilization" as a form of Choctaw exceptionalism vis-à-vis other Indian nations—a rhetoric of nation-building that hinged on a form of colonial mimicry. Couched in the language of progress and civilization, Pitchlynn's speeches on education reflect that nineteenth-century nationalisms were typically driven by the economic and political interests of elites and intellectuals, who tapped into community sentiments to advance their own leadership positions, all the while promoting projects of institutional and economic reform.[111] Calling for the modernization of the Choctaw Nation, Pitchlynn's fraught rhetoric of progress engaged the ideological tensions in the debate over Indian education during the era of removal. For Pitchlynn these concerns were not purely an intellectual matter but also immediately practical. Wielding political agency in projects of education and reform, Pitchlynn defended a vision of change and modernization that his own life and career bore witness to.

"The Blessings Which We Are Now Enjoying" | 153

GLOOMY FOREBODINGS: INDIAN TERRITORY AND
THE "REMONSTRANCE" OF PETER PITCHLYNN

By the time the 1840s drew to a close, Peter Pitchlynn's work as a diplomat to the United States extended his efforts to promote tribal control over the Choctaws' educational and governmental institutions. In the early years of the decade, the General Council had appointed him to make frequent trips to Washington, for negotiations about annuities, educational expenses, and land claims. He had also been involved in the diplomatic negotiations with the Chickasaw Nation, who came to live on the Choctaw Nation's western lands in Indian Territory after removal.[112] Established as something of a career diplomat, in 1848 he published a collaboratively written critique of American policy proposals regarding the administration of Indian Territory. That year, the US House of Representatives considered a bill to reorganize Indian Territory, proposing that the different nations who lived there be united under one territorial government, with representation in Congress. In protest against this bill, Pitchlynn cowrote and delivered a speech titled the "Remonstrance of Col. Peter Pitchlynn, Choctaw Delegate." Arguing for the insurmountability of intertribal differences, Pitchlynn's "Remonstrance" protested the bill on nationalist grounds, prioritizing Choctaw sovereignty over a remapping of Indian country that would only be expedient to the American government. Through this collaborative project, Pitchlynn turned his critique of the Congressional proposal into an intellectual defense of Choctaw sovereignty.

Delivered by Pitchlynn in the House of Representatives in January 1849, the speech was written collaboratively with unknown coauthors; historian W. David Baird notes that the "inspiration" and "imagery" may have been Pitchlynn's but the statement was drafted by others, as was the case with many of his state papers.[113] The congressional bill was defeated that same year, although it probably never stood much of a chance to begin with.[114] Moreover, the 1848 proposal was nothing new, as the political organization of Indian Territory had been a matter of debate in Congress for decades. In 1834, it was in fact Isaac McCoy who proposed a congressional bill to establish a territorial government in Indian Territory, and similar bills had been considered in 1836, 1837, and 1838, although none of them had passed.[115] The 1848 proposal—meant to "provide for the organization of an Indian Territory west of the Mississippi River"—was the work of the Committee on Indian Affairs in the House of Representatives, headed by the Pennsylvania Whig Abraham McIlvaine, whose short career in the House was unremarkable except for an impassioned speech in 1847 against the Mexican-American War.[116] McIlvaine's bill proposed that the territories west of Missouri and Arkansas—between the Platte River and the Mexican border—would be organized as a territory "reserved for the use of the various Indian tribes," who would retain a legal right to the lands within its boundaries.[117] The different nations' councils would still be able to conduct "such government for the regulation of their internal affairs as to them may seem proper," as far as this was consistent with the United States constitution and laws.[118] But the Territory would also have a governor and a secretary, appointed by the president of the United States, as well as a general council of representatives who would meet yearly to make laws governing "the intercourse among the several tribes."[119]

Despite the odds being against the congressional bill from the beginning, the "Remonstrance" is significant in its argument for placing Native leaders front and center in governmental decision-making about Indian country. Pitchlynn's speech was eloquent on the colonial imposition that the territorial reorganization represented: "We look with gloomy forebodings to the passage of this bill," Pitchlynn wrote, "and should it be the pleasure of Congress to enact it we earnestly pray that we (the Choctaws) may be excluded from the operations of it. Bad men will use it as a means of introducing discord and confusion among our people, and finally driving them from their present happy home to wander on the shores of the Pacific, or sink in its deep waters."[120] Pitchlynn saw the territorial scheme as "evil to all the Indian tribes," but he specifically urged against it "in behalf of my own people."[121] In the first place, the plan looked like a potential repeat of the State of Mississippi extending its laws over the Choctaws in 1830, which had originally driven them from their homelands. He recalled the violence of removal, when "for a mere pittance we yielded to you our country in Mississippi, the most beautiful and productive, rendered dear to us by the associations of our youth, the traditions of our people, and the graves of our fathers."[122] Using the intimate language of nationhood—"our country," "our youth," "our people," "our fathers"—Pitchlynn's remonstrance protested the territorial scheme as a potential repeat of a historical injustice that had a profound impact on people's lives. Imagining that the bill would again "drive them from their present happy home," Pitchlynn used the history of removal in a typological move, suggesting that the only prospect would be more removals, which would perpetuate a wandering state that was incompatible with Choctaw civilization.

This collaborative diplomatic text echoed Pitchlynn's long-standing ideas about Choctaw civilization, which he considered foundational to the Nation's political status and its claim to their lands in Indian Territory. He argued that the Choctaws were at a different stage of "civilization" compared to other Indian nations in the region, and he mobilized this idea once again to assert a notion of

Choctaw exceptionalism. Their success in establishing Euro-American practices and institutions rendered their reform complete: "Schools, civilization upon Christian principles, agriculture, temperance and morality are the only politics we have among us; and adhering to these few primary and fundamental principles of human happiness, we have flourished and prospered: hence we want none others."[123] Pitchlynn argued that these institutions and ideologies were central to Choctaw nationhood, and because their history of institution-building distinguished them from other nations in Indian Territory, they should not be organized as one political unit: "There is no community of interest among them ... for that which will promote the interest of the hunters, induced the agriculturists to idle their time and neglect their farms.... Their laws and customs are wholly different—that which is regarded as a virtue by the civilized Indians, being considered as a weakness by the hunters; and those actions which are regarded as manly and heroic by the wandering tribes, are vices of the darkest character among the others."[124] In short, their different places on an imagined scale of civilization made their interests too different to be governed by a single state. Although "beautiful in theory," he argued, the bill would be "destructive to all the long cherished hopes of the friends of the red men, as it would introduce discord, dissensions, and strife among them."[125]

Of course, the Choctaws were not unique in Indian Territory in their adoption of new forms of education, political organization, and alphabetic writing—the hallmarks of Pitchlynn's "civilization." But Pitchlynn emphasized intertribal differences as a means to amplify Choctaw national character. In doing so, he modified the paradigm of what Maureen Konkle names the "theory of Indian difference." Formulated by the Scottish Enlightenment historian William Robertson in *History of the Discovery and Settlement of North America* (1777), the idea of "Indian difference" presumed the moral inferiority of Native Americans that kept them from rising from a state of nature, as it made them ill-disposed to labor, intellectual improvement, or political organization beyond small communities.[126] As a colonial ideology, the theory of Indian difference influenced American policymakers who sought a justification for extinguishing native land title.[127] Pitchlynn's argument against the congressional bill reappropriated the notion of a civilization gap—one that existed not between whites and Native Americans, but between the "civilized" Choctaws and the "wandering" tribes within the borders of Indian Territory. Pitchlynn measured these intertribal differences on a temporal scale, where different nations occupied "different platforms in civilization; some being nearly wholly civilized, others partially so, and others, again, retaining the wandering habits of their fathers."[128] Articulating this idea of intertribal difference, Pitchlynn rejected American political ideas that rendered the situation of all Indian nations as the same.

Pitchlynn saw the differences among these nations in terms of their diplomatic histories: the territorial scheme was sure to fail since different nations had experienced different histories and signed different treaties, which would frustrate the project of territorial reorganization. "Each of these tribes," Pitchlynn wrote, "hold the country they occupy by tenures differing from the others, and according to the terms of the several treaties by which they have acquired them from the United States, and all independent of each other."[129] As the different nations' presence in Indian Territory testified to different histories of Indian diplomacy and treaty-making, the political schemes of American politicians proved necessarily shortsighted in an intertribal geography configured by a complex overlay of different histories of treaty-making. In the end, then, he argued for a form of Choctaw separatism: "We wish simply to be left alone, and permitted to pursue the even tenor of our way."[130] Pitchlynn's concept of Indian sovereignty was the right and ability to be left alone with the Choctaw Nation. It would be naïve, however, to consider this demand for being left to their own devices as a project purely of indigenous separatism. Even if his "remonstrance" did not mention it, the issue of slavery probably weighed heavily on his defense of the present form of Choctaw political organization. Following the end of the Mexican-American war in 1848, American westward expansion spurred national debate on whether slavery would expand in western territories, and Pitchlynn's call to "pursue the even tenor of our way" probably mattered in the context of the Nation's dependence on slave labor: it is likely that Pitchlynn feared that the reorganization of Indian Territory would threaten the legality of slavery in indigenous nations. In this respect, Pitchlynn's pragmatic nationalism was tied in material ways to the interests of elite, property-owning Choctaws whose voice carried great weight in these scenes of Indian diplomacy.

The "Remonstrance of Col. Peter Pitchlynn, Choctaw Delegate" challenged the long history of congressional proposals to reorganize Indian Territory in ways that might sideline the sovereign status of Indian nations. Speaking out against such plans wholesale, Pitchlynn staged a high-profile intervention in US-Choctaw diplomacy, anchoring his arguments in treaty discourse and the rhetoric of his people's exceptionalism. His writing and oratory articulated a nationalist project that ostensibly sought to defend the interests of all tribal nations in Indian Territory while maintaining the status quo of Choctaw governance. Pitchlynn's "Remonstrance" is a reminder that the literatures of Indian diplomacy were defined not only by the colonial dynamics of US settler colonialism, but by intertribal relations and domestic debates over tribal governance and economic interests.

As he brought his "Remonstrance" to the seat of the US government, Pitchlynn insisted on a future in which the Choctaw people would continue to have the last word in such debates. However, in an American empire in which race-based hierarchies determined social and political life, Pitchlynn also gave carte blanche to ideas of race and property that undergirded the history of racialized dispossession and disenfranchisement in the nineteenth century.

A CONTEST OF INTERPRETATION: DIPLOMACY AND
THE LITIGATION OF INDIAN REMOVAL

Peter Pitchlynn's long career as a diplomat illustrates that by the middle of the nineteenth century, a generation of American Indian activists emerged who found new ways to negotiate the place of Indian nations in US empire. Through the channels of Indian diplomacy, indigenous intellectuals and tribal leaders devised new strategies of Native representation in colonial networks. In *This Indian Country*, historian Frederick Hoxie traces a generation of activists who were formally educated and drew on new strategies and legal arguments to make their cases, in diplomatic settings and in public discourse. As Hoxie writes, these activists "rose to positions of community leadership, and decided to enter the nation's political arena—as lawyers, lobbyists, agitators, and writers—to defend their communities. They argued that Native people occupied a distinct place inside the borders of the United States and deserved special recognition from the federal government. Undaunted by their adversary's military power, these activists employed legal reasoning, political pressure, and philosophical arguments to wage a continuous campaign on behalf of Indian autonomy, freedom, and survival."[131] Although it may be a stretch to call him an "activist," there are parallels between this cohort of activists and the diplomatic projects of Peter Pitchlynn. In the early 1840s he established himself as a lawyer and began a decades-long campaign at the seat of the United States government to represent the claims of Choctaw people who had been defrauded out of land in the wake of removal. In 1854, several years after his protest against the congressional bill on Indian Territory, Pitchlynn traveled to Washington as the leader of a delegation that contested the legacies of the Treaty of Dancing Rabbit Creek (1830), an effort that cemented his status as a political figure. In carrying out this diplomatic work—through speeches, petitions, negotiations, and letter-writing—Pitchlynn embraced Euro-American ideologies that saw indigenous lands not through the lens of traditional values but through a discourse on property rights that was linked materially to Choctaw institution-building. Defying static notions of culture and community, Pitchlynn reiterated his ideas about a pragmatic Choctaw nationalism, and if he generated anticolonial critiques of the practice of treaty-making, he also defended education as a resource for indigenous self-determination. Bringing his long-standing ideas about Choctaw nationhood into the arena of Indian diplomacy, he spearheaded a collaborative project that reconciled colonial critique with the object of Choctaw nation-building.

When they traveled to Washington in 1854, Pitchlynn and his fellow delegates sought to contest a history of land grabs that had taken place two decades earlier, in the wake of the Treaty of Dancing Rabbit Creek, the Choctaw removal treaty. Namely, Article Fourteen of the treaty stipulated that every Choctaw citizen who chose to remain in Mississippi would receive a "reservation of land" if they registered with the Indian agent. After five years, they would get American citizenship while also retaining their privileges as Choctaw citizens, in effect becoming dual citizens. Yet as historian Arthur DeRosier writes, the Indian agent William Ward had been "ardent in his wish to see no Indian remain in the state" and "put off registering the Choctaws as long as he could, pretending at times to be ill, and occasionally going into hiding." Although Ward "reluctantly registered a few Choctaws out of token compliance," he found different ways to "defraud the Indians."[132] Because of Ward's corruption, many Choctaw individuals lost significant amount of lands that they were not compensated for in any way. When the US government first investigated Ward's conduct in 1838, it found "obvious and overwhelming" evidence of fraud and launched several subsequent investigations.[133] In short, if Article Fourteen had held out the possibility for a continuous Choctaw community in Mississippi, after 1830 those Choctaw people who remained were exposed to "an orgy of white theft and violence" that eradicated their land title in ways that exceeded even the terms of the Treaty of Dancing Rabbit Creek.[134] During the 1854 delegation, Pitchlynn and his collaborators claimed that the "net proceeds" from these Mississippi lands ought to be paid in a lump settlement, which they sought to secure through a new treaty that would "combine all the individual claims against the United States into one large demand" of three million dollars. The financial settlement would then be "administered locally by the tribal council."[135]

This collaborative project represented a new and important type of Indian diplomacy, one in which indigenous delegates drew on legal expertise and political lobbying to litigate a past history of dispossession. The Choctaw General Council approved the delegation in November 1853, and they appointed Pitchlynn, his brother-in-law Samuel Garland, the Reverend Israel Folsom, and the attorney Dickson W. Lewis. To help with the diplomatic work of navigating Washington political networks, they collaborated with a number of men from outside the Choctaw Nation, who helped to strategize their negotiations at the seat of the

US government. First, they employed Albert Pike, a charismatic Arkansas lawyer and poet who advised them on the protocols of diplomacy in Washington. Pike was already familiar with the Choctaw claims case and arranged the assistance of three other collaborators: the attorney John Cochrane; Luke Lea, the former commissioner of Indian Affairs; and Douglas Cooper, the Indian agent to the Choctaws.[136] These collaborators focused on different aspects of the delegation, with Pike outlining the overall strategy, Cochrane conducting many of the correspondences, and Cooper overseeing the financial investigation into the Choctaw claims. Meanwhile the Choctaw delegates provided additional information on the case and Pitchlynn made the speeches in Washington.[137] In the US government, the delegates interacted mainly with George Washington Manypenny, who served as the commissioner of Indian Affairs. At that point, the Office of Indian Affairs had been transferred from the War Department to the Department of the Interior, which meant that Manypenny reported to the Secretary of the Interior, Robert McClelland. The delegates' aim to negotiate a new treaty was not a long shot, as Manypenny was notably open to renegotiating treaties and amending the workings of annuity payments: by the end of his tenure in 1857, he had overseen fifty-two new treaties.[138]

In their diplomatic writings, the Choctaw delegates emphasized the injustice of Choctaw removal and criticized the American government's lack of accountability for its history of treaty-making. But what did it mean for Pitchlynn and his collaborators to seek justice in this case? To argue that the 1830 treaty was invalid altogether would have been a dangerous gamble, since the status of Indian treaties was the basis for the recognition of indigenous sovereignty under American law. In a memorial to Manypenny, therefore, the delegates held that it was "the fixed sentiment of our people, that scarcely one of its executive stipulations has been carried out by the government in a manner to do justice."[139] In other words, the issue was not the treaty itself but the breaking of its terms immediately after. Characterizing the treaty as a living, breathing document, the delegates argued that its history still shaped the Choctaw Nation's current precarious situation. The ongoing disputes about the stipulations of Article Fourteen perpetuated a colonial situation: "Nearly twenty-four years have elapsed since that treaty was made, during the whole of which time there have been contests and disputes ... in regard to the execution of its different stipulations, which ... have kept our people in a state of perplexity, uncertainty, and dependence, extremely embarrassing and prejudicial to their interests and welfare."[140] The treaty of 1830, in other words, was still the cause of social unrest because the government's failure to act on its stipulations compromised the meaning of the treaty and, thereby, the diplomatic relationship that profoundly shaped Choctaw social and economic life.

Put briefly, the delegates argued that the United States had failed to do justice to the profound sacrifices the Choctaw Nation had made in 1830. Removal had been forced on the Choctaws as an impossible choice between two bad options: to become subjects of the state of Mississippi or to be removed to Indian Territory and remain organized as a sovereign nation. This choice, moreover, had been made in the context of unceasing pressure on Choctaw lands from white settlers and the Mississippi government. Pitchlynn therefore argued that although the "great body" of the Nation had "yielded to the policy and solicitations of the government, and consented to remove west," the American government had failed to uphold its end of the bargain. The Choctaws were supposed to have "ample time to prepare" for removal, but the American government had used "every means and appliance ... to hurry us off," making the process of removal "disastrous in the extreme in the loss of both life and property."[141] Meanwhile, when white land-jobbers illegally took the lands of Choctaws who had chosen to stay in Mississippi, the US government had failed to implement justice. "These reservations were sold from them by the government as public land," Pitchlynn wrote, "or they were forcibly disposed of, or by threats and intimidations driven from them, by heartless and lawless white men ... justice required that it should repossess [the Choctaws] of their property, but no effort for that purpose was made." Instead, Choctaw landowners "were told that their reservations were gone, and could not be restored."[142]

Seeking redress for this history of land theft, the end game of the delegates was clear: they sought three million dollars in compensation for lands stolen from Choctaw landowners, to be paid collectively to the nation, separately from their annuities. This meant, of course, that the delegates' understanding of "land" in these negotiations was not cultural or spiritual, nor primarily about political sovereignty or territoriality. Their address worked from a concept of land that was sectioned off, surveyed, and conveyed in monetary terms: the Mississippi lands were the Choctaw homelands, but they were now also understood as property. This translation of land into property also meant that the delegates' rhetoric of "our people" in fact referred to a more exclusive group of property-owning tribal members. Yet the delegates translated this exclusive notion of justice into a public good, as the compensation for lost lands would serve as a material resource for Choctaw nation-building. They stressed the Choctaws' devotion to educational projects in the Nation, finding that it was "time that all matters between [the Choctaws] and the United States were finally settled" and time to "turn their whole attention and efforts to the improvement of their people, by the extension of schools, and other means of enlightenment and civilization. It is of consequence to them to know what resources they will have to rely upon. It is their wish and intention to devote all their means to that great object."[143] As such, the delegates tried to negotiate not only the payment of their claims, but the conditions under which the resulting funds would be administered. By using the funds for a national project of education, the delegates looked to make a legacy of colonialism into a framework for investing in indigenous nationalism.

When in June 1854 Secretary of the Interior Robert McClelland rejected the Choctaws' claims, the delegates used various tactics to promote their case publicly. McClelland argued that the Treaty of Dancing Rabbit Creek did not conclusively state that the proceeds from the Mississippi lands were to be paid to their original owners, separately from the Choctaw annuity payments.[144] In their response, the delegates claimed that the US government had unfairly ruled against them, since they were a southern slave-holding nation. They remarked that nonslaveholding nations had been more successful in obtaining restitution and asked "whether under a northern administration of Indian affairs we are to fail in our efforts to obtain justice for our people. We are beginning to feel there is, somehow, a difference in the present disposition in policy of the government towards the tribes inhabiting different latitudes."[145] Stepping above McClelland's authority, the delegates appealed to President Franklin Pierce in February 1855, with Pitchlynn asking the president to "interfere and cause justice and liberality to be extended towards us."[146] Although the president did not have the legal power to intervene, this tactic was an instance of an older tradition in which Native delegates "ultimately looked to the president for the enforcement of their treaties whether or not he personally had the power, political or otherwise, to uphold the treaties."[147]

The speech to President Pierce generated wider circulation when the Congressional printer Alfred Nicholson reprinted Pitchlynn's address in a Washington newspaper called the *Daily Union*. Nicholson described Pitchlynn's speech as "a most touching and eloquent address" by which the President "found himself much gratified."[148] In it, Pitchlynn argued that although history could not be reversed, it could be reinterpreted, and doing so would make the country accountable in the present for injustices of the past. In spite of the injustices of Choctaw removal and the subsequent history of land theft, a "fair and just interpretation" of the treaty could still give the Choctaw claimants "the value of the lands ceded by it."[149] The heart of the matter, then, was a contest of historical interpretation. After the 1830 council at Dancing Rabbit Creek, the written terms in the treaty ended up being "less specific than the promises of the commissioners" who were present. And, importantly, it was on these *oral* promises that "our people relied in hastily signing the treaty without its being read to them."[150] As written treaties represented an agreement made in an oral context—and were thus prone to misunderstanding and coercion—the historical interpretation of the treaty therefore ought to take Native people's contestations more seriously than the original treaty commissioners had, especially if there was ambivalence in the language of the treaty. Pitchlynn recognized the problematic relationship between written treaties and the context of their signing, so he argued that "in case of doubt or obscurity" the Choctaws should have "the right, by a well-established principle of interpretation, to go back and refer to the facts ... connected with the formation of the treaty." In particular, to understand the treaty in light of the "promise of the commissioners" would help "to show its meaning and intent."[151]

Explaining the intent of the treaty called for more than simply looking at its text in isolation. Interpreting the treaty also meant contextualizing the time pressures and misunderstandings that surrounded the treaty negotiations, as well as the discrepancies between the written text and the spoken promises of the treaty commissioners, John Eaton and John Coffee. Historical context mattered, and renegotiating the removal treaty was a debate over colonial inequality, in which the inherently asymmetrical power relations between Indian nations and the United States meant that Native people's claims ought to be addressed more seriously than other legal claims. Between countries of equal stature, Pitchlynn argued, treaties should be reexamined "only on the most clear and undoubted grounds."[152] In the context of Indian diplomacy, however, unequal power relations dictated that Indian nations' claims ought to be addressed more quickly and thoroughly: "Between a great, powerful, and enlightened government such as the United States, and a weak, helpless, and comparatively ignorant people like the Choctaws, it is one which should be conceded on the slightest grounds of doubt. We humbly submit that it would ill-become the dignity, honor, and fair fame of this 'great republic' to stand upon technicalities in such a case."[153] By positioning them as "weak" and "helpless," Pitchlynn mobilized colonial tropes of the Choctaws as "weakened" and unenlightened compared to the United States, in effect echoing an understanding of Indian nations as "domestic dependent nations." However, in his speech to Pierce he also insisted on the American government's accountability in reexamining past treaties, by making the colonial relationship between the two nations the central concern.

More than a financial settlement over lost property, the object of the Choctaw delegation was to turn the broken treaty into a public good. They argued that a renegotiated treaty could be a springboard for securing the "means and resources" for advancing the civilizing mission through education. "The future of the Choctaws," they argued, "materially depends upon what is now done, or omitted to be done, for them. They have arrived at a critical point in their history. They have made great advances in civilization. This has been done mainly by education. To promote this great cause, they have exerted every energy, and used all the means and resources they could command, for the purpose."[154] At this "critical point" in history, renegotiating the treaty directly affected the welfare of the Choctaws in the present, and this very moment would determine the nation's future course. They warned that their investment in education was subject to an economy of energy and fatigue and therefore time-sensitive, and the "public spirit" in support of education, they argued, was "in danger of languishing." The Choctaws were "becoming discouraged, and retrograding," realizing "how slow is their progress, and how little is accomplished, compared with what might be effected if their means were more ample."[155] The delegates appealed to what was a common feature of Indian treaties, namely, their rhetoric about American support for Native education as a means to promote their national interest. Indeed, the Treaty of Dancing Rabbit Creek provided for twenty years of financial support for school buildings and teachers in Choctaw Nation, as well as an elite education program "under the direction of the President and at the expense of the US [for] forty Choctaw youths for twenty years."[156] The treaty proclaimed this support for education to be for the "benefit and advantage of the Choctaw people, and to improve their condition"—a notion that Pitchlynn and his delegation eagerly reappropriated two decades later. Working within the framework set forth by the treaty of 1830, the delegates did not undo the imperial logics by which the treaty forced removal and transformed their Mississippi lands into private property, but if Choctaw nationalism was located in political institutions and schools, their negotiations in Washington could be seen as a project of Choctaw nation-building.

When a new treaty was signed in 1855, the delegates had only limited success, securing about $900,000 in payments "for purposes of education" and thereby the "improvement, welfare, and happiness of the Choctaw people and their descendants."[157] The Choctaws' original claim was $3 million, and it was lowered to $2.3 million in the course of the delegation. While their lobbying efforts mattered in direct, financial ways, the delegation still testified to the limited power of Indian nations in relation to the United States. At the same time, the collaborative publications that came out of the 1854 delegation testified to a new type of Indian diplomacy, in which the authorized agents of the Choctaw nation took on the critical examination of past treaties, with an eye on both the historical (and colonial) context of their signing and their promise as a political tool in the present. Pitchlynn's diplomacy was based in what Frederick Hoxie describes as "the proposition that Native futures could be secured by the laws and institutions of the American state," and that Indian nations might "reclaim some portion of their original homeland by invoking the laws and values of their dispossessors."[158] The delegation's criticism of treaty-making did not offer the spectacle of the Native speaker who cursed the American government where it lived. Pitchlynn's appeal worked through rather prosaic means of diplomatic negotiation—through a team of lawyers and an Indian agent—and aimed to secure financial compensation for property.

Renegotiating the treaty did not undo the commodification of land as property or the dispossession of the Choctaws, nor did his reading of removal history offer an alternative to rhetorics of civilization and progress. Like Pitchlynn's 1849 protest against the congressional bill on Indian Territory, this revisiting of Choctaw removal was shaped by situational, multiparty negotiations and the diplomatic conventions in colonial institutions of government. By critiquing the history of treaty-making, however, the delegates traded on the possibility that treaty-stipulated rights might become a vital resource for the project of Choctaw nation-building. These efforts were not the type of colonial resistance that made it into history books or compendiums of "Indian eloquence," but they were an important precedent for contesting the legacies of removal to secure the Choctaws' future in Indian Territory.

"TAKE ME TO MY NATION"

His diplomatic trips to Washington must have caused Peter Pitchlynn to reflect frequently on the differences between Choctaw Nation and the United States, since he captured his ruminations on this subject in one of his more belletristic writings. In around 1850, Pitchlynn wrote a poem that imagines his daughter Rhoda's time away from Choctaw Nation while attending school in Virginia.[159] The poem's persona is a Choctaw girl who is quite literally in a country not her own, and who recognizes the lands in Indian Territory as her familial and ancestral home—the place of her immediate family, her mother's grave, and her "race and kindred":

> My mother's grave is yonder,
> And there it must remain;
> My father's care is tender,
> I wish for home again!
> O, take me to my Nation,
> And let me there remain;
> This other world is strange, strange—
> I wish for home again.[160]

The linking of "home" and "nation" in "Song of a Choctaw Girl" surely calls to mind the history of Choctaw removal, and perhaps this imagery offers a more familiar cultural narrative than Pitchlynn's political writings. After all, over the course of his career as an educator and diplomat, Pitchlynn's ideas about Choctaw nationalism were more prosaic, prioritizing modes of self-definition that were tethered to Euro-American ideologies of land, property, race, and "civilization." For Pitchlynn and his generation of Choctaw leaders, appealing to Indian nationalism meant not only evoking it in an affective sense but also by codifying laws, establishing schools, renegotiating treaties, and—more generally—imagining tribal-national futures beyond the violence of Indian removal.

Pitchlynn's writings remind us that in the nineteenth century, Indian diplomacy played a constitutive role in the emergence of Native American nationalisms as an intellectual tradition. In his diplomatic writings he expressed a concept of Choctaw peoplehood that had a powerful anticolonial purchase, but that also hinged on ideas of civilization and exceptionalism that extended the racial logics of nineteenth-century American empire. In this respect, Pitchlynn's writings reflect that nationalist ideologies do not simply articulate the cultural coherence of a unified, preformed concept of "the nation." As the literary scholar Adam Spry remarks, nationalism is "not an identity but an ideology, a set of political convictions about the right of certain peoples to continue to exist as self-defining, self-governing political bodies."[161] Pitchlynn promoted a concept of Choctaw nationhood that served to advance institutions of government and education as well as the Choctaw Nation's claims to land—those in Indian Territory and those in Mississippi that they had been forced to leave behind. Navigating the networks of Indian diplomacy, Pitchlynn articulated a notion of Choctaw nationhood that was shaped by moments of political opportunity and by colonial ideologies of civilization and progress.

By endorsing a politically expedient notion of Choctaw nationalism, Peter Pitchlynn ignored existing social hierarchies among his people and prioritized the interests of elites whose appeals to justice were rooted in often exclusive claims to property, class, and political power. Yet these appeals to justice also harbored forms of anticolonial critique, and it is precisely this tension that makes Pitchlynn's state papers such an invaluable historical and literary archive. His collaborative publications deserve critical attention because they offer a crucial perspective on how Native tribal leaders and intellectuals asserted indigenous nationalism in all its forms. Pitchlynn's writings contested the colonial practice of treaty-making and claimed political recognition for Choctaw rights within settler institutions. Yet these diplomatic writings also expressed a larger political project—one based less in notions of ancestry or tradition and more in ideas about property and economic opportunity, not to mention ideologies of race and masculinity. They remind us that the literatures of Indian diplomacy were a fraught recourse for contesting the histories of indigenous dispossession.

CHAPTER 4

Rewriting the Native Diplomat

Community and Authority in Ojibwe Letters

In nineteenth-century literary culture, the representation of indigenous politics was deeply shaped by familiar images of the *Indian*. Theater audiences consumed the drama of John Augustus Stone's *Metamora* (1829), readers of novels sympathized with Uncas and Chingachgook in Cooper's *The Last of the Mohicans* (1826), and art lovers admired the portraits of celebrated "chiefs" and "braves" by George Catlin and Charles Bird King. During this age of Native dispossession and settler expansion, stories and images of conquered warrior-leaders offered a means for white settlers to access feelings of guilt and catharsis over a history of colonialism.[1] A key trope in the cultural imagination of the settler state, the figure of the Indian chief became increasingly detached from indigenous nations' own histories and their political status as sovereign nations. To be sure, some writers and historians made serious attempts to write tribal histories based on historical research. In *The Life and Adventures of Black Hawk* (1838), for instance, the historian Benjamin Drake showed a critical stance toward the Americans' conduct in the Black Hawk War and took seriously the ideas and actions of Native leaders and councils.[2] But more typically, as Jean O'Brien demonstrates for New England, the writing of Native history wrote indigenous people "out of existence," by commemorating the "last" Native people to inhabit areas now settled by white Americans, even in places where American Indians were still very much present.[3] Given the prevalent narrative of indigenous erasure and replacement, the figure of the "Indian chief" was popularized not as someone who generated political discourse, but as the subject of art, anthropology, literature, and local history.

As it was taken up in US culture, the figure of the Indian diplomat became less a signifier of sovereign indigenous nationhood than an emblem of American nationalism and empire. This is why the Pawnee delegate Petalesharo was celebrated as a potent symbol for "friendly" tribes in the trans-Mississippi West, and why the Sauk warrior Black Hawk came to be remembered as another iteration of the conquered vanquished warrior-hero. Against this impulse, however, Native speakers themselves continually re-inscribed the figure of the Indian chief with something more politically meaningful. This chapter explores how various Ojibwe writers and orators complicated the representation of tribal political authority in American literary culture, reasserting the political value of Indian diplomacy in a new publication landscape.[4] From Ojibwe communities in different parts of the Great Lakes region, Jane Johnston Schoolcraft, Peter Jones, and George Copway published texts—poetry, autobiography, pamphlets, and speeches—in which the depictions of Indian chiefs and tribal councils spoke to a more grounded vision of US-Ojibwe diplomacy. Their publications examined the life and history of Ojibwe communities whose ancestral connections to the land had been uprooted by settler expansion. At a time when the cultural representation of Indian diplomacy became more and more the purview of fiction and history, their writings staked out a place in American letters where the figure of the Native diplomat retained its role as a signifier of a political indigenous voice.

For the Ojibwe people, the crisis of removal was about the fate of communities marked by locality, language, and shared cultural practices, even as their physical territory stretched far across the Great Lakes region and the border between the United States and British Canada—from the east of Lake Ontario to the west of Lake Manitoba. Against this vast geography, however, the political life of the Ojibwe was rooted in a multitude of smaller communities, whose place in North America was in dialectical opposition to the industrializing United States and the expansion of white settlement in Upper Canada. In this respect, the history of Ojibwe diplomacy registers a central dynamic of nineteenth-century history and culture. According to the cultural theorist Raymond Williams, it was in the nineteenth century that the concept of community came to evoke something more "immediate than society," a form of cultural belonging that stood in contrast to the "state or organized society."[5] As Williams notes, the idea of a "community" is marked by "immediacy and locality" and a "sense of common identity and characteristics," evoking a form of social life that is distinct from "larger and more complex" industrialized and urbanized societies.[6] Since the nineteenth century, indigenous literatures have borne witness to the interplay between indigenous communities and the administration of the settler state. In *That the People Might Live*, Jace Weaver traces a centuries-old tradition of Native literature that expresses "communitism," a community-oriented activism that championed indigenous peoplehood by emphasizing locality and culturally specific practices and beliefs.[7] Even for writers whose homelands stretched across different regions and were part of a transatlantic world of exchange, the representation of Native life spoke to the needs of communities that stood in direct contrast to an expansive American empire.

The representation of Ojibwe diplomacy became a contested site in nineteenth-century American literary culture. Two American writers who worked as Indian Office administrators, Henry Rowe Schoolcraft and Thomas McKenney, brought these negotiations into an expansive print culture. In their works of history and ethnology, Schoolcraft and McKenney co-opted the representation of Indian diplomacy by making the figure of the Ojibwe chief a metonym for indigenous community assent to colonial projects of treaty-making. However, the writings of Schoolcraft's wife, Jane Johnston Schoolcraft, complicated these tropes by recognizing the networks of family and government that were central to indigenous life and diplomacy in the Great Lakes. Likewise, in a wider print culture, Ojibwe authors fashioned publication projects that challenged the cultural translation of Indian diplomacy in governmental and religious networks. In speeches, autobiographies, and published journals, Peter Jones and George Copway asserted notions of indigenous leadership that resisted the colonial narrative in which Ojibwe chiefs stood in for fragile and anachronistic communities that would inevitably be incorporated into a settler regime. While they worked as missionaries within transatlantic networks of reformers, Copway and Jones challenged religious discourses of "pity" and paternalism to enact new forms of Indian diplomacy, asserting rhetorical control over Indian reform in the Great Lakes. Seen together, their publication projects modified the popular metonymy of the Indian chief, offering alternative scripts for understanding the relation between Native leadership, tribal sovereignty, and community life. Put forward as "authorized agents" in new scenes of diplomatic negotiation, Copway and Jones elaborated a politicized Ojibwe voice that negotiated between the need to channel local community interests and to stand in for the abstraction of the Indian *nation*—thus expressing an ambivalent space between community and sovereign indigenous nationhood. As they carried community politics into the realm of public lectures and print publishing, they reauthorized the Indian chief in ways that escaped the romanticizing logics of a colonial culture.

REMEMBERING WAUBOJIIG IN HENRY ROWE SCHOOLCRAFT'S *Literary Voyager*

When it comes to the literary representation of Ojibwe culture in the nineteenth century, the historical and linguistic studies of Henry Rowe Schoolcraft (1793–1864) remain a looming presence. Throughout his career as an explorer, ethnologist, and administrator of Indian affairs, he became the foremost authority on indigenous cultures of the Great Lakes region in the nineteenth century, and the field of Native American studies has long grappled with his vexed legacy. In particular, Schoolcraft became the most prominent curator of Ojibwe language and culture with works such as *Algic Researches* (1839), *The Red Race of America* (1847), and *The Myth of Hiawatha* (1856). Perhaps most famously, his work influenced the American poet Henry Wadsworth Longfellow, who drew on Schoolcraft's writings for the bestselling narrative poem *The Song of Hiawatha* (1855). Schoolcraft's literary career originated in his diplomatic work in the Great Lakes region, where his career as an Indian agent began with an exploratory expedition to Michigan Territory in 1818, led by territorial governor Lewis Cass. Four years later, Cass appointed Schoolcraft as subagent at the Lake Superior Indian agency near Sault Ste. Marie, on St. Mary's River, on the border with British Canada. There he managed the political relations between American traders and indigenous leaders, by enforcing fur-trade regulations and keeping tabs on the conflicts between the Ojibwe and the Sioux, who were long-time adversaries.[8] Schoolcraft's work as Indian agent was part of a larger effort to assert American hegemony in the Lake Superior region. The area around Sault Ste. Marie had been part of Michigan Territory since 1805, and in 1820 Cass tried to open up the region for white settlement. Notwithstanding the imperial aspirations of the United States, it remained predominantly Native space, and historian Michael Witgen has documented Cass's repeated failure to assert American sovereignty in Michigan Territory. Although in 1820 the Americans established Fort Brady near the American settlement at Sault Ste. Marie, fewer than 9,000 Americans lived in Michigan, "a far cry from the 60,000 white male citizens required to form a state under the provisions of the Northwest Ordinance."[9]

With these tenuous inroads of American hegemony, the practice of Indian diplomacy was a crucial focus point for American administrators, and Schoolcraft's career as Indian agent was much helped by his marriage, in 1823, to Jane Johnston (Bamewawagezhikaquay, 1800–1842), who belonged to a prominent Ojibwe family in the area.[10] Her mother Susan Johnston (Ozhaguscodaywayquay, c. 1775–c. 1840) was the daughter of the Ojibwe leader Waubojiig, while her father John Johnston (1762–1828), born in Ireland, was a prominent fur trader in the Sault Ste. Marie region. The Johnston household was an important site of US-Ojibwe diplomacy: in 1820 Susan Johnston had played a crucial role in Henry Schoolcraft's political career when her house was the setting for a peace treaty between the Americans and the Ojibwe of Sault Ste. Marie. When territorial governor Lewis Cass pressured a war leader of the Crane *doodem* (clan) into accepting American supremacy, the negotiations between the Ojibwe and the United States had started off badly. As a woman of social prominence and the daughter of a famous civil chief, Susan Johnston managed to achieve an agreement with the Americans and maintain peace: historian Michael Witgen writes that by working with her son George Johnston and the war leader Shingwaukonse, she "built consensus around the idea of accommodating an American presence at Bow-e-ting [Sault Ste. Marie]." She also held a second council with Lewis Cass at her house, where they agreed that the Ojibwe would sell the Americans a tract of land along St. Mary's River, and in return get financial compensation while retaining hunting and fishing rights "in perpetuity."[11] Through this treaty the Americans claimed a "token degree of American sovereignty at Bow-e-ting," a testament to the role Susan Johnston and her children played as "important cultural brokers." Although the Ojibwe "recognized the potential power of the American state," Witgen notes, the 1820 treaty testified to the fact that the Americans' liminal inroads in Michigan depended on their relations with mixed-race fur-trading families like the Johnstons.[12]

Henry Rowe Schoolcraft's marriage to Jane thus played a crucial role in gaining access to a family that carried "political and social influence" in the Great Lakes region, which Robert Dale Parker describes as a "trilingual Ojibwe, French, and English world of commerce, cultural exchange, government, and daily life."[13] For his literary work, too, Schoolcraft drew heavily on the work of his Ojibwe wife, who wrote some fifty poems during her life and recorded traditional Ojibwe stories and songs.[14] Henry's writings on philology and ethnology became the most visible—and perhaps infamous—literary engagement with Ojibwe history and culture, and Jane's writings also began to catch the interest of a wider literary world. Her records of Ojibwe legends and stories appeared in works such as Chandler Gilman's *Life on the Lakes* (1836) and Anna Brownell Jameson's *Winter Studies and Summer Rambles* (1838), and, a year after Jane Schoolcraft's death, in Margaret Fuller's *Summer on the Lakes, in 1843* (1844).[15]

The connections between literature and diplomacy are a crucial dynamic in the Schoolcrafts' *Muzzeniegen, or, The Literary Voyager*, a manuscript magazine the couple circulated in 1826 and 1827. The publication of the *Literary Voyager* testifies to Henry Schoolcraft's dependence on the Johnstons' knowledge and networks, not only for his work as an Indian agent but for his efforts to establish himself as a "man of letters." He had already tried to launch a print magazine with specimens of what he called "Indian eloquence" that he hoped would present "honorable testimonials of Indian genius and valor" and a "defence of their character."[16] Although his plans for a print magazine faltered, from December 1826 to April 1827 Schoolcraft cowrote and edited the *Literary Voyager* to pass the time during the harsh, isolating winter in Sault Ste. Marie.[17] As Laura Mielke describes it, the manuscript magazine "included local news, Ojibwe stories, commentary on American Indian languages, and poems" and was "circulated among his neighbors at Sault Sainte Marie and among his peers in Detroit and various eastern cities."[18] It grew out of a literary society the Schoolcrafts had inaugurated in 1826, which Henry described as a "little means of supporting existence in so remote a place, and keeping alive . . . the sparks of literary excitement."[19] While it is tempting to attribute to Jane Johnston Schoolcraft an active role as editor and compiler of the magazine, beyond her contribution of various writings, the editorial work was done by Henry, who controlled the overall content of the magazine.[21] The bulk of the magazine was comprised of Henry Schoolcraft's writings on American Indian customs, traditions, languages, and history. But he also included writings by his wife Jane and her family—who contributed as poets, storytellers, translators, and writers—and several other acquaintances, including a friend in Vermont, a

FIGURE 4.1
Portrait of Ozhaguscodaywayquay (Woman of the Green Glade), wife of John Johnston. Unknown date and artist. Johnston Family Papers, Box 1, HS17258. Bentley Historical Library, University of Michigan.

merchant who sold supplies at Fort Brady, and Zina Pitcher, an army surgeon who later became the mayor of Detroit.[20]

The *Literary Voyager* extended the diplomatic relations forged by Henry's connections to the Johnstons, and in this regard, the magazine's reflection on their family history was also an engagement with the history of Indian diplomacy in the Great Lakes region. Over three issues, Schoolcraft included a historical account of the Ojibwe civil chief Waubojiig (1747–1793), Jane's grandfather on her mother's side. Jane's mother, Susan Johnston, narrated the story to him, and since she did not speak English and Henry's knowledge of Anishinaabemowin was rudimentary, it is likely that one of her children—Jane, George, or William—interpreted for them.[22] Writing the *Literary Voyager* was "a family activity," to use Laura Mielke's words, and the narrative was further embellished with Waubojiig's "war song," which was written by Jane's father, John Johnston. Introducing Susan Johnston as the narrator, Schoolcraft described her both as a representative informant from a larger cultural group ("a female of Chegoimegon on Lake Superior, the ancient capital of the Chippewa nation") and as a person of elevated status (the "daughter of the reigning chief of that place"). Noting that she had "every means of learning their traditions," Schoolcraft gave "full credence ... to the general incidents of her narrative," and added that her marriage to Johnston did not diminish her attachment to her community.[23] Although her marriage had led her to move "to the comforts and conveniences of a civilized dwelling," she still "remained firmly attached to the traditions of her people, and continued to speak only the Indian language."[24] In other words, Schoolcraft's introduction established Susan Johnston as the *author* of the text, identifying her as the narrator while testifying to the reliability of her narrative based on her social status, her knowledge of the Ojibwe language, and her authentic attachment to the "traditions of her people."

As transcribed by Schoolcraft, Susan Johnston rendered a textured history of Ojibwe settlement in the Great Lakes region, situating Waubojiig's life in the context of profound social and political changes. Her account covered everything from the Ojibwe system of *doodemag* (clans) to the geopolitics of the Seven Years War, the Battle of Quebec, ecological changes, intertribal conflicts (with the Sioux, Sauk, and Meskwaki Nations), historical migrations, the successes and failures of diplomacy, US-Indian councils, and commerce. Amid all of this, Waubojiig emerges as the central actor of this history and as a natural embodiment of Ojibwe peoplehood. Well before Thomas Carlyle's articulation of the "Great Man Theory," Schoolcraft editorialized about the "effect of great personal prowess, and a reputation for bravery and sagacity, among savage nations."[25] He argued that the "whole power and destiny of such nations" depended on the "private character of a few great men," and Waubojiig was able to "rouse and direct the energies" of his people, and to see their true needs where they could not: "His views were enlightened, compared with the mass of Indians who surrounded him. He saw the true situation, not only of his relatives, but of the whole nation; and he resolved to use all of his influence to rouse them to a true sense of it. With this view he admonished them to be active and diligent. To hunt well, and to fight well, were the cardinal maxims of his life, upon which he believed the happiness and independence of the nation to depend."[26] In this transcript of Susan Johnston's narrative, Waubojiig's legitimacy as an Ojibwe leader depends not only on his supposedly more "enlightened" thinking, but on his adherence to codes of hunting and warfare—signifiers of national character that Waubojiig expressed through his "respectable powers as an orator."[27] In this respect, his authority was encoded in his very physiognomy: his "ready flow of words" was complemented by his imposing "stature of 6 feet 6 inches in height," his "keen searching black eye," and his overall "countenance and bearing commanding high respect."[28]

Henry Rowe Schoolcraft's transcript of the narrative imagines a metonymic link between the political representation of Native communities and the figure of the eloquent male Indian orator. Likewise, in his poem "The Otagamiad"—included in the March 1827 issue of the *Literary Voyager*—a fictionalized version of Waubojiig emerges as the warrior-leader who embodies his community's virtues. In heroic couplets and iambic pentameter, Schoolcraft's poem gives an account of a warrior named "Ojeeg" and his war council, tapping into a well-established tradition of neoclassical verse about American Indian leaders. Translating into verse form the types of negotiations that Schoolcraft knew intimately from his work as Indian agent, the opening lines set the action at La Pointe, the historical Waubojiig's home on Chequamegon Bay, on the southwest shore of Lake Superior:

> In northern climes there liv'd a chief of fame,
> La Pointé his dwelling, and Ojeeg his name,
> Who oft in war had rais'd the battle cry,
> And brav'd the rigors of an Arctic sky[29]

Because of his accomplishments in both wartime and peacetime, Ojeeg is lifted to his "simple forest throne," and when he sees his nation "hem'd around by foes" he convenes a war council. Different council members offer their thoughts on the prospect of war: Camudwa, "fam'd for eloquence of tongue," urges not war but to use "pliant speech, to gain our purpos'd will," while the "sage" Canowakeed preaches "calm judgment."[30] As Maureen Konkle puts it, the poem offers a narrative of democratic deliberation, building toward the moral that "these Indian warriors are too philosophical to murderously take up the tomahawk and scalping knife."³¹ The council's commitment to democratic process delays the decision on whether to go to war, and the poem ends on a lack of resolution:

> Each for himself, both knows & feels & sees,
> The growing evils of a heartless peace,
> And the sole question, of this high debate,
> Is—shall we longer suffer—longer wait,
> Or, with heroic will, for strife prepare,
> And try the hazard of a gen'ral war! ³²

Even as Canowakeed leans toward warfare, the council offers a display of "high debate," a form of rational political discourse through which Schoolcraft evokes an ideal of democratic deliberation. In true republican fashion, the council gathers together to weigh the decision, "each for himself" bringing their private thoughts and emotions to the table. Together the council members embody a variation on the Fergusonian noble savage, whose civic-mindedness is both the origin of

FIGURE 4.2
Photograph of a portrait of Jane Johnston Schoolcraft. Unknown date and artist. Johnston Family papers, Box 1, HS156. Bentley Historical Library, University of Michigan.

and model for democratic sentiment, and thereby a natural representation of an American Indian community.[33] Fictionalizing this scene of indigenous politics, Schoolcraft made the Ojibwe council a vehicle for a romanticized image of the Native leader, whose commitment to democratic process makes him a safe arbiter of political and military decisions.

Yet the *Literary Voyager* was also a dialogic space that decentered Henry Schoolcraft's interpretations, and the same issue of March 1827 included a poem by Jane Johnston Schoolcraft that brought the representation of Waubojiig back into an intimate family setting. According to the date below the poem, Jane's "Invocation to My Maternal Grandfather, on Hearing His Descent from Chippewa Ancestors Misrepresented" was written a few years earlier, in 1823. Written under the pen name "Rosa," her poem corrects a form of misinformation, speaking back to the rumor that her grandfather Waubojiig was not of Ojibwe but Sioux ancestry, and thus belonged to an enemy nation. As Robert Dale Parker writes, the poem suggests a "commitment to family history and pride" but also "worry about betrayal ... rumor, and slander," as well as a "vulnerability over family reputation in [Jane Johnston Schoolcraft's] and her mother's Ojibwe world."[34] An "invocation" typically evokes a poet's summoning of a muse or deity, but the opening lines of Schoolcraft's poem call on a deceased loved one: "Rise bravest chief! of the mark of the noble deer." This invocation establishes Waubojiig both as a member of the *doodem* (clan) of the reindeer and as the poem's intimate audience.[35] In this intimate, familial setting, the persona challenges the spoken rumors about his lineage, suggesting that the "foes of thy line / With coward design / Have dar'd, with black envy / to garble the truth."[36] The words of Waubojiig's slanderers have lingering effects in the present, as they "stain, with a falsehood, thy valorous youth." Yet the next stanza conveys a marked contrast between the "warlike" Ojibwe chief and the "impotent" words of his detractors:

> They say, when a child, thou wer't taken from the Sioux,
> And with impotent aim,
> To lessen thy fame,
> Thy warlike lineage basely abuse,
> . . . .
> And thou noble chieftain! art nerveless and dead,
> The bow all unstrung, and thy proud spirit fled.[37]

Rendering an intimate conversation between an Ojibwe writer and her grandfather, Schoolcraft's "Invocation" challenges outsiders' understanding of who Waubojiig was and how he was remembered. If the *Voyager*'s historical narrative—as narrated by Susan Johnston—presented oral transmission as a reliable source of information, Jane's poem evokes the potential for misinformation within spoken discourse. Correcting the misrepresentation of her grandfather's lineage, her poem claims Waubojiig not only as a historical figure of great political significance, but as a member of an Ojibwe family that still held a crucial position in the political landscape of the Sault Ste. Marie region.

The different accounts of Waubojiig connected the Johnstons' family networks to a history of Ojibwe government and diplomacy, representing their Ojibwe ancestor in a way that appealed to the most positive connotations of indigenous community: connectedness, democratic deliberation, and a natural relationship between community members and tribal leadership. But if the *Voyager* traded on the romance of the Indian chief as an indicator of community sentiment and innate democratic virtues, it also offered a more dialogic representation of the overlapping spheres of family networks and Great Lakes Indian diplomacy. Her husband made the eloquent male tribal leader central to the drama of Indian diplomacy, but Jane's poem is a reminder that at least in Sault Ste. Marie, such figures were also members of extended family networks. This is not to suggest that the juxtaposition of the Schoolcrafts' writings in the *Literary Voyager* register a conflict between Henry's "official" public voice as Indian agent and Jane's "private" voice as his wife. It is important not to romanticize Jane Johnston Schoolcraft as representing a poetic form of "resistance" against her husband's work as a purveyor of ethnological knowledge about the Ojibwe. Moreover, as it bridges family networks and diplomatic traditions, the *Literary Voyager* refuses a binary in which Susan Johnston and her daughter Jane represent Ojibwe "culture" and Henry Rowe Schoolcraft represents American bureaucracy and diplomacy. After all, Native women like Susan Johnston performed crucial roles in Indian diplomacy, and her narration of Waubojiig's life was a repository of political-historical information. The *Literary Voyager* thus extended the fluid logics of Indian diplomacy at Sault Ste. Marie, in which governmental and family networks were tightly interwoven and in which Henry Rowe Schoolcraft carried his work as Indian agent into literary and philological conversations. Rooted in the life of an Ojibwe family and the world of Great Lakes indigenous politics, the *Voyager* captured a dimension of indigenous life that could not be reduced to any facile notion of Native community.

PICTURING SHINGABAWOSSIN: SCHOOLCRAFT, MCKENNEY,
AND THE METONYMY OF THE OJIBWE CHIEF

If Henry Rowe Schoolcraft's writings on Waubojiig detailed an already distant history of Ojibwe diplomacy, he also commented on living political leaders with whom he had sat in council as an Indian agent. In the second issue of the

Literary Voyager, Schoolcraft included a biographical piece on the civil chief Shingabawossin (c. 1763–1830), interpreting his life and political career into a signifier of indigenous community sentiment and political authority. A civil chief of the Crane *doodem* who lived along St. Mary's River, Shingabawossin ("The Figured Stone") had fought alongside the British in the War of 1812, but he was also a signatory of the 1820 treaty at Sault Ste. Marie and the 1825 treaty at Prairie du Chien. Schoolcraft had conducted interviews with him on multiple occasions, and his narrative represented Shingabawossin as a logical embodiment of Ojibwe authority, being a "dignified & majestic man," at once "respectful and respected."[38] His appearance matched this status. Schoolcraft described him as "six feet three inches in height and well proportioned, erect in his carriage, and of a commanding and dignified aspect." Schoolcraft saw in Shingabawossin a dedicated public servant, whose commitment to democratic process held a promise for intertribal peace. He had given up his time to attend "the public councils convened under the authority of government to secure a permanent peace, with the tribes with whom the Chippewas are at variance." As a "man of policy" he had recognized early on that the "prosperity of his nation depended upon peace, and an assiduous attention to their ordinary occupations," by which Schoolcraft presumably meant trade and agriculture. This "good sense," Schoolcraft argued, pointed him to the "proper course to be pursued by his band," and his "kindness, and benevolence rendered him beloved."[39] Like Waubojiig before him, Shingabawossin fit the bill for representing Schoolcraft's favored notion of the democratically minded Indian chief.

In the *Literary Voyager*, Schoolcraft romanticized Shingabawossin as an embodiment of community sentiment, encoding his collaboration with US treaty commissioners as Ojibwe "assent" to the US colonial project in the Great Lakes. He imagined Shingabawossin as the "organ of expressing the wants of his band, and the medium through which they received advice and aid from the officers of government."[40] Reconciling Ojibwe "wants" with American "advice and aid," Schoolcraft's account of Shingabawossin located the validity of treaty-making in the character of this sympathetic Ojibwe chief. In Schoolcraft's eyes, given the "qualities both of his head and heart," Shingabawossin's signing of the 1820 treaty was simply an act of reason and good intentions. The same held true for the treaty of Fond du Lac of 1826, which stipulated the Americans' right to engage in mineral mining in Ojibwe lands in present-day Wisconsin and Minnesota. Schoolcraft recalled that it was Shingabawossin who suggested that the American treaty commissioners insert "a provision for calling together the body of the Chippewa nation at Fond du Lac," to "procure their assent" to the articles of the treaty. According to Schoolcraft, Shingabawossin did so because he was simply "a prudent ruler, who was sensible of the true interests of his tribe."[41]

Yet Schoolcraft's interpretation belied a more complex process by which Shingabawossin was "authorized" as a representative of the Ojibwe people. During the negotiations at Fond du Lac in 1826, Shingabawossin's role as signatory depended more on the strategies of American treaty commissioners than on Ojibwe community authorization. As historian Michael Witgen argues, the US commissioners at Fond du Lac had tried to make different Ojibwe leaders "acknowledge that they spoke for all of the Chippewa people" and ultimately designated Shingabawossin as "first chief of the Chippewa nation." By elevating the chief's status, the commissioners recognized that he was a "prominent civil leader at Sault Sainte Marie, a village of enormous political, spiritual, and cultural importance to the Anishinaabeg." But in doing so, they also tried to "simplify the complex leadership patterns and social relationships" of the Ojibwe people in an effort to make them "governable."[42] Extending the logics of these treaty negotiations, Schoolcraft's sketch of Shingabawossin overlooked the decentered politics of Ojibwe government in order to render dispersed Ojibwe communities as a coherent "nation." This coherent and expansive idea of the Ojibwe "nation" was a form of mistranslation that was convenient to US administrators; by interpreting Shingabawossin's individual reason as an expression of community-based decision-making, Schoolcraft saw the Ojibwe leader as a signifier of community assent to US colonial claims, as tenuous as those were on St. Mary's River.

From an American perspective, then, there was a real political value in representing Ojibwe leaders through the trope of the sympathetic Indian chief. In this regard, it is not surprising that Shingabawossin entered a wider print culture, through the writings of Thomas McKenney and the portraits of James Otto Lewis. As the first head of the Indian Office, McKenney had appointed Lewis to make portraits of Native American leaders at different treaty councils in the West— including those at Prairie du Chien (1825) and Butte Des Morts (1827)—and he made the portrait of Shingabawossin the frontispiece in his travelogue *Sketches of a Tour to the Lakes* (1827). Written as a series of letters to Secretary of War James Barbour, McKenney's exhaustive book recount his travels in Michigan Territory during the same time that Lewis Cass sought to solidify the American presence there. The frontispiece was a reproduction of a portrait that James Otto Lewis made of Shingabawossin at the Treaty of Fond du Lac (1826). A decade later, in 1837, McKenney collaborated with the lawyer James Hall on the first volume of his *History of the Indian Tribes of North America* (1838), which included a lithograph adaptation of the same portrait. As such, Shingabawossin became part of a landmark compendium of portraits and biographies of Native leaders and diplomats—including Petalesharo, Keokuk, Shaumonekusse, and Hayne Hudjihini—richly illustrated with portraits by Lewis and Charles Bird King.

FIGURE 4.3
Shin-gua-ba-wossin, after James Otto Lewis. In Thomas L. McKenney, *Sketches of a Tour to the Lakes, of the Character and Customs of the Chippeway Indians, and of Incidents Connected with the Treaty of Fond du Lac* (Baltimore, 1827). Archives and Special Collections, University of Louisville.

FIGURE 4.4
Shin-ga-ba-w'ossin, Image stone, after James Otto Lewis. Lithograph. In Thomas L. McKenney, *History of the Indian Tribes of North America, with Biographical Sketches and Anecdotes of the Principal Chiefs*, vol. 1 (Philadelphia, 1838). Archives and Special Collections, University of Louisville.

The 1827 and 1837 versions of Shingabawossin's portrait—in McKenney's *Tour to the Lakes* and *History of the Indian Tribes*—reflect the recurring tropes by which indigenous leaders like Shingabawossin were represented visually. As in many of the diplomatic portraits by Lewis and Charles Bird King, a central element is the peace medal around Shingabawossin's neck, although the medal is more clearly defined in the 1837 version. A staple of US-Indian diplomacy in the early republic, peace medals were "ritual objects in a complex performance of power and allegiance" and underscored "the close relationship of international diplomacy and friendship discourse."[43] Although the object was a recurring trope of these portraits, they carried profound significance for McKenney and Michigan's territorial governor, Lewis Cass. Historian Herman J. Viola writes that at the Fond du Lac council of 1826, Cass and McKenney had tried to assert "American sovereignty over the Chippewas by collecting British medals and flags," and anytime one of them "saw an Indian with a British medal, he would ask the owner to exchange it for an American medal."[44] The more prominent depiction of the friendship medal in *History of Indian Tribes* amplified McKenney's interest in Shingabawossin as an Ojibwe leader committed to the diplomatic project of asserting American jurisdiction in Michigan Territory. In the iconography around Shingabawossin, this standard visual token of the relationship between diplomacy and friendship projected what was an otherwise insecure claim to American hegemony in the Sault Ste. Marie region.[45]

In the biographical narrative that accompanied Shingabawossin's portrait in *History of the Indian Tribes*, McKenney extended this metonymy of the Ojibwe leader as a signifier of community assent. Like Schoolcraft in his account of Waubojiig, McKenney approached Native leaders and diplomats, to use historian Steven Conn's phrase, as "distinguished individuals" who were "the central actors in history." Even though McKenney wrote at length about political and diplomatic careers of his subjects, the biographies in *History of the Indian Tribes* had a metonymic function, preserving "the likeness of significant, individual representatives of the 'race.'"[46] McKenney based his biography of Shingabawossin on information he gathered when he visited the Schoolcrafts at Sault Ste. Marie in 1826. He wrote that Shingabawossin had fought in battle under Waubojiig, whose name, he noted, "was never spoken but in connection with some tradition exemplifying his great powers as a chief and warrior."[47] Emphasizing Shingabawossin's participation in the treaty councils at Prairie du Chien (1825), Fond du Lac (1826), and Butte des Morts (1827), McKenney noted that he "gave much of his time to attending the public councils convened under the authority of our government."[48] Shingabawossin endeared himself to McKenney by using his eloquence to keep peace and to help American commissioners forge treaties with different Ojibwe communities. McKenney cited his importance in negotiating a "half-breed tract" for mixed-race Ojibwe people, and for being the "patron of the school that has since been established at the Sault for the education of Indian children." Although Shingabawossin was "not an advocate for school knowledge," he nevertheless "remarked that some of the Chippewas might profit by it," thereby giving "proof of his disinterestedness."[49]

Significantly, Shingabawossin's cooperation with American treaty commissioners was directly tied to the land-centered project of US settler colonialism, particularly Lewis Cass's pursuit of large deposits of copper in Ojibwe country. At the Fond du Lac council, Cass explained to the Ojibwe representatives that the Great Father in Washington wanted "the right to search the Chippewa country for copper rock which could then be made into kettles and other useful things." At that time, Shingabawossin came out with the strongest support for the governor's request, stating that "our Fathers have come here to embrace their children. Listen to what they say. It will be good for you. If you have any Copper on your lands, I advise you to sell it. It is of no advantage to us. They can convert it into articles for our use."[50] In the *History of Indian Tribes*, McKenney suggested that Shingabawossin had hereby "placed himself above the *superstitions* of his people, who regard this mass of copper as a *manitou.*"[51] McKenney understood that the treaty negotiations translated the copper deposits from a spiritually animate, culturally meaningful site into an economic resource, a translation that was sanctioned by Shingabawossin's consent to the treaty. In McKenney's reading, the Ojibwe leader represented a modernizing influence, but as a natural embodiment of Ojibwe community sentiment he could afford to transgress traditional Ojibwe beliefs without alienating himself from his own people, and offer aid to the Americans without being reduced to an interloper who betrayed his community.

Drawing from the scripts of Indian diplomacy, Thomas McKenney's writings brought the political world of the Great Lakes into a colonial mapping of Indian country. In his hands, Shingabawossin came to represent an idealized version of the "authorized agent," a tribal leader who represented indigenous cooperation with the Americans, while simultaneously embodying Ojibwe community sentiment. His participation in US-Ojibwe diplomatic interactions made him legible to McKenney as an exemplar of the sympathetic Native leader whose natural authority was a potent resource in seeking indigenous assent to US colonial claims. The writings of Schoolcraft and McKenney—aided by the reproduction of James Otto Lewis's portrait—brought a tribally specific history of diplomacy into a wider print culture, offering a narrative of a growing American influence in Ojibwe country. Failing to capture the decentralized nature of Ojibwe politics and government, these histories offered romanticized and politically convenient ideas about the representational role of indigenous leaders in spheres of Indian diplomacy. The works of Henry Rowe Schoolcraft and Thomas McKenney concreted the cultural trope of the enlightened, sympathetic male Native leader who represented indigenous assent to colonial claims, an ideological construct that complemented the figure of the Native leader as a belligerent (or vanquished) foe. This image of the Indian chief as authorized agent offered a carefully crafted defense of the colonial project, but it was also a meaningful site of contestation for Native writers who sought to correct the representation of indigenous nations.

PETER JONES'S TRANSNATIONAL COMMUNITY
AND THE "UTILITY OF NATIVE AGENCY"

The writings of Henry Rowe Schoolcraft and Thomas McKenney reflect that in the nineteenth century, the figure of the Native American chief became a frequent subject of art and ethnology and an emblem of American historical consciousness. The potency of this cultural emblem, however, was also recognized by a new cohort of Ojibwe writers who found their way into a transatlantic print culture. The 1830s and 1840s saw the rise of several Ojibwe writers, intellectuals, and performers who successfully navigated the lecture circuit and a growing market for printed books. There was Peter Jones (Kahkewāquonāby, 1802–1856), a Methodist missionary in Upper Canada whose memoirs and historical writings were published by his wife after his death in 1856. There was Jones's former convert, George Copway (Kahgegagahbowh, 1818–1869), whose 1847 account of his life and work as a Methodist missionary was the start of a string of print publications, including a newspaper and an account of his European travels. And there was George Henry (Maungwudaus, c. 1807–c. 1851), Copway's cousin and a Methodist missionary, who in 1848 published a short account of his travels in Europe as an entertainer.[52] The careers of Jones and Copway in particular—as missionaries, activists, and public intellectuals—took shape through their involvement with missionary organizations that elaborated a far-reaching market of evangelical print. Making use of these religious networks and their opportunities for publication, Jones and Copway brought alternative representations of Ojibwe culture and politics into a wider media landscape.

The literary career of Peter Jones reflects the transnational dimensions of Ojibwe writing in the era of removal. Where Waubojiig and Shingabawossin had been reinterpreted by Schoolcraft and McKenney as authorized agents who ultimately underwrote a national American narrative, Jones's writings challenged the coherence of the settler nation as the framework for US-Indian relations. As Adam Spry argues, Ojibwe literature has always been inherently transnational in scope, representing forms of cultural exchange that defy Native-settler binaries and cut across the US-Canadian border.[53] Likewise, the activism of Peter Jones reflected the complex geography and political situation of the Ojibwe Nation, which was comprised of communities on both sides of the US-Canadian border, across present-day Minnesota, Wisconsin, Michigan, and Ontario. His career further testifies to the transatlantic dimensions of Ojibwe literature in English, since Jones traveled and lectured extensively in Europe, engaging networks of reformers on both sides of the Atlantic. Through oratory, diplomatic visits, petitions, and journals, Jones modeled what can be seen as the representation of Ojibwe authority within a new form of Indian diplomacy—one that was not dependent on the figure of the Indian chief as an embodiment of community sentiment, but on a more active forging of new connections between missionary groups, government officials, tribal leaders, and indigenous community members. Recognizing the complexities of representing indigenous affairs in a transatlantic world of exchange, Peter Jones re-inscribed the figure of the "authorized agent" with a politicized understanding of indigenous community.

Peter Jones was born in 1802 among the Mississauga, the British designation for the Ojibwe people who lived on the north shore of Lake Ontario.[54] He was the son of an Ojibwe woman, Tuhbenahneequay, and Augustus Jones, a Welsh farmer who was legally married to an Iroquois woman. Jones spent his childhood in a Mississauga community much affected by the War of 1812 and the subsequent influx of white settlers in the province of Upper Canada, later known as Canada West (1841) and Ontario (1867). He converted to Methodism at a camp meeting in 1823 and began a career as an exhorter in Ojibwe and Iroquois communities. In 1826 Jones helped the Methodist Church establish a mission station at the Credit River community of the Mississauga. As Donald Smith notes, the mission, which began with forty families and twenty log cabins, was located on 200 acres of land along the Credit River in Upper Canada. Jones served as pastor to the community and was elected as one of three chiefs in 1829. Working closely with the missionaries William Case and Egerton Ryerson, he helped to set up a school for Ojibwe children that offered instruction in English as well as Anishinaabemowin. In 1830 Jones was ordained as a deacon of the Wesleyan Methodist Conference and became the first First Nations Methodist minister three years later.[55] Over the next two decades Jones kept a journal of his work as a missionary, educator, and tribal leaders, which was published posthumously in 1860 at the request of the Wesleyan Methodist missionary Egerton Ryerson. After his death in 1856, Jones's widow Eliza handed her late husband's manuscripts over to the Methodist minister Enoch Wood; the resulting volume was published in 1860 as *Life and*

Journals Kah-Ke-Wa-Quo-Na-By, the bulk of which is comprised of Jones's (edited) journal entries, reflecting on three decades of missionary work and activism.[56]

This work bridged his political engagement at the level of the Credit River Mission and at the level of indigenous-British relations. In Jace Weaver's words, Jones espoused an ideal of Native community "in his praxis as well as his writing," and his missionary journals record the career of an activist whose promotion of Indian reform worked through the networks of missionary organizations in Upper Canada and Great Britain.[57] Over the course of several decades, Jones traveled to England three times to preach, to raise money for the education of Native children, and to pressure the colonial government to recognize the Credit River community's legal title to their lands. As a leader in the Credit River community, Jones brought this ethics of community activism into a practice of diplomacy that was both local and transatlantic in scope. In 1831, he joined Egerton Ryerson on a year-long visit to England, giving public lectures and sermons and meeting with prominent figures in civil society. Participating in an economy of exchange and philanthropy, he spent his time in England "preaching, speaking both about the 'superstitions' of the Indians and what the Gospel has done for them; asking not just for funds but ... for local wares, such as joiners' tools and cutlery [and] writing to the committees of the Sunday School Union and the Sunday School Society for books for Indian Sunday schools."[58] His travels in England included an audience with King William IV and Queen Adelaide in 1832, during which he offered the King a copy of his Ojibwe translation of the Gospel of St John. Jones asked the Queen whether she had received the "few articles of Indian work" by "the Indian women of Canada," which Jones had asked Lord Goderich to send to them in advance of his trip to England.[59] In return, the King gave Jones a peace medal, an illustration of which was later included in his *History of the Ojebway Indians* (1861).[60]

While adhering to established protocols, Jones re-inscribed these diplomatic interactions with a politicized understanding of the Credit River community's situation. When he traveled to England for a second time in 1837 and 1838, Jones had a brief audience with Queen Victoria at Windsor Castle. At that point, the Credit River community were still waiting for the colonial government to follow up on their promise to grant them a permanent title deed to their lands. Jones was presented to the Queen in the presence of Lord Glenelg, the secretary of war and the colonies. Although the audience did not last for more than five minutes, Jones claimed a measure of control over the meeting by offering the Queen the text of a petition that he had sent the government previously. The petition asked the governor of Upper Canada for the Credit River community's title deed, and a string of white and black wampum was affixed to the petition. Jones proclaimed to be "happy to say Lord Glenelg (pointing to his Lordship,) had already granted the prayer of the petition, by requesting the Governor of Upper Canada, to give the Indians the title-deeds they asked for."[61] By offering Queen Victoria the petition, he handed her an urgent and political written artifact, and by doing so in the presence of Lord Glenelg, he impressed on them the secretary's accountability to both the Queen and her "red children." Moreover, Jones explained the symbolism of the wampum: the white beads expressed "loyalty of good feeling which prevails amongst the Indians towards her Majesty and Her Government," while the black beads meant that "their hearts were troubled on account of their having no title-deeds for their lands." He told the Queen that he had brought the petition in case the Queen "might be pleased to take out all the black wampum, so that the string might be all white."[62] By presenting the petition and the wampum, Jones amplified the political dimensions of his travels to England, insisting on a more responsive diplomatic relationship between the Ojibwe and the colonial government, in which the political claims of indigenous nations would carry more weight.

Yet although Queen Victoria and Lord Glenelg authorized the title deeds, the efforts to obtain them failed when the secretary's term in office ended not long after the meeting. Given the wave of white settlement in Upper Canada, this situation made the Credit River community's land tenure an insecure prospect. As diplomacy between the British crown and indigenous communities had lost much political weight, Jones turned mostly to religious and philanthropic publics to secure support for Ojibwe projects of nation-building. For instance, in his journal he reflected on a meeting in 1832 with the English author and philanthropist Hannah More. A well-known writer of religious and moral literature, More was a noted supporter of Bible and missionary societies and received frequent visitors in spite of her declining health.[63] Jones's account of the meeting emphasized the intimate character of the exchange: frequently taking hold of Jones's arm "in an affectionate manner," she was "wholly engaged on the subject of religion and literary information." More invited him into one corner of the room and presented him with a volume of her moral sketches, *The Spirit of Prayer* (1825), and a five-pound note for the Canadian missions.[64] Besides gifts of clothes and articles, Jones received manuscripts and books, including an original manuscript letter by John Wesley, a "fine edition" of *Pilgrim's Progress*, a Bible containing marginal notes by a late friend of his, and a copy of George Stanley Faber's *The Origins of Pagan Idolatry* (1816).

Such exchanges of books were not an ephemeral practice in nineteenth-century lettered social circles but a common practice of social and economic exchange, elaborating an important sense of social reciprocity.[65] But gift exchanges were also an established practice of diplomacy in indigenous nations, and among the Ojibwe gift-giving had long reinforced kinship, economic, and diplomatic relations with European and indigenous nations.[66] By exchanging gifts, Bruce M. White notes, Ojibwe leaders gave "material demonstration of concern for the welfare" of others in their family or the larger community, showing themselves "worthy, generous, and unselfish." These practices of exchange strengthened ties to nonkin and were the means by which foreigners such as fur traders and government officials hoped to achieve their political goals.[67] By the 1830s, however, the Ojibwe's political position relative to the settler population in Canada had weakened their diplomatic status on the world stage. Tim Fulford notes that the power of indigenous nations was "so reduced that whites no longer needed their military aid, feared their opposition, or relied upon their trade goods," and Jones operated from a position of weakness in which he "could only appeal to people's goodwill and compassion."[68] As such, the philanthropic sentiments of European benefactors did not necessarily contribute to significant political change. If Ojibwe nation-building was about the political issue of title deeds and the political recognition of indigenous sovereignty, Jones's fundraising also registers that his national projects were primarily seen as an object of charity in an unequal economy of benevolence. Although these gift exchanges cemented Jones's relations with philanthropists and fellow Methodists, his work within their circles suggests that this benevolent work was less about structural political changes and more about what Susan M. Ryan terms "the direct dispensation of aid."[69] Despite Jones's call for lasting political reform, benevolent societies typically viewed indigenous communities as objects of pity: in Laura Stevens's words, Indians proved "useful to feel with" and functioned as a vehicle for exercising religious obligation and consolidating a transatlantic religious community.[70]

In his *Life and Journals*, then, Jones tested the possibilities and limits of his work in navigating governmental and religious networks. While he performed this diplomatic work from a position of little political power, when Jones visited Britain for a third time, from 1844 to 1846, he fashioned a politicized representation of his Ojibwe community that was also effective for the purposes of fundraising and institution-building. As he traveled through Ireland and England, he gave talks on the "Customs, Manners, and Religion of his North American Brethren" and circulated a pamphlet—signed on Boxing Day, 1844—to solicit support for Ojibwe education. In the pamphlet, Jones used the language of civilization and "Indian degradation" to insist on the "importance of such schools being established amongst them; in order to effect their entire civilization, and thus to raise them from their present indolent and degraded state."[71] The plan involved establishing two schools: one for male and one for female students, a hundred each. Aside from their instruction in reading and writing, their education would be divided along gender lines: the boys were to be instructed in "a common English education, the art of Farming and useful trades," while the girls would be taught skills in "domestic economy, sewing, knitting, spinning; so as to qualify them to become good wives and mothers."[72] The schools would also be a steppingstone for talented boys and girls toward becoming missionaries, to "select from each School the most promising boys and girls, with a view of giving them superior advantages, so as [to] qualify them for Missionaries and School teachers among their brethren." For Jones, the plan held the potential to improve the representation of Native people in Methodist missionary networks—because "no one can doubt the importance and utility of Native agency, in carrying forward the work of reformation amongst the pagan nations of the earth."[73]

To persuade his readers to support the Credit Mission financially, Jones's "Appeal to the Christian Public" listed the donors and subscribers who had already committed financially to the proposed schools, sketching a network of patrons and supporters that stretched across Brighton, Southampton, Canterbury, Tottenham, and London, among other cities. Jones appealed to the British as a nation of benevolence, arguing that their abolition of slavery had proven that it had "manifested a kind and sympathizing feeling towards the oppressed and degraded of every clime."[74] However, tapping into this register of sympathy and benevolence also meant translating the Credit River Ojibwe community into more generic tropes of the *Indian* as an object of white philanthropy. Jones characterized the Ojibwe as being in a situation of dependency, playing into a sentimental notion of the "poor Indian" as an object of missionary discourse and benefaction. "These remnant children of the forest," Jones wrote, "now call upon their rich kind Christian friends in England and Ireland, to help to rescue their descendants from utter ruin and extinction."[75]

However, Jones ensured that any evocation of Ojibwe community included the expression of political sovereignty, so that his representation of community deliberation could not be reduced to a romanticized or stereotypical image of indigenous societies. Jones signed his pamphlet as an "Indian Missionary and Chief" who had been "duly appointed" by both his "fellow Chiefs and Countrymen in Canada" and the "Missionary society under whose direction I have been laboring for many years."[76] To make this concrete, Jones's "Appeal" was authorized by the chiefs Nawahjegezhegwabe (Joseph Sawyer) and Thayendenegea (John Jones), in the presence of "twenty-two Warriors" and the missionary Samuel Belton. This ad hoc council commissioned Jones to "solicit the aid of all Christian people on behalf of the poor Red Men of the forest." A second statement of leaders from the Munceytown community—made up in the presence of an Indian Department clerk and signed by Bwunowashkung (John Riley) and "four other chiefs"—stated that "we authorize you on our part to plead for us."[77] Furthermore, the pamphlet noted that "His Excellency Sir Charles Metcalfe, Governor General of Canada, has expressed his entire approval, and kindly given his name as a subscriber." Finally, Jones's "Appeal" constructed a notion of "the Indian parents" who endorsed his scheme to raise money for the manual labor schools: "The Indian parents have repeatedly acknowledged and mourned over their want of government, and knowledge of bringing up their children in the way they should go; especially to teach them the habits of industry." To make this construct of the "Indian parents" concrete, he reproduced extracts of personal testimony from Ojibwe parents, to be shared with "Christians of every class and denomination" in the United Kingdom and Ireland.[78]

In short, Jones's pamphlet carried four different layers of authorization: from Ojibwe leaders (in different communities), missionary organizations, the colonial government and the Indian Department, and Ojibwe community members. This layering of authorization did more than simply make the fundraising appear "legitimate." First, it represented the Ojibwe community beyond the tropes of objects of pity, as a "real" community that was also a *political* community. Second, it captured Jones's position in navigating these different publics, in a practice of Indian diplomacy that connected indigenous and colonial audiences more intimately. In doing so, Jones's petition negotiated between, on the one hand, the trope of the *Indian* as an object of sympathy and benevolence, and on the other hand, a truer representation of the Ojibwe leaders and community members who sponsored the petition. Rendering a political dimension to the Credit River community, it decentered the global network of benevolent societies as the only framework for cross-cultural sympathy. Outlining an ethics of community between Jones, the parents, and the Ojibwe leadership, the pamphlet invited British benefactors to become an extension of this community through their contributions.

Through this project of Christian reform, Jones carried out a form of activism that was both community-based and transnational in scope. Well informed about Indian removal in the United States, Jones recognized its ripple effects in Upper Canada, and as historian Donald B. Smith writes, he imagined the Ojibwe homelands as "a place of refuge" for indigenous people across the Great Lakes, thousands of whom had already "emigrated from the American side of the Great Lakes to avoid relocation."[79] For Jones, "Indian unity" was key in the political struggle to secure title deeds for indigenous communities, and he saw Methodism as an organizational framework for claiming a place for the Credit River nation and advancing the prospects of indigenous people in the Great Lakes.[80] Paradoxically, his Methodism offered a framework to re-affirm the traditional indigenous ethics of community, and throughout his life Jones believed that Ojibwe values were "compatible with those of Christians."[81] In this respect, while Jones's spiritual commitment to his Christian faith was undoubtedly sincere, his Methodism also reflected what scholars have called "retraditionalization," an effort to integrate preexisting ethics of care and community into new frameworks, responding to contemporary contexts.[82] Originally developed by Teresa LaFromboise to describe Native women's extension of "traditional care-taking and cultural transmission roles to activities in predominantly non-Native settings," retraditionalization points to the continuation of the traditional ethics of community in the context of cultural or religious change.[83] As Laura Donaldson has argued, Methodist practices often "extended rather than subsumed" existing cultural practices of community and care in indigenous nations.[84] Extending these logics, Jones's writings articulated a project of Indian reform that involved transatlantic religious networks but was also rooted in local, indigenous ethics of community.

Like his *Life and Journals*, Jones's "Appeal to the Christian Public" expressed the politics of Indian reform in a transatlantic culture of philanthropy, in which indigenous people had become an emblem of "need" and, as such, objects of pity. Jones mobilized this image for practical purposes, appealing to a sense of reciprocity in a colonial culture that was marked by inequality. But his representation of Ojibwe community—to British and Irish readers—also activated a complex authorization that depended on community sentiments as well as the systems of authorization that existed in Ojibwe and British government. In Jones's *Life and Journals* and his "Appeal to the Christian Public," the figure of the Indian chief as a signifier of community sentiment made way for a new kind of "authorized agent," who publicly performed a politicized Indianness through the imbricated roles of tribal leader, activist, educator, and missionary. Channeling these roles into new projects of reform, Jones bridged the transnational discourses of philanthropy and the local politics of indigenous leaders and organizers.

GEORGE COPWAY'S CHIEFS: AUTOBIOGRAPHY AND THE PROJECT OF OJIBWE REFORM

Peter Jones's journals and pamphlet remind us that printed artifacts played an important role in cross-cultural diplomacy: as instruments of political and philanthropic action, books were central commodities in economies of cultural exchange. Indigenous intellectuals realized that print publication could be an important physical testament to authority and expertise, a form of social capital that could help one establish a reputation and navigate networks of sponsors, policymakers, and benefactors. One of Peter Jones's Methodist converts, the

Canadian-born George Copway (Kahgegagahbowh), achieved a significant moment of literary fame as a lecturer and as the author of a widely read autobiography, *The Life, History, and Travels of Kah-Ge-Ga-Gah-Bowh* (1847). Like the work of Peter Jones, George Copway's writing and organizing was embedded in the history of Methodist mission work in Ojibwe country. He was born in 1818 in the Mississauga Ojibwe community of Rice Lake, near present-day Trenton, Ontario, and it was in fact Peter Jones who converted his family to Methodism in 1827. After attending a local mission school, Copway began work as a missionary himself among native communities across Michigan, Wisconsin, Minnesota, Iowa, and Illinois. He attended school at Ebenezer Academy in Illinois in 1838 and 1839, and by the early 1840s he was combining his missionary work with public lectures on American Indian affairs and temperance. He moved to New York and became a much-sought-after speaker on the history and political situation of American Indians in Canada and the United States.

A controversial figure, Copway (1818–1869) has often been regarded as a writer who promoted the assimilation of American Indians and played along with American plans for removal. After all, he wrote about his own conversion, worked as a missionary, and endorsed a plan for a separate "Indian State" in the Dakotas that would have facilitated large-scale removals if it had materialized.[85] Moreover, the means by which Copway advanced his writing career has often made him a somewhat suspect figure in critical review. As Scott Richard Lyons points out, literary critics have often suggested that his increasing detachment from Ojibwe community life led him to prioritize his own celebrity as an author over his commitment to indigenous populations.[86] These critiques point to a lingering idea that the works of Native writers necessarily represent a narrowly defined notion of indigenous communities, in which only the author's original community should be seen as the framework for interpreting their work and their political commitments. Indeed, Copway's work deliberately defies the expectation that American Indian spokespersons were supposed to be "authentic" representations of their tribal culture. His autobiography *Life, History, and Travels* challenges the expedient image of the Indian chief as an index of indigenous community sentiment, updating it with depictions of Ojibwe chiefs and councils who embraced new forms of diplomacy and promoted new tribal institutions. And if Copway relished the imagery of the "authorized agent," perhaps he was also one of the first writers to deconstruct this trope, as his writings scrutinize the representational politics of indigenous writing and organizing within religious, philanthropic, and governmental networks.

Copway's significant if short-lived literary career was cemented with the publication of his most popular work, his autobiography, *Life, History, and Travels*

(1847). Reprinted seven times, it was republished in 1850, under different titles, in England and the United States. Fashioning a career as a "man of letters," Copway was endorsed by prominent writers such as James Fenimore Cooper, the historian Francis Parkman, the ethnologist Lewis Henry Morgan, and Henry Rowe Schoolcraft. Copway buttressed his status as a public speaker with a string of publications that included his *Traditional History and Characteristic Sketches of the Ojibway Nation* (1850) and a short-lived newspaper titled *Copway's American Indian* (1851). In 1850, Copway published *The Ojibway Conquest: A Tale of the Northwest*, an epic poem narrating a tale of romance set against the backdrop of the wars between the Ojibwe and the Eastern Dakota. Although the title page boasted Copway's name and portrait, the poem was actually written by Julius Taylor Clark, a Wisconsin lawyer who had worked as a teacher among the Ojibwe at La Pointe in the mid-1840s.[87] The last major publication of his career was *Running Sketches of Men and Places* (1851), a travel account that details his participation in the Universal Peace Congress in Frankfurt.

In his 1847 autobiography, *The Life, History, and Travels of Kah-Ge-Ga-Gah-Bowh*, Copway considers the role of tribal leaders in Ojibwe communities that were undergoing profound historical, religious, and political change. Copway's

FIGURE 4.5 Portrait of George Copway, from a daguerreotype by McClees & Germon. Engraved by T. B. Welch. Frontispiece of George Copway, *The Ojibway Conquest, A Tale of the Northwest* (New York, 1850). Author's collection.

book is often read—quite rightly—as primarily an account of his early childhood, his conversion to Methodism, his missionary work among Indian nations in the West, and his ethnological account of Ojibwe culture. However, in several important moments in his book, Copway points out the imbrication of missionary work with the practice of intertribal diplomacy. In particular, he describes his work among Ojibwe and Sioux communities in the Great Lakes in the 1840s, at a time when these communities were affected by the frequent border wars between the Ojibwe and the Eastern Dakota. This long-standing series of conflicts played a major part in Copway's commitment to peace and Indian reform, and in *Life, History, and Travels* he recounts his efforts to set up a new school in an Ojibwe community on Lac Court Oreilles, in Wisconsin Territory. During his travels in the territory, he meets with the Ojibwe chief Moose Tail (Mo-so-ne) of the Catfish Clan, and is confronted with the realities of the Ojibwe-Dakota wars at Ottawa Lake, which, as Donald B. Smith notes, was located in the "war zone between the Ojibwe and the eastern Dakota, the Ojibwe's hereditary enemies."[88] When the people of Ottawa Lake show him the battlegrounds, Moose Tail shares his recollections about the site: "The Chief, pointing to a certain spot, observed, 'There I killed two Sioux, about thirteen winters ago; I cut open one of them; and when I reflected that the Sioux had cut open my cousin, but a year before, I took out his heart, cut a piece from it, and swallowed it whole. I scooped some of his blood, while warm, with my hand, and drank as many draughts as the number of friends who had perished by their hands.' As he spoke, the fierceness of the Indian gleamed from his countenance."[89] Of course, Moose Tail's gruesome memory is mediated by Copway's narration, which was crafted several years after this encounter. Nevertheless, the passage problematizes the link between the figure of the Indian chief and the notion of civic roundedness that American commentators such as Henry Rowe Schoolcraft and Thomas McKenney promoted. While recognizing Moose Tail's hospitality and describing him as "particularly kind," Copway associates the Ojibwe leader with a deleterious history of intertribal warfare.

Copway similarly resists such romanticized representations of tribal leaders when he recalls an encounter with the Ojibwe chief Bagone-giizhig while working at the Rabbit River mission in present-day Minnesota. Known also as Hole-in-the-Day the Elder, Bagone-giizhig was an influential Ojibwe chief at the Sandy Lake community, north of Mille Lacs and west of Duluth. As the anthropologist Anton Treuer notes, Bagone-giizhig rose to power after his predecessor Babiiziginibe (Curly Head) appointed him chief of Sandy Lake in the 1820s, along with his brother Zoongakamig (Strong Ground). Over the course of the next twenty years, however, Bagone-Giizhig claimed solitary power, not only over the Sandy Lake community but over the Ojibwe across the entire upper Mississippi region.⁹⁰ In *Life, History, and Travels*, Copway remarks that the chief "had always been kind to me and mine," but he also suggests that Bagone-giizihg was more concerned with the wars between the Ojibwe and the Eastern Dakota. Discussing "the importance of true religion," Bagone-giizhig "became much troubled, and admitted that his own religion was not as good as the religion of the Bible; but, said he, 'I will embrace your religion when I shall have returned from one more battle with the Sioux; and I will then advise my people to embrace it too.' What a struggle this poor fellow had within!"⁹¹ Copway presents this anecdote with a sense of humor, but it also registers a criticism of the Ojibwe chief. If Bagone-giizhig understands the premises of Copway's evangelizing, his lingering attachment to the tenets of a warrior culture make him a problematic indicator of community sentiment. Situating these Ojibwe leaders in a wider landscape of intertribal warfare, Copway suggests that they are overly preoccupied with political and military pursuits that he hopes will soon be a thing of the past.

Refusing to idealize the roles of these chiefs, Copway narrates his own experience of being thrust into the world of Ojibwe-Dakota conflict, reflecting how much his work as a missionary in indigenous communities intersected with the regional politics of intertribal diplomacy. He recounts how, after his interactions with Bagone-Giizhig, he travels by himself to the St. Peters Sioux Indian agency on the Minnesota River, near present-day Minneapolis. On the way, he comes across a war party—presumably of the Mdewakanton Santee Sioux—which is planning to "murder all the Ojebwas they could find," and Copway follows them in order to warn Bagone-giizhig and the people at his mission, including his wife and children. He seeks help from a Mdewakanton Santee leader along the way, but when informed of the situation he instructs Copway to "tell Hole-in-the-sky, I am coming to get his scalp."⁹² When Copway fears the Sioux war party will take him prisoner, he overhears one war chief say " 'if you kill these men, the Great Spirit will be angry, and he will send his white children to kill us, and our children."⁹³ Although the attack ultimately does not come to pass, Copway considers the country "a dangerous place for the Ojebwa Missionaries," and the war party reminds him "much of his Satanic and fiendish majesty, rejoicing over a damned spirit in hell."⁹⁴ In this episode, Copway has no qualms about evoking the Eastern Dakota as a representation of savagery, which offers justification for his own project of missionizing and reform in Indian country. Like Ongpatonga and Keokuk before him, Copway locates the cause of warfare and other social problems with the Sioux, whom he describes as a threatening, militarized presence in the Mississippi Valley. On another level, however, this account is more than simply a sensational account of warfare, as it shows the extent to which Copway's missionary work was shaped by intertribal politics, in which the traditional figure of the Ojibwe chief played what he considered to be a problematic role.

Tracing a breakdown of diplomatic relations in this intertribal geography, Copway's *Life, History, and Travels* promotes the political work of other Christianized Ojibwe leaders and missionaries that he worked with. If Moose Tail and Bagone-giizhig—and their association with scenes of warfare—make them poor indicators of Ojibwe community sentiment, Copway locates more meaningful forms of tribal authority in the General Council of Christianized Ojibwas, of which he was vice president in the early 1840s. The General Council was a gathering of converted Methodist Ojibwe leaders from different communities in Canada West, which was previously called Upper Canada. Presided over by Joseph Sawyer (Nawahjegezhegwabe), the head chief of Peter Jones's Credit River community, the General Council brought together representatives from St. Clair, Huron, Ontario, and Simcoe Lakes, and also from the Rice Lake and Mud Lake communities. In the latter chapters of his *Life, History and Travels,* Copway reflects on an 1845 meeting of the General Council at Saugeen in Canada West, where they discussed the prospect of relocating all Ojibwe communities to Saugeen, to bring them together as one single nation.

Although these plans never materialized, in his book Copway celebrates the council's model of modern government, and his account of the meeting integrates familiar images of the "Indian chief" with a representation of midcentury innovations in Ojibwe leadership structures. On the one hand, he echoes a romanticized image of Native leadership when he describes the visual spectacle of the "uncommonly eloquent" leader and missionary John Sunday (Shah-wun-dais). Trading on the metonymy of the eloquent Indian body, Copway highlights Sunday's "keen black eyes, flashing fire," and the way he held his "large brawny arms extended" to give "great effect to his speech."[95] On the other hand, this spectacle of the eloquent Indian body takes place in the context of decidedly modern and businesslike proceedings. Copway emphasizes that the council is conducted "in the same manner as public and other business meetings are conducted among the whites," namely, by following a numbered agenda. As reprinted in Copway's *Life, History, and Travels*, John Jones of the Owen Sound reserve proposed the following considerations:

1 Whether it would not be better for the whole Ojebwa Nation to reside on this, our territory.
2 Would it not be well to devise ways and means to establish Manual Labour Schools for the benefit of the nation.
3 Ought not a petition to be drawn up and presented to our Great Father [the Governor General,] for the purpose of fixing upon a definite time for the distribution of the annual "presents," and the small annuities of each tribe.

>   4 Is it not desirable to petition to the Governor General, to appoint a resident Indian interpreter, to assist the agent in Toronto.
>
>   5 As we [the Christian part of our nation] have abandoned our former customs and ceremonies, ought we not to make our own laws, in order to give character and stability to our chiefs.[96]

If not exactly quotidian, these were the pragmatic concerns that together constituted nation-building: claiming a territory, establishing a school, managing the annuity payments, appointing an interpreter, and establishing tribal laws.

Copway follows this agenda with a draft of the council's petition to Lord Metcalf, the governor-general of British North America, pleading for the uninterrupted land rights to the reservation near Saugeen and Owen Sound:

> Father—Your petitioners are very anxious that the reserve (now still known as the Indian Territory) be a perpetual reserve; as a future refuge for a general colonization of the Ojebwa Nation, comprising the scattered Tribes in Canada West;
>
> Father—And that these lands may now and for ever be opened to all the Tribes; that whenever any tribe is disposed to move. That they may have nothing to fear, but have access to any of the good lands to settle upon;
>
> Father—You have settled your white children on those lands that once were our fathers; we ask now to let us have the only remaining land we have, to ourselves, unmolested.[97]

Reflecting on this collaborative publication project, Copway captures the desperate situation and limited choices that the General Council was now faced with in securing a permanent land title for the Ojibwe. At the same time, by including the petition immediately after the summary of the council meeting, he shows the General Council to be efficient and action-driven in its businesslike approach, quickly translating their deliberations into immediate political action. In other words, the General Council is *organized*. In a culture in which the figure of the Indian chief was associated with a nostalgic vision of an organic community, Copway instead sees the participants in the council meeting as organizers who mediated between Ojibwe leadership, the networks of the Canada Conference of Methodists, and the colonial government, and thereby modeled a new relation between indigenous community and political representation.

This representation of Ojibwe authority, of course, was in its own ways reductive: since the council was composed only of the "Christian part of our nation," this political body represented the different Ojibwe communities only in a limited sense. Nevertheless, in *Life, History, and Travels*, Copway locates in this democratic body a more legitimate representation of Ojibwe collectivity, and he praises the modernizing impulse underway in the General Council:

> Never was I more delighted than with the appearance of this body. As I sat and looked at them, I contrasted their former (degraded) with their present (elevated) condition. The Gospel, I thought, had done all this. If any one had told me twenty years ago, that such would be their condition, I should have ridiculed the idea, and set the narrator down for a fool or a maniac. The assembly was not convened for the purpose of devising schemes of murder; plans by which the could kill their enemies; but to adopt measures by which peace, harmony, and love, might be secured, and a "smooth and straight path" made for their children.[98]

This reflection is typical of Copway's writing, communicating a message of evangelization that simultaneously bears witness to political mobilization and nation-building. Just as Peter Jones saw the framework of Methodism as being compatible with Ojibwe ethics of community and care, Copway sees the tenets of the Gospel as compatible with the Ojibwe's desire for "peace, harmony, and love" in a time of warfare. His reflections on the General Council therefore contrast this body with images of a former "degraded" form of tribal politics, associated with the scenes of warfare he had witnessed.

Yet the General Council was not the only framework for Copway's missionary work and activism. As a self-professed "authorized agent" to the Ojibwe, he developed ambitious plans for reorganizing US-Indian relations on a national scale, particularly in the face of Indian removal. He was well informed about this policy, which was affecting Indian nations in dramatic ways. Scott Richard Lyons notes that Copway had witnessed two treaty signings—at Fort Snelling (1837) and La Pointe (1842)—that "ceded vast tracts of land in Wisconsin, Minnesota, and the Upper Peninsula of Michigan" to the United States, and that spurred the Commissioner of Indian Affairs, William Medill, "to send agents to the Lake Superior region to begin removing the Ojibwe to lands west of the Mississippi."[99] In 1850, an executive order from President Zachary Taylor further annulled Ojibwe land rights in Wisconsin and Michigan, and ushered in a three-year crisis during which thousands of Ojibwe people were forced to relocate to Sandy Lake, in the Territory of Minnesota. These removal efforts were halted in 1853 after many petitions and a delegation of the Lake Superior Ojibwe to Washington, but by then some 400 Ojibwe people had died because of governmental negligence, in what came to be known as the Sandy Lake Tragedy.[100]

It was in this context that Copway promoted a project he called "Kahgega," a proposal for the organization of Indian nations under a territorial government, with the goal of establishing an independent Indian state. In Kahgega, Native people from different tribes would have political representation at the federal level, while also becoming individual landowners and US citizens. As Lyons writes, Kahgega was "basically an Indian colonization plan" that would offer "relief from the racial conflicts of the nineteenth century and protect them from future removals."[101] Copway promoted this plan to several state legislatures, and in 1850 he presented to the US Congress a "bill to provide for the organization of an Indian Territory east of the Missouri River."[102] Similar ideas had been debated as congressional bills in the 1830s and 1840s (including the one protested by the Choctaw diplomat Peter Pitchlynn), and, as Donald B. Smith notes, Copway's outline bore similarities to the 1841 proposal of Duane Doty, the governor of Wisconsin Territory.[103] His plan relied on the key idea that the current organization of Indian country, in the middle of the continent, was a problem, since he predicted (correctly, one might add) that Native people would just be removed again as white settlers moved west and built canals, railroads, and military thoroughfares through Indian country. The scheme did not materialize—due in part to the opposition of Commissioner of Indian Affairs William Medill—but as Copway promoted his plans, he garnered support from many prominent writers and politicians who were committed to Indian reform.[104]

The Life, History, and Travels of Kah-ge-ga-gah-bowh includes an early version of these plans, in a form that mirrors the proceedings of the General Council. Although Copway promoted his territorial scheme independently from the council, his description of it echoes its businesslike character, organized as a numbered list outlining his own plans for Indian reform. Explaining "the reason that the Indians are diminishing in numbers in the midst of their white neighbors," he offers the following condensed explanation of the problems facing Indian nations:

1 The introduction of King Alcohol among them.
2 The introduction of new diseases ...
3 Their inability to pursue that course of living, after abandoning their wigwams, which tends to health and old age.
4 Their spirits are broken down in consequence of seeing that their *race* are becoming homeless, friendless, moneyless, and trodden down by the whites.
5 Their future prospects are gloomy and cheerless—enough to break down the noblest spirits.[105]

Copway mirrors this "gloomy and cheerless" list with one that offers a concrete plan of action to achieve Indian nations' economic and social regeneration:

1 They should establish missions and high schools wherever the whites have frequent intercourse with them.
2 They should use their influence, as soon as the Indians are well educated ... to have them placed on the same footing as whites.
3 They should try to procure for them a territorial or district government, so that they may represent their own nation.
4 They should obtain for them, deeds of their own lands; and ... urge their right to vote.[106]

Breaking down complex information into succinct and concrete components, Copway's list echoes the action-driven voice of the Ojibwe council, taking stock of present conditions and projecting future possibilities. In moments such as this, Copway's narrative escapes the bounds of autobiography and suggests a blueprint for a larger project of reform.

In the final chapter of *Life, History, and Travels*, Copway maps this project of Indian reform onto the transnational geography of the Ojibwe Nation. Titled "A Geographical Sketch of the Ojebwa, or Chippeway, Nation," the last chapter abandons the autobiographical narrative altogether to tackle the complex geographical terrain of the nation, which consists of communities far dispersed "within the bounds of the two Governments—the American and the British." Of the Ojibwe communities in the United States, he briefly notes that they "inhabit all the northern part of Michigan, or the south shore of Lake Huron; the whole northern part of Wisconsin Territory; all the south shore of Lake Superior, for eight hundred miles; the upper part of the Mississippi, and Sandy, Leach, and Red Lakes."[107] This description makes an interesting geographical move. First, Copway begins with the Ojibwe's location within the boundaries of the settler states. Second, he locates Ojibwe communities in the United States with reference to American territorial mappings: Wisconsin Territory and the State of Michigan. Third, Copway presents a more traditional mapping that references the proximity of these Ojibwe communities to different bodies of water: the Great Lakes, the Mississippi, and several smaller lakes. In this respect, even as he presents a scheme that is rooted in a settler colonial mapping of the Ojibwe homelands, Copway also superimposes a community-based understanding of indigenous space.

Turning to the Canadian communities, Copway overlays his view of the Ojibwe Nation with a fourth discourse of space, mapping a network of mission stations that connect these dispersed communities. Here Copway includes several excerpts from the "Report on the Affairs of the Indians in Canada" by the Bagot

Commission (1842–44), which was presented to the Legislative Assembly of Canada in 1845 and laid out a proposal for federally run religious and agricultural instruction for Native people in Canada.[108] These excerpts essentially map fifteen different Ojibwe communities in Canada West, noting their geographical location, their demographics, the schools already established in them, and the resources they still require. Outlining the inroads of Methodist, Presbyterian, Episcopalian, Baptist, and Roman Catholic missions, the report points out the existing gaps: "Those who are not under religious instruction ... are wandering without the gospel. There is a field in the Territory of Wisconsin where missionaries should be sent. There are Indians all around the shores of Lake Superior who have, from time to time, called for missionaries, and have not yet been supplied."[109] Offering a bird's-eye view of the dispersed communities that make up the Ojibwe Nation, Copway's reprinting of the Bagot report maps the terrain, points out available resources, identifies existing gaps, and, finally, imagines a cross-regional project of organizing. First, his overview of the fifteen Ojibwe communities includes the names of the tribal leaders there, listing them as points of contact in a wider mapping of missionaries and reformers.[110] Second, he sees the dispersed Ojibwe communities as being united by a historical narrative centered on the "greater advancement in religion, literature, and the arts and sciences," which will lead them away from "their wigwams, their woods, and the chase."[111] The tension in Copway's work, then, is that it sees this project of religious and cultural assimilation—for indeed, this was very much the goal of the Bagot Commission—as being simultaneously a project of community organization and economic reform.

As Copway navigated indigenous, Methodist, and governmental networks, he mapped the work that was involved in organizing projects of reform in dispersed Ojibwe communities. The promotion of this scheme depended on a new figure of the "authorized agent": not the Indian chief who metonymically embodied community sentiment, but an indigenous diplomat-missionary-intellectual who was situated within a network of institutions and organizers. In this regard, Copway displayed little nostalgia for the old image of the Indian chief or—more problematically—for the Ojibwe's traditional modes of living. Instead, he endorsed projects of Indian reform that hinged on Christianization and agricultural education, and in his autobiography he concretely mapped the individuals and networks that would enable the work involved. A central tension in Copway's work is that this assimilationist bent in his writing—his promotion of Christianity and cultural change—aligned with visions of Indian reform as governmental and missionary organizations promoted it, but also with a newly emerging strand of reformist politics among Ojibwe tribal leaders. Through the publication of his *Life, History, and Travels*, George Copway created a discursive space for negotiating these intersecting projects, by envisioning new possibilities for Indian diplomacy in an expansive print culture.

"HIGH TONED UPRIGHT INDEPENDENT INDIAN":
THE DELEGATE AS ORGANIZER IN GEORGE COPWAY'S
Running Sketches of Men and Places

By bringing the logics of Indian diplomacy into a wider market for Native American life writing, George Copway's literary projects placed him in a network of intellectuals and political leaders, many of whom had published authoritative accounts of American Indian life. Copway's connection to his literary peers is evident from his short-lived newspaper, *Copway's American Indian*, which ran from July to late September 1851. When he solicited support for his newspaper, he sought the support of "men of standing and talent" and listed the writers James Fenimore Cooper, William Gilmore Simms, Henry Rowe Schoolcraft, and Washington Irving among the "names that are at my command to write for and contribute to its columns."[112] Moreover, in seeking patronage for his project, Copway captured the rhetoric of publication that was expected of a "man of letters" partaking in the nineteenth-century public sphere. In a letter to the Philadelphia poet Henry Beck Hirst, he assured that his project would be "devoted entirely to the claims of the Indian Race" and "independent of all creeds and isms of every description," and would "follow the morals of the Bible and the dictates of common sense."[113] Serving a public cause while remaining politically impartial, his "high toned upright independent Indian paper" would remain "aloof from all political questions of a local nature" and "present the good intentions of the government to the Indians."[114] Copway imagined a dual audience for his newspaper, which would be "a channel of information for the American people and to the Indian Race," to "give them a better idea of each other." Constructing a cross-cultural public, his newspaper was to be a comprehensive means to Native people's "moral and physical elevation," and Copway imagined sending "several thousand copies into the country where they live gratuitously." By planning to "send 5,000 prospectuses over the city and nearly as many in the country," he championed an effort to connect urban readers with American and indigenous readers in the territories.[115]

Although *Copway's American Indian* was not a commercial success—it folded within three months—Copway clearly imagined himself playing a role as a communication link between American and Native readers, distributing indigenous knowledge in a growing market for print. If the newspaper folded, however, this was still a period of much activity for Copway: in 1850 he also reissued his autobiography as *The Life, Letters, and Speeches of Kah-Ge-Ga-Gah-Bowh*, and published *The Ojibwe Conquest* and *The Traditional History and Characteristic Sketches of the Ojbway Nation*. Copway's written work continued to extend his political activism, as he also published an important pamphlet on the "Organization of a new Indian territory, east of the Missouri river" (1850), based on arguments he made before Congress that year. In the course of these activities, Copway eagerly embraced recent innovations in mass printing to ensure a place for indigenous people in public discourse. This project was also at the heart of Copway's fourth and final book, a travelogue titled *Running Sketches of Men and Places, in England, France, Germany, Belgium, and Scotland*, published in 1851. An account of his travels in Europe and his participation in the Universal Peace Congress in Frankfort, Germany, in 1850, *Running Sketches* is in part a dissection of Copway's own role as speaker, writer, and political organizer. Advertised on the title page as written by "George Copway, (Kah-Ge-Ga-Gah-Bowh), chief of the Ojibway Nation, North American Indians," his travelogue presents Copway as a bridge between the nineteenth-century "man of letters," the figure of the Indian "chief," and the "North American Indian" more generally. *Running Sketches* simultaneously embraces and deflates the paradigmatic role of the Native intellectual as a representative of "his people": Copway's book caters to cultural expectations around indigenous orators as a variation on the "Indian chief," but it also decenters this trope to offer more idiosyncratic critiques of colonialism. Reflecting on the organizational dimensions of his travels and lectures, *Running Sketches* considers a new role for the authorized agent as a public indigenous intellectual, in a world of transnational exchange and organizing.

Copway's careers as a public speaker and author extended the mix of religion and politics that characterized the work of evangelical organizations, which were some of the most influential actors in creating a national reading public in the nineteenth-century United States. For reform-minded intellectuals like Copway, the networks of religious organizations represented an important political presence in the world, as their infrastructure sustained the reform efforts he championed and the publication landscape he sought to be a part of. Debates on all the pressing social issues of the time—slavery, women's rights, the "Indian question"—took place in publications sponsored by evangelical organizations and associations. The emergence of a cross-regional readership for print in the nineteenth century depended greatly on evangelical organizations that pioneered an infrastructure for mass publication. Bible and tract societies helped to disseminate reading materials across dispersed geographical locations, and evangelical publishers worked toward establishing a unified, cross-regional religious community. After the American

Tract Society invented a national distribution system based on salaried line employees and managers, by 1850 an elaborate system of colportage distribution was in use by Baptists, Presbyterians, and Methodists. As tract societies grew into major publishing houses, they laid the groundwork for what would become the first mass media in North America.[116] Moreover, as Phillip H. Round notes, not only did evangelical organizations determine how books circulated in North America, in the western territories "Christian missions and their books were significant 'points of contact.' "[117] In this regard, Copway's work as a missionary and his success as an author depended on such innovations in publishing and religious organizing, which connected the work of missions in the West to reading audiences on the East Coast.

Yet Copway's celebrity as an author did not depend on the printed word alone, since it grew out of his work as a public speaker on the lecture circuit. Like Peter Jones before him, Copway traveled to Europe in 1850, giving lectures in several countries and participating as a delegate to the Third International Peace Congress in Frankfurt am Main in Germany. He was invited by the famous philanthropist Elihu Burritt, one of the main organizers of the Congress and a prominent figure in the nineteenth-century peace movement. Organized by "American Quakers, European republicans, and British radical bourgeoisie," the Universal Peace Congress was held yearly between 1848 and 1853, and its organizers tried to initiate "a lasting international institution of dispute resolution."[118] Among the participants in the Frankfurt congress were the French author Victor Hugo, the English radical political activist Richard Cobden, the French polemicist Émile de Girardin, and a host of abolitionists. En route to the Peace Congress in Frankfurt, Copway lectured throughout England at meetings of such organizations as the Temperance Society, carrying letters of introduction from the poet Henry Wadsworth Longfellow and the historian Francis Parkman. His published account of these travels, *Running Sketches of Men and Places*, became the first book-length travel narrative by a Native American author, detailing his lecture tour in England, his participation in the Peace Congress in Frankfort, and his miscellaneous observations on European customs, institutions, scenery, and celebrities.

Throughout *Running Sketches*, Copway includes excerpts from other publications, which give a glimpse into how he navigated this transatlantic network of readers, spectators, and philanthropists, with particular attention to the use of new communication technologies. His account of his time in Liverpool, for instance, includes a substantial notice from the newspaper the *Mercury*, which had reviewed one of his lectures at the Mechanics' Institute in the city. The article dramatizes Copway's work to raise public notice around US-Indian relations, which depended on a range of communication technologies:

> If he could get, say £2,500 ... he would return to Washington again, and he intended to send out three of his brethren to deliver addresses throughout the country, and at the time have blank petitions circulated, and at a certain given time ... he wanted to touch the wires which vibrated from one end of the country to the other, he wanted to besiege the white house of the Government of the United States, and knock at the door of the American Government, that justice might be done to the Indian by giving him a home from which he shall never be removed again.[119]

By including this excerpt, Copway maps the communication circuits in which he operated, emphasizing the importance of newspapers such as the *Liverpool Mercury* and the *London Times* in "plac[ing] me before the citizens of Liverpool and the British public in general." In other words, *Running Sketches* narrates Copway's entry into a transatlantic community of benevolence, not as an object of white sympathy but as a link in a communication circuit. Playing on ideas about American Indians in the popular imagination, he notes that he was expected to "send '*paper talk*' to my American friends," and that he "*hunted* among those to whom I carried letters" to find someone who might "invite me to attend church with him."[120] Highlighting such efforts to carry letters between people in the United States and England, Copway embraced this role as a node in a wider system of communication.

Copway's travelogue draws out these communication circuits—rooted in interactions that were both face-to-face and mediated—and suggests that there is a potential for anticolonial organizing within them. He notes that his wealthy benefactors (John Prescott Bigelow, Amos Lawrence, Julius Palmer, and Reuben H. Walworth) expressed their "good-will to my race ... notwithstanding all the many aggravated wrongs which my poor brethren have received from the hands of the Pale face."[121] While Copway hints at a history of injustice, his idiomatic use of the phrase "pale face" is also an instance of him putting on the *Indian*: a slippage into a familiar, perhaps even cliché, rhetoric for writing about US-Indian encounters. In a similar fashion, Copway plays into feelings of colonial guilt by describing the moment just before he departs for England, and his anticipation is interrupted by news of the death of President Zachary Taylor. Copway again casts himself as a node in a transatlantic information circuit: perceiving "quite a commotion among the boarders," he finds out that "General Zachariah Taylor is no more! and we shall take to Europe the news of his death." But he also politicizes this moment, as he offers a brief anticolonial critique by remembering Taylor's involvement in the killing of Native Americans, as he expresses his hope that the "Great Spirit had forgiven him for killing so many of the red men of my country."[122] Presumably, Copway here refers to Taylor's order for Ojibwe removal in 1850, or perhaps to his participation in the Black Hawk War (1832) and the Second Seminole War (1838–1840). In either case, this passage does triple duty: Copway simultaneously performs a role as *Indian*, as a "neutral" carrier of information passing along the news of Taylor's death, and as an open-minded critic willing to pray for the president's forgiveness, despite the wrongs he committed to Native people. In moments like this, *Running Sketches* introduces something novel, as Copway emphasizes the idiomatic quality of his anticolonial arguments. Remixing familiar tropes in the representation of Native people, Copway touches on a history of colonialism while resisting the pathos of the "poor Indian" as an object of white sympathy.

Despite its novelty, *Running Sketches* received a muted reaction, probably in no small part because of its excessive excerpting from other volumes. Copway includes many long passages copied from tourist guides and magazines and newspaper articles, which give information on the places he visited, the people he met, and his own appearances on the lecture circuit. A reviewer of the *New York Tribune* wrote that there was "too much book-making in the volume, even for a Yankee compiler, to say nothing of an Indian chief, and a great portion of the extracts from common-place sources would have been better omitted."[123] For these reasons, critics have often approached *Running Sketches* as a rushed afterthought to his autobiography: Bernd Peyer notes that it is his "most pompous" and "least accomplished" publication, while A. LaVonne Brown Ruoff has called it "primarily a collection of quotations from local guidebooks" that fails to live up to the "narrative power of his autobiography."[124] More recently, however, critical commentary has recognized the significance of Copway's often idiosyncratic commentary on the relation between Native people and modernity. Kate Flint sees Copway's reprinting of different texts as "an acknowledgment of the need for a fluidity of styles and registers" in an attempt to make "some kind of sense and order of modern, urban existence." And Scott Richard Lyons argues that the *heteroglossia* on display in *Running Sketches*—its "radical interplay of different 'voices' "—offers a reflection on modernity and actively affirms native people's presence *in* modernity.[125] Indeed, it is this multivoiced composition that also allows Copway to capture the networked dynamics behind the organization of his lecture tour and his participation in the Universal Peace Congress.

Besides the effect of his excerpting, Copway's commentary in *Running Sketches* is amplified by his choice of the literary sketch as a framing device, which allows him to combine fragmentary observations of "men and places" with a measure of social commentary. As a genre, the literary sketch typically denotes a brief and usually entertaining account of characters, travels, locales, or stories, often about foreign or even exotic places. According to Kristie Hamilton, the literary sketch became a staple of magazine publishing in the nineteenth century. Their brevity and fragmentary form catered as easily to escapism as to social realism: literary sketches could alternately represent "inescapably nostalgic ways of seeing 'the country' " or scenes of "urban poverty, crowds and crowded conditions, labor exploitation, and the plight of immigrants."[126] Reflecting this duality, *Running Sketches* caters equally to a general interest in picturesque European locations and to a subtle commentary on ideologies of the *Indian*. For instance, in his account of his travels along the Rhine, Copway observes the landscape to point out that Europeans held on to more "superstitious" ideas than American Indians did: "Tales and Legends are told at each crevice of the rocks," he observes. "Wonders and displays of miraculous power, and a great deal of superstition, much more than the North American Indians ever had."[127] He points out the visible remnants of warfare in the Rhine Valley, and when he observes a royal "review of the soldiers," he suggests that while warfare is a thing of the past in Ojibwe country, it is still a present reality in Europe. "These soldiers make a brilliant and formidable appearance," he notes, "but such things are altogether repugnant to my feelings since my warrior's creed has been changed to a harmless one."[128] Copway invites his readers to admire the military spectacle, but then dismisses it as merely a state-sanctioned form of savagery: militarism and violence are the purview of the Western nation-state, he implies, but not of modern Indian nations.

Copway's first-person narrator blends the perspective of a traveling commentator—who makes sly and ironic critiques in passing—with a new variation on the Indian diplomat. In *The Transatlantic Indian*, Kate Flint notes that the volume displays a "fluidity of styles and registers" in order to engage white audiences that had difficulty distinguishing the "symbolic and the historical" when it came to their ideas about Native people.[129] As Copway shifts between these textual personae—the traveler and the chief—*Running Sketches* captures the ambiguities of his ability as a narrator to "represent" the Ojibwe or Native people in general. For instance, the title page introduces the author with some exaggeration as "Chief of the Ojibway Nation," and throughout the book he excerpts newspaper commentaries that also describe him as "chief." Although he was briefly vice president of the General Council of Christianized Ojibwas, Copway was never chief, yet *Running Sketches* evokes the figure of the "Indian chief" as a token of his authority on the lecture circuit and in print culture, to present himself as an authorized agent of the Ojibwe people and Native Americans generally. At the Universal Peace Congress of 1850, too, Copway was introduced as "lately a chief of the Red Indian tribes," and was asked to proclaim the Congress's fifth resolution on "the principle of non-intervention" and "the sole right of every state to regulate its own affairs."[130] According to the official proceedings of the Peace Congress, Copway gave a forty-minute speech that echoed familiar tropes of Indian diplomacy, for instance by presenting the organizers with a peace pipe: "When I left my country in the West, my aged father came to me and said, 'Here, my son, take this'—(unrolling the Indian pipe of peace)—yes, when I took my seat at this table, many persons seemed afraid to sit near me, as if I had arms in my hand; but Mr. President, it is not a weapon of war, it is a weapon of peace, which, in the name of my countrymen, I present to you—it is our calamet."[131] Copway argued that the Ojibwe's path to peace set an example for the "state of Europe, and the difficulties to have been overcome ... in the way of civilization." He asked if the time would soon come "when all the courts of Europe will send its representatives to this Congress, even from Rome itself?"[132] As transcribed in the proceedings, Copway's speech relished in his role as a delegate of the "Red Indians," representing a people who signed off on the project of peace and "civilization" *before* European nations did.

In *Running Sketches*, Copway's account of the Peace Congress downplays the importance of this diplomatic performance and conveys the ambiguous representational role that he wielded in Frankfort. Indeed, it is striking that no space is allotted for his own speech, especially in a book that reproduces so many different excerpts from letters, newspapers, and tour guides. Instead, Copway simply notes that his oratory at the Peace Congress was "his poorest speech," and explains that he will not "trouble the reader with even an outline of the remarks with which I endeavored to enforce the resolution."[133] In place of the speech, he includes a newspaper article about the Peace Congress, which amplifies the *visual* spectacle of Copway's oratory. For instance, the excerpt recounts that among the various speakers, "none seemed to attract more notice than an Indian Chief, with the noble Roman profile, and the long, shining, black hair," even if the "Frankforters are sorry that he wears a modern hat, instead of a cap with feathers."[134] Copway's practice of excerpting Copway simultaneously mobilizes and deflates paradigmatic ideas of the *Indian*, inviting reflection on the politics of representation for indigenous people in the modern world. Elsewhere, however, he refuses the European gaze. Recounting his travels in Belgium, Copway pauses on a moment of being recognized as an *Indian* by European bystanders: while waiting at the railway station in Liège about to board for Cologne, "for the first time the people recognized me as being the Indian from America. They came and stood in groups just by, and watched me as I paced the platform of the station."[135] His commentary on the situation ends immediately after this, however, and Copway does not dwell on the implications of being recognized as an "Indian from America." Instead, he describes being introduced to the American poet and painter Thomas Buchanan Read and a friend of the poet Ferdinand Freilingrath's. The move is telling: rather than commenting on the matter of being read as the *Indian* as an anomaly in European society, Copway emphasizes his inclusion in a network of poets and artists. His elliptical narrative refutes the assumption that his representational role—and that of the Native orator generally—is simply to be admired as an object of exoticism. By highlighting this network of hosts and fellow writers he claims a place among his literary peers.

Copway's play with such moments of recognition amplifies the book's meditation on the politics of representation for indigenous writers and speakers. *Running Sketches* exposes the tensions between its author's ability to speak freely as a public figure and the bounds on that freedom for people of color within a racialized regime of representation. He makes this duality explicit in an early chapter of the book, in which he defines his own role as a carrier of information from America to England. Declaring a set of rules that he intends to adhere to, Copway avows that

> I will have one invariable set of rules to observe wherever I shall be during my stay in this country—and it is this. I will uphold my race—I will endeavor never to say nor do anything which will prejudice the mind of the British public against my people—In this land of refinement I will be an Indian—I will treat everybody in a manner that becomes a gentleman—I will patiently answer all questions that may be asked me—I will study to please the people, and lay my own feelings to one side.[136]

Copway's list of rules pulls in two different directions. On the one hand, he casts aside his own feelings in order to be seen as a disinterested participant in a transatlantic public sphere. On the other hand, his avowal to "uphold my race" and "endeavor never to say nor do anything which will prejudice the mind of the British public" means that his participation is already shaped by a colonial relationship in which Native people are not perceived as impartial. Copway's list stages a central tension: can he, as a Native intellectual, comment impartially on the world around him? And if he approaches his subject with gentlemanly impartiality, can he still "be an Indian"? As laid out on the printed page, Copway's answer may be read as a tentative *yes*. He organizes his list horizontally rather than vertically, in a seemingly unordered fashion, and since Copway was notably fond of the numbered list, its absence here is striking. By presenting these different goals without apparent organization, he hints that they might stand in tension with one another. At the same time, Copway's words suggest that there is no reason to doubt that indigenous intellectuals can represent their people while also being committed to disinterested discourse—that the categories of intellectual and *Native* intellectual are not mutually exclusive.

It would be a stretch to call *Running Sketches* Copway's declaration of intellectual independence, if only because so many of Copway's ideas and paragraphs are borrowed from other publications. But as a self-conscious reflection on his own work as an organizer and writer, *Running Sketches* traces his complicated entry as an autonomous intellectual into a transnational public sphere, who published anticolonial critiques while being circumscribed by whites' expectations about how his work related to the life of indigenous communities. In this light, one problem that critics have tended to diagnose in Copway's work—the notion that he became increasingly "separated from his tribal origins"—may in fact be an effect of his turn toward different modes of organizing.[137] Copway's role as an authorized agent was not beholden to the representation of discrete, local indigenous communities, but he embraced a more mobile and perhaps ambiguous role as a node in a larger network of reformers, writers, politicians, and missionaries. *Running Sketches* critically examines this aspect of his own brief career as a public intellectual who navigated religious and governmental groups to pursue efforts of anticolonial organizing. Playing the role of the Indian diplomat in a transatlantic culture of print and performance, George Copway celebrated new practices of diplomacy and brought them into an important tradition of Native American publishing.

"MAKE SOME AMENDS"

If George Copway's *Running Sketches* offers an innovative representation of the Indian chief, he did not altogether abandon the type of romanticizing of tribal leaders that was such a commonplace in nineteenth-century American letters. In the concluding chapter of *The Life, History, and Travels of Kah-Ge-Ga-Gah-Bowh*, Copway praises a slew of Native leaders and warriors who were being lionized in the pages of American history books. Like Thomas McKenney and Henry Rowe Schoolcraft, Copway holds these figures up as emblems of the moral sentiment to be found in Indian nations. "Is it not well known that the Indians have a generous and magnanimous heart?" Copway asks. "I feel proud to mention in this connection, the names of a Pocahontas, Massasoit, Skenandoah, Logan, Kusic, Pushmataha, Philip, Tecumseh, Osceola, Petalesharro, and thousands of others. Such names are an honor to the world! ... Is it for the deeds of a Pocahontas, a Massassoit, and a host of others, that we have been plundered and oppressed, and expelled from the hallowed graves of our ancestors?"[138] Given the fact that he dedicated his book to Thomas McKenney, Copway had probably delved into the biographies in his *History of the Indian Tribes of North America*, finding deep moral values in its sketches of these famous Native Americans. But more than just a source of cultural pride, Copway sees the stories of these famous chiefs and diplomats as a call to action. "If help cannot be obtained from England and America," he asks, "where else can we look? Will you then, lend us a helping hand; and make some amends for past injuries?"[139] In Copway's eyes, the history and legacy of these chiefs and diplomats were important arguments in his call for anticolonial organizing, in Indian nations and in transnational networks of benevolence.

Copway's question captures a wider project of nineteenth-century Native literature in English, asking how the history of Native dispossession could be told in a way that recognized Indian nations' particular histories and their future prospects. Through acts of writing and public speaking, George Copway and Peter Jones expressed the tensions between, on the one hand, American understandings of Indian diplomacy as a corollary to US empire, and, on the other hand, the organization of political power in Ojibwe communities, which was located in complex networks of indigenous leaders, councils, missionaries, and reformers. Just as the *Literary Voyager* testified to Susan Johnston and Jane Johnston Schoolcraft's intimate knowledge of the relation between tribal authority, family networks, and community politics, Jones and Copway sketched a new imbrication of religious, political, and philanthropic networks in the work of Indian diplomacy. But perhaps the writings of American commentators such as Henry Rowe Schoolcraft and Thomas McKenney had the most lasting impact on the cultural legacy of nineteenth-century tribal leaders. As they wrote about the lives of diplomats, including Waubojiig and Shingabawossin, they rendered them as convenient vehicles for legitimizing American influence in Ojibwe country, belying the decentralized nature of indigenous politics and diplomacy in the Great Lakes. Over the course of the removal era, such interpretations dovetailed with the ways that the image of the Indian chief became a widely recognized yet ultimately effete symbol in American culture—either an emblem of a US national sentiment or a means to channel settlers' ambivalent feelings about the displacement of American Indians.

In this light, the fact that George Copway creatively styled himself a "chief" makes more sense, considering that the most culturally resonant figure of the indigenous orator was the Native American diplomat and tribal leader. His publications offered a counterpoint to the representation of the Ojibwe diplomat in American literature—a new iteration of the "Indian chief" that might gain purchase in a modern world of transnational cultural and literary exchange. Like Peter Jones before him, he interrogated his own role as an "authorized agent," whose words were assumed to represent the affairs of Ojibwe communities within philanthropic networks. In their own ways, Jones and Copway reinvented this representational role as they brought new forms of diplomatic exchange into the lecture circuit and a bourgeoning market for print. While examining their own movements through these networks, they contested knowledge about American Indians while promoting projects of reform that were responsive to the needs of indigenous communities. Their publications epitomize how nineteenth-century indigenous authors turned histories of cultural exchange into politically charged critiques of colonialism. Notwithstanding the limitations of their work, their representations of Native North America escaped facile understandings of Indian nations as culturally interesting yet politically invisible communities. Sending forth texts that knowingly reflected on the circulation of indigenous writing, they carried the work of Indian diplomacy into new realms of public discourse.

AFTERWORD

The Indians in the Lobby

Almost two centuries after Indian removal became a cornerstone of American nation-building and territorial expansion, still relatively few Native writers from this period have become part of its literary history. In surveys of Native American literature, authors such as Black Hawk and Elias Boudinot have long stood in for the full breadth of Indian nations that bore the brunt of removal policy in the nineteenth century. The surge in scholarship that seeks to broaden the archive of nineteenth-century Native American literature is therefore a development to be celebrated.[1] But the literary history of Indian removal also poses interpretive challenges. For how do we read removal-era writings without finding in them only an index of indigenous territorial and cultural loss? And how do we interpret a record of American expansion and indigenous dispossession without simply reifying the ascent of the settler state? In this book I have tried to show that the practice of Indian diplomacy played an integral part in shaping the literatures of Native North America, and that indigenous writers gave new meaning to this tradition as they confronted the crisis of removal and the ongoing pressures of settler colonialism. At a time when removal policy and settler expansion upended Native people's relationships to lands, economies, and cultural practices, diplomatic exchanges were a means for Native intellectuals and tribal leaders to protest the colonial policies of the settler state, while also advancing indigenous projects of education and institution-building. Some of these efforts had only limited effect and many were misinterpreted by policymakers and American reading audiences. But together these projects enacted a sphere of public discourse in which the concerns of Indian nations remained a central focus of debate and organizing, despite a rapidly transforming cultural landscape.

By the time the 1850s drew to a close, however, the routines of Indian diplomacy had become less central to the social and political lives of Native communities. Particularly after the American Civil War, the militarization of American society changed the dynamics of US-Indian relations in drastic ways. Gold rushes and the collapse of the powerful Comanche empire led to the rapid white settlement of the West, and brought the United States to engage in more frequent "Indian wars" and commit massacres of Native people.[2] As the American government began to see the "Indian problem" as one to be solved through military intervention, the long and ongoing contestations with Indian nations over land title and sovereignty became less and less important to its approach to Indian affairs. In 1871 the US Congress formally declared the end of the practice of making treaties with Indian nations, further dismantling the already-limited diplomatic power that indigenous people held. The government's changing approach to settler colonial conflict ushered in an increasingly restrictive reservation system and the assimilation programs of the late nineteenth century. If the literatures of Indian removal already testified to the dramatic land loss and displacement of indigenous people, by the turn of the twentieth century these forms of diplomatic negotiation had become a distant memory.

From this perspective, the literatures at the center of this book represent a pivotal generation of Native American authors whose work reflects a transition from older models of Indian diplomacy to the activism of late-nineteenth-century authors, who often performed anticolonial critiques outside the purview of US-Indian diplomatic relations.[3] For removal-era authors, navigating institutions of Indian diplomacy took many different forms and meant more than simply acquiescence to colonial pressures and ideologies. To contest US-Indian relations was to enter debates about how to manage Indian nations' investment in education, how to organize their economic activities, how to reconcile intertribal and US-Indian diplomacy, and how to make philanthropic projects responsive to the demands of Native communities. The history of nineteenth-century Native American literature is the history of indigenous authors who turned to a range of media to grapple with the question of how to arrive at meaningful social and institutional change. These projects responded to a longer history of dramatic and violent dispossession that was shaped not only by isolated moments of removal but by structural patterns of capitalist trading practices, commercial agriculture, land speculation, militarization, and bureaucratic mismanagement. Even if these projects failed to present any radical opposition to American ideas or institutions, they consistently performed meaningful critical work: they outlined and intervened in existing debates, they narrated complex histories of colonialism, and they critically reflected on the politics of representation within diplomatic networks.

This means that indigenous publication projects of the removal era were about crucial matters of land and dispossession, but not exclusively so. The diplomatic writings at the heart of this book also confronted the lived realities of the removal era by considering the place of Native people in a new landscape of social and political institutions. As Kate Flint argues in *The Transatlantic Indian*, in the nineteenth century Native people found themselves responding to a range of new pressures and changes, including "demographic upheavals" and their severance from ancestral homelands and from "traditional connections to both space and time."[4] At the same time, indigenous people experienced a broader set of changes that came with the onset of the modern nation-state and global capitalism: a closer relationship to "world markets and industrialization," new roles as "subjects, rather than agents" in the development of the nation-state, and "subjection to externally imposed bureaucracy." Finally, the nineteenth century brought on new ways of thinking about the self and others, through "the growth of the rhetoric of individuality," the "articulation of various freedoms" (including freedom of speech), and the incorporation of Native people into "systems of mass communication."[5] If these characteristics of modernity sound familiar, perhaps it is because they represent some of the fault lines that shape global conflicts, crises, oppressions, and opportunities to this very day. In this respect, Native authors engaged with the political crisis of Indian removal while they alternately embraced and resisted the global currents of life in the modern age.

The literatures of Indian diplomacy reflect the extent to which Native people were able to wield control over such changes and pressures, and in doing so they expressed inherently future-oriented visions of Native people's place in modern life. Projecting in concrete terms a social and political place in North America, they refused the notion that their future as autonomous Indian nations was incompatible with the onset of modernity. As a growing body of scholarship in Native studies has emphasized, indigenous nations have always been innovative and future-oriented agents in the making of the modern world, and indigenous authors responded to historical changes not only by either resisting or accommodating change, but by building or endorsing new institutions, ideologies, concepts, and alliances.[6] Such endorsements of new ideas and institutions represent what Scott Richard Lyons terms "x-marks," the decisions that Native people made in a colonial context of limited choices and even coercion, but that nevertheless signal their assent to what they deemed the best choices available, and that held the potential to work out positively for Native communities.[7] Of course, signing on to new institutions and ideas did not undo a violent history of dispossession, but it contradicted colonial narratives in which Indian nations are incongruous with change, modernity, and futurity. More than subjects of a colonial regime, they were global actors who made and remade the fabrics of modern life by negotiating indigenous futures.

As they engaged the crisis of Indian removal, Native diplomats and writers were participants in transnational debates over sovereignty and empire in a rapidly changing world. This is not to suggest, however, that Euro-American narratives of temporality are the only framework for understanding indigenous people's relation to time and futurity. In *Beyond Settler Time*, Mark Rifkin argues that examining indigenous "persistence, adaptations, and innovation" within modernity risks reaffirming settler conceptions of temporality, in which the history of the settler state is the only context by which to count historical time. It is imperative, Rifkin suggests, to attend to "discrepant temporalities" that may not be "mergeable into a neutral common frame—call it time, modernity, history, or the present."[8] This important caveat notwithstanding, it is worth remembering that the denial of Native people's place in modernity was not primarily about time but about place. The idea that American Indians were doomed to either assimilate or fade away in light of "civilization" legitimized to settlers and policymakers the expropriation of indigenous lands, presupposing a historical narrative in which settler societies had a future in North America and indigenous societies did not. The perception of Indian nations as incompatible with modernity rendered them inherently vulnerable and offered the ideological rationale for extinguishing indigenous land title. In the face of historical ruptures that caused sudden and dramatic change—opening up some possibilities while foreclosing others—Native writers and speakers sought to claim a social and political place for Indian nations that was not marked by fragility or temporariness. Through the workings of US-Indian diplomacy, they asserted these anticolonial ideas within American institutions of government and civil society.

In studies of Native American literature, however, indigenous writing that was produced through the networks of colonial institutions is often regarded with a measure of skepticism. For instance, in his seminal study *The People and the Word*, Robert Allen Warrior names William Apess as "a turning point in the history of Native writing" because his work was published "without the benefits of institutional or programmatic support," and therefore stands as a "model for contemporary work."[9] In this reading, the work of Apess represents a form of individual expression that was free from the trappings of institutional support, suggesting that Native authors' relationships to existing institutions are merely a matter of somewhat unfortunate context. Still, I would argue that it is necessary to attend to the institutional contexts of Native writing beyond the extent to which authors escaped or refused them. We risk disregarding important avenues of indigenous publication if we dismiss them too quickly as colonial projections or as forms of cultural-political translation. To claim such collaborative and institutionally embedded writings as part of a body of Native American literature does not mean we should try to "filter out" the distortions produced by their publication context or to isolate a purely indigenous speech act from them. Rather, they represent an inherently dialogic writing tradition that negotiated indigenous sovereignty, land-centered histories of settler colonialism, and transnational forms of exchange. The challenge is to see such institutionally embedded writings as more than inherently suspect collaborations or as vehicles for US imperial projections, and to attend to the ways in which they carried out indigenous projects of publication.

Despite the long tradition of Indian diplomacy, the image of Native people who navigated colonial institutions is one that American culture tends to shy away from. Consider, for example, the following scene from Aaron Sorkin's TV drama series *The West Wing*. An episode titled "The Indians in the Lobby," which originally aired on the eve of Thanksgiving 2001, opens with two Native activists from the Stockbridge-Munsee community who are standing in the White House lobby. They have been stood up by a staffer who was supposed to discuss with them a petition that their tribe had submitted more than a decade ago, but although the meeting has been canceled, the activists refuse to leave the premises of the White House. Press secretary C. J. Cregg (Allison Janney) is asked to defuse a potentially bad PR situation by engaging the activists—Maggie Morningstar-Charles (Georgina Lightning) and Jack Lonefeather (Gary Farmer)—as they stand quietly in the lobby while staffers and visitors buzz around them. Even when C.J. invites them into her office, they decline to leave their spot, and when she insists, Jack parries, "Then you can forcibly remove us. I've noticed that correspondents from the Times, Reuters, CNN, and the Miami Herald are here." C.J. backs off: "This is gonna have something to do with us screwing you out of all your land, isn't it?"[10] It is a strong opening. The delegates are savvy: they know the importance of media representation and they know how to leverage the little power they have. Their very presence disrupts the normal proceedings at the White House as they stick to their principles in service of their cause. By the end of the episode, however, the show seems oddly comfortable leaving these activists intact as *outsiders*: even in the final scenes they are still standing, tired yet defiant, in the lobby, presenting an image of Native American representatives who are always standing just outside of the room where decisions are made.

This scene resonates because it aligns with dominant ideas about the relation between Indian nations and American institutions of government. This representation of Indian delegates in Washington reaffirms notions of what Philip J. Deloria terms "Indians in unexpected places," cultural "anomalies" that ultimately re-inscribe rather than disrupt the normative expectations of American society.[11] The "Indians in the lobby" offer a powerful image of protest, but it is also clear that at the end of the day, they do not have a seat at the negotiating table. Given the contours of such narratives, the idea of Indian diplomacy may call to mind a hazily remembered history of treaties once made, rather than the ongoing negotiations between Indian nations and settler governments about issues including education, healthcare, natural resources, housing, or indigenous government. Against this lacuna, scholarship in Native American studies has offered new views of what historian Kevin Whalen calls the "relationships between indigenous peoples and the state structures that aimed at different times to control, improve, and erase them."[12] Indeed, our understanding of the relationships between Native communities and institutional structures is inherently bound up with the question of how indigenous people intervened in them, in the past and in the present. This is all the more relevant since to this day, institutions of various kinds—from tribal colleges and cultural centers to universities and the Bureau of Indian Affairs—play crucial roles in such issues as Native American language preservation, cultural revival, healthcare, education, and social and economic justice.

To take Indian diplomacy seriously as an important site of colonial contestation may just broaden our understanding of what indigenous resistance to settler colonialism looks like. For instance, the groundbreaking political work of the "Red Power" movement in the 1960s and 1970s is closely associated—quite logically so—with the direct activism of the American Indian Movement (AIM). Yet this history of activism emerged in part from a longer tradition of Indian diplomacy, in which not only tribal governments but organizations such as the National Congress of American Indians (NCAI) and the National Indian Youth Council (NIYC) performed a pivotal role. James H. Cox argues in *The Red Land to the South* that the work of these organizations was characterized by "slow, cautious, and tedious negotiations" within governmental networks, contrasting sharply with "popular depictions of the direct actions of the Red Power period."[13] As Cox notes, even Vine Deloria Jr., who is often regarded as "the quintessential Red Power intellectual voice," favored more established routes of diplomacy over direct action.[14] More than that, the most widely covered moments of direct protest during the Red Power era were also interwoven with diplomatic forms of negotiation. The occupation of Alcatraz Island by activists of Indians of All Tribes, from November 1969 to June 1971, is well known as an event that led to widespread media coverage and renewed the commitments of activists and policymakers to the political recognition of tribal sovereignty. But the occupation also led to sustained negotiations about making the island a place to serve American Indian communities and commemorating their history, with a museum, a cultural center, statues, and a "state-of-the-art transportation system."[15] And besides the high-profile activism of the Trail of Broken Treaties (1972) and the Wounded Knee occupation (1973), American Indian Movement (AIM) activists also navigated a range of organizations and government institutions to establish community-centered education programs for Native people in the Twin Cities.[16] The history of Red Power activism, then, was also in part a history of projects that were aimed at building new institutions and remaking existing ones.

To critically examine such forms of institutional negotiation is to refuse what Gerald Vizenor calls "terminal creeds" for thinking about indigenous people's historical agency. Terminal creeds are narrative patterns that always situate American Indians in fixed subject positions, in which they signify only the *Indian*—a colonial simulation of indigenous people devoid of history or active presence.[17] When it comes to the topic of Native people's relation to colonial institutions, such simulations run deep. Consider the American poet Philip Freneau, whose 1788 poem "The Indian Student" expresses an enduring idea of Native people's role in existing institutions. In it, a Native American boy encounters a missionary who convinces him to go to college in the East. He departs to Cambridge to trade in the "silver stream" and "limpid lake" for "musty books, and college halls." But when he arrives there, the Indian student finds nothing of use to him and returns to "nature's ancient forests," where this particular Vanishing Native American finds a more fitting environment:

> 'My heart is fix'd and I must go
> To die among my native shades.'
> He spoke, and to the western springs
> (His gown discharged, his money spent
> His blanket tied with yellow strings,)
> The shepherd of the forest went.[18]

"The Indian Student" reveals more about white Americans' longing for an imagined past than about Native American education, but it is nevertheless a revealing text. Freneau imagines an unbridgeable distance between indigenous people's experiences and the possibility of transforming colonial institutions or using them to pursue self-defined goals. This is the image of the *Indian* for whom navigating colonial spaces is always a loss of authenticity, and this is also a terminal creed. If we fail to recognize how Native writers and speakers have always used, critiqued, and adapted the institutions that shape US-Indian relations even to this day, Freneau's "Indian Student" will have cast a long shadow indeed.

The literatures of Indian diplomacy are an essential site for reexamining the histories of Native-settler relations and how we tell them in the present. The economic and political marginalization of Native people over the past centuries has engendered a public discourse in which Indian affairs are often understood as a distant history instead of a continuous colonial relationship between indigenous nations and settler states. And as Craig Womack suggests, the idea of Native resistance to colonialism is often associated only with "plains warriors on horseback" and histories of direct military action.[19] Scholars of Native American and indigenous studies still find themselves at the forefront of deconstructing the tropes by which settler-indigenous relations are typically understood, to insist on new narratives that reflect that, in Frederick Hoxie's words, "Native people spent far more time negotiating, lobbying, and debating than they spent tomahawking settlers or shooting at soldiers."[20] If Indian diplomacy evokes a hazily remembered history of treaties once made, its literary record suggests a more telling story about indigenous writers and orators who produced critical records of institutional wrangling—negotiations about place and power in a colonial culture. Their collaborative acts of publication carried the work of Indian diplomacy into a wider cultural sphere and gave shape to an important tradition of indigenous literature. Envisioning new indigenous futures in North America, they spoke back to institutions that played a central role in a history of dispossession. To claim a voice in these spaces was to carry out an ongoing project of Native American writing.

NOTES

NOTES TO INTRODUCTION

1. "Indian Eloquence," *Richmond Enquirer* (Richmond, VA), December 6, 1821. The same speech was printed in numerous other newspapers that year. The editorial note reads, "The following speech was delivered by Shun-kah-kihe-gah, (the Child Chief), Second Chief of the Grand Pawnees, Agent for Indian affairs on the Missouri, at Fort Atkinson, on the 10th June, 1821, on the subject of the Pawnee Loups, plundering and insulting some Americans on the Arkansas River." "Grand Pawnee" was the Americans' designation for the Pawnee band typically known as the Chaui Pawnees. The rendering of indigenous names by newspapers editors is notoriously unreliable, so it is possible that "Shun-kah-kihe-gah" is the same person referred to as "Shinggacahega" in an 1818 treaty between the Chaui Pawnee and the United States. See "Treaty with the Grand Pawnee, 1818," in *Indian Affairs: Laws and Treaties*, vol. II, *Treaties*, ed. Charles J. Kappler (Washington, DC: Government Printing Office, 1904), 156–57.

2. "Indian Eloquence."

3. Ibid.

4. Ibid.

5. I use the term "Indian diplomacy" to denote the diplomatic relations between Indian nations and settler nations in North America. For the majority of the analyses in this book, this involves relations between the United States and various Indian nations. However, since this book also covers diplomacy among different Indian nations as well as diplomacy between Indian nations and Great Britain, I favor the term "Indian diplomacy" over "US-Indian diplomacy."

6. "Indian Eloquence." Emphasis in original.

7. Philip H. Round, *Removable Type: Histories of the Book in Indian Country, 1663–1880* (Chapel Hill: University of North Carolina Press, 2010), 103.

8. Richard White, *The Middle Ground: Indians, Empires, and Republics in the Great Lakes Region* (Cambridge, UK: Cambridge University Press, 1991). Although White himself has noted that the concept of the "middle ground" is not as mobile as it has sometimes been given credit for—it being more unique to the geographical region he termed the *pays d'en haut*—his work underscores that Indian diplomacy forged a new world of intercultural traditions from political recognition and mutual misinterpretation. See Philip J. Deloria, "What Is the Middle Ground, Anyway?" *William and Mary Quarterly*, Third Series, 63, no. 1 (2006): 15–16.

9. For a history explaining how national identities were projected onto more loosely confederated bands and families, see Michael Witgen, "The Rituals of Possession and the Problems of Nation," ch. 2 of *An Infinity of Nations: How the Native New World Shaped Early North America* (Philadelphia: University of Pennsylvania Press, 2012), 69–107. For an analysis of how national identities emerged via the projections of American empire as well as the newly forged connections between indigenous families and American traders, see Anne F. Hyde, *Empires, Nations, and Families: A History of the North American West, 1800–1860* (Lincoln: University of Nebraska Press, 2011).

10. György Ferenc Tóth, *From Wounded Knee to Checkpoint Charlie: The Alliance for Sovereignty Between American Indians and Central Europeans in the Late Cold War* (Albany: State University of New York Press, 2016), 15.

11. In this respect, the participation in Indian diplomacy itself was what Scott Richard Lyons calls an "x-mark." Referring to the method by which most Native treaty signatories signed US-Indian treaties, Lyons defines "x-marks" as an analytical concept that points to moments of Native American agency in situations where such agency signifies both Native assent and colonial coercion. As markers of the interplay between Native agency, colonial pressures, and cultural "contamination," x-marks reflect "the political realities of the treaty era." Scott Richard Lyons, *X-Marks: Native Signatures of Assent* (Minneapolis: University of Minnesota Press, 2010), 1

12. Matt Cohen and Jeffrey Glover, eds., *Colonial Mediascapes: Sensory Worlds of the Early Americas* (Lincoln: University of Nebraska Press, 2014), 5–7.

13. Andrew Newman, *On Records: Delaware Indians, Colonists, and the Media of History and Memory* (Lincoln: University of Nebraska Press, 2012); Birgit Brander Rasmussen, *Queequeg's Coffin: Indigenous Literacies and Early American Literature* (Durham, NC: Duke University Press, 2012).

14. Craig Womack, *Red on Red: Native American Literary Separatism* (Minneapolis: University of Minnesota Press, 1999), 15; Matt Cohen, *The Networked Wilderness: Communicating in Early New England* (Minneapolis: University of Minnesota Press, 2010), 7.

15. Here it is important to recognize Trish Loughran's argument in *The Republic in Print* that despite the "techno-mythology" of print culture being tied directly to US national origins, "there was no 'national' print culture before the industrial revolution slowly centralized literary production in the 1830s, '40s, and '50s" (3). Furthermore, Loughran's work shows that when centralized literary production did develop in the mid-nineteenth century, it did not bring about national unification but rather regional and political division. In this respect, the increasingly expansive, cross-regional reach of print was not "national" in any homogenous sense. See Trish Loughran, *The Republic in Print: Print Culture in the Age of U.S. Nation Building, 1770–1870* (New York: Columbia University Press, 2007).

16. Michael Warner, *The Letters of the Republic: Publication and the Public Sphere in Eighteenth-Century America* (Cambridge, MA: Harvard University Press, 1992).

17. The *Cherokee Phoenix*, first edited by Elias Boudinot (1802–1839), was the first Native American newspaper, published in New Echota, the capital of Cherokee Nation. Its first run, before it was revived in the twentieth century, lasted from 1828 until 1834. See Theda Perdue, ed., *Cherokee Editor: The Writings of Elias Boudinot* (Athens:

University of Georgia Press, 1996); Lyon, *X-Marks*, 127–29; Round, *Removable Type*, 124–49; Theresa Strouth Gaul, "Editing as Indian Performance: Elias Boudinot, Poetry, and the *Cherokee Phoenix*," in *Native Acts: Indian Performance, 1603–1832*, ed. Joshua David Bellin and Laura L. Mielke (Lincoln: University of Nebraska Press, 2011), 281–307; Megan Vallowe, "The Long Arm of the *Phoenix* in Nineteenth-Century Political Reprinting," *American Periodicals* 28, no. 1 (2018): 41–55.

18. Black Hawk, *Life of Ma-ka-tai-me-she-kia-kiak or Black Hawk, embracing the tradition of his nation—Indian wars in which he has been engaged—cause of joining the British in their late war with America, and its history—description of the Rock-River village—manners and customs—encroachments by the whites, contrary to treaty—removal from his village in 1831. With an account of the cause and general history of the late war, his surrender and confinement at Jefferson Barracks, and travels through the United States. Dictated by himself*, ed. J. B. Patterson (Cincinnati, 1833).

19. Elizabeth Maddock Dillon, "John Marrant Blows the French Horn: Print, Performance, and the Making of Publics in Early African American Literature," in *Early African American Print Culture in Theory and Practice*, ed. Lara Cohen and Jordan Stein (Philadelphia: University of Pennsylvania Press, 2012), 338.

20. Eric Cheyfitz, "The (Post)Colonial Construction of Indian Country," in *The Columbia Guide to American Indian Literatures of the United States since 1945*, ed. Eric Cheyfitz (New York: Columbia University Press, 2006), 87.

21. Arnold Krupat, *For Those Who Come After: A Study of Native American Autobiography* (Berkeley: University of California Press, 1985), 7–8.

22. Susan Manning, "Performance," in *Keywords for American Cultural Studies*, ed. Bruce Burgett and Glenn Hendler (New York: New York University Press, 2007), 177–78.

23. For further background on Apess and the Mashpee Revolt, see Lisa Brooks, *The Common Pot: The Recovery of Native Space in the Northeast* (Minneapolis: University of Minnesota Press, 2008), 163–97; Philip F. Gura, *The Life of William Apess, Pequot* (Chapel Hill: University of North Carolina Press, 2015). 77–99; and Drew Lopenzina, *Through an Indian's Looking Glass: A Cultural Biography of William Apess, Pequot* (Amherst: University of Massachusetts Press, 2017), 169–209; and Barry O'Connell, "Introduction," in *On Our Own Ground: The Complete Writings of William Apess* (Amherst: University of Massachusetts Press, 1992), xiii–lxxviii.

24. Kiara M. Vigil, *Indigenous Intellectuals: Sovereignty, Citizenship, and the American Imagination, 1880–1930* (Cambridge, UK: Cambridge University Press, 2015), 12.

25. Sandra Gustafson, "American Literature and the Public Sphere," *American Literary History* 20, no. 3 (2008): 467–70. A substantial body of work on the history of the book in North America has shown that the production of early American periodicals and novels was rooted in the conversational modes and belletrist practices of urban elites. Crucially, Caroline Wigginton argues that in early America, the circulation of letters and materials among Native, black, and white women were acts of "relational publication." Marked by intimacy and particularity, such exchanges between women were foundational in fashioning an alternative to the abstract and masculinist sphere of republican print culture. See Caroline Wigginton, *In the Neighborhood: Women's Publication in Early America* (Amherst: University of Massachusetts Press, 2016), 7–13. For other analyses

of the relational dimensions of writing and publication, see also David Shields, *Civil Tongues and Polite Letters in British America* (Chapel Hill: University of North Carolina Press, 1997); Bryan Waterman, *Republic of Intellect: The Friendly Club of New York City and the Making of American Literature* (Baltimore: Johns Hopkins University Press, 2007); Catherine O'Donnell Kaplan, *Men of Letters in the Early Republic: Cultivating Forums of Citizenship* (Chapel Hill: University of North Carolina Press, 2008); Mary Kelley, *Learning to Stand and Speak: Women, Education, and Public Life in America's Republic* (Chapel Hill: University of North Carolina Press, 2008).

26. See Robert Lawrence Gunn, *Ethnology and Empire: Languages, Literature, and the Making of the North American Borderlands* (New York: New York University Press, 2015); Sean P. Harvey, *Native Tongues: Colonialism and Race from Encounter to the Reservation* (Cambridge, MA: Harvard University Press, 2015); Susan Scott Parrish, *American Curiosity: Cultures of Natural History in the Colonial British Atlantic World* (Chapel Hill: University of North Carolina Press, 2006); Sarah Rivett, *Unscripted America: Indigenous Languages and the Origins of a Literary Nation* (Oxford, UK: Oxford University Press, 2017); Kelly Wisecup, *Medical Encounters: Knowledge and Identity in Early American Letters* (Amherst: University of Massachusetts Press, 2013).

27. Richard Brodhead, *Cultures of Letters: Scenes of Reading and Writing in Nineteenth-Century America* (Chicago: University of Chicago Press, 1995), 8.

28. Gunn, *Ethnology and Empire*, 5

29. Ibid., 10.

30. Brooks, *The Common Pot*, 229.

31. Phillip H. Round, *Removable Type: Histories of the Book in Indian Country, 1663–1880* (Chapel Hill: University of North Carolina Press, 2010), 102–3.

32. Nancy Fraser, "Rethinking the Public Sphere: A Contribution to the Critique of Actually Existing Democracy," in *Habermas and the Public Sphere*, ed. Craig Calhoun (Cambridge, MA: MIT Press, 1992), 132–36.

33. James H. Cox, *The Red Land to the South: American Indian Writers and Indigenous Mexico* (Minneapolis: University of Minnesota Press, 2012), 112, 113.

34. David Alff, *The Wreckage of Intentions: Projects in British Culture, 1660–1730* (Philadelphia: University of Pennsylvania Press, 2017), 7.

35. Alfred Schütz, *The Phenomenology of the Social World*, translated by George Walsh and Frederick Lehnert, 1932 (Evanston: Northwestern University Press, 1967), 57–91.

36. Ann Mische, "Projects and Possibilities: Researching Futures in Action," *Sociological Forum* 24, no. 3 (2009): 696. See also Ann Mische and Philippa Pattison, "Composing a Civic Arena: Publics, Projects, and Social Settings," *Poetics* 27, nos. 2–3 (2000): 163–94.

37. Relatedly, Elizabeth Povinelli's work on indigenous communities in Australia considers "social projects" as the group-based, projective imagining of alternative lifeworlds. See Elizabeth Povinelli, *Economies of Abandonment: Social Belonging and Endurance in Late Liberalism* (Durham, NC: Duke University Press, 2011), 6–9.

38. In their definition of the project as a temporary organization, Ralf Müller and J. Rodney Turner argue that "a project is a temporary organization to which (human, material, and financial) resources are assigned to undertake a unique, novel,

and transient endeavor . . . to deliver beneficial objectives of change." Ralf Müller and J. Rodney Turner, "On the Nature of the Project as a Temporary Organization," *International Journal of Project Management* 21, no. 1 (2003): 7. Organization theorists have consistently grappled with a theorization of "the project," and define it as a relatively short-term, transient employment of effort and resources that works both by the virtue of, and as a means to *intervene in*, larger organizational structures. For a chronological overview of definitions of *projects* from organization theory, see François Chiochhio, E. Kevin Kelloway, and Brian Hobbs, *The Psychology and Management of Project Teams* (Oxford, UK: Oxford University Press, 2015), 7.

39. Cheyfitz, "(Post)Colonial Construction of Indian Country," 8.

40. Ibid., 7.

41. Maureen Konkle, *Writing Indian Nations: Native Intellectuals and the Politics of Historiography, 1827–1863* (Chapel Hill: University of North Carolina Press, 2004), 26–41.

42. Cheyfitz, "(Post)Colonial Construction of Indian Country," 110n6.

43. Cherokee Women and Nancy Ward, [Petition to the Cherokee National Council, 30 June 1818], in *Native American Women's Writing: An Anthology*, ed. Karen L. Kilcup (Oxford, UK: Blackwell, 2000), 29.

44. Ibid., 26.

45. Ibid., 30.

46. Stuart Banner, *How the Indians Lost Their Land: Law and Power on the Frontier* (Cambridge, MA: Harvard University Press, 2005), 193.

47. Ibid., 194.

48. William E. Unrau, *The Rise and Fall of Indian Country, 1825–1865* (Lawrence: University Press of Kansas, 2007), 7.

49. Banner, *How the Indians Lost Their Land*, 217.

50. Andrew Jackson, from State of the Union Address, 6 December 1830, in *The Cherokee Removal: A Brief History with Documents*, ed. Theda Perdue and Michael D. Green, 3rd ed. (Boston: Bedford/St. Martin's Press, 2016), 121.

51. Unrau, *Rise and Fall of Indian Country*, 3.

52. Christina Snyder, *Great Crossings: Indians, Settlers, and Slaves in the Age of Jackson* (Oxford, UK: Oxford University Press, 2017), 145.

53. Ibid., 145.

54. John P. Bowes, *Land Too Good for Indians: Northern Indian Removal* (Norman: University of Oklahoma Press, 2016), 51.

55. Ibid., 58.

56. For Jeremiah Evarts's critical writings against removal, see especially his *Speeches on the Passage of the Bill for the Removal of the Indians, Delivered in the Congress of the United States, April and May 1830* (Boston, 1830) and *Essays on the Present Crisis in the Condition of the American Indian, First Published in the National Intelligencer under the Signature of William Penn* (Philadelphia, 1830). The latter volume's "William Penn" essays were republished in Francis Paul Prucha, ed., *Cherokee Removal: The "William Penn" Essays & Other Writings by Jeremiah Evarts* (Knoxville: University of Tennessee Press, 1981).

57. See Isaac McCoy, *Remarks on the Practicability of Indian Reform, Embracing their Colonization* (New York: Gray and Dunce, 1829).

58. For influential histories of Indian removal, see Grant Foreman, *Indian Removal: The Emigration of the Five Civilized Tribes* (Norman: University of Oklahoma Press, 1953); Ronald N. Satz, *American Indian Policy in the Jacksonian Era* (Lincoln: University of Nebraska Press, 1974); and Francis Paul Prucha, *The Great Father: The United States Government and the American Indians*, abridged edition (Lincoln: University of Nebraska Press, 1984), 64–121. Following Ronald Satz's *American Indian Policy in the Jacksonian Era*, a dominant narrative of removal has been that the federal government's inaction rather than action was the cause of removal being as widespread as it was. Stephen Rockwell argues against this notion, noting that the federal policy of removal was precisely engineered to engage a wide range of agencies at different levels in the process of removal. See Stephen J. Rockwell, *Indian Affairs and the Administrative State in the Nineteenth Century* (Cambridge, UK: Cambridge University Press, 2010), 111. The role of local and regional interests in removal in the Midwest is dealt with sensitively and critically in Susan Gray, "Limits and Possibilities: White-Indian Relations in Western Michigan in the Era of Removal," *Michigan Historical Review* 20, no. 2 (Fall 1994): 71–91; Gray, "Of Two Worlds and Intimate Domains," in *Beyond Two Worlds: Critical Conversations on Language and Power in Native North America*, ed. James Joseph Buss and C. Joseph Genetin-Pilawa (Albany: State University of New York Press, 2014), 161–80; John P. Bowes, "Indian Removal beyond the Removal Act," *NAIS* 1, no. 1 (2014): 65–87; and Bowes, *Land Too Good for Indians*.

59. Throughout this book, my use of the words "settler" and "indigenous" refers to terms that denote a settler colonial relationship. I understand settler colonialism as a particular form of colonialism centered on extinguishing indigenous land title and eroding Indian sovereignty. It differs from exploitation colonialism in that it hinges not primarily on the extraction of indigenous labor, but on the expropriation of native land. As Lorenzo Veracini puts it, if in exploitation colonialism the relation between colonizer and colonized can be captured by the phrase "you, work for me," settler colonialism operates by the logic of "you, go away." This particular colonial relationship shapes the dialectic between "settler" and "indigenous," and both are analytical distinctions rather that categories of ethnic or racial identity. See Lorenzo Veracini, "Introducing Settler Colonial Studies," *Settler Colonial Studies* 1, no. 1 (2011): 1.

60. Patrick Wolfe, "Settler Colonialism and the Elimination of the Native," *Journal of Genocide Research* 8, no. 4 (2006): 393.

61. Carole Pateman, "The Settler Contract," *Contract and Domination*, ed. Carole Pateman and Charles W. Mills (Cambridge, UK: Polity Press, 2007), 46–53.

62. Amanda J. Cobb, "Understanding Tribal Sovereignty: Definitions, Conceptualizations, and Interpretations," *American Studies* 46, no. 3–4 (2005): 115–16.

63. See Vine Deloria, Jr., and Clifford T. Lytle, "American Indians in Historical Perspective," ch. 1 in *American Indians, America Justice* (Austin: University of Texas Press, 1983), 2–8; Francis Paul Prucha, *Great Father*, 72–77; Konkle, *Writing Indian Nations*, 17–18.

64. Audra Simpson, *Mohawk Interruptus: Political Life Across the Borders of Settler States* (Durham, NC: Duke University Press, 2014), 11.

65. Kevin Bruyneel, *The Third Space of Sovereignty: The Postcolonial Politics of US-Indigenous Relations* (Minneapolis: University of Minnesota Press, 2007).

66. Scott Richard Lyons, "Rhetorical Sovereignty: What Do American Indians Want from Writing?" *College Composition and Communication* 51, no. 3 (2000): 447–68; Robert Warrior, *Tribal Secrets: Recovering Native American Intellectual Traditions* (Minneapolis: University of Minnesota Press, 1995).

67. See Michelle Raheja, *Reservation Reelism: Redfacing, Visual Sovereignty, and Representations of Native Americans in Film* (Lincoln: University of Nebraska Press, 2013); Tahu Kukutai and John Taylor, eds., *Indigenous Data Sovereignty: Toward an Agenda* (Acton: Australian National University Press, 2016); and Mark Rifkin, *Beyond Settler Time: Temporal Sovereignty and Indigenous Self-Determination* (Durham, NC: Duke University Press, 2017). In addition, the 2017 and 2018 meetings of the Native American and Indigenous Studies Association included papers or panels on "sonic sovereignties," "seed sovereignty," "research sovereignty," and "screen sovereignty," testifying to the central place of indigenous sovereignty as a concept in Native American and indigenous studies scholarship.

68. See Lucy Maddox, *Removals: Nineteenth-Century American Literature and the Politics of Indian Affairs* (Oxford, UK: Oxford University Press, 1991); Susan Scheckel, *The Insistence of the Indian: Race and Nationalism in Nineteenth-Century American Literature* (Princeton: Princeton University Press, 1998); Cheyfitz, "(Post)colonial Construction of Indian Country" and "The (Post)colonial Predicament of Native American Studies," *Interventions: International Journal of Postcolonial Studies* 4, no. 3 (2002): 405–27. For a recent example of a study that successfully takes the contestation of opposing land claims as a framework for thinking about Delaware and American literatures, see Andrew Newman, *On Records: Delaware Indians, Colonists, and the Media of History and Memory* (Lincoln: University of Nebraska Press, 2012).

69. For brevity and readability, I hereafter refer to the Office of Indian Affairs as the "Indian Office."

70. Qtd. in Herman Viola, *Thomas McKenney: Architect of America's Early Indian Policy: 1816–1830* (Chicago: Sage, 1974), 202.

71. See Viola, *Thomas McKenney*. In *The Great Father*, Francis Paul Prucha points out the evolution of Thomas McKenney's ideas about removal. First he regarded it as necessary only in cases where he deemed Indian nations' surroundings to be detrimental to their happiness. Gradually, however, he came to see no potential whatsoever for Indian nations to remain in their homelands, given what he called the "degradation" of Eastern tribal nations. See Francis Paul Prucha, *The Great Father: The United States Government and the American Indians* (Lincoln: University of Nebraska Press, 1984), 54–57, 72.

72. Viola, *Thomas McKenney*, 95; Robert M. Kvasnicka, "George W. Manypenny," in *The Commissioners of Indian Affairs, 1824–1977*, ed. Herman J. Viola and Robert M Kvasnicka (Lincoln: University of Nebraska Press, 1979), 60.

73. Rockwell, *Indian Affairs and the Administrative State*, 111.

74. Bowes, "Indian Removal beyond the Removal Act," 67.

75. Antonio Gramsci, *Selections from the Prison Notebooks*, ed. Quintin Hoare and Geoffrey Nowell Smith (New York: International Publishers, 1971), 247–53.

76. Edward Said, *Orientalism* (New York: Vintage, 1978), 6–7.

77. William J. Novak, "The American Law of Association: The Legal-Political Construction of Civil Society," *Studies in American Political Development* 15, no. 2 (2001): 163.

78. See Rockwell, *Indian Affairs*, 150; Jon Reyhner and Jeanne Eder, *American Indian Education: A History* (Norman: University of Oklahoma Press, 2015), 43.

79. See Hyde, *Empires, Nations, and Families*, passim.

80. Rockwell, *Indian Affairs and the Administrative State*, 47.

81. Michael Denning, "The Peculiarities of the Americans: Reconsidering *Democracy in America*," in *Culture in the Age of Three Worlds* (London: Verso, 2004), 201.

82. Stuart Hall. "Gramsci's Relevance for the Study of Race and Ethnicity," *Journal of Communication Inquiry* 10, no. 5 (1986): 19.

83. Frederick E. Hoxie, "Retrieving the Red Continent: Settler Colonialism and the History of American Indians in the US," *Ethnic and Racial Studies* 31, no. 6 (2008): 1157.

84. Donald B. Smith, *Mississauga Portraits: Ojibwe Voices from Nineteenth-Century Canada* (Toronto: University of Toronto Press, 2013), 182.

85. Ibid., 184–85.

86. George Copway, *The Life, History, and Travels of Kah-Ge-Ga-Gah-Bowh (George Copway), A Young Indian Chief of the Ojibwa Nation*, vol. II (Philadelphia, 1847), 138.

87. Ibid., 138.

88. Phillip H. Round, "Indian Publics," in *Native Acts: Indian Performance, 1603–1832*, ed. Joshua David Bellin and Laura L. Mielke (Lincoln: University of Nebraska Press, 2011), 251.

89. William H. Sewell, Jr., "A Theory of Structure: Duality, Agency, and Transformation," *American Journal of Sociology* 98, no. 1 (1992): 20.

90. Ibid. Social theorists Ann Mische and Mustafa Emirbayer similarly consider agency as an interplay between actors and larger structures, and the exigencies of a given historical moment. They define *agency* as "the temporally constructed engagement by actors of different structural environments," which can both reproduce and transform those structures "through the interplay of habit, imagination, and judgment," in response to "the problems posed by changing historical situation." Mustafa Emirbayer and Ann Mische, "What Is Agency?" *American Journal of Sociology* 103, no. 4 (1998): 970.

91. Beth H. Piatote, "The Indian/Agent Aporia," *The American Indian Quarterly* 37, no. 3 (2013): 46.

92. Ibid., 49.

93. Walter Johnson, "On Agency," *Journal of Social History* 37, no. 1 (2003): 119.

94. Ibid., 116.

95. Konkle, *Writing Indian Nations*, 26–34.

96. For the role of women in the fur trade, see Sylvia Van Kirk, *Many Tender Ties: Women in Fur-Trade Society, 1670–1870* (Norman: University of Oklahoma Press, 1983); Jennifer S. H. Brown, *Strangers in Blood: Fur Trade Company Families in Indian Country* (Norman: University of Oklahoma Press, 1996); Susan Sleeper-Smith, *Indian Women and French Men: Rethinking Cultural Encounter in the Western Great Lakes* (Amherst: University of Massachusetts Press, 2001); and Hyde, *Empires, Nations, and Families*.

97. Glen Coulthard, *Red Skin, White Masks: Rejecting the Colonial Politics of Recognition* (Minneapolis: University of Minnesota Press, 2014).

NOTES TO CHAPTER I

1. For a detailed analysis of Samuel F. B. Morse's *The House of Representatives*, see Elisa Tamarkin, *Anglophilia: Deference, Devotion, and Antebellum America* (Chicago: University of Chicago Press, 2008), xv–xxii. Tamarkin points out that the clock above the doorway suggests it is 6:13 in the evening and that the painting includes portraits of "sixty-eight congressmen, six justices of the Supreme Court, a sergeant-at-arms, a Pawnee chief, and Morse's father," even though the painting stills "feels empty" due to the size of the chamber (xv).

2. Not only did King's portrait of Petalesharo lay the basis for Samuel Morse's figure in *House of Representatives*, his father Jedidiah Morse used it as the frontispiece for his report on Indian country when it was published as a book in 1822. Jedidiah Morse, *Report to the Secretary of War, of the United States, on Indian Affairs: Comprising a Narrative of a Tour Performed in the Summer of 1820* (New Haven, 1822). For more information on the history of the "Indian gallery," see Herman J. Viola, *The Indian Legacy of Charles Bird King* (Washington, DC: Smithsonian Institution Press, 1976), 15–21, and Steven Conn, *History's Shadow: Native Americans and Historical Consciousness in the Nineteenth Century* (Chicago: University of Chicago Press, 2004), 49–50.

3. C. Joseph Genetin-Pilawa, "The Indians' Capital City: Diplomatic Visits, Place, and Two-Worlds Discourse in Nineteenth-Century Washington, DC," in *Beyond Two Worlds: Critical Conversations on Language and Power in Native North America*, ed. James Joseph Buss and C. Joseph Genetin-Pilawa (Albany: State University of New York Press, 2014), 114.

4. Genetin-Pilawa, "Indians' Capital City," 114.

5. Ibid., 117, 119.

6. John Calhoun to Benjamin O'Fallon, 8 March 1819, Letters Sent, Records of the Secretary of War related to Indian Affairs, 1800–1824. Microfilm Publications, National Archives and Records Administration, RG75, M15. Roll 5, vol. D.

7. Christopher Deventer to William Clark, 23 June 1818, LS-SWIA, Roll 5, vol. D.

8. Treaty between the United States and the Piitahawiraata Pawnee, *American and Commercial Daily Advertiser* (Baltimore), February 1, 1819. The language of the treaties signed with the Pawnee nations was identical to that in Clark and Chouteau's treaties with the Iowa, various Sioux nations, and the Otoes, Poncas, Menominee, and Quapaw.

9. Francis Paul Prucha, *The Great Father: The United States Government and the American Indian*, vols. 1 and 2 unabridged (Lincoln: University of Nebraska Press, 1984), 175.

10. Anne F. Hyde, *Empires, Nations, and Families: A History of the North American West, 1800–1860* (Lincoln: University of Nebraska Press, 2011), 294.

11. Richard Edward Oglesby, *Manuel Lisa and the Opening of the Missouri Fur Trade* (Norman: University of Oklahoma Press, 1963), 153–54; Tanis C. Thorne, *The Many Hands of My Relations: French and Indians on the Lower Missouri* (Columbia: University of Missouri Press, 1996), 157.

12. Hyde, *Empires, Nations, and Families*, 49.

13. For a more detailed discussion of this system, see Hyde, *Empires, Nations, and Families*, 243–44.

14. William S. Belko, "John C. Calhoun and the Creation of the Bureau of Indian Affairs: An Essay on Political Rivalry, Ideology, and Policymaking in the Early Republic," *South Carolina Historical Magazine* 105, no. 3 (2004): 173. For a historical analysis of the factory system during these historical developments, see Hyde, *Empires, Nations, and Families*, 255–262.

15. Herman J. Viola, *Diplomats in Buckskins: A History of Indian Delegations in Washington City*, 1981 (Bluffton, SC: Rivolo, 1995), 25.

16. Prucha, *Great Father*, 84.

17. John Calhoun to Benjamin O'Fallon, May 22, 1821, LS-SWIA, Roll 5, vol. E; John Calhoun to O'Fallon, August 18, 1821, LS-SWIA, Roll 5, vol. E.

18. John Calhoun to O'Fallon, 18 August 1821, LS-SWIA, Roll 5, vol. E.

19. John Calhoun to O'Fallon, 10 October 1821, LS-SWIA, Roll 5, vol. E.

20. In identifying the names of these delegates, I have chosen to use the spellings most consistently used in the historical record and scholarship. There is little historical evidence, however, that the commentators at the time accurately captured the names or titles of the delegates. In this light, I use these names as a means to identify a more complex author function that was prone to error on the part of scribes or translators. On a related note, the historian George Hyde identifies two delegates named "Pitalesharo" who came to Washington in 1821–22, one a Skidi Pawnee and one a Kithehaki Pawnee. It is possible that the Kithehaki delegate refers to the same delegate McKenney calls "Peskelachaco." See George E. Hyde, *The Pawnee Indians*, 1951 (Norman: University of Oklahoma Press, 1974), 175.

21. Herman J. Viola, "Invitation to Washington—A Bid for Peace," *The American West* IX, no. 1 (1972): 21. Herman Viola writes that while Benjamin O'Fallon was put up at the luxurious Indian Queen Hotel in Washington, the delegates stayed in George Miller's tavern, known as an establishment where slave-owners often housed their slaves while visiting the capital (24–25).

22. Richard White, *The Roots of Dependency: Subsistence, Dependency, and Social Change among the Choctaws, Pawnees, and Navajos* (Lincoln: University of Nebraska Press, 1983), 154–56; 162. Even the very name *Pawnee* loomed large in the American cultural imagination: in newspapers and reports from traders it became a generic term for any hostile band that Americans were unfamiliar with, and perpetrators of attacks on American traders would often be casually identified as "Pawnee," whether or not they belonged to any Pawnee band. Many thanks to Susan Sleeper-Smith for pointing this out to me.

23. Pekka Hämäläinen, *The Comanche Empire* (New Haven: Yale University Press, 2008), 159.

24. "From the Council Bluffs," *Daily National Intelligencer* (Washington), November 14, 1821. The entry is dated "St. Louis, Oct. 13."

25. Hyde, *Empires, Nations, and Families*, 244.

26. Ibid.

27. Susan M. Ryan, *The Grammar of Good Intentions: Race and the Antebellum Culture of Benevolence* (Ithaca, NY: Cornell University Press, 2003), 27.

28. William E. Unrau, *The Rise and Fall of Indian Country, 1825–1855* (Lawrence: University Press of Kansas, 2007), 48.
29. Unrau, *Rise and Fall of Indian Country*, 48.
30. Hyde, *Empires, Nations, and Families*, 273. See also T. F. Morrison, "Mission Neosho: The First Kansas Mission," *The Kansas Historical Quarterly* 4, no. 3 (1935), 227–34.
31. "Indian Deputation," *Religious Intelligencer*, vol. 6 (January 1822), 576. The Committee of Missions was an association of Presbyterian, Reformed Dutch, and Associate Reformed missionaries; the UMFS was a Presbyterian missionary society.
32. "Indian Deputation," *American Missionary Register, for the Year 1823*, vol. IV (New York, 1823): 576.
33. Joseph Lancaster, *The British System of Education: Being a Complete Epitome of the Improvements and Inventions Practised by Joseph Lancaster: to which is Added, a Report of the Trustees of the Lancaster School at Georgetown, Col.* (Washington, 1812), 122. According to a report of the school's trustees, in 1812 the Lancaster school in Georgetown already had 370 students a year after its opening.
34. The Lancaster method was first introduced in the United States in 1806 with the establishment of the public-school system in New York. See Phillip H. Round, "America's Indigenous Reading Revolution," in *Why You Can't Teach United States History Without American Indians*, eds. Susan Sleeper Smith et al. (Chapel Hill: University of North Carolina Press, 2015), 167–68, and Patricia Crain, *Reading Children: Literacy, Property, and the Dilemmas of Childhood in Nineteenth-Century America* (Philadelphia: University of Pennsylvania Press, 2016), 12–13, 63–78.
35. Hilary Wyss, *English Letters and Indian Literacies: Reading, Writing, and New England Missionary Schools* (Philadelphia: University of Pennsylvania Press, 2012), 133.
36. "Indian Deputation," *American Missionary Register* IV, no. 1 (January 1823): 14.
37. Ibid., 15.
38. See Mary Black-Rogers, "Varieties of 'Starving': Semantics and Survival in the Subarctic Fur Trade, 1750–1850," *Ethnohistory* 33, no. 4 (1986): 353–83; Bruce M. White, "'Give Us a Little Milk': The Social and Cultural Meanings of Gift-Giving in the Lake Superior Trade," *Minnesota History* 48, no. 2 (1982), 60–71; Bruce White, "A Skilled Game of Exchange: Ojibway Fur Trade Protocol," *Minnesota History* 50, no. 6 (1987), 229–40.
39. "Indian Deputation," *American Missionary Register*, 15.
40. Viola, "Invitation to Washington," 21.
41. "Indian Deputation," 15. While the Chaui Pawnee speaker is unnamed in the *Register*'s report, there is reason to assume that this speaker was Sharitarish, since he was the main delegate of the Chaui Pawnee.
42. "Indian Deputation," *American Missionary Register*, 15.
43. Ibid., 17.
44. Ibid., 17.
45. "Indian Deputation," *Religious Intelligencer* VI, no. 34 (January 19, 1822): 538.
46. "Indian Deputation," *American Missionary Register*, 16–17.
47. Ibid., 17.
48. Philip J. Deloria, *Playing Indian* (New Haven: Yale University Press, 1998), 21.

49. In the early US republic, newspapers writings were not produced by professional journalists, but depended on intimate epistolary networks. Newspaper articles were often contributed by "friends" writing personal letters to editors, often with the explicit request or expectation that their letters would be published in their newspapers. In the absence of copyright law, such contributions were then often reprinted in other newspapers and magazines, either with or without an acknowledgment of the original source. These could achieve region-wide circulation within days while maintaining the character of personal communications.

50. William Faux, *Memorable days in America: being a journal of a tour to the United States, principally undertaken to ascertain, by positive evidence, the condition and probable prospects of British emigrants; including accounts of Mr. Birkbeck's settlement in the Illinois: And intended to show Men and Things as they are in America* (London, 1823), 378.

51. "Aboriginal Deputation," *Washington Gazette* (Washington), November 29, 1821.

52. Faux, *Memorable days in America*, 378.

53. Ibid., 381.

54. Shari M. Huhndorf, *Going Native: Indians in the American Cultural Imagination* (Ithaca, NY: Cornell University Press, 2001), 20.

55. *Daily National Intelligencer* (Washington), February 11, 1822. The article is dated 6 February 1822.

56. Ibid.

57. As Karen Halttunen writes, "costume, manner, body markings, and linguistic patterns could indicate status or rank, occupation, nationality, and . . . moral character." See Karen Halttunen, *Confidence Men and Painted Women: A Study of Middle-class Culture in America, 1830–1870* (New Haven: Yale University Press, 1982), 36.

58. In this respect, the position of Native orators was similar to that of nineteenth-century African American orators, whom white audiences expected to perform their humanity through the display of the "eloquent body." As Robert Fanuzzi argues in *Abolition's Public Sphere*, the oratory of black abolitionists constituted a "visual sphere" in which "white audiences occupied the omnipotent, disembodied position of spectator and trained their eyes on the orator's black body." Frederick Douglass's audiences, for instance, "sharpened their observations of the black orator, whose every anatomical feature and gesture could signify the superiority of abolitionist principles." Robert Fanuzzi, *Abolition's Public Sphere* (Minneapolis: University of Minnesota Press, 2003), 83–84.

59. *Daily National Intelligencer* (Washington), February 11, 1822.

60. Ibid.

61. Ibid.

62. David Waldstreicher, *In the Midst of Perpetual Fetes: The Making of American Nationalism, 1776–1820* (Chapel Hill: University of North Carolina Press, 1997), 2–3, 12.

63. Susan G. Davis, *Parades and Power: Street Theatre in Nineteenth-Century Philadelphia* (Philadelphia: Temple University Press, 1986), 4.

64. "Indian Dance," *Washington Intelligencer* (Washington), March 7, 1822.

65. Ibid.

66. *Baltimore Patriot and Mercantile Advertiser* (Baltimore), Feb. 14, 1822. Charles Durang (1796–1870) was an American dancer, actor, and stage manager.
67. Ibid.
68. Ibid.
69. "Indian Dance," *Essex Register* (Salem, MA), February 23, 1822. According to an editorial note, this was an "extract of a letter" originally sent to the editor of the *Providence American*.
70. *Daily National Intelligencer* (Washington), February 11, 1822.
71. Robert Lawrence Gunn, *Ethnology and Empire: Languages, Literature, and the Making of the North American Borderlands* (New York: New York University Press, 2015), 75.
72. Several years after the delegation, in the fall of 1825, there is a record of Petalesharo and his father signing a treaty at Fort Atkinson that guaranteed Americans safe passage on the Santa Fe Trail. Hyde, *Pawnee Indians*, 179.
73. The painter Charles Bird King referred to him as "Terrekitauahu" ("Generous Chief"), and the name Petalesharo seems to be an Americanization of "Piitariisaaru" ("Man Chief"). See also Mark van de Logt, "Brides of the Morning Star: The Petalesharo Legend and the Skiri Pawnee Rite of Human Sacrifice in American Popular Fiction," in *The Challenges of Native American Studies: Essays in Celebration of the Twenty-fifth American Indian Workshop*, ed. Barbara Saunders and Lea Zuyderhoudt (Leuven, Belgium: Leuven University Press, 2004), 207.
74. James F. Brooks, *Captives and Cousins: Slavery, Kinship, and Community in the Southwest Borderlands* (Chapel Hill: University of North Carolina Press, 2002), 11.
75. Ibid., 13–14.
76. Ibid., 14–15.
77. Ibid., 16.
78. "Anecdote of a Pawnee Chief," *Daily National Intelligencer* (Washington), 29 January 1822.
79. Ibid.
80. Brooks, *Captives and Cousins*, 14. This is also the interpretation in Hyde, *Pawnee Indians*, 160.
81. Edwin James, *Account of an Expedition from Pittsburgh to the Rocky Mountains: Performed in the Years 1819 and '20 by Order of the Hon. J. C. Calhoun, Secretary of War: Under the Command of Major Stephen H. Long*, vol. I (Philadelphia, 1823), 358.
82. Hyde, *Pawnee Indians*, 160–61.
83. Richard White, *Roots of Dependency*, 174.
84. Melburn D. Thurman, "The Skidi Pawnee Morning Star Sacrifice of 1827," *Nebraska History* 51 (1970): 272–76.
85. [Mary Rapine], "Address," *Ladies' Literary Cabinet, Being a Repository of Miscellaneous Literary Productions, Both Original and Selected, in Prose and Verse*, vol. V (New York, 1822), 141. The report of Rapine and Petalesharo's speeches was published earlier in the *Georgetown Metropolitan* of March 2, 1822. For studies of women's seminaries and the participation of women in public life, see Mary P. Ryan, *Cradle of the Middle Class: The Family in Oneida County, New York, 1790–1865* (Cambridge, UK: Cambridge University Press, 1983) and Mary Kelley, *Learning to Stand and Speak:*

Women, Education, and Public Life in America's Republic (Chapel Hill: University of North Carolina Press, 2006).

86. For more details about the friendship medal that the seminary students gave to Petalesharo, see Viola, *Indian Legacy of Charles Bird*, 31.

87. [Rapine], "Address," 141.

88. Ibid.

89. Ibid.

90. Gayatri Chakravory Spivak, "Can the Subaltern Speak?" in *Colonial Discourse and Post-Colonial Theory*, ed. Patrick Williams and Laura Chrisman (New York: Columbia University Press, 1994), 93.

91. "The Pawnee's Reply," *Ladies' Literary Cabinet*, vol. V (New York, 1822), 141.

92. Ibid., 141. In a reflection on the event published some fifteen years later, Thomas McKenney paraphrased Petalesharo's speech in a slightly different way: "This [medal] brings rest to my heart. I feel like the leaf after a storm and when the wind is still. I listen to you. I am glad. I love the pale faces more than I ever did, and will open my ears wider when they speak. I am glad you heard of what I did. I did not know the act was so good. It came from my heart. I was ignorant of its value. I now know how good it was. You make me know this by giving me this medal." See Thomas McKenney, "Petalesharo," in *History of the Indian Tribes of North America*, vol. I, 1836 (Philadelphia: D. Rice, 1872), 149.

93. Huhndorf, *Going Native*, 20.

94. *Daily National Intelligencer* (Washington), February 11, 1822.

95. Ibid.

96. American newspaper and magazine articles bearing the title "Indian Eloquence" or "Aboriginal Eloquence" had a long history, the most prominent example being the speech of the Mingo chief Logan, famously reprinted in Thomas Jefferson's *Notes on the State of Virginia* (1782). For two perceptive recent discussions of Logan's speech, see Gordon M. Sayre, *The Indian Chief as Tragic Hero*, 162–202; Carolyn Eastman, "The Indian Censures the White Man: 'Indian Eloquence' and American Reading Audiences in the Early Republic," *William & Mary Quarterly*, Third Series, 65, no. 3 (2008): 535–63; Gunn, *Ethnology and Empire*, 74–75.

97. Steven Conn, *History's Shadow: Native Americans and Historical Consciousness in the Nineteenth Century* (Chicago: University of Chicago Press, 2004), 93. See also Eastman, "Indian Censures the White Man," 537–38.

98. For instance, in 1820 the author and politician Caleb Atwater proposed a volume of Indian oratory arguing that it was "high time, before it be forever too late, to collect into one body, specimens of Indian eloquence." Caleb Atwater, "Indian Eloquence," *City of Washington Gazette* (Washington), June 28, 1820. The *City of Washington Gazette* attributes the article to the *National Gazette*. See also Gunn, *Ethnology and Empire*, 73–75.

99. Qtd. in Morse, *Report to the Secretary of War*, 283.

100. *Fletcher v. Peck*, 10 U.S. (6 Cranch) 87 (1810).

101. Eric Cheyfitz, "The (Post)Colonial Construction of Indian Country," 110n6.

102. Jodi Byrd, *The Transit of Empire: Indigenous Critiques of Empire* (Minneapolis: University of Minnesota Press, 2012), xiii.

103. *Daily National Intelligencer* (Washington), February 11, 1822.
104. Ibid.
105. Morse, *Report to the Secretary of War*, 244.
106. See W. C. Vanderwerth, ed., *Indian Oratory: Famous Speeches by Noted Indian Chieftains* (Norman: University of Oklahoma Press, 1971), 79; "Petalesharo," *Norton Anthology of American Literature*, vol. B: *1820–1865*, 9th ed., ed. Michael A. Elliott, Sandra M. Gustafson, Amy Hungerford, and Mary Loeffelholz (New York: Norton, 2017), 313. The cause of the confusion is unclear, but it probably has to do with the fact that Sharitarish's oratory was usually reprinted in newspapers anonymously. Also, in Jedidiah Morse's *Report to the Secretary of War* (1822), the frontispiece features Petalesharo's portrait, with an asterisk referring to a section of the book in which Sharitarish's speech is printed prominently.

107. Frederick Turner, ed., *The Portable North American Indian Reader* (New York: Viking, 1973), 247; Colin Calloway, *Our Hearts Fell to the Ground: Plains Indian Views of How the West Was Lost* (Boston: Bedford/St. Martin's, 1996), 56. Although there does not seem to be direct evidence that the "Speech by the Pawnee Chief" was spoken by Sharitarish, several circumstantial factors make Sharitarish a more likely source. The Chaui delegate would probably have been the first to speak after President Monroe, as the Chaui Pawnee were the most prominent and influential band. Second, Sharitarish had been instrumental in facilitating the relations between the Chaui Pawnee and Benjamin O'Fallon, showing himself more willing than other tribal leaders—including the head chief Tarecawawaho—to engage in US-Indian diplomacy. Third, in several newspapers and volumes that reprint the delegates' speeches, the first and longer speech is given as the speech of a "Pawnee Chief," while a second, much shorter speech is given more specifically as a "Pawnee Loup Chief." For these reasons, it is reasonable to conclude that the first speech was given by the main Chaui Pawnee representative, Sharitarish.

108. Hyde, *Pawnee Indians*, 152.

109. Dougherty was born in Kentucky in 1791 and came to St. Louis in 1808, where he signed on with the Missouri Fur Company. Over the next ten years he worked as a trapper and trader near the mouth of the Big Horn River, in what is now Wyoming and Montana. In 1819 he was a member of Major Stephen H. Long's Yellowstone Expedition, which came to the Upper Missouri Indian Agency at Council Bluffs, near present-day Omaha, Nebraska. He stayed there to serve as the interpreter for the US Office of Indian Affairs, working for the Indian agent Benjamin O'Fallon as subagent and interpreter until 1827.

110. David Bernstein, *How the West Was Drawn: Mapping, Indians, and the Construction of the Trans-Mississippi West* (Lincoln: University of Nebraska Press, 2018), 141–44. However, it is worth noting that at least two different newspaper sources give a similar account of the Pawnee speech. A summary of the council with President Monroe—also published in the *National Intelligencer* and dated February 6, 1822—includes a substantial paraphrase of the oratory of a Pawnee chief, which corresponds to the contents of the published speech.

111. Michael Foucault, "What Is an Author?" in *Language, Counter-Memory, Practice: Selected Essays and Interviews*, ed. Donald F. Bouchard (Ithaca, NY: Cornell University Press, 1977), 113–38.

112. *Daily National Intelligencer* (Washington), February 11, 1822.
113. More, *Report to the Secretary of War*, 244–45.
114. Ibid., 245.
115. Ibid., 245.
116. Hyde, *Pawnee Indians*, 175.
117. Loretta Fowler, *The Columbia Guide to American Indians of the Great Plains* (New York: Columbia University Press, 2003), 45, 58.
118. Lorenzo Veracini, "Introducing Settler Colonial Studies," *Settler Colonial Studies* 1, no. 1 (2011): 14.
119. White, *Roots of Dependency*, 199.
120. Morse, *Report to the Secretary of War*, 244. Italics in original.
121. Ibid., 245.
122. White, *Roots of Dependency*, 199–203.
123. Bernstein, *How the West Was Drawn*, 141.
124. Ibid., 143.
125. Mary Black-Rogers, "Varieties of 'Starving': Semantics and Survival in the Subarctic Fur Trade, 1750–1850," *Ethnohistory* 33, no. 4 (1986): 358.
126. White, *Roots of Dependency*, 154–56, 162.
127. Ibid., 199.
128. Morse, *Report to the Secretary of War*, 245.
129. Ibid.
130. To gather data for his study, Jedidiah Morse toured the former Northwest Territory, the Great Lakes region, Canada, and the Mississippi River Valley. See Hyde, *Empires, Nations, and Families*, 282. One source of information for Morse was the journal of Captain John R. Bell, who had accompanied Stephen Harriman Long on his expedition of 1819–1820. Morse furnishes information about the Pawnees from Bell's journal, as well as information on other tribal nations. For the regions he did not visit, Morse relied on materials from traders, Indian agents, and military officers.
131. Morse, *Report to the Secretary of War*, 241.
132. Ibid.
133. Johannes Fabian, *Time and the Other: How Anthropology Makes Its Object*, 1983 (New York: Columbia University Press, 2002), 25–36.
134. Morse, *Report to the Secretary of War*, 246.
135. Ibid., 246–47.
136. "Aboriginal Eloquence," *Daily National Intelligencer* (Washington), February 16, 1822.
137. For a historical analysis of territorial expansion of the Western Sioux, see Richard White, "The Winning of the West: The Expansion of the Western Sioux in the Eighteenth and Nineteenth Century," *Journal of American History* 65, no. 2 (1978): 319–43.
138. Morse, *Report to the Secretary of War*, 246.
139. Ibid.
140. I. G. Hutton, "The Generous Chief" (Washington: 1824), William L. Clements Library, University of Michigan.
141. See Wayne Franklin, *James Fenimore Cooper: The Early Years* (New Haven: Yale University Press, 2007), 478.

142. James Fenimore Cooper, *Notions of the Americans: Picked up by a Travelling Bachelor* (London, 1828), 381.
143. Ibid., 381.
144. Ibid., 369.
145. Ibid., 380.

NOTES TO CHAPTER 2

1. Henry Rowe Schoolcraft, *Personal Memoirs of a Residence of Thirty Years with the Indian Tribes on the American Frontiers* (Philadelphia, 1851), 216.
2. In the records of the Indian Office, the Meskwaki people were typically referred to as the Fox people, and presently the largest of the three federally recognized tribes of the Sauk and Meskwaki is also called the Sac and Fox Nation. I use "Sauk" and "Meskwaki" to acknowledge that the history at the center of this chapter is the history of the Sauk and Meskwaki people more broadly, beyond that of the Sac and Fox Nation in Oklahoma.
3. Mark Rifkin, "Documenting Tradition: Territoriality and Textuality in Black Hawk's Narrative," *American Literature* 80, no. 4 (2008): 695.
4. Thomas Burnell Colbert, " 'The Hinge on Which All Affairs of the Sauk and Fox Indians Turn': Keokuk and the United States Government," in *Enduring Nations: Native Americans in the Midwest*, ed. Russell David Edmunds (Urbana: University of Illinois Press, 2008), 55. For instance, in 1955 Donald Jackson described Keokuk as "a smooth talker and a politician who planned to co-exist with the Americans," whereas Black Hawk was "a bull-headed fighter who chose a bitter last stand against extinction." And Joshua David Bellin's analysis of the *Life* characterizes Keokuk as one of the "puppet leaders" who falsely assumed tribal leadership and unwittingly promoted the projects of the settler state. Donald Jackson, "Introduction," *Black Hawk: An Autobiography*, 1833, ed. Donald Jackson (Urbana: University of Illinois Press, 1955), 31. Joshua David Bellin, "How Smooth Their Language: Masculinity and Self-Performance in the *Life of Black Hawk*," *American Literature* 65, no. 3 (1993): 486.
5. Colbert, "Keokuk and the United States Government," 55.
6. Ibid., 55.
7. Ibid., 55.
8. William T. Hagan, *The Sac and Fox Indians* (Norman: University of Oklahoma Press, 1958), 94–95.
9. J. Gerald Kennedy, "Introduction," in Black Hawk, *Life of Black Hawk, or Ma-ka-tai-me-she-kia-kiak. Dictated by Himself*, ed. J. Gerald Kennedy, 1833 (New York: Penguin, 2008), ix. See also Roger L. Nichols, *Black Hawk and the Warrior's Path* (Arlington Heights, IL: Harlan Davidson, 1992), 27–28.
10. For a detailed account of this history of removal, see Hagan, "Iowa Interlude," ch. 16 in *The Sac and Fox Indians*, 205–24.
11. Michael Witgen, *An Infinity of Nations: How the Native New World Shaped Early North America* (Philadelphia: University of Pennsylvania Press, 2012), 346.
12. Colbert, "Keokuk and the United States Government," 57.

13. Ibid., 56. Colbert notes that Secretary of War Calhoun drew up a new treaty that paid the tribes for the disputed lands and established a reservation for mixed-blood Sauks and Meskwakis in southeast Iowa.

14. Jay Buckley, *William Clark: Indian Diplomat* (Norman: University of Oklahoma Press, 2010), 147.

15. Ibid., 148.

16. Council with the Sacs & Foxes, St. Louis, 27 March 1830. Letters Received Office of Indian Affairs. Roll 728, Sac and Fox Agency, 1824–1833.

17. Ibid.

18. Colbert, "Keokuk and the United States Government," 58.

19. Council with the Sacs & Foxes, St. Louis, 27 March 1830.

20. Ibid.

21. Stephen J. Rockwell, *Indian Affairs and the Administrative State in the Nineteenth Century* (Cambridge, UK: Cambridge University Press, 2010), 62.

22. Council with the Sacs & Foxes, St. Louis, 14 June 1830, LROIA, Roll 728, Sac and Fox Agency, 1824–1833.

23. Ibid.; Colbert, "Keokuk and the United States Government," 58. Colbert also notes that at intertribal councils, Keokuk was prone to arrive by boat at a moment when all the other nations would already be present, while dressed in war regalia and singing war songs (56–57).

24. Council with the Sacs & Foxes, St. Louis, 14 June 1830. According to Thomas McKenney in *History of the Indian Tribes of North America*, Peahmuska was killed by a Menominee war party—not Sioux. See McKenney, *History of the Indian Tribes in North America*, vol. I, 396–97.

25. Council with the Sacs & Foxes, 14 June 1830.

26. Ibid.

27. Ibid.

28. Ibid.

29. Ibid.

30. Ibid.

31. Colbert, "Keokuk and the United States Government," 58–59.

32. Cheyfitz, "(Post)Colonial Construction of Indian Country," 7.

33. John A. Wakefield, *History of the War Between the United States and the Sac and Fox Nations of Indians, and Parts of Other Disaffected Tribes of Indians, in the Years Eighteen Hundred and Twenty-Seven, Thirty-One, and Thirty-Two* (Jacksonville, IL, 1834), 107–8.

34. Qtd. in Buckley, *William Clark*, 209.

35. Patrick J. Jung, *The Black Hawk War of 1832* (Norman: University of Oklahoma Press, 2007), 172.

36. Treaty with the Sauks and Foxes, 1832, in *Indian Affairs: Laws and Treaties*, vol. II, ed. Charles J. Kappler (Washington, DC: Government Printing Office, 1904), 349. Referring to "the Sac and Fox nation," the treaty institutionalized a singular national identity onto the two confederated tribes, thereby claiming dominion over more loosely confederated bands or tribes. For a discussion of how this played out in the Great Lakes region in the seventeenth century, see Michael Witgen, "The Rituals of Possession: Native

Identity and the Invention of Empire in Seventeenth-Century Western North America," *Ethnohistory* 54, no. 4 (2007): 639–68.

36. Treaty with the Sauks and Foxes, 350.

37. Ibid.

38. Ibid.

39. For a discussion of the group of prisoners, their confinement, and their tour of the East Coast, see Donald Jackson, "Introduction," *Black Hawk: An Autobiography*, 1833 (Urbana: University of Illinois Press, 1955), 1–15; and Tena L. Helton, "What the White 'Squaws' Want from Black Hawk: Gendering the Fan-Celebrity Relationship," *American Indian Quarterly* 34, no. 4 (2010): 498–520.

40. Kennedy, "Introduction," xiv.

41. David Claypoole Johnston, "The Grand National Caravan Moves East," 1833[?], lithograph, Library of Congress, Washington DC.

42. "Black Hawk and the President," *Niles' Register* (Baltimore), April 5, 1833.

43. *New York Evening Post* (New York), June 11, 1833, "Blackhawkiana," in *American Indians of Illinois*, University of Illinois Online, <https://cdn.citl.illinois.edu/courses/aiiopcmpss/BH-Myth/blackhawkiana/military.htm>.

44. *Niles' Register* (Baltimore), July 20, 1833.

45. *New York Evening Post* (New York), June 28, 1833, *American Indians of Illinois*.

46. *Washington Globe* (Washington), June 26, 1833, *American Indians of Illinois*.

47. "Blackhawkiana," *Niles' Register* (Baltimore), June 29, 1833.

48. Black Hawk, *Life of Ma-ka-tai-me-she-kia-kiak or Black Hawk, embracing the tradition of his nation—Indian wars in which he has been engaged—cause of joining the British in their late war with America, and its history—description of the Rock-River village—manners and customs—encroachments by the whites, contrary to treaty—removal from his village in 1831. With an account of the cause and general history of the late war, his surrender and confinement at Jefferson Barracks, and travels through the United States. Dictated by himself*, ed. J. B. Patterson (Cincinnati, 1833), 9–10.

49. Gordon M. Sayre, *The Indian Chief as Tragic Hero: Native Resistance and the Literatures of America, from Moctezuma to Tecumseh* (Chapel Hill: University of North Carolina Press, 2005), 10–13.

50. Benjamin Drake, *The Life and Adventures of Black Hawk, with Sketches of Keokuk, the Sac and Fox Indians, and the Late Black Hawk War* (Cincinnati, 1838); Elbert Herring, *Ma-ka-tai-me-she-kia-kiak; or, Black Hawk, and Scenes in the West. A National Poem: In Six Cantos* (New York, 1848).

51. Timothy Sweet, "Masculinity and Self-Performance in the Life of Black Hawk," *American Literature* 65, no. 3 (1993): 478.

52. Charles Snyder, "Antoine LeClaire, the First Proprietor of Davenport," *Annals of Iowa* 23, no. 2 (1941): 85–93.

53. During the Black Hawk War, Patterson had joined the Illinois volunteer army as regimental printer; John Lee Allaman, "The Patterson Family of Oquawka," *Western Illinois Regional Studies* 11 (Spring 1988): 57. Allaman notes that Patterson was related to the Davenport family, although it is not clear what the family connection was.

54. Ann Fabian, *The Unvarnished Truth: Personal Narratives in Nineteenth-Century America* (Berkeley: University of California Press, 2002).

55. William Boelhower, "Saving Saukenuk: How Black Hawk Won the War and Opened the Way to Ethnic Semiotics." *Journal of American Studies* 25, no. 3 (1991): 336.

56. Black Hawk, *Life*, 99.

57. Schmitz, *White Robe's Dilemma*, 71.

58. Black Hawk, *Life*, 101.

59. Ibid., 100.

60. Ibid., 104.

61. Mark Rifkin, *Manifesting America: The Imperial Construction of US National Space* (Oxford, UK: Oxford University Press, 2009), 101.

62. Arnold Krupat, "Patterson's *Life*; Black Hawk's Story; Native American Elegy," *American Literary History* 22, no. 3 (2010): 527.

63. Black Hawk, *Life*, 98–99.

64. Bellin, "How Smooth Their Language," 494–95; Rifkin, "Documenting Tradition," 695.

65. Black Hawk, *Life*, 98.

66. Sweet, "Masculinity and Self-Performance," 485.

67. Rifkin, *Manifesting America*, 100.

68. Black Hawk, *Life*, 111–12.

69. Ibid., 112.

70. Ibid., 112.

71. Ibid., 112.

72. Alvin Josephy, *The Patriot Chiefs: A Chronicle of American Indian Leadership* (New York: Viking Press, 1961), 209.

73. Hagan, *Sac and Fox Indians*, 205.

74. Arnold Krupat, "Native American Literary Criticism in Global Context," in *The World, the Text, and the Indian: Global Dimensions of Native American Literature*, ed. Scott Richard Lyons (Albany: State University of New York Press, 2017), 65–66.

75. Flint, *The Transatlantic Indian*, 84.

76. Gregory Dowd, *A Spiritual Resistance: The North American Indian Struggle for Unity, 1745–1815* (Baltimore, MD: Johns Hopkins University Press, 1992), 3.

77. Michael Witgen, *An Infinity of Nations: How the Native New World Shaped Early North America* (Philadelphia: University of Pennsylvania Press, 2011), 52.

78. Ibid., 52.

79. Substance of a Talk made to Gen'l Joseph M. Street Indian Agent, by the Chiefs and principal men of the united tribes of Sac and Fox Indians, at Rock Island the 19 August 1834, LROIA, Roll 729, Sac and Fox Agency, 1834–1837.

80. Ibid.

81. Ibid.

82. Keokuk to William Clark, 19 December 1832, LROIA, Roll 728, Sac and Fox Agency, 1824–1833.

83. Ibid.

84. Ibid.

85. Minutes of a Talk held at Jefferson Barracks Missouri on the 27th of March 1834, by General H. Atkinson with Keokuck and other principal Chiefs of the Sac & Fox Nations, LROIA, Roll 729. Sac and Fox Agency, 1834–1837.
86. Extract from talks delivered by Keokuck to Superintendent, on 25th & 27th March 1833, LROIA, Roll 728, Sac and Fox Agency, 1824–1833.
87. Ibid.
88. Keokuk et al. to William Clark, 28 January 1834, LROIA, Roll 729, Sac and Fox Agency, 1834–1837.
89. Minutes of a Talk held at Jefferson Barracks Missouri on the 27th of March 1834.
90. Ibid.
91. Colbert, "Keokuk and the United States Government," 58.
92. Minutes of a Talk held at Jefferson Barracks Missouri on the 27th of March 1834.
93. Ibid.
94. Keokuk et al. to William Clark, 28 January 1834, Letters Received Office of Indian Affairs, Roll 729, Sac and Fox Agency, 1834–1837.
95. At a talk held with the confederated Tribes of Sac and Fox Indians, in St. Louis, 24 June 1837, LROIA, Roll 729, Sac and Fox Agency, 1834–1837.
96. Ibid.
97. When in 1837 he sat in council with the Indian agent Joseph Street before going on a delegation to Washington, Keokuk showed him a peace pipe that he had received from the Sioux, which he held up as a physical testament to their broken promises. Keokuk told Street that "if you wish it, I will take this pipe to Washington and tell its history to the President." Substance of a Talk held with the Sac and Fox Indians, at Saint Louis, 27 June 1837, by Genl. Jos. M. Street Indian Agent, LROIA, Roll 729, Sac and Fox Agency, 1834–1837.
98. Ibid.
99. Ibid.
100. Frederick Jackson Turner, "The Significance of the Frontier in American History," ch. 1 in *The Frontier in American History* (New York: Henry Holt, 1920), 11.
101. Ibid., 3.
102. William Cronon, *Nature's Metropolis: Chicago and the Great West* (New York: Norton and Company, 1991), 47–52.
103. Hagan, *Sac and Fox Indians*, 215.
104. Memorandum of a Talk with all the chiefs and principal men of the united Tribes of Sac and Fox Indians held at Fort Armstrong, 30 May 1836, LROIA, Roll 729, Sac and Fox Agency, 1834–1837.
105. Ibid.
106. Substance of a talk made by the principal chiefs, 19 August 1834.
107. Ibid.
108. Ibid.
109. Nichols, *Black Hawk and the Warrior's Path*, 154–55.
110. Hagan, *Sac and Fox Indians*, 215–17.
111. Ibid., 213.

112. Although as the head of the Ioway delegation Na'hjeNing'e presented the map to American treaty commissioners, Mary Kathryn Whelan writes that "there is no evidence that he drew it." See Mary Kathryn Whelan, "The 1837 Ioway Indian Map Project: Using Geographic Information Systems to Integrate History, Archaeology and Landscape" (master's thesis, University of Redlands, 2003), 27. See also David Bernstein, *How the West Was Drawn: Mapping, Indians, and the Construction of the Trans-Mississippi West* (Lincoln: University of Nebraska Press, 2018), pp. 36–38.

113. Adam Jortner, "The Empty Continent: Cartography, Pedagogy, and Native American History," in *Why You Can't Teach United States History without American Indians*, ed. Susan Sleeper-Smith, Juliana Barr, Jean M. O'Brien, Nancy Shoemaker, and Scott Manning Stevens (Chapel Hill: University of North Carolina Press, 2015), 75, 73.

114. Whelan, "1837 Ioway Indian Map," 8; Bernstein, *How the West Was Drawn*, 41–42.

115. Greg Olson, *The Ioway in Missouri* (Columbia, MO: University of Missouri Press, 2008), 120.

116. Olson, *Ioway Life: Reservation and Reform, 1837–1860* (Norman: University of Oklahoma Press, 2016), 84.

117. Walter Johnson, "On Agency," *Journal of Social History* 37, no. 1 (2003): 113–24.

118. Hagan, *Sac and Fox Indians*, 217.

119. Michael D. Green, "The Sac-Fox Annuity Crisis of 1840 in Iowa Territory," *Arizona and the West* 16, no. 2 (1974): 143.

120. Michael D. Green, "'We Dance in Opposite Directions': Mesquakie (Fox) Separatism from the Sac and Fox Tribe," *Ethnohistory* 30, no. 3 (1983), 134.

121. Extract from talks of Keokuck to Supt. Ind. Affs. St Louis, 25 and 27 March 1833, LRAOI, Roll 728, Sac and Fox Agency, 1824–1833.

122. Ibid.

123. Council of the Sacs & Foxes, held at the Indian Agency at Rock Island, 18 June 1833, LROIA, Roll 728, Sac and Fox Agency, 1824–1833.

124. Extract from talks of Keokuck to Supt. Ind. Affs., 25 and 27 March 1833.

125. Letter from A-pe-noose, Fox chief, to the President of the United States, 22 September 1834, LROIA, Roll 729.

126. Colbert, "Keokuk and the United States Government," 62.

127. Green, "Sac-Fox Annuity Crisis," 147.

128. Memorial of the Chiefs, &c. of the Fox Tribe of Indians, 7 January 1835, LROIA, Roll 729, Sac and Fox Agency, 1834–1837. The memorial was made up in the presence of J. B. Patterson, William Cousland, Alexis Phelps, and the interpreter Joseph Cota.

129. "A Notice to the Public," *Iowa Territorial Gazette*, February 29, 1840. LROIA, Roll 730, Sac and Fox Agency, 1838–1840.

130. "Notice to the Public"; Green, "Annuity Crisis," 150.

131. Green, "Annuity Crisis," 145.

132. Petition of the Sauk and Fox Chiefs, 22 April 1840, LROIA, Roll 730, Sac and Fox Agency, 1838–1840.

133. Petition to the President of the United States, 5 May 1840, Letters Received Office of Indian Affairs, Roll 730, Sac and Fox Agency, 1838–1840.

134. Lisa Brooks, *The Common Pot: The Recovery of Native Space in the Northeast* (Minneapolis: University of Minnesota Press, 2008), 224.

135. Ibid., 225.

136. Daniel Carpenter, "Recruitment by Petition: American Antislavery, French Protestantism, English Suppression," *Perspective on Politics* 14, no. 3 (2016): 701.

137. Ibid., 701.

138. Petition to the President of the United States; Lucas, "Indian Affairs," 263–64. If the signatures were real, Lucas argued, the Sauk and Meskwaki nations must have experienced astronomic population growth in just one year. Michael Green argues that Lucas's accusation is "open to question." As Green writes, "evidence ... suggests that the Keokuk faction possibly did outnumber the Hardfish group. There are no official population statistics for the Sacs and Foxes in 1840, but a careful enumeration in September of 1842 revealed 2,348 people—1,146 males and 1,202 females. This number ... was only 48 above the October 1841 figure. Of the total, 498 were children under ten years. Assuming no radical population shift occurred from 1840 to 1841 (and assuming one-half the children were boys), the total Sacs and Foxes numbered 897 males over ten years in 1840. If Lucas correctly estimated 250 chiefs and warriors in the Hardfish faction, that leaves 647 males, 503 of which could have signed the May petition to support the money chiefs." See Green, "Annuity Crisis," 151.

139. Petition of Iowa settlers to President Van Buren, 5 August 1840, LROIA, Roll 730, Sac and Fox Agency, 1838–1840.

140. Green, "Sac-Fox Annuity Crisis," 150.

141. Colbert, "Keokuk and the United States Government," 65–66; Green, "Sac-Fox Annuity Crisis," 155.

142. Robert Lucas, "Indian Affairs of Iowa in 1840," *Annals of Iowa: A Historical Quarterly*, Third Series, XV, no. 4 (April 1926): 262.

143. Ibid. 262.
144. Ibid., 264.
145. Ibid., 264.
146. Ibid., 264.
147. Ibid., 272.
148. Ibid., 273.
149. Ibid., 272–73.
150. Ibid., 275.
151. Ibid., 278.
152. Hagan, *Sac and Fox Indians*, 206.
153. Ibid., 206.
154. Lucas, "Indian Affairs," 278.
155. Green, "Annuity Crisis," 149.
156. Robert Lucas, "Third Annual Message, November 3, 1840," in *The Messages and Proclamations of the Governors of Iowa*, ed. Benjamin F. Shambaugh (Iowa City: State Historical Society of Iowa, 1903), 151.

157. Ibid., 151–152.
158. Ibid., 152.
159. Colbert, "Keokuk and the United States," 65.

160. Hagan, *Sac and Fox Indians*, 223–24.
161. Ibid.
162. Philip J. Deloria, "From Nation to Neighborhood: Land, Policy, Colonialism, and Empire in US-Indian Relations," in *The Cultural Turn in US History: Past, Present, Future*, ed. James W. Cook, Lawrence B. Glickman, and Michael O'Malley (Chicago: University of Chicago Press, 2008), 353.

NOTES TO CHAPTER 3

1. Alexis de Tocqueville, *Democracy in America and Two Essays on America*, ed. Isaac Kramnick, trans. Gerald E. Bevan, 1835 (London: Penguin, 2003), 380.
2. Ibid., 380.
3. See Gerald Vizenor, "Wistful Envies," chapter 2 in *Fugitive Poses: Native American Indian Scenes of Absence and Presence* (Lincoln: University of Nebraska Press, 1998), 81–84; Kate Flint, *The Transatlantic Indian, 1776–1930* (Princeton, NJ: Princeton University Press, 2009), 147–48; Jace Weaver, *The Red Atlantic: American Indigenes and the Making of the Modern World, 1000–1927* (Chapel Hill: University of North Carolina Press, 2014), 24, 104.
4. Peter Pitchlynn, "Song of the Choctaw Girl" and ["Will you go with me"], in *Changing Is Not Vanishing: A Collection of American Indian Poetry to 1930*, ed. Robert Dale Parker (Philadelphia: University of Pennsylvania Press, 2010), 135–37.
5. Charles Dickens, *American Notes for General Circulation*, vol. II (London, 1842), 99. Richard Mentor Johnson to John C. Spencer, 26 November 1841, Richard Mentor Johnson Papers, The Filson Historical Society, Louisville, Kentucky.
6. Craig Womack, *Red on Red: Native American Literary Separatism* (Minneapolis: University of Minnesota Press, 1999), 1–24.
7. Christina Snyder, *Great Crossings: Indians, Settlers, and Slaves in the Age of Jackson* (Oxford, UK: Oxford University Press, 2017), 21.
8. Ibid., 20.
9. James Taylor Carson, *Searching for the Bright Path: The Mississippi Choctaws from Prehistory to Removal* (Lincoln: University of Nebraska Press, 2003), 87–89.
10. Snyder, *Great Crossings*, 104.
11. *Report of the American Board of Commissioners Foreign Missions, Compiled from Documents Laid Before the Board, at the Eighteenth Annual Meeting* (Boston, 1827), 122–23.
12. Peter Pitchlynn, *A Gathering of Statesmen: Records of the Choctaw Council Meetings, 1826–1828*, ed. and trans. Marcia Haag and Henry J. Willlis (Norman: University of Oklahoma Press, 2013), 45–46.
13. Ibid., 49–50.
14. Snyder, *Great Crossings*, 26.
15. Angie Debo, *The Rise and Fall of the Choctaw Republic*, 1934, 2nd ed. (Norman: University of Oklahoma Press, 1961), 45; Clara Sue Kidwell, *Choctaws and Missionaries in Mississippi, 1818–1918* (Norman: University of Oklahoma Press, 1995), 65–67.
16. Kidwell, *Choctaws and Missionaries*, 57.

17. Herman J. Viola, *Thomas McKenney: Architect of America's Early Indian Policy, 1816–1830* (Chicago: Sage, 1974), 189; W. David Baird, *Peter Pitchlynn: Chief of the Choctaws* (Norman: University of Oklahoma Press, 1972), 24.

18. Baird, *Peter Pitchlynn*, 23. Richard Mentor Johnson (1780–1850) was a long-serving US congressman who had consistently run on a platform of representing the "common man" in Congress, not only supporting legislative acts against imprisonment for debt, but defending settlers' rights to public lands. Johnson was related to the Indian agent to the Choctaw and adapted his plantation house to accommodate students. See Ronald Rayman, "Joseph Lancaster's Monitorial System of Instruction and American Indian Education, 1815–1838," *History of Education Quarterly* 80, no. 4 (1981): 402. See also Steven Crum, "The Choctaw Nation: Changing the Appearance of American Higher Education, 1830–1907," *History of Education Quarterly* 47, no. 1 (2007), 49–51, and Snyder, *Great Crossings*, passim.

19. Viola, *Thomas McKenney*, 189–90.
20. Baird, *Peter Pitchlynn*, 23–24.
21. Ibid., 53.
22. Ibid., 28–30.
23. Richard Mentor Johnson to the Professors of Transylvania University, 11 March 1827, Peter Pitchlynn Collection, Box 1, Folder 10, Western History Collection, University of Oklahoma, Norman, Oklahoma. Philip Lindsley of the University of Nashville also testified to Pitchlynn's "uniformly good moral character," commenting on his "amiable, correct, & gentlemanly" behavior and "respectable proficiency" as a scholar. See President Lindsley to unidentified, 15 April 1828, Peter Pitchlynn Collection, Box 1, Folder 13, Western History Collection, University of Oklahoma, Norman, Oklahoma.
24. "Answer of the Choctaw Chiefs to Colonel McKenney," 17 October 1827, in Thomas McKenney, *Memoirs, Official and Personal: with Sketches of Travels among the Northern and Southern Indians* (New York, 1846), 338. The district chiefs were encouraged by Richard Mentor Johnson—the overseer of Choctaw Academy—who "quietly supported removal" and framed it as an "exploratory expedition with no strings attached." Snyder, *Great Crossings*, 130.
25. These details on the composition of the expedition party are based on John Francis McDermot (ed.), "Isaac McCoy's Second Exploring Trip in 1828," *Kansas Historical Quarterly* 13, no. 7 (1945): 416; Speer Morgan and Greg Michalson, "A Man Between Nations: The Diary of Peter Pitchlynn," *The Missouri Review* 14, no. 3 (1991): 56; Baird, *Peter Pitchlynn*, 31–33; and Snyder, *Great Crossings*, 130.
26. Isaac McCoy, *Remarks on the Practicability of Indian Reform, Embracing their Colonization* (New York, 1829), 25.
27. Peter Pitchlynn, "Typescript of original document—diary of Peter P. Pitchlynn," 1828–29, Peter Perkins Pitchlynn Papers, Box 5, Folder 2, Western History Collections Online, University of Oklahoma, Norman, OK. Entry dated November 7, 1828.
28. McDermot, ed. "Isaac McCoy's Second Exploring Trip in 1828," 435.
29. Archivist's note in Pitchlynn, "Diary of Peter P. Pitchlynn."
30. Snyder, *Great Crossings*, 131.
31. Pitchlynn, "Diary of Peter P. Pitchlynn," undated pages.
32. Pitchlynn, "Diary of Peter P. Pitchlynn," undated pages.

33. R. David Edmunds, *The Shawnee Prophet* (Lincoln: University of Nebraska Press, 1985), 170–75. For historical accounts of Tecumseh and Tenskwatawa's religious movement and political resistance, see also Richard White, *The Middle Ground: Indians, Empires, and Republics in the Great Lakes Region, 1650–1815* (Cambridge, UK: Cambridge University Press, 1991), 469–516; and Gregory Evans Dowd, *A Spirited Resistance: The North American Indian Struggle for Unity, 1745–1815* (Baltimore: Johns Hopkins University Press, 1993), 123–90.

34. Pitchlynn, "Diary of Peter P. Pitchlynn," undated pages.

35. Ibid.

36. Peter P. Pitchlynn, "Talk to the Osage," [November 21, 1828], in "Diary of Peter P. Pitchlynn."

37. Ibid.

38. Ibid.

39. Pitchlynn, "Diary of Peter P. Pitchlynn," undated pages.

40. Ibid.

41. Snyder, *Great Crossings*, 131.

42. Pitchlynn, "Diary of Peter P. Pitchlynn," November 28, 1828.

43. Ibid.

44. Ibid.

45. Michael Denning, "Peculiarities of the Americans," 206–7.

46. Carole Pateman, "The Settler Contract," *Contract and Domination*, ed. Carole Pateman and Charles W. Mills (Cambridge, UK: Polity Press, 2007), 46–53.

47. Stuart Banner, *How the Indians Lost Their Land: Law and Power on the Frontier* (Cambridge, MA: Harvard University Press, 2005), 191–2.

48. Snyder, *Great Crossings*, 135.

49. Ibid., 136.

50. George Harkins, "To the American People," *Niles' Weekly Register* (Baltimore), February 25, 1832.

51. Ibid.

52. Snyder, *Great Crossings*, 141–42.

53. Choctaw council to John Eaton, 16 January 1831, in *Correspondences on the Subject of the Emigration of the Indians*, vol. III (Washington, 1835), 393; Peter Pitchlynn to Lewis Cass, *The Papers of Andrew Jackson*, vol. 8, *1830*, ed. Daniel Feller, Laura-Eve Moss, and Thomas Coens (Knoxville: University of Tennessee Press, 2010), 395.

54. Arthur H. DeRosier, *The Removal of the Choctaw Indians* (Knoxville: University of Tennessee Press, 1970), 141–46.

55. Snyder, *Great Crossings*, 25. Snyder notes that it is possible that Lincecum was Pitchlynn's first teacher during his teenage years.

56. Gideon Lincecum, "Phrenological Character of Mr. P. P. Pitchlynn," Peter Pitchlynn Papers, 1846, Folder 532, Gilcrease Museum and Archives, Tulsa, OK.

57. Ibid.

58. Karen Halttunen, *Confidence Men and Painted Women: A Study of Middle-class Culture in America, 1830–1870* (New Haven: Yale University Press, 1982), 40.

59. Sharrona Pearl, *About Faces: Physiognomy in Nineteenth-Century Britain* (Cambridge, MA: Harvard University Press, 2010), 8.

60. Robert E. Bieder, *Science Encounters the Indian: The Early Years of American Ethnology* (Norman: University of Oklahoma Press, 1986), 59.
61. Britt Rusert, *Fugitive Science: Empiricism and Freedom in Early African American Culture* (New York: New York University Press, 2017), 122.
62. Bieder, *Science Encounters the Indian*, 59.
63. Ibid., 59–64; Ann Fabian, *The Skull Collectors: Race, Science, and America's Unburied Dead* (Chicago: University of Chicago Press, 2010).
64. Rusert, *Fugitive Science*, 125.
65. Lincecum, "Phrenological Character of Mr. P. P. Pitchlynn."
66. Ibid.
67. Ibid.
68. Dana D. Nelson, *National Manhood: Capitalist Citizenship and the Imagined Fraternity of White Men* (Durham, NC: Duke University Press, 1998), 14.
69. Lincecum, "Phrenological Character of Mr. P. P. Pitchlynn."
70. Ibid.
71. Dickens, *American* Notes, 184.
72. Clara Sue Kidwell, *The Choctaws in Oklahoma: From Tribe to Nation, 1855–1970* (Norman: University of Oklahoma Press, 2007), 9.
73. Ibid., 54–63.
74. Ibid., 10.
75. Ibid., 9
76. Ibid.
77. Peter Pitchlynn, "Draft of address to the Choctaw General Council," 7 August 1841, Peter Pitchlynn Papers, Folder 289, Gilrease Museum and Archives, Tulsa, OK.
78. Ibid.
79. Ibid.
80. Josiah Gregg, *Commerce of the Prairies*, vol. II (New York, 1844), 261.
81. Richard Mentor Johnson to John C. Spencer, 26 November 1841, Richard Mentor Johnson Papers, Filson HS. See also Baird, *Peter Pitchlynn*, 58–61.
82. See Philip J. Deloria, Jr., *Indians in Unexpected Places* (Lawrence: University Press of Kansas, 2004), 4–7.
83. Pitchlynn, "Draft of address to the Choctaw General Council."
84. Ibid.
85. Ibid.
86. Donna Akers, *Living in the Land of Death: The Choctaw Nation, 1830–1860* (East Lansing: Michigan State University Press, 2004), 34–35.
87. Richard White, *The Roots of Dependency: Subsistence, Dependency, and Social Change among the Choctaws, Pawnees, and Navajos* (Lincoln: University of Nebraska Press, 1983), 118–19.
88. Ibid.
89. For more historical background on slavery in the Choctaw Nation, see Snyder, *Great Crossings*, 20–21, 290–93. For histories of slavery in Indian country, see Barbara Krauthammer, *Black Slaves, Indian Masters: Slavery, Emancipation, and Citizenship in the Native American South* (Chapel Hill: University of North Carolina Press, 2012); Tiya Miles, *Ties that Bind: The Story of an Afro-Cherokee Family in Slavery*

and Freedom (Berkeley: University of California Press, 2005); and Tiya Miles, *The House on Diamond Hill: A Cherokee Plantation Story* (Chapel Hill: University of North Carolina Press, 2010).

90. Peter Pitchlynn, "Substance of a Lecture Delivered by P. P. Pitchlynn at the Temperance Celebration upon the Subject of Patriotism," 25 June 1842, Peter Pitchlynn Papers, Folder 362, Gilcrease Museum and Archives, Tulsa, OK.

91. Ibid.

92. Ibid.

93. Peter Pitchlynn, "Notes of a speech delivered by Pitchlynn in Eagletown Debating Society," [undated], Peter Pitchlynn Papers, Folder 646, Gilcrease Museum and Archives, Tulsa, OK.

94. Homi K. Bhabha, "Of Mimicry and Man: The Ambivalence of Colonial Discourse," in *The Location of Culture*, 1994 (London: Routledge, 2004), 122.

95. Donna Akers, "Peter P. Pitchlynn: Race and Identity in Nineteenth-Century America," in *The Human Tradition in Antebellum America*, ed. Michael A. Morrison (Wilmington: Scholarly Resources, 2000), 132–33.

96. Elias Boudinot, "An Indian's Address to the Whites," *North American Review* vol. XXIII (Boston, 1826): 471.

97. Ibid.

98. This topic was apparently suggested to him by his friend, the Presbyterian minister Israel Folsom. Israel Folsom to Peter P. Pitchlynn, 14 June 1842, Peter Perkins Pitchlynn Papers, Western History Collections, University of Oklahoma, Norman, OK.

99. Pitchlynn, "Substance of a Lecture Delivered by P. P. Pitchlynn."

100. Ibid. For clarity, I have silently changed the periods in the original text to question marks.

101. Ibid.

102. Although traditional accounts vary, the Choctaws entered the world either from Nanih Waiya—also known as the "Mother Mound"—or from a cave nearby. Akers, *Land of Death*, 2–3.

103. Pitchlynn, "Substance of a Lecture Delivered by P. P. Pitchlynn."

104. Frantz Fanon, "On National Culture," in *The Wretched of the Earth*, 1961, translated by Richard Philcox (New York: Grove Press, 2004), 168.

105. Qtd. in Scott Richard Lyons, *X-Marks: Native Signatures of Assent* (Minneapolis: University of Minnesota Press, 2010), 119.

106. Homi K. Bhabha, "DissemiNation: Time, Narrative, and the Margins of the Modern Nation," in *The Location of Culture*, 201.

107. Gregg, *Commerce of the Prairies*, 261–62.

108. Benedict Anderson, *Imagined Communities: Reflections on the Origin and Spread of Nationalism*, 1983 (London: Verso, 2006), 22–26.

109. Peter Pitchlynn, "Substance of a Lecture Delivered by P. P. Pitchlynn."

110. Ibid.

111. See Lyons, *X-Marks*, 121–32.

112. Baird, *Peter Pitchlynn*, 54.

113. Ibid., 69.

114. Ibid., 69.

115. Debo, *Choctaw Republic*, 67; Grant Foreman, *Advancing the Frontier*, 1933 (Norman: University of Oklahoma Press, 1968), 182–88.

116. Abraham Robinson McIlvaine, "Speech of Hon. A. R. McIlvaine, of Pennsyl'A, on the Mexican War, delivered in the House of Representatives, February 4, 1847" (Washington, DC, 1847).

117. "A Bill to provide for the Organization of an Indian Territory West of the Mississippi River," June 27, 1848, House of Representatives, 30th Congress, 1st Session, Report no. 736, 12.

118. Ibid., 13.

119. Ibid.

120. Peter Pitchlynn, "Remonstrance of Col. Peter Pitchlynn, Choctaw Delegate," 3 February 1849, House of Representatives, 30th Congress, 2nd Session (Misc. Documents 35): 3.

121. Ibid., 2.

122. Ibid., 3.

123. Ibid., 3.

124. Ibid., 2.

125. Ibid., 1.

126. Maureen Konkle, *Writing Indian Nations: Native Intellectuals and the Politics of Historiography, 1827–1863* (Chapel Hill: University of North Carolina Press, 2004), 10.

127. Ibid., 11–13.

128. Pitchlynn, "Remonstrance of Col. Peter Pitchlynn," 1.

129. Ibid., 1.

130. Ibid., 3.

131. Frederick Hoxie, *This Indian Country: American Indian Activists and the Place They Made* (New York: Penguin, 2012), 4.

132. DeRosier, *Removal of the Choctaw Indians*, 135.

133. Ibid., 136.

134. Snyder, *Great Crossings*, 142.

135. Baird, *Peter Pitchlynn*, 99.

136. Ibid., 97–98.

137. Ibid., 100–104.

138. Robert M. Kvasnicka, "George W. Manypenny," in *The Commissioners of Indian Affairs*, ed. Robert M. Kvasnicka and Herman J. Viola (Lincoln: University of Nebraska Press, 1979), 58–60.

139. Peter Pitchlynn et al. to George Washington Manypenny, 5 April 1854, in *Papers relating to the claims of the Choctaw nation against the United States, arising under the treaty of 1830* (Washington, 1855), 13. Library of Congress, Washington DC.

140. Ibid.

141. Ibid.

142. Ibid., 14.

143. Pitchlynn et al. to George W. Manypenny, 30 May 1854, *Claims of the Choctaw Nation*, 40.

144. R. McClelland to Charles E. Mix, 20 June 1854, *Claims of the Choctaw Nation*, 41–42.

145. Peter Pitchlynn, Samuel Garland, and Dickson Lewis to C. E. Mix, 11 July 1854, *Claims of the Choctaw Nation*, 47.

146. Peter Pitchlynn, "Colonel Pitchlynn's address, delivered to President Pierce, upon presenting the appeal of the Choctaw delegation for a settlement with the government," *Claims of the Choctaw Nation*, 3.

147. Vine Deloria, Jr., and Clifford Lytle, *American Indians, American Justice* (Austin: University of Texas Press, 1983), 36.

148. *Daily Union* (Washington), February 6, 1855.

149. Pitchlynn et al., "To his Excellency General Franklin Pierce, President of the United States," *Claims of the Choctaw Nation*, 10

150. Ibid., 10

151. Ibid., 6

152. Ibid., 6.

153. Ibid., 10.

154. Ibid., 12.

155. Ibid., 12.

156. Treaty with the Choctaw, 1830, in *Indian Affairs: Laws and Treaties*, vol. II, ed. Charles J, Kappler (Washington, DC: Government Printing Office, 1904), 315.

157. Baird, *Peter Pitchlynn*, 99; Treaty with the Choctaws and Chickasaws, 1855, in *Indian Affairs: Laws and Treaties*, vol. II, *Treaties*, ed. Charles J. Kappler (Washington, DC: Government Printing Office, 1904), 709–10.

158. Hoxie, *This Indian Country*, 97.

159. See Baird, *Peter Pitchlynn*, 90–91.

160. Peter Pitchlynn, "Song of a Choctaw Girl," in *Changing Is Not Vanishing*, ed. Parker, 136.

161. Adam Spry, *Our War Paint Is Writers' Ink: Anishinaabe Literary Transnationalism* (Albany: State University of New York Press, 2018), 99.

NOTES TO CHAPTER 4

1. Gordon M. Sayre, *The Indian Chief as Tragic Hero: Native Resistance and the Literatures of America, from Moctezuma to Tecumseh* (Chapel Hill: University of North Carolina Press, 2005), 5–8.

2. Benjamin Drake, *The Life and Adventures of Black Hawk, with Sketches of Keokuk, the Sac and Fox Indians, and the Late Black Hawk War* (Cincinnati, 1838).

3. Jean O'Brien, *Firsting and Lasting: Writing Indians Out of Existence in New England* (Minneapolis: University of Minnesota Press, 2010).

4. I use the word "Ojibwe" to signal that the authors I study in this chapter identified as belonging to communities—organized according to traditional clan structures but recognized politically as nations—of Ojibwe people (often spelled as "Ojibwa" or "Ojibway" or designated by the anglicized "Chippewa" or "Chippeway"). The Ojibwe people belong to the culturally and linguistically related indigenous people of the Great Lakes region, the Anishinaabeg, which also includes Potawatomi, Cree, Odawa, and Algonquin people.

5. Raymond Williams, *Keynotes*, 1976 (New York: Oxford University Press, 1983), 75.

6. Ibid.

7. Jace Weaver, *That the People Might Live: Native American Literatures and Native American Community* (Oxford, UK: Oxford University Press, 1997).

8. Philip P. Mason, "Introduction," in Henry Rowe Schoolcraft, *The Literary Voyager or Muzzeniegun*, ed. Philip P. Mason (East Lansing: Michigan State University Press, 1962), xix.

9. According to Michael Witgen, the Native population outnumbered the white population by more than three times, and most of them "lived on lands to which they retained legal title." Witgen, *Infinity of Nations*, 339.

10. Maureen Konkle, "Recovering Jane Schoolcraft's Cultural Activism," in *The Oxford Handbook of Indigenous American Literature*, ed. James H. Cox and Daniel Heath Justice (Oxford, UK: Oxford University Press, 2014), 84.

11. Michael Witgen, *An Infinity of Nations: How the Native New World Shaped Early North America* (Philadelphia: University of Pennsylvania Press, 2012), 342.

12. Ibid., 343.

13. Robert Dale Parker, "Introduction: The World and Writings of Jane Johnston Schoolcraft," in *The Sound the Stars Make Rushing Through the Night; The Writings of Jane Johnston Schoolcraft*, ed. Robert Dale Parker (Philadelphia: University of Pennsylvania Press, 2007), 6.

14. Ibid., 1.

15. See Anna Brownell Jameson, *Winter Studies and Summer Rambles in Canada*, vol. III (New York: Wiley and Putnam, 1839), and Chandler Robbins Gilman, *Life on the Lakes, Being Tales and Sketches Collected during a Trip to the Pictured Rocks of Lake Superior* (New York: George Dearborn, 1836).

16. Henry Rowe Schoolcraft, *Personal Memoirs of a Residence of Thirty Years with the Indian Tribes on the American Frontiers: with Brief Notices of Passing Events, Facts, and Opinions* (Philadelphia, 1851), 203.

17. Parker, "World and Writings of Jane Johnston Schoolcraft," 34.

18. Laura Mielke, *Moving Encounters: Sympathy and the Indian Question in Antebellum Literature* (Amherst: University of Massachusetts Press, 2008), 139.

19. Philip P. Mason, "Introduction," xxvi.

20. As Robert Dale Parker notes, the main title of the magazine, *Muzzeniegun*, is the Ojibwe word for "book" while the word "voyager" is a pun on the French *voyageurs* in North America. See Parker, "World and Writings of Jane Johnston Schoolcraft," 34.

21. I am grateful to Robert Dale Parker for suggesting this point to me.

22. Konkle, "Recovering Jane Johnston Schoolcraft's Cultural Activism," 85.

23. Henry Rowe Schoolcraft, "Waub Ojeeg, or The Tradition of the Outagami and Chippewa History No. 1," *The Literary Voyager*, no. 1 (December 1826). Photostatic Copy. Henry Rowe Schoolcraft Papers, Bentley Historical Library, University of Michigan.

24. Ibid.

25. Schoolcraft, "Waub Ojeeg, or The Tradition of the Outagami and Chippewa War No. 3," *The Literary Voyager*, no.4 (12 January 1827), HRS Papers, Bentley Historical Library.

26. Ibid.
27. Ibid.
28. Ibid.
29. Henry Rowe Schoolcraft, "Otagamiad," *Literary Voyager*, no. 13 (10 March 1827), HRS Papers, Bentley Historical Library.
30. Ibid.
31. Konkle, *Writing Indian Nations*, 174.
32. Schoolcraft, "Otagamiad."
33. Adam Ferguson, *An Essay on the History of Civil Society*, ed. Fania Oz-Salzberger, 1767 (Cambridge, UK: Cambridge University Press, 1995), 74–106.
34. Parker, *The Sound the Stars Make*, 102.
35. Ibid., 100.
36. Jane Johnston Schoolcraft, "Invocation, To My Maternal Grandfather, On Hearing His Descent from Chippewa Ancestors Misrepresented," no. 13 (10 March 1827), HRS Papers, Bentley Historical Library.
37. Ibid.
38. Henry Rowe Schoolcraft, "Shingaba Wossin," *The Literary Voyager*, no. 2 (October 1826), HRS Papers, Bentley Historical Library.
39. Ibid.
40. Ibid.
41. Ibid.
42. Witgen, *Infinity of Nations*, 349.
43. Ivy Schweitzer, *Perfecting Friendship: Politics and Affiliation in Early American Literature* (Chapel Hill: University of North Carolina Press, 2006), 18.
44. Herman J. Viola, *Thomas McKenney: Architect of America's Early Indian Policy: 1816–1830* (Chicago: Sage Books, 1974), 145.
45. See Witgen, *Infinity of Nations*, 322–58.
46. Steven Conn, *History's Shadow: Native Americans and Historical Consciousness in the Nineteenth Century* (Chicago: University of Chicago Press, 2004), 52–53.
47. Thomas McKenney and James Hall, "Shingabawossin," in *History of the Indian Tribes of North America: with biographical sketches and anecdotes of the principal chiefs*, 1836 (Philadelphia: D. Rice, 1872), 154.
48. Ibid., 156.
49. Ibid., 159.
50. Qtd. in Viola, *Thomas McKenney*, 147.
51. McKenney and Hall, "Shingabawossin," 160.
52. Maungwudaus (George Henry), *An Account of the Chippewa Indians, who have been travelling among the Whites, in the United States, England, Ireland, Scotland, France and Belgium; with very interesting incidents in relation to the general characteristics of the English, Irish, Scotch, French, and Americans, with regard to their hospitality, peculiarities, etc.* (Boston, 1848).
53. Adam Spry, *Our War Paint Is Warrior's Ink: Anishinaabe Literary Transnationalism* (State University of New York Press, 2018), passim.
54. Donald B. Smith, *Mississauga Portraits: Ojibwe Voices from Nineteenth-Century Canada* (Toronto: University of Toronto Press, 2013), 3–32. According to Smith, "the

British Canadians' minimal interest in Ojibwe language and history best explains their designation of these Ojibwe as Mississauga." Smith notes that Jones wrote in *History of the Ojebway Indians; with Special reference to their Conversion to Christianity* (1861), "a 'common mistake is, that the Messissauga Indians are distinct from the Ojibways, whereas they are a part of that nation, and speak the same language.' In their own tongue, these Ojibwe-speakers called themselves, 'Anishinabe,' or in its plural form, 'Anishinabeg' " (xvi). Since Peter Jones himself mostly uses the word "Ojebway" throughout his writings, I use the modern spelling "Ojibwe" of that name in this chapter, unless there is reason to use a different term.

55. Smith, *Mississauga Portraits*, 16–19. On the Credit Mission, see pp. 52–55.

56. Peter Jones, *Sacred Feathers: The Reverend Peter Jones (Kahkewaqunaby) and the Mississauga Indians* (Toronto: University of Toronto Press, 1987), 246.

57. Weaver, *That the People Might Live*, 64.

58. Kate Flint, *The Transatlantic Indian, 1776–1930* (Princeton: Princeton University Press, 2009), 211.

59. Jones, *Life and Journals*, 342.

60. Ibid., 314, 318.

61. Ibid., 407.

62. Ibid., 407–8.

63. For Hannah More's interest in missionary and Bible societies, see Mary Gwladys Jones, *Hannah More* (Cambridge, UK: Cambridge University Press, 1952), 208–11.

64. Jones, *Life and Journals*, 306–7.

65. Leon Jackson, "Making Friends at the Southern Literary Messenger," in *The History of the Book in America*, vol. II, *An Extensive Republic*, ed. Robert Gross and Mary Kelley (Chapel Hill: University of North Carolina Press, 2010), 421.

66. See Bruce M. White, " 'Give Us a Little Milk': The Social and Cultural Meanings of Gift-Giving in the Lake Superior Trade," *Minnesota History* 48, no. 2 (1982), 60–71; and Bruce White, "A Skilled Game of Exchange: Ojibway Fur Trade Protocol," *Minnesota History* 50, no. 6 (1987), 229–40.

67. White, "Give Us a Little Milk," 71.

68. Tim Fulford, *Romantic Indians: Native Americans, British Literature, and Transatlantic Culture, 1756–1830* (Oxford, UK: Oxford University Press, 2006), 260.

69. Susan M. Ryan, "Reform," in *Keywords in American Cultural Studies*, ed. Bruce Burgett and Glenn Hendler (New York: New York University Press, 2007), 197.

70. See Laura M. Stevens, *The Poor Indians: British Missionaries, Native Americans, and Colonial Sensibility* (Philadelphia: University of Pennsylvania Press, 2004), 137.

71. Peter Jones, "An Appeal to the Christian Public of Great Britain & Ireland, in behalf of the Indian Youth in Upper Canada" (London, 1844). National Archives of Canada, Ottawa.

72. Ibid.
73. Ibid.
74. Ibid.
75. Ibid.
76. Ibid.
77. Ibid.

78. Ibid.
79. Smith, *Sacred Feathers*, 172–74.
80. Ibid., 75.
81. Smith, *Mississauga Portraits*, 18
82. Laura Donaldson, "Making a Joyful Noise: William Apess and the Search for Postcolonial Method(ism)," in *Messy Beginnings: Postcoloniality and Early American Studies*, ed. Malani Johar Schueller and Edward Watts (New Brunswick, NJ: Rutgers University Press, 2003), 38–39.
83. Ibid., 40.
84. Ibid., 36.
85. George Copway, *Organization of an Indian Territory East of the Missouri River, Arguments and Reasons Submitted to the Honorable the Members of the Senate and House of Representatives of the 31st Congress of the United States* (New York, 1850); Smith, Mississauga Portraits, 190–91.
86. For further discussion of the criticism that Copway's work has often met from literary critics, see Konkle, *Writing Indian Nations*, 189; and Scott Richard Lyons, "Migrations to Modernity: The Many Voices of George Copway's *Running Sketches of Men and Places, in England, France, Germany, Belgium, and Scotland*," in *The World, the Text, and the Indian: Global Dimensions of Native American Literature*, ed. Scott Richard Lyons (Albany: State University of New York Press, 2017), 145–46.
87. In 1843 Julius T. Clark was appointed as an educator to the Ojibwe at La Pointe, where he worked alongside the Indian agent Alfred Brunson and the missionaries Bishop Baraga and Sherman Hall. Elisha Williams Keyes, "Julius T. Clark," in *Proceedings of the Historical Society of Wisconsin at its Fifty-Sixth Annual Meeting*, ed. Rueben Gold Thwaites and Mary Elizabeth Haines (Madison: Wisconsin Historical Society, 1908), 141–42. Clark had once shown the poem to Copway, who asked for the right to publish the book and share in the profits. When Copway found it "difficult to accomplish his purpose," however, Clark let Copway publish it in his own name, since the Ojibwe writer was at that point a marketable author. Julius Taylor Clark, "Preface," *The Ojibue Conquest; an Indian Episode. With Other Waifs of Leisure Hours* (Julius Taylor Clark, 1898), v–vi.
88. Smith, *Mississauga Portraits*, 175.
89. George Copway, *The Life, History, and Travels of Kah-Ge-Ga-Gah-Bowh (George Copway), A Young Indian Chief of the Ojibwa Nation*, vol. II (Philadelphia, 1847), 81.
90. Anton Treuer, *The Assassination of Hole in the Day* (St. Paul, MN: Borealis Books, 2011), 36–62.
91. Copway, *Life, History, and Travels*, vol. II, 116.
92. Ibid., 118.
93. Ibid., 119.
94. Ibid., 120.
95. Ibid., 138. As Scott Richard Lyons suggests, such passages reflect "a particular rhetorical strategy that was often employed in the nineteenth century by literary nationalists of many origins: namely, [Copway's] description of Indian bodies as metaphors for nationhood." Lyons argues that in his work of history, *Traditional and Characteristic Sketches of the Ojibway Nation* (1850), Copway frequently uses

this language metaphorically, in keeping with "synecdochic portrayals common to much nineteenth-century nationalist rhetoric." Scott Richard Lyons, *X-Marks: Native Signatures of Assent* (Minneapolis: University of Minnesota Press, 2010), 130.

96. Ibid., 134.
97. Ibid., 135–36.
98. Ibid., 136.
99. Lyons, "Migrations to Modernity," 150.
100. Treuer, *Assassination of Hole in the Day*, 101–7.
101. Lyons, "Migrations to Modernity," 164.
102. George Copway, *The Organization of an Indian Territory, East of the Missouri River* (New York, 1850).
103. Smith, *Mississauga Portraits*, 190.
104. Ibid., 190.
105. Copway, *Life, History, and Travels*, vol. II, 139.
106. Ibid., 141.
107. Ibid., 142.
108. Smith, *Mississauga Portraits*, 183.
109. Copway, *Life, History, and Travels*, vol. II, 143.
110. Ibid., 144.
111. Ibid., 145.
112. George Copway to H. B. Hirst, 12 June 1851, Edward Ayer Collection, Ms. 3051, Newberry Library, Chicago.
113. Ibid.
114. Ibid.
115. Ibid.
116. See Shelby Balik, " 'Scattered as Christians Are in This Country': Layfolk's Reading, Writing, and Religious Community in New England's Northern Frontier," *New England Quarterly* 83, no. 4 (2010), 604–40; Barbara Sicherman, "Ideologies and Practices of Reading," in *The History of the Book in America*, vol. 3, *The Industrial Book, 1840–1880* (Chapel Hill: University of North Carolina Press, 2007), 297–302; Candy Gunther Brown, *The Word in the World: Evangelical Writing, Publishing, and Reading in America, 1790–1880* (Chapel Hill: University of North Carolina Press, 2004); David Nord, *Faith in Reading: Religious Publishing and the Birth of Mass Media in America* (Oxford, UK: Oxford University Press, 2004).
117. Phillip H. Round, *Removable Type: Histories of the Book in Indian Country, 1663–1880* (Chapel Hill: University of North Carolina Press, 2010), 76–77. In Round's words, for Native people the advent of stereotype printing and centralized methods of distribution "came to mean preserving tribal sovereignty, protecting traditional religions, and mediating imperial power" (96).
118. Lyons, "Migrations to Modernity," 155.
119. George Copway, *Running Sketches of Men and Places, in England, France, Germany, Belgium, and Scotland* (New York, 1851), 63.
120. Ibid., 44.
121. Ibid., 18.
122. Ibid., 13.

123. Qtd. in Donald B. Smith, *Mississauga Portraits*, 198.

124. See Bernd Peyer, *The Tutor'd Mind: Indian Missionary-Writers in Antebellum America* (Amherst: University of Massachusetts Press 1997), 254; LaVonne Brown Ruoff, "The Literary and Methodist Contexts of George Copway's *Life, Letters and Speeches*," in George Copway, *Life, Letters, and Speeches*, 1850, ed. A. LaVonne Brown Ruoff and Donald B. Smith (Lincoln: University of Nebraska Press, 1997), 19.

125. Flint, *Transatlantic Indian*, 217; Lyons, "Migrations to Modernity," 146.

126. Kristie Hamilton, *America's Sketchbook: The Cultural Life of a Nineteenth-Century Literary Genre* (Athens: Ohio University Press, 1998), 6.

127. Copway, *Running Sketches*, 199–201.

128. Ibid., 254–55.

129. Flint, *Transatlantic Indian*, 217–18.

130. Copway, *Running Sketches*, 218.

131. Charles Gilpin, *Report of the Proceedings of the Third General Peace Congress, Held in Frankfort on the 22nd, 23rd, and 24th August 1850* (London, 1851), 42.

132. Ibid.

133. Copway, *Running Sketches*, 221, 222.

134. Ibid., 227–28. I would argue that Copway's comment on the spectators' disappointment about his "modern" hat is another sly reversal, suggesting that while Indian nations had committed themselves fully to modern ideas and institutions, Europeans still fetishized the premodern.

135. Ibid., 186.

136. Ibid., 55.

137. Qtd. in Lyons, "Migrations to Modernity," 145.

138. Copway, *Life, History, and Travels*, vol. II, 155–56. Since Copway's autobiography quotes at length Thomas McKenney's *Memoirs, Official and Personal* (1846), it is highly likely that Copway was familiar with McKenney and Hall's *History of the Indian Tribes of North America*, and that Copway based his examples on the biographies included in this volume.

139. Ibid., 155–56.

NOTES TO AFTERWORD

1. Here I consider such works as Robert Dale Parker's groundbreaking edition of Jane Johnston Schoolcraft's poetry and his anthology of early Native American poetry, as well as critical editions of the works of writers such as William Apess, Black Hawk, Elias Boudinot, and George Copway, which have made their writings accessible to wider audiences. See Black Hawk, *Life of Black Hawk, or Ma-ka-tai-me-she-kia-kiak. Dictated by Himself*, ed. J. Gerald Kennedy, 1833 (New York: Penguin, 2008); George Copway, *Life, Letters, and Speeches*, ed. A. LaVonne Brown Ruoff and Donald B. Smith (Lincoln: University of Nebraska Press, 1997); Barry O'Connell, ed., *On Our Own Ground: The Complete Writings of William Apess* (Amherst: University of Massachusetts Press, 1992); Robert Dale Parker, *The Sound the Stars Make in the Night: The Writings of Jane Johnston Schoolcraft* (Philadelphia: University of Pennsylvania Press, 2008); Parker, *Changing Is Not Vanishing: A Collection of American Indian Poetry to 1930* (Philadelphia: University

of Pennsylvania Press, 2012); and Theda Perdue, *Cherokee Editor: The Writings of Elias Boudinot* (Athens: University of Georgia Press, 1996). In addition, I consider critical studies that have done much to broaden our understanding of the archive of Native American literature, including Lisa Brooks, *The Common Pot: The Recovery of Native Space in the Northeast* (Minneapolis: University of Minnesota Press, 2008); Ryan Carr, "Lyric X-Marks: Genre and Self-Determination in the Harp Poems of John Rollin Ridge," *MELUS* 43, no. 3 (Fall 2018): 42–63; Alanna Hickey, " 'Let Paler Nations Vaunt Themselves': John Rollin Ridge's "Official Verse" and Racial Citizenship in Gold Rush California," *Studies in American Indian Literatures* 27, No. 4 (Winter 2015): 66–100; Maureen Konkle, *Writing Indian Nations: Native Intellectuals and the Politics of Historiography, 1827–1863* (Chapel Hill: University of North Carolina Press, 2004); Phillip H. Round, *Removable Type: Histories of the Book in Indian Country, 1663–1880* (Chapel Hill: University of North Carolina Press, 2010); and Kelly Wisecup, "Practicing Sovereignty: Colonial Temporalities, Cherokee Justice, and the 'Socrates' Writings of John Ridge," *NAIS: Journal of the Native American and Indigenous Studies Association* 4, no. 1 (Spring 2017): 30–60.

2. For instance, see Jeffrey Ostler, *The Plains Sioux and U.S. Colonialism from Lewis and Clark to Wounded Knee* (Cambridge, UK: Cambridge University Press, 2004); Ned Blackhawk, *Violence Over the Land: Indians and Empires in the Early American West* (Cambridge, MA: Harvard University Pres, 2008), 176–266; and Roxanne Dunbar-Ortiz, *An Indigenous Peoples' History of the United States* (Boston: Beacon Press, 2014), 137–196.

3. For studies of American Indian activists who wrote, published, and lobbied the US government later in the nineteenth century and in the early twentieth century, see Kristina Ackley and Cristina Stanciu, Eds., *Laura Cornelius Kellogg: Our Democracy and the American Indian and Other Works* (Syracuse: Syracuse University Press, 2015); Cari M. Carpenter and Carolyn Sorisio, Eds., *The Newspaper Warrior: Sarah Winnemucca Hopkins's Campaign for American Indian Rights, 1864–1891* (Lincoln: University of Nebraska Press, 2015); C. Joseph Genetin-Pilawa, *Crooked Paths to Allotment: The Fight over Federal Indian Policy after the Civil War* (Chapel Hill: University of North Carolina Press, 2014); Frederick Hoxie, *This Indian Country: American Indian Activists and the Place They Made* (New York: Penguin, 2012); Tadeusz Lewandowski, *Red Bird, Red Power: The Life and Legacy of Zitkala-Ša* (Norman: University of Oklahoma Press, 2016); and Kiara M. Vigil, *Indigenous Intellectuals: Sovereignty, Citizenship, and the American Imagination, 1880–1930* (Cambridge, UK: Cambridge University Press, 2015).

4. Kate Flint, *The Transatlantic Indian, 1776–1930* (Princeton, NJ: Princeton University Press, 2009), 84.

5. Ibid.

6. Among such works, I consider Philip J. Deloria, *Indians in Unexpected Places* (Lawrence: University Press of Kansas, 2004); Flint, *The Transatlantic Indian*; Pekka Hämäläinen, *The Comanche Empire* (New Haven: Yale University Press, 2008); Konkle, *Writing Indian Nations: Native Intellectuals and the Politics of Historiography, 1827–1863* (Chapel Hill: University of North Carolina Press, 2004); Scott Richard Lyons, *X-Marks: Native Signatures of Assent* (Minneapolis: University of Minnesota Press, 2010); Kyle T. Mays, *Hip Hop Beats, Indigenous Rhymes: Modernity and Hip Hop in Indigenous North*

America (Albany: State University of New York Press, 2018); Tiya Miles, *The House on Diamond Hill: A Cherokee Plantation Story* (Chapel Hill: University of North Carolina Press, 2012); Jean O'Brien, *Firsting and Lasting: Writing Indians Out of Existence in New England* (Minneapolis: University of Minnesota Press. 2010); Coll Thrush, *Indigenous London: Native Travelers at the Heart of Empire* (New Haven: Yale University Press, 2016); Jace Weaver, *The Red Atlantic: American Indigenes and the Making of the Modern World, 1000–1927*; and Michael Witgen, *An Infinity of Nations: How the Native New World Shaped Early North America* (Philadelphia: University of Pennsylvania Press, 2012).

7. Lyons, *X-Marks*, esp. 1–34.

8. Mark Rifkin, *Beyond Settler Time: Temporal Sovereignty and Indigenous Self-Determination* (Durham, NC: Duke University Press, 2017), 3.

9. Robert Allen Warrior, *The People and the Word: Reading Native Nonfiction* (Minneapolis: University of Minnesota Press, 2005), xiii.

10. Aaron Sorkin, "The Indians in the Lobby," *The West Wing*, season 3, episode 7, aired November 21, 2001.

11. Deloria, *Indians in Unexpected Places*, 4–7.

12. Kevin Whalen, *Native Students at Work: American Indian Labor and Sherman Institute's Outing Program, 1900–1945* (Seattle: University of Washington Press, 2016), 157.

13. James H. Cox, *The Red Land to the South: American Indian Writers and Indigenous Mexico* (Minneapolis: University of Minnesota Press, 2012), 108.

14. Ibid.,108.

15. Paul Chaat Smith and Robert Warrior, *Like a Hurricane: The Indian Movement from Alcatraz to Wounded Knee* (New York: New Press, 1996), 78. For a longer history of these negotiations, see pp. 70–79 in particular.

16. See Julie L. Davis, *Survival Schools: The American Indian Movement and Community Education in the Twin Cities* (Minneapolis: University of Minnesota Press, 2013).

17. Gerald Vizenor, *Manifest Manners: Narratives on Postindian Survivance*, 1994 (Lincoln: University of Nebraska Press, 1999), 11.

18. Philip Freneau, "The Indian Student: or, The Force of Nature," in *The Poems of Philip Freneau: Poet of the American Revolution*, vol. II, ed. Fred Lewis Pattee (Princeton: University Library, 1903), 373–74.

19. Craig Womack, *Red on Red: Native American Literary Nationalism* (Minneapolis: University of Minnesota Press, 1999), 3.

20. Hoxie, *This Indian Country*, 4.

INDEX

Note: numbers in italics refer to figures

activism, community, 169, 185, 189–90
"Act Making Provisions for the Civilization of the Indian Tribes," 41
Adams, John Quincy, 59
agency, 11, 75–76, 215, 222n11; and agent *vs.* subject, 215; authorized, 23–27, 62, 183, 188–89, 191; as charged term, 24–25; continuity as goal of, 109–10; definition of, 24, 229n90; as fiction, 92; and Indian Agents, 25; institutional context of, 216–18; intersectionality and, 26–27; resistance and, not identical, 25–26; strategic, 12; tenuousness of, 58; terminal creeds regarding, 219
agriculture: as civilizing, 41, 64; education in, 41–45; land rights and, 59, 104; removal and the adoption of, 131, 134
Akers, Donna, 147, 149
Alcatraz Island occupation, 218
alcohol, 198; agents blaming, 118; annuities and, 112; temperance and, 127, 191
Alff, David, 11
Allaman, John Lee, 239n53
"American," becoming, 1–2
American Indian Movement (AIM), 218–19
American Notes (Dickens), 124, 144
American Tract Society, 202–3
ancestry, 125, 148–151; connection to land, 168
Anderson, Benedict, 152
Anishinaabeg, 250n4, 253n54

annuities, 37, 110–12, 114–17, 119–22; compromise on, 115; debts exceeding, 121; intratribal conflict over, 111–12, 114–16, 120–21; Lucas using, for removal, 119–21
Apess, William (Pequot), 7, 8–9, 216
Appanoose (Meskwaki), 112–13, 116, 118
"Appeal to the Christian Public" (Jones), 188–90
assimilation: Copway accused of, 191, 200; of diplomats, 29–30, 125, *128*; *vs.* nationalism, 147, 152; programs, 147, 191, 200–201, 214
association, 9, 21, 22, 57, 202
Atkinson, Henry, 85, 100
Atwater, Caleb, 234n98
author function, 61–62
authority: and authorship, 23–30; commissioners interfering in, 179; layers of, 188–89; mimicry and, 149; questioning, 23–24, 83, 114
autobiographies: of Black Hawk, 5, 7, 75–76, 89–95; critique embedded in, 8, 23, 75–76, 91–92, 93–94, 95; as self-defense, 23
autonomy, 66, 92, 113, 148, 215

Babiiziginibe (Ojibwe), 193
Bagone-giizhig (Ojibwe), 193–94
Bagot Commission, 199–200
Baird, W. David, 153
Bamewawagezhikaquay. *See* Schoolcraft, Jane Johnston (Ojibwe)
Banner, Stuart, 15, 138

259

Baraga, Bishop, 254n87
Baricou, J., *135*
Bell, John, 53, 130, 236n130
Belle Oiseau (Osage), 134–35
Bellin, Joshua David, 237n4
Belton, Samuel, 188
"benevolence," 41, 56, 187–89, 204
Bernstein, David, 61, 64–65
Berthollet, J. L., 140, *141*
Bhabha, Homi K., 149, 151
Bieder, Robert, 140, 142
Big Elk. See Ongpatonga (Omaha)
Biography and History of the Indians of North America (Drake), 52
bison scarcity, 63, 64
Black Hawk (Sauk), 28, 75–76, 84–95, *90*, 237n4; Gaines and, 92–93; Hardfish and, 110, 113; Keokuk and, disagreements between, 77, 93–94, 95; *Life* of, 5, 7, 75–76, 89–95, 122; ridicule of, 89; Saukenuk defended by, 85–86, 93; speech of, 87; as symbol, 168; tour of, 87–89, *88*; Washington delegation including, 105
"Blackhawkiana," 86, 89
Black Hawk War, 75–76, 77, 85–86, 95, 122, 167, 205
"Black Peter," 131
Black-Rogers, Mary, 65
bodies: of African-American orators, 232n58; of chiefs, 174, 178, 195, 254n95; gender and, 49–51; rhetoric of, 48–52; scrutiny of, 48–52, 144, 207–8, 232n57
Boelhower, William, 91
borderlands, 9–10
borders, 76–77, 79–81, 83, 99, 101, 107, 137
Boudinot, Elias (Cherokee), 7, 149, 222n17
Bowes, John P., 17
"braves," 55
Brodhead, Richard, 9
Brooks, James F., 53
Brooks, Lisa, 10, 115
Brunson, Alfred, 254n87
Bruyneel, Kevin, 19
Buckley, Jay, 79

bureaucracy, 10, 11, 21, 74, 90–92, 94–95, 215
Burritt, Elihu, 203
Byrd, Jodi, 59–60

Calhoun, John C., 15, 34, 37–39, 62, 238n13
Camudwa, 174
Canada: Bagot Commission and, 199–200; General Council of Christianized Ojibwas in, 195–97; Ojibwe lands in, 189, 199–200; white encroachment in, 184
Canowakeed, 174, 175
capitalism, 21–22, 37, 150, 214–15. *See also* trade
captivity, economy of, 53
Carpenter, Daniel, 115
Carson, James Taylor, 127
Cass, Lewis, 134, 170, 171, 179, 181, 182
Catlin, George, *80, 128*, 167
ceremony, 4, 47, 50, 52–53, 55–57
character, physiognomy and, 140–43, *141*
Cherokee Nation, 14–15, 17, 25, 29
Cherokee Nation v. Georgia, 25, 59
Cherokee Phoenix (newspaper), 7, 222n17
Cheyfitz, Eric, 7, 13, 59, 84
Chickasaw Nation, 153
Chinn, Julia, 129
Chippewa. See Ojibwe Nation
Choctaw Academy, 129–30, 145–46, 151, 245n24
Choctaw language, 129, 151
Choctaw Nation: Chickasaw Nation and, 153; as "civilized," 137–38, 139–40, 146–47, 154–55; cultural assimilation of, 146–48; defrauded, 157–64; districts of, 127; education in, 125, 129, 144–52, 160–61, 162–63; emergence story of, 151, 248n102; exceptionalism of, 29, 137–38, 152, 154–56, 165; expeditions in, 130–34, 245n24; futurity of, 145, 147, 164; General Council of, 127–29, 130, 145, 153; in Indian Territory, 126–38; Lighthorse, 126, 127; Mississippi state law and, 138–39, 154; modernization of,

125–26, 127–29, 149–50, 155, 160, 162–63; Osage and, 134–35; political power in, shifting, 126; removal of, 17, 123–24, 130, 137–39, 157–64; slavery in, 124, 126, 127, 147, 156, 161; stratification of, 126–27, 129, 147, 165; US compared to, 164–65; written laws of, 127–29
Choctaw nationalism, 29, 123–65; education and, 29, 125, 129, 144–52, 160–61, 162–63; exceptionalism in, 137–38, 152, 154–55; Indian Territory in, 150–51; "progress" and, 148–50, 154–55; separatism and, 156; treaties and, 125–26, 157–64
Choncape (Otoe), 39
Chouteau, Pierre, 35, 37, 229n8
Christianity: Choctaw nationalism and, 147; as civilizing influence, 40–41, 46, 147, 155, 196–97, 200; denominations of, 200; and the General Council of Christianized Ojibwas, 195–97, 206
Civilization Fund, 21
civilization program, 40–46; Christianity as part of, 40–41, 46, 147, 155, 196–97, 200; delegations introduced to, 34; failures of, 69; Hardfish's Town and, 117–18; judging Native receptiveness to, 48–49, 51–52, 57; missionaries in, 21, 41–43, 69, 105, 131; openness to, 66; Petalesharo as figurehead for, 55–57; policies, 21, 25; resistance to, 28, 64–66, 67–70, 105; rhetoric of, 14–15, 26, 64, 187. *See also* education
Clark, Julius Taylor, 192, 254n87
Clark, William, 34–35, 37, *80,* 118; Black Hawk and, 85, 92; Keokuk and, 77, 79–84, 94, 98, 100; Pitchlynn and, 134, 135; treaties made by, 37, 229n8. *See also* Lewis and Clark expedition
Cobb, Amanda J., 18
Cochrane, John, 159
Coffee, John, 162
Cohen, Matt, 6, 7

Colbert, Thomas Burnell, 75, 76, 80, 100, 238n13, 238n23
collaboration, 153–54, 178, 179, 216–17, 220; authorship and, 26; coercion as, 84; and collaborative speech, 80–81; definition of, 7–8, 84; delegations as, 69, 72; legal, 157–65; with non-Natives, 91, 94–95, 110, 121–22, 140–44, 158–59; on physiognomy, 142–44; projects as, 11–12, 72; Sauk, 75–76, 91, 94–95, 99, 110, 111, 114–22; types of, 6
colonialism, 14–22; bureaucracy of, 10, 75, 96, 101–2, 125, 215; catharsis over guilt of, 167; diplomatic resistance to, 19, 75–76, 110, 125–26, 202, 219–20; gender and, 27, 56–57, 143–44; indigenous writing shaped by, 12–13; politics of recognition and, 27; and politics of representation, 207–9, 210–11, 214; replacement narrative of, 47, 64, 137–38, 167; settler *vs.* extraction-based, 18, 226n59; "weakness" as trope of, 162. *See also* settler colonialism
"colonial mediascapes," 6
colonization plan, Kahgega as, 198
Committee of Missions, 231n31
Committee on Indian Affairs, 153–54
communication: controlling, 100–101, 125; cross-cultural, 6–7; networks, 9–10, 94, 232n49; publication as, 12; technologies, 100–101, 203–4, 215
"communitism," 169, 185, 189–90
community: as concept, 168–69; *vs.* empire, 168–69; literature serving, 177; Methodism as framework for, 189–90; organizers, 196–97; politicized, 184, 185, 189; *vs.* settler state, 169; sovereignty and, 188–89
Conn, Steven, 59
continuity: agency used for, 109–10; ancestry and, 151; *vs.* progress, 149–50
Cooper, Douglas, 159
Cooper, James Fenimore, 71–72, 167
copper mining, 182

Copway, George (Ojibwe), 23–24, 25, 27, 29, 168, 190–211, *192*; anticolonial critique by, 204–5; as assimilationist, 191, 200; background of, 190–91, 192–93; detachment of, from Ojibwe life, 191, 209; on Eastern Dakota "savagery," 194; endorsements of, 192; on European superstitions, 206; European travels of, 203, 206–9, 256n134; and the General Council, 195–97; on Indian chief figures, 193–94, 195, 200, 254n95; on indigenous leadership, 169; *Life of*, 23, 191–95, 196–201, 209–10; oratory of, 207; Peace Congress attended by, 202, 203, 206–7; removal and, 191, 197–98, 204–5; *Running Sketches* of, 192, 201–9; on US-Indian relations, 203–4
Copway's American Indian (newspaper), 192, 201–2
Cornstalk, Peter (Shawnee), 132, 135
cosmopolitans *vs.* primordialists, 127, 129
Coulthard, Glen, 27
Council Bluffs agency. *See* Upper Missouri Agency (Council Bluffs)
Council of the Sacs and Foxes, at Washington City, 106
"covering the dead," 112
Cox, James H., 10, 218
Crane *doodem*, 171
Credit River Mission, 184, 185–86, 187–89, 195
Creek Nation, 136–37
Cronon, William, 102–3
culture, 9, 144, 149–52. *See also* print culture

dance, intertribal, 50–51, 233n69
Dancing Rabbit Creek treaty, 17, 126, 139, 157–64; education and, 160–61, 162–63; McClelland and, 161; update to, 163–64; US failure to implement, 158, 159–60
Davenport, George, 91, 92, 97–98
Davis, Susan G., 50
debt, 22, 81, 102, 118–19, 121
decision-making, Native, 44–46; on ceremonies, 55; conflicts in, 93, 110–16, 120–21; localized, 20–21, 44–46, 69; Ojibwe, decentered nature of, 179; Pitchlynn on, 154; US ignorance of, 95
decision-making by Indian Office, 20–21, 81–82
delegations to Washington, 31–72, 74; indigenous mapping by, 107–9, *108*; local knowledge shared by, 34; meaning of, to Native diplomats, 33
Deloria, Philip J., 47, 122, 217
Deloria, Vine, Jr., 218
Denning, Michael, 22, 137
Department of War, 32, 33, 34
dependency, rhetoric of, 19, 162, 188
DeRosier, Arthur, 158
Dickens, Charles, 124, 144
Dillon, Elizabeth Maddock, 7
diplomacy, 2–3; as agency, 4, 222n11; ceremony as part of, 4, 47, 50–51; chiefs decentered from, 184; colonial hierarchies reproduced in, 93–94; decision-making in, 44–46, 95, 97, 175; definition of, 221n5; failures of, 93–95, 100–101, 121; gift exchanges in, 186–87; as indigenous publics, 10–11, 121; intertribal aspects of, 96, 109, 153–57, 193, 194; journalistic coverage of, 46–53, 58–59, 86–87, 94–95, 203–4, 221n1, 232n49, 234n96; as legal proceedings, 157–65; *Literary Voyager* and, 173; local nature of, 34, 45–46, 70; and military power, relationship between, 28, 38–40, 91–92, 94, 213–14; mock, 50–51, 87; Native control over, 62–63; as the performance of nationhood, 5, 125; persistence of, in Red Power movement, 218–19; post-Civil War, 213–14; relegated to fiction or history, 167–68; treaties re-interpreted in, 157–64; in US propaganda, 86–87; US representatives' ignorance of, 92–93; wampum in, 185–86; women in, 14–15, 27, 170–71, 177. *See also* petitions
"diplomatic publics," 10
diplomats: collaborating with non-Natives, 91, 94–95, 110, 121–22,

140–44, 158–59; colonists recognizing, 27; Euro-American ideologies of, 125–26, 129, 147–49, 154–55, 157–58, 165; idealized, from US perspective, 182–83; missionaries as, 200–201, 209, 210; presumed to be representatives, 44, 69; ridicule of, 89; settler colonialism challenged by, 20, 22; skepticism of writings of, 216; as slaveholders, 124, 126, 131, 147, 156; sovereignty affirmed by, 3–4; status of, 14, 26, 27, 76–77, 89, 157, 173
disease, 198
displacement, 14–15, 63
Dodge, Henry, 103
Donaldson, Laura, 190
doodem (clan), 171, 173
Doty, Duane, 198
Dougherty, John, 42, 61, 235n109
Douglass, Frederick, 232n58
Dowd, Gregory, 96
Drake, Benjamin, 90, 167
Drake, Samuel Gardner, 52
Durang, Charles, 233n66

Easterly, Thomas M., 78
Eastern Dakota. *See* Sioux Nations
Eaton, John, 162
ecological changes, 63, 64, 119
economy: annuities and, 110–12, 114–17, 119–20, 121–22; collapse of, 121; horticulture and hunting, 63, 64–66; indigenous *vs.* settler, 102–5; land use and, 28, 63, 102–5; seasonal variations in, 103–4, 107; trading houses' role in, 21–22, 28, 104, 118–19
education, 5–6; agricultural, 41– 45; AIM negotiating for, 218; away from home, 164–65; Choctaw nationalism and, 29, 125, 129, 144–52, 160–61, 162–63; class and, 147; contingent on future conditions, 67–68, 69–70; gender and, 188; indigenous control of, 145, 146–47; Lucas on, 117; mission schools, 41, 44, 129, 191; Ojibwe, 182, 184, 187–89, 193, 195, 199; resistance to, 66, 105;

in US interest, 163. *See also* civilization program
"emigration," 119
Emirbayer, Mustafa, 228n90
encroachment. *See* white encroachment
England, indigenous relations with, 185–89
ethnic cleansing, 16, 18
the "ethnie," 151
Euro-American ideologies, 125–26, 129, 147–49, 154–55, 157–65
evangelical organizations, 202–3
Evarts, Jeremiah, 17
exceptionalism, 29, 137–38, 152, 154–55, 173–74
expansion: critiques of, 87, *88*; intertribal conflict and, 68; O'Fallon delegation and, 33
exploratory expeditions, 15, 22, 34; in Choctaw territory, 130–34, 245n24; Native members of, 130–31

Fabian, Johannes, 67
factory system, 37, 40
Fanon, Frantz, 151
Fanuzzi, Robert, 232n58
Faux, William, 47–48
Fenderich, Charles, *128*
Ferguson, Adam, 175
fiction, 167, 174–76
Fields, Richard (Cherokee), 135
"Five Civilized Tribes," 17
Fletcher v. Peck, 18–19, 59
Flint, Kate, 96, 205, 206, 214–15
Folsom, David, 126
Folsom, Israel, 158, 248n98
Folsom, Rhoda, 126
Folsom, Sophia, 126
Fontanelle, Lucien, 37
Forsyth, John, *106*
Forsyth, Thomas, 77, 91
Fort Armstrong, 91
Fort Brady, 170
Fort Osage mission school, 44–45
Foucault, Michel, 61–62
Fowler, Loretta, 63
Fraser, Nancy, 10
Freneau, Philip, 219

"frontier," 28, 102–3; definition of, 102; homeland turned into, 85; racial imaginary of, 111, 119–21, 122; westward shift of, 63
"frontier violence," narrative of, 94, 119–21
Fulford, Tim, 187
Fuller, Margaret, 171
fur trade. *See* trade
futurity, Native, 67–68, 69–70, 215–16, 220

Gaines, Edmund P., 85, 92–93
Garland, Samuel, 158
gender, 26–27, 49–51, 52–53, *54*, 55–57, 143–144. *See also* women; masculinity, politics of
General Council of Christianized Ojibwas, 195–97, 206
"The Generous Chief" (song), 52, *54*, 71
Genetin-Pilawa, C. Joseph, 33
geography: indigenous representations of, 107–9, *108*; of Ojibwe Nation, 184, 199–200; of removal, 17–18; tribal, of Indian Territory, 77, 79, 132
Giddings, Salmon, 41
gift exchanges, 186–87
Gilman, Chandler, 171
Girl Child, 53
Glenelg, Lord. *See* Grant, Charles (Lord Glenelg)
Glenelg, Lord (Charles Grant), 185–86
Glover, Jeffrey, 6
Gramsci, Antonio, 21, 22
The Grand National Caravan Moving East, 87, *88*
Grant, Charles (Lord Glenelg), 185–86
Graves, James, 39
Gray, Susan, 226n58
Great Nehama Agency, 105, 107
Great Spirit, 14, 43, 55–56, 61, 67, 194, 204
Green, Michael, 115, 243n138
"guest-keepers," 76
Gunn, Robert Lawrence, 9–10, 51

Habermas, Jürgen, 7
Hagan, William T., 95
Haley, David W., 130

Hall, James, 179
Hall, Sherman, 254n87
Hall, Stuart, 22
Halttunen, Karen, 48, 140, 232n57
Hamilton, Kristie, 206
Hardfish (Sauk), 28, 75, 76, 117–21, 122; on annuities, 114; Black Hawk and, 110, 113; Keokuk allying with, 121; Lucas and, 114–15, 119, 120; as principal chief, 113; publication projects of, 111, 114–15
Hardfish's Town, 113, 117–18, 119
Harkins, George W., 139
Harmony Mission school, 41
Harris, Carey Allen, 105, *108*
Harvey, Sean, 9
Hatchootucknee ("The Snapping Turtle"). *See* Pitchlynn, Peter (Choctaw)
Hayne Hudjihini (Otoe), 39, 47–48, *49*, 49–50
health care, 198
Henry, George (Ojibwe), 183
historical romance, *54*
History of the Indian Tribes (McKenney), 52, *53*, *60*, 179–81, *180*, 182, 256n138
History of the Ojebway Indians (Jones), 185, 253n54
Honoré, Louis T., 39
Hood, Washington, 130
House of Representatives, 31–32, *32*, 72, 153–54
House of Representatives (Morse), 31–32, *32*, 229nn1–2
Hoxie, Frederick, 22, 157, 163, 220
Huhndorf, Shari M., 48, 57
humanitarianism, rhetoric of, 16, 20, 71–72, 92, 131
human rights, Black Hawk and, 87, *88*
hunting, 42, 77, 79, 98–100, 119
Hush-ook-wa, 126
Hutton, Isaac Garner, 52, *54*, 71
Hyde, Anne F., 35, 222n9
Hyde, George, 230n20

identity, 92–93, 149
Illinois, statehood of, 84–85, 99
imagination, 11
imagined community, 151–52

Index | 265

Indian agents, 25, 91–92, 104; trade overseen by, 40, 170; turnover among, 118. *See also* Forsyth, Thomas; O'Fallon, Benjamin; Schoolcraft, Henry Rowe; Street, Joseph; Ward, William
"Indian chief," 43, 175–211; challenging images of, 191, 210; Copway as, 23–24, 202, 206–7, 210; Copway on, 209–10; decentered, 184; empire symbolized by, 168, 169, 183, 210; in popular culture, 167, 174–76; and "public Indianness," 24, 190; romanticization of, 52, 169, 176, 178, 181, 182–83, 195; as warrior, 193–94
"Indian country," definition of, 16
"Indian Eloquence," 58–59, 234n96, 234n98
Indian Office. *See* Office of Indian Affairs
Indian policy, US, 5, 13; as collaborative literature, 13; debt in, 22, 81, 118–19, 121; as decentralized, 21, 22; as influence, 40; removal as, 15; Supreme Court rulings on, 18–19, 25, 59–60; treaties as, 34–35
Indian Removal Act, 15–16, 87, 138
"An Indian's Address to the Whites" (Boudinot), 149
"The Indians in the Lobby," 217
"Indian State," 191, 197–99
"The Indian Student" (Freneau), 219
Indian Territory: Choctaw Nation in, 126–38; living conditions in, 135–36; "reorganization" of, 153–57, 198; slavery in, 156; tribal geography of, 77, 79, 132
Indian Trade and Intercourse Act, 16
Indian wars, era of, 213–14
indigenous, definition of, 226n59
indigenous publication projects: 22, 26–28, 30, 72, 75, 84, 95, 110–11, 114, 120, 121, 126, 169, 196, 214–15; definition of, 12–13
indigenous religions, 29, 53; dismissed as superstition, 182. *See also* Great Spirit
individuality, rhetoric of, 215
institutional contexts of writing, 216–17

institutions of Indian policy, 3, 217–18
intellectual sovereignty, 19
intermarriage, 21; diplomacy and, 170–71; as strategy, 37, 126; Susan Johnston on, 173
interpreters, 90, 97–98, 196; backgrounds of, 235n109; implicated in injustice, 5, 91, 94. *See also* translation
intertribal conflicts, 77, 79, 193–94; conquests in, 109; over hunting grounds, 79, 98–99, 100, 107–9, 119; US expansion affecting, 68, 76, 96, 99–100
intertribal difference, theory of, 155–56
intertribal geography, shifting of, 96
intratribal conflict, 111–12, 114–16, 120–21
"Invocation to My Maternal Grandfather" (J. J. Schoolcraft), 176–77
Iowa Territory, 95, 114, 116, 118, 120, 121
Ioway Nation: map of, 107–9, *108*, 242n112; Sauk taking land from, 109; Washington delegation and, 105, 107, 242n112

Jackson, Andrew, 15–16, 87, *88*, 138
Jackson, Donald, 237n4
Jameson, Anna Brownell, 171
Johnson, Richard Mentor, 129, 130, 146, 245n18, 245n24
Johnson, Walter, 25, 110
Johnson v. M'Intosh, 59
Johnston, David, 87, *88*
Johnston, George (Ojibwe), 171
Johnston, John, 170–71, 173
Johnston, Susan (Ojibwe), 29, 170–71, *172*, 173–74, 176–77, 210
Jones, Augustus, 184
Jones, John (Ojibwe), 188, 195–96
Jones, Peter (Ojibwe), 5–6, 29, 168, 183–90, 210, 253n54; authority of, establishing, 188–89; background of, 184–85; in Europe, 184, 185, 187–89; fundraising work of, 186–89; on indigenous leadership, 169; *Life* of, 184–85, 187, 190; schools founded by, 187–89
Josephy, Alvin M., 95

Kahgega, 191, 197–99
Kahgegagahbowh. *See* Copway, George (Ojibwe)
Kahkewāquonāby. *See* Jones, Peter (Ojibwe)
Kanza, 32
Kennedy, J. Gerald, 86
Kennerly, George H., 130
Keokuk (Sauk), 5, 28, 29, 76–84, *78*, 121–22; on annuities, 111–12; Black Hawk and, disagreements between, 77, 93–94, 95; challenges to, 74–75, 110–11, 113–15; civilization resisted by, 105; Clark and, 77, 79–84, 94, 98, 100; drama of, 82, 238n23; Gaines and, 92; goals of, 109–10; Hardfish allying with, 121; land sales and, 102, 103–5; life of, 76–77; negative portrayals of, 75, 237n4; oratory of, 73, 74–77, 93, 95–101, 109–10, 122; Pilcher and, 111; at Prairie du Chien, 73–75, 77, 79, 82–84; reputation of, damaged, 115–16, 118, 243n138; Sioux and, 73, 79, 98–100, 105, 241n97; trading houses and, 116, 118–19; Van Buren petitioned by, 115; Washington delegation including, 105, *106*; Washington delegation urged by, 79–80, 94; and the written word, 100–101
Kidwell, Clara Sue, 129
Kilgo, Dolores Ann, *78*
King, Charles Bird, 31, 33, 167; Black Hawk portraits by, 86, 105; Petalesharo portrait by, 52, *53*, *54*, 229n2, 233n73
Konkle, Maureen, 13, 25, 155, 174–75
Krupat, Arnold, 8, 92, 96

Lachelesharo (Pawnee), 52
LaFromboise, Teresa, 190
Lancaster method, 41, 231n34
Lancaster schools, 41–42, 231n33
land: adopting Euro-American perspectives on, 157–64; ancestral connections to, uprooted, 168; boundary lines, 99; commodification of, 164, 182; conquest of, 109; debt and, 22, 81, 102, 121; economic activity and, 28, 63, 102–5; futurity and, 122, 196, 216; intertribal conflicts over, 77, 79, 96, 98–100, 107–9, 119; loss, "vanishing Indian" and, 216; military intervention over, 214; sale of, pressured, 81–82, 102, 103–4; theft, 160–61; value of, as more than monetary, 103–4, 164. *See also* white encroachment
land title: diplomats betraying, 93; as hunting rights, 59; Indian unity and, 189; Ojibwe, 195–96, 197, 199; president annulling, 197; settler contract and, 137; as temporary, 18–19, 59–60
language: Choctaw, 129, 151; manipulation of, 93, 101; Ojibwe, 170, 173, 253n54; of Pawnee groups, 35; of resistance, 17. *See also* interpreters; translation
La Pointe, 174
The Last of the Mohicans (Cooper), 167
law and legal proceedings, 17, 157–63, 164
Lea, Luke, 159
LeClaire, Antoine, 91; Black Hawk and, 75, 90, 91, 94–95; Keokuk and, 97–98
Lesslie, Jonathan, 41
Lewis, Dickson W., 158
Lewis, James Otto, *74*, *135*, 179, *180*
Lewis and Clark expedition, 15
The Life, History, and Travels of Kah-Ge-Ga-Gah-Bowh (Copway), 23, 191–95, 196–201, 209–10
The Life, Letters, and Speeches of Kah-Ge-Ga-Gah-Bowh, 202
Life and Adventures of Black Hawk (Drake), 90, 167
Life and Journals of Kah-Ke-Wa-Quo-Na-By (Jones), 184–85, 187, 190
Life of Ma-ka-tai-me-she-kia-kiak, 5, 7, 75–76, 89–95, 122; Indian Agency critiqued in, 91–92
Lighthorse, 126, 127
Lincecum, Gideon, 140, *141*, 142–43, 246n55
Lindsley, Philip, 130, 245n23

Lisa, Manuel, 37
literacy, orality and, 6–7, 101, 161–62
literary separatism, 125–26
literary sketches, 205–6
Literary Voyager, 171–78, 251n20
literature: evangelical organizations and, 202–3; institutional contexts of, 216–17; multimedia, 6–7; Ojibwe, Indian chiefs in, 168, 173, 189–90; petitions as genre of, 114–15; publication of, 6–13; scribal contributions to, 113; skepticism of, 216; transatlantic, 183, 184–90, 192; as transnational, 10, 96, 183–84, 189–90. *See also* collaboration
locality, 168–69
Logan (Mingo), 234n96
Long, Stephen Harriman, 15, 34, 236n130
Longfellow, Henry Wordsworth, 170
Loughran, Trish, 222n15
Lucas, Robert, 114–18, *116,* 243n138; Hardfish and, 114–15, 119, 120; Sauk removal promoted by, 119–21
Lyons, Scott Richard, 191, 197, 198, 205; on rhetoric, 19, 254n95; on the "x-mark," 215, 222n11

Ma-ka-tai-me-she-kia-kiak. *See* Black Hawk (Sauk)
Ma-ka-tai-me-she-kia-kiak (Smith), 90
manidoo, 96–97
manual labor schools, 21, 23, 189, 195
Manypenny, George Washington, 159
mapping, US, 75, 96, 112; alternatives to, 10, 107–9, *108,* 199–200; problems caused by, 96, 100, 112
Marshall, John, 18–19, 59
"Marshall trilogy," 19, 59
masculinity, politics of, 27, 140, 143–44, 165
Mashpee Wampanoag, 8–9
Maungwudaus. *See* Henry, George (Ojibwe)
McClelland, Robert, 159, 161
McCoy, Isaac, 17, 131, 132, 153
McKenney, Thomas, 20, 40–46, 209, 210; and Choctaw removal, 130; Copway's familiarity with, 256n138;

History of the Indian Tribes by, 52, *53, 60,* 179–81, *180,* 182, 256n138; Ojibwe chief figure coopted by, 169; on Peahmuska, 238n24; Petalesharo and, 56–57, 234n92; Pitchlynn and, 129; on removal, changing thoughts on, 227n71; Shingabawossin and, 179–83, *180*
Medals. *See* peace medals
Medill, William, 198
Meskwaki Nation, 74–75, 81, 82–83, 237n2
Metamora (Stone), 167
Metcalfe, Charles, 189, 196
Methodism, 8–9, 23–24, 183–84, 186–91; and the General Council of Christianized Ojibwas, 195–97; as organizational framework, 189–90; sovereignty and, 195–96; *vs.* warrior culture, 194
metonymy, 42, 43, 44, 169
Meumbane (Omaha), 37
Mexico, trade with, 40
Michigan Territory, 170–71, 251n9
"middle ground," 4, 221n8
Mielke, Laura, 172
military power, waning of, 28, 102
militias, settler, 120, 139
Milledoler, Philip, 41
mimicry, 149
mineral rights, 178–79, 182
Mische, Ann, 11, 228n90
missionaries: agricultural education and, 41–45; as authorized agents, 200–201, 209, 210; civilization program depending on, 21, 41–43, 69, 105, 131; government encouraging involvement of, 21; intertribal diplomacy by, 193, 194; Native, 23, 169, 183–211; in removal debates, 17, 131; tracts and, 202–3
mission schools, 41, 44, 129, 191
Mississauga, 184, 253n54
Mississippi, 138–39, 154, 158, 160
Missouria, 32
Mitain (Omaha), 37
modernity, 65, 68, 205, 215–16
Monchousia (Kanza), 39, 43, 44–45
Monroe, James, 15, 33, 48, 49–50, 58–70

268 | Index

Moose Tail (Ojibwe), 193
More, Hannah, 186
Morning Star ceremony, 52–53, *54*, 55–57
Morse, Jedidiah, 31–32, *32*, 229n2; *Report* of, 31, 53–55, 66, 69, 229n2, 235n106
Morse, Samuel F. B., 31–32, *32*, 229n1; *House of Representatives* by, 31–32, *32*, 229nn1–2
Morton, Samuel G., 142
Müller, Ralf, 11–12, 224n38
Munceytown community, 188–89
Mushulatubbee (Choctaw), 126

nahikut, 55
Na'hjeNing'e (Ioway), 107, *108*, 109, 242n112
Nanih Waiya (Mother Mound), 151, 248n102
Nasheaskuk (Sauk), 86
National Congress of American Indians (NCAI), 218
National Indian Youth Council (NIYC), 218
nationalism: American, 50, 70, 168; indigenous, 29, 125, 146, 149, 151, 161, 165; literary, 125; as performance of national identity, 50. *See also* Choctaw nationalism
nation-building: and bodies as metaphors for nationhood, 254n95; centralization as tool of, 127; colonial ideologies informing, 165; institutional focus of, 151–52; maps and, 107–9, *108*; mission schools as tools of, 129; and national culture, 151; Ojibwe, 195–96; privileged centered in, 124, 126, 129; teleology of, 102, 148–49; written laws in, 127–29
nations: as construct, 5, 13; as "domestic dependent nations," 19, 162; local community interests and, 169; political representation of, 198; US legal system and, 59–60; US understanding of, 44–45. *See also specific nations*
Native Americans: diminishing numbers of, 71, 198; Eastern *vs.* Western, 72; as global actors, 215; "legal wardship" of, 25; place of, in new landscape, 214–15; settlers and, binaries of, 183–84; stereotypes of, challenging, 29, 30; as US citizens, 198, 199; written out of history, 167. *See also* stereotypes of Native Americans
Neapope (Sauk), 86, 94
Nelson, Dana, 143
networks, 9–10, 12, 13, 207–8; of agents, traders, and interpreters, 90–92, 94–95; family, 44, 169, 177; Indian agents depending on, 35, 37; missionary, 43–44; overlapping, 177; of print culture, 223n25
Newman, Andrew, 6
newspapers, 1, 2, 7, 33, 40–41, 47–48, 50, 52–53, 56, 58–59, 61, 87, 204, 207, 221n1, 230n22, 232n49, 235n106, 235n107
Nicholson, Alfred, 161
Northwest Ordinance, 170
Notions of the Americans (Cooper), 71–72
Novak, William, 21

O'Brien, Jean, 167
O'Fallon, Benjamin, 1, 2, 32, *36*, 62, 70; appointment of, 34; diplomacy as strategy of, 38–39; early life of, 35, 37
O'Fallon, John, 37
O'Fallon delegation, 31–72; ceremony and, 50–51; decision-making among, 44–46, 69; gifts from, 67; interpreters for, 39, 42, 61–62, 235n109; at Lancaster School, 41–42; lodgings for, 230n21; McKenney meeting, 40–44; meaning of, 33–34; Monroe meeting, 33, 48, 49–50, 58–70, 235n107, 235n110; names of, 230n20; O'Fallon trusted by, 45–46; organizing, 34–40; Petalesharo's role in, 52–58, 61; physical scrutiny of, 46–52; social events for, 47
Office of Indian Affairs, 20; failures of, 82–83, 98–100; funding, 37–38; and localized decision-making, 20–21; as loose network, 82; mismanagement of, 91, 94, 98–99; reorganization of, 97; St. Louis office of, 79, 80,

Index | 269

81–83; transferred to Interior Department, 159
The Ojibway Conquest (Copway and Clark), 192, *192*, 202, 254n87
Ojibwe language, 170, 173, 253n54
Ojibwe Nation, 18, 29, 167–211; annulment of land title of, 197; as civilized, 196–97; decentered politics of, 179, 181, 182, 188–89, 191, 210; education in, 182, 184, 187–89, 193, 195, 199; England and, 185–87, 253n54; geography of, 184, 199–200; gift exchanges in, 186–87; mineral rights and, 178–79, 182; as more civilized than Europe, 207; name of, 250n4, 253n54; nation-building, 195–96; peace treaty with US, 171; reform of, 169, 190–201, 202, 210–11; religion of, 194; relocation campaign, 195–96; removal of, 168, 197, 204–5; Sandy Lake community of, 193–94; and Sioux, conflict between, 170, 173, 176, 193–94; small communities forming, 168–69; traditional values of, 173–74, 190, 200; transnational literature of, 183–84; US influence in, growing, 182–83; white encroachment on, 168, 170, 171, 184; in white fiction, 174–76
Olson, Greg, 109
Omaha, 32; futurity, 67–68; O'Fallon delegation speech, 67–69; peacefulness of, 68–69; Sioux and, relations between, 68
Ongpatonga (Omaha), 28, 37, *38*, 39, 44, 70; on O'Fallon, 45–46; speech of, 67–69
orality and literacy, 6–7, 101, 161–62
oral performance, 6, 8
oratory, 58–70; depiction of, in fiction, 174–76; as institutional intervention, 82; physical scrutiny *vs.*, 58–59, 232nn57–58; suspicion of, 75
"Organization of a new Indian territory" (Copway), 202
organization theory, 11–12, 224n38
Osage Nation, 134
"The Otagamiad" (H. R. Schoolcraft), 174–76

Otherness, 48, 51, 61, 91
Otoe, 32
Ozhaguscodaywayquay (Ojibwe). *See* Johnston, Susan (Ojibwe)

pacification, narratives of, 57, 71, 86–87, 96
Pamaho (Sauk-Winnebago), 86
Panic of 1819, 37
parades, 1, 4, 50, 87, *88*
Parker, Robert Dale, 124, 171, 176, 251n20
Parrish, Susan Scott, 9
Pashepaho (Sauk), 99
Pateman, Carole, 18, 137
paternalism, 16, 42–43, 57, 169
Patterson, John Barton, 75, 89, 91, 94–95, 239n53
"Pawnee chief," speech of. *See* Sharitarish (Pawnee)
Pawnee Nation, 1–2; Chaui band, 32, 35, 221n1; crises facing, 63–65; diversity among, 35; futurity, 67; importance of, in Upper Missouri, 39; Kítkehahki band, 32, 35, 230n20; languages spoken by, 35; Morning Star ceremony of, 52–53, *54*, 55–57; and name "Pawnee," 230n2; Pitahawirata band, 35; Skidi band, 2, 32, 35; traders raided by, 39
peace, 98–99; pipe, 207, 241n97; rhetoric, 71, 135, 178. *See also* peace medals
peace medals, 35, 52, 56, 57, *180*, 181, 185
Peahmuska (Meskwaki), 82–83, 238n24
Peat-Tshe-Noi (Sauk), 99
peoplehood, 151–52
performance, 6, 8, 47–50
Perry, William (Shawnee), 132, 135
Peskelechaco (Pawnee), 39, 230n20
Petalesharo (Pawnee), 31, *32*, 33, 39, 52–58, 70–72, 233n72; ceremony interrupted by, 52–53, *54*, 55–57; cult of, 71–72; McKenney and, 56–57, 234n92; name of, 233n73; portraits of, 52, *53*, *54*, 229n2, 235n106; speech of, 57, 61, 233n85, 234n92; as symbol, 168

petitions, 8, 14, 114–15; to England, 185–86, 195–96; Keokuk organizing, 115, 243n138; as recruitment documents, 115; as sign of organization, 196
Pettrich, Ferdinand, *106*
Peyer, Bernd, 205
philanthropy, 186, 187, 188, 190, 203
phrenology, 140–42, *141*
physiognomy, 140–42, *141*, 174, 178
Piatote, Beth H., 24–25
Pierce, Franklin, 161
Pike, Albert, 159
Pilcher, Joshua, 111
Pitcher, Zina, 173
Pitchlynn, John, 126
Pitchlynn, Peter (Choctaw), 5, 26, 29, 123–65, 245n23; background of, 126–27, 129–30, 246n55; as chief, 139–44; on Choctaw superiority, 29, 137–38, 152, 154–56, 165; on civilization, 136–37, 145, 147; as controversial, 124–26; Dancing Rabbit Creek treaty and, 157–64; diary of, 131–38, *133*, 150; Dickens and, 124, 144; on education and nationalism, 144–52, 158; at General Council, 127–29, *128*, 131; identity of, 149–50; on Indian Territory, 131–32, 150–51, 153–57; as a lawyer, 157–64; Native Americans' appearance described by, 135–36; oratory of, 144–52, 161–62; papers of, 124; physiognomical examination of, 140–43, *141*; on race, 124, 136–38, 140, 147–48, 157, 165; on the Sioux, 136; as slaveholder, 124, 126, 131, 147, 156; on traditional knowledge, 151–52; US and Choctaw Nation compared by, 164–65
Pitchlynn, Rhoda, 164
"pity," 5–6, 43, 169
Poinsett, Joel, *106*, 109
political and civil society, 21
politics of representation, 207–9, 210–11
popular culture, the "Indian" in, 3, 47–52, 167

Porter, Peter B., 131
portraiture: Black Hawk in, *90*; Congress commissioning, *128*; Copway in, *192*; Indian Office commissioning, 179–81, *180*; Keokuk in, *78*, 105; Petalesharo in, 31, 52, *54*, 229n2, 235n106; Pitchlynn in, *128*; popularity of, 31, *78*, 167; Shingabawossin in, 179–81, *180*, 182; Susan Johnston in, *172*; Tenskwatawa in, *135*; tropes of, 181; War Department commissioning, 33
postal service, 100–101
Povinelli, Elizabeth, 224n37
power: 80; gradations of, 97; as relational, 96–97; unequal relations of, 162
Poweshiek (Meskwaki), 100
The Prairie (Cooper), 71
Prairie du Chien treaty councils, *74*, 98–99; failure of, 100; Keokuk at, 73–75, 77, 79, 82–84; treaties of, *80*, 82, 178, 179
primordialists *vs.* cosmopolitans, 127, 129
print culture, 7; authority of, 190; evangelical organizations spreading, 202–3; networks of, 223n25; sovereignty and, 255n117; "techno-mythology" of, 222n15
prisoners of war, 86–87
progress, rhetoric of, 102, 147–48, 149, 151–52, 164
"project," 11–12, 224nn37–38
Prucha, Francis Paul, 227n71
publication, 6–13; innovations in, 202–3; opaque process of, 58; as relational act, 7–10, 223n25; stereotype printing and, 255n117
"publication events," 7
publication projects. *See* indigenous publication projects
"public Indianness," 24, 190
publics: cross-cultural, 201; diplomatic, 10, 121; religious and philanthropic, 186, 187–90; strong *vs.* weak, 10
the "public sphere," 7
public *vs.* private, 81–83

Quàshquàme, 77

race: class, political power, and, 126–27, 165; judging strangers by, 48–50; and masculinity, 143–44; Mississippi laws on, 138–39; Pitchlynn on, 124, 136–38, 140, 147–48, 157, 165; and racial mixing, 50–51, 136–37; and scientific racism, 16, 140, 142, 143; and spiritual effects of racism, 198

Rapine, Daniel, 56

Rapine, Mary, 56, 57, 233n85

raripakusus, 55

Rasmussen, Birgit Brander, 6

Red Power, 218–19

reform: Ojibwe rhetoric of, 169, 190–201, 202, 210–11; removal tied to, 131

"Remonstrance of Col. Peter Pitchlynn," 153–57

removal: agriculture and, 131, 134; Black Hawk War and, 75; bureaucracy of, 91–92, 94; of Choctaw Nation, 17, 123–24, 130, 137–39, 157–64; as "emigration," 119; era, 14–22; era, authorship and authority in, 23–30; as ethnic cleansing, 16; federal inaction *vs.* action causing, 226n58; as humanitarian, 16, 20, 71–72, 92, 131; hurried nature of, 160; litigating, 157–64; McKenney's evolution on, 227n71; negotiating, at local level, 20–21; prevention of, 198; provisions for, insufficient, 139; reform tied to, 131; settlements for, 124; as unending process, 154, 198

"Report on the Affairs of the Indians in Canada," 199–200

Report to the Secretary of War (Morse), 31, 53–55, 66, 69, 229n2, 235n106

representation: contested, 75–76, 81; of diplomats, presumed, 44, 69; politics of, 207–9, 210–11

reservations, 16, 25, 214

resistance: agency and, 25–26, 30; to education, 66; language of, 17; recognizing, 109–10, 164, 218; and the "third space of sovereignty," 19

retraditionalization, 190

Reynolds, John, 85

rhetoric: of benevolence, 41, 56, 188; bodily, 48–52; of civilization, 14–15, 26, 64, 187; clichés in, 204; of dependency, 19, 162, 188; failure of, 46; of humanitarianism, 16, 20, 71–72, 92, 131; of identity, 92–93; of individuality, 215; metaphor in, 42; metonymy in, 42, 43, 44, 169; of peace, 71, 135, 178; of pity, 5–6, 43, 169; of progress, 147–48, 149, 151–52, 164, 169; and rhetorical sovereignty, 19; of separatism, 61; of starvation, 65; of wants, 64, 65, 81, 178

Rifkin, Mark, 75, 92, 93–94, 216

Riley, John, 189

Robertson, William, 155

Rock Island Agency, 90–91

Rockwell, Stephen J., 20, 82, 226n58

Round, Phillip H., 3, 10, 24, 203, 255n117

Running Sketches of Men and Places (Copway), 192, 201–9

Ruoff, A. LaVonne Brown, 205

Rusert, Britt, 142

Ryan, Susan M., 41, 187

Ryerson, Egerton, 184, 185

"Sac and Fox Nation." *See* Meskwaki Nation; Sauk Nation

Sandy Lake Ojibwe community, 193–94

Sandy Lake Tragedy, 197

Santa Fe trail, 40, 233n72

Satz, Ronald, 226n58

Saukenuk, 76–77, 85–86

Sauk Nation, 28, 73–122, 237n2; Black Hawk War and, 75; captivity tour, 87–89, *88*; civilization program resisted by, 105; collectivity of, 95; conquest by, 109; cornfields of, destroyed, 91; decline of, 116–17; delegation, 79; dispossession of, 75, 77, 95–96; futurity of, 76, 122; Iowa River reservation, sale of, 102, 103–4; Lucas reporting on, 115–18; petition, 115, 243n138; population of, 243n138; removal of, 119–21; Sioux and, 79, 80, 82, 98–100, 105, 119, 241n97;

Sauk Nation (*cont'd*)
  treaties of, 77, 82, 85–87, 95, 101, 111, 113, 121–22, 238n13, 238n36; white encroachment on, 99, 101–10
Sault Ste. Marie, 170–72
Sawyer, Joseph (Ojibwe), 23, 188, 195
Sayre, Gordon M., 90
scarcity of game, 64, 65, 97, 107
Schmitz, Neil, 91
Schoolcraft, Henry Rowe, 73, 210; *Literary Voyager* of, 170–78; on Ojibwe chiefs, 169, 177–83; on Ojibwe language and culture, 170, 171; on Shingabawossin, 177–79, 183; Susan Johnston transcribed by, 173–74
Schoolcraft, Jane Johnston (Ojibwe), 29, 168, *175*, 210; on Ojibwe networks, 169; poetry of, 176–77; writings of, 171, 172, 176–77
schools: Choctaw Academy, 129–30, 145–46, 151, 245n24; Choctaw tribal, 145–46, 163; Fort Osage, 44–45; in Hardfish's Town, 117; Harmony Mission, 41; Lancaster, 41–42, 231n33; for manual labor, 21, 23, 189, 195; mission, 41, 44, 129, 191; Peter Jones founding, 184, 187–89; public, 231n34. *See also* education
Schütz, Alfred, 11
scientific racism, 16, 140, 142, 143
Second Seminole War, 205
semiotics of embodiment, 51
separatism, rhetoric of, 61
settler colonialism: Black Hawk resisting, 84–95; as decentralized, 21, 22; definition of, 18, 226n59; diplomats abetting, 75; diplomats challenging, 20, 121, 156–57, 216–17; diplomats constrained by, 101–10; " Indian chief" trope in, 167, 179–83; land value and, 103–4; literary history challenging, 213; militias and, 120, 139; Ojibwe challenges to, 183–84; and politics of recognition, 27; "saving" Natives, 64; strict *vs.* tempered logic of, 18; time in, 215–16

settlers: definition of, 226n59; economy of, encroaching, 102–5; Native Americans and, as binaries, 183–84; and settler exceptionalism, 137–38
Sewell, William H., 24
Sharitarish (Pawnee), 28, 37, 39, 41–42, 49, *60*; speech by, 61, 62–67, 231n41, 235n110, 235nn106–7
Shaumonekusse (Otoe), 39, 47–48
Shawnee Nation, 132, 134
Shingabawossin (Ojibwe), 177–83; McKenney and, 179–81, *180*; peace medal worn by, *180*, 181
Shinggacahega, 221n1
Shingwaukonse (Ojibwe), 171
Shun-kah-kihe-gah (Pawnee), 1–2, 3, 221n1
Simpson, Audra, 19
Sioux Nations: and Ojibwe, 170, 173, 176, 193–94; and Omaha, 68; Peahmuska killed by, 82–83; Pitchlynn on, 136; raids by, 63, 194; and Sauk, 79, 80, 82, 98–100, 105, 119, 241n97
Sketches of a Tour to the Lakes (McKenney), 179–81, *180*
slavery: in Choctaw Nation, 124, 126, 127, 147, 156, 161; and diplomats as slaveholders, 124, 126, 131, 147, 156
smallpox, 63
Smith, Anthony, 151
Smith, Donald B., 189, 198, 252n54
Smith, Elbert Herring, 90
Snyder, Christina, 16, 127, 129, 132, 246n55
social action, 11–12
social organization, changing, 63
"social projects," 224n37
social stratification, 27, 126–27, 129
A Son of the Forest (Apess), 8
sovereignty: Christianity and, 195–96; community and, 188–89; as critical heuristic, 19, 227n67; defining, 18–19; diminished form of, 5, 18; diplomats affirming, 3–4, 13, 33–34, 44–45, 92; "nested," 19; political, 19–20; print culture and, 255n117; treaties contesting, 13, 18–19

speech, collaborative, 80–81
Spencer, John, 146
Spencer Academy, 145, 146
Spivak, Gayatri Chakravorty, 56
Spry, Adam, 165, 183–84
starvation, 64–65
stereotype printing, 255n117
stereotypes of Native Americans, 3, 47–52, 167; as cultural anomalies, 217–18; as morally inferior, 16, 71; as outsiders, 48, 85; in replacement narratives, 47, 64, 137–38, 167. *See also* vanishing Indian trope
Stevens, Laura, 187
Stone, John Augustus, 167
Street, Joseph, 97–98, 102, 113, 241n97
St. Vrain, Felix, 91–92
Sully, Robert, 86, *90*
Sunday, John (Ojibwe), 195
Supreme Court rulings, 18–19, 25, 59–60
Sweet, Timothy, 90, 93

Tamarkin, Elisa, 229n1
Tarecawawaho (Pawnee), 37, 61, 235n107
Taylor, Zachary, 197, 204–5
Tecumseh (Shawnee), 132
temperance, 127, 191
Tenskwatawa (Shawnee), 132, 134, *135*
terminal creeds, 219
"third space of sovereignty," 19
Thurman, Melburn, 55
time, 215–16
de Tocqueville, Alexis, 123–24
Todson, George P., 130
Tóth, György Ferenc, 5
tracts, 202–3
trade, 21–22, 28, 37; agencies linked with, 91, 94, 104–5, 170; alcohol and, 118; debt incurred in, 22, 81, 116, 118–19, 121; decline of, 37–38; "dependency" on, 116, 118–19; illegal trading in, 37; Indian agents overseeing, 40, 170; in Michigan Territory, 170–71; proximity to, 104–5, 119. *See also* traders
traders: attacks on, 39; as diplomats, 21–22, 34–35; implicated in injustice, 91; intermarriage with, 21, 37, 126; safe passage for, 35, 39–40; starvation rhetoric of, 65
trading houses, economy and, 21–22, 28, 104, 118–19
Traditional History and Characteristic Sketches of the Ojibway Nation (Copway), 192, 202
Trail of Tears, 15, 17
translation, 62; of the Bible, into Ojibwe, 185; of O'Fallon delegates, 39, 42, 61–62, 235n109; political aims of, 43–44. *See also* interpreters
treaties: of 1804, 85, 95; of 1832, 86, 94, 113; of 1842, 121; alteration of, one-sided, 101; annuities in, 37, 111; Butte Des Morts (1827), 179, 181; critiques of, by diplomats, 125, 126; Dancing Rabbit Creek, 17, 126, 139, 157–64; Doak's Stand (1820), 130, 134; era of, ending, 19, 214; Fond du Lac (1826), 178–79, 181; Fort Snelling (1837), 197; fraud and, 158; ineffectiveness of, 35, 38; La Pointe (1842), 197; and legal rights, 157, 164, 165; mineral rights, 178–79, 182; negotiating, 20, 162; negotiation of, conditions around, 162; New Echota, 15, 17; Ojibwe, 171, 178–79, 181–82, 197; oral vs. written, 161–62; Pawnee, 1, 221n1, 229n8; Pitchlynn critiquing, 157–58, 161–62; portraits commemorating, 179; Prairie du Chien (1825), *80*, 82–83, 98, 99, 178, 179, 181; re-interpreting, 161–62; renegotiating, 157–64; romanticization of, 3; Sauk, 77, 82, 85–87, 95, 101, 111, 113, 121–22, 238n13, 238n36; Sault Ste. Marie (1820), 171, 178; settler colonialism and, 18, 19, 214; signatories' roles in, 178–79; and "treaty literature," 10; Washington (1837), 111; Washington City (1825), 130, 134; William Clark's role in, 79
Treuer, Anton, 193
Tuhbenahneequay (Ojibwe), 184
Turner, Frederick Jackson, 102
Turner, J. Rodney, 11–12, 224n38

United Foreign Mission Society (UFMS), 41, 42, 44–46, 69, 231n31
United States: Choctaw Nation compared to, 164–65; economy of, 28; indigenous critiques of, 2, 3–4, 5, 33; as protector, 1–2; sanitizing colonialism of, 3. *See also* Indian policy, US
Universal Peace Congress, 202, 203, 206–7
"unorganized territory," 85
Unrau, William E., 16, 41
Upper Missouri Agency (Council Bluffs), 1–2, 32, 35, 38, 39–40, 69, 235n109. *See also* O'Fallon delegation
Upper Missouri Valley, 28, 34, 62, 63, 68. *See also* O'Fallon delegation

Van Buren, Martin, 87, *88,* 115
Vanderwerth, W. C., 61
vanishing Indian trope, 42, 48, 59–60; countering, 60–65, 67–68, 69–70, 72; the "frontier" in, 102; in histories, 167; land loss and, 216; and publishing Indian oratory, 60. *See also* stereotypes of Native Americans
Veracini, Lorenzo, 64, 226n59
Victoria, Queen, 185–86
Vigil, Kiara M., 9
Viola, Herman J., 181, 230n21
Vizenor, Gerald, 219

Wabokieshiek (Sauk-Winnebago), 86, 94
Wahcamme (Sauk), 99
Wakashawske (Meskwaki), 100
Waldstreicher, David, 50
wampum, 10, 185–86
wants, rhetoric of, 64, 65, 81, 178
Wapello (Sauk), 92, 118
Ward, Nancy (Cherokee), 14–15, 27
Ward, William, 139, 158
wardship, 25
Warner, Michael, 7
War of 1812: Black Hawk and, 84; Sauk and, 76; Tecumseh and, 132
Warrior, Robert, 19, 216

Washington. *See* delegations to Washington
Waubojiig (Ojibwe), 170, 173–77, 181
Weaver, Jace, 169, 185
The West Wing, 217
Whalen, Kevin, 218
Whelan, Mary Kathryn, 107, 242n112
White, Richard, 55, 64, 65; on Choctaw nationalism, 147; on the "middle ground," 4, 221n8
white encroachment: in Canada, 184; Cass inviting, 170, 171; on Choctaw land, 160; on Ojibwe land, 168, 170, 171, 184; on Sauk land, 99, 101–10; scarcity caused by, 64; in Upper Missouri, 28, 62, 63, 68
white philanthropy, 186, 187, 188, 190, 203
Wigginton, Caroline, 223n25
Williams, Raymond, 168
Wisconsin Territory, 95, 103, 110, 118
Wisecup, Kelly, 9
Witgen, Michael, 96–97, 170, 171, 179, 251n9
Wolfe, Patrick, 18
Womack, Craig, 6, 125, 219–20
women: as diplomats, 14–15, 27, 170–71, 177; publication by, 223n25; retraditionalization work by, 190; sacrifice and, 52–53, *54,* 55–57; scrutiny of, 49–50
Wood, Enoch, 184
Wopeshiak (Meskwaki), 100
Worcester v. Georgia, 59
writing: accountability through, 100–101; cultural context of, 9, 13; publication, 6–13, 58, 202–3, 223n5, 255n117. *See also* communication; print culture

x-marks: signatures, 115; as analytical term, 215, 222n11

Yewell, Robert H., *116*
"Young Lochinvar," *54*

Zoongakamig (Ojibwe), 193

www.ingramcontent.com/pod-product-compliance
Lightning Source LLC
Chambersburg PA
CBHW030529230426
43665CB00010B/822